The Perennial Philosophy

Series

About this Book

"Ananda K. Coomaraswamy is in the very first rank of exceptional men, such as René Guénon and Frithjof Schuon, who in our 'dark age' have permitted us to rediscover the great truths of sacred Tradition, to relearn what a civilization, a society, and a world are that conform to this Tradition ... The masterful work of Ananda K. Coomaraswamy is one of the most suitable to enlighten the minds and hearts of 'men of good will.'"

—**Jean Hani**, author

"This anthology is comprised of essays on a variety of subjects, from art and literature through philosophy to myth, religion and metaphysics, setting forth, not simply the informed opinions of its author, but indeed the timeless and inspired wisdom of mankind. Given the immensity of Ananda K. Coomaraswamy's literary output, the present compilation constitutes a welcome and much-needed contribution to the perennialist literature."

—**Wolfgang Smith**, scientist and mathematician, author of *Cosmos and Transcendence: Breaking Through the Barrier of Scientistic Belief*

"This book is important to anyone who intends to grasp the roots of culture both in the East and in the West and how they inter-relate in their intellectually vital aspects. Exemplary and flawless use of language makes this book an inspiring evaluation and contemplation of the meaning of culture in both its Oriental and Western manifestations."

—**Frederick Franck**, artist and author of *The Zen of Seeing* and *Messenger of the Heart: The Book of Angelus Silesius*

"Coomaraswamy's work is as important as that of Joseph Campbell or Carl Jung, and deserving of the same attention. *The Essential Ananda K. Coomaraswamy* is a good way to approach his extensive writings that explore in depth and in detail the essence of culture and spirituality both East and West, both ancient and modern."

—**David Frawley**, author of *Yoga and Ayurveda* and *From the River of Heaven: Hindu and Vedic Knowledge for the Modern Age*

"Like St. Augustine, Ananda K. Coomaraswamy wrote in order to perfect his own understanding. He sought to know the whatness and principial roots of things, above all of himself. In doing so, he collaterally provided access to a fundamental intellectual itinerary which unfailingly beckons all who recognize in themselves an intrinsic regard for Truth. This itinerary is eloquently epitomized in the twenty essays of this book, essays as delightful as they are perennial."

> —**Alvin Moore, Jr.**, co-editor of *Selected Letters of Ananda Coomaraswamy*

"After having read Ananda K. Coomaraswamy, the distinction between Oriental and Occidental thought hardly has any more meaning. He is a tireless 'ferryman' between one and the other side of the same transcendent [reality]."

> —**Jean Canteins**, author

"The pioneering and interdisciplinary essays of Ananda K. Coomaraswamy on medieval Christian and Oriental art have shed so much light on religious symbolism and iconography, and given such profound metaphysical insight into the study of aesthetics and traditional folklore, that if contemporary art history does not take [his] challenges and contributions into account, it will inevitably fall prey to ideological reductionisms and degrade the ancient and perennial language of art forms into a mere archaic system of lifeless symbols with [no] meaning."

> —**Ramon Mujica Pinilla**, art historian, Universidad Mayor de San Marcos, Lima, Peru

"Coomaraswamy's essays [give] us a view of his scholarship and brilliant insight."

> —**Joseph Campbell**, author of *The Hero with a Thousand Faces* and *The Masks of God*

"In Coomaraswamy ... all the religious traditions of the world meet."

> —**Jean Borella**, author of *The Secret of the Christian Way* and *The Sense of the Supernatural*

World Wisdom
The Library of Perennial Philosophy

The Library of Perennial Philosophy is dedicated to the exposition of the timeless Truth underlying the diverse religions. This Truth, often referred to as the *Sophia Perennis*—or Perennial Wisdom—finds its expression in the revealed Scriptures as well as the writings of the great sages and the artistic creations of the traditional worlds.

The Perennial Philosophy provides the intellectual principles capable of explaining both the formal contradictions and the transcendent unity of the great religions.

Ranging from the writings of the great sages of the past, to the perennialist authors of our time, each series of our Library has a different focus. As a whole, they express the inner unanimity, transforming radiance, and irreplaceable values of the great spiritual traditions.

The Essential Ananda K. Coomaraswamy appears as one of our selections in The Perennial Philosophy series.

The Perennial Philosophy Series

In the beginning of the Twentieth Century, a school of thought arose which has focused on the enunciation and explanation of the Perennial Philosophy. Deeply rooted in the sense of the sacred, the writings of its leading exponents establish an indispensable foundation for understanding the timeless Truth and spiritual practices which live in the heart of all religions. Some of these titles are companion volumes to the Treasures of the World's Religions series, which allows a comparison of the writings of the great sages of the past with the perennialist authors of our time.

Cover Reference:
Eleven-headed Juichimen-Kannon (Avalokiteshvara),
9th century, Nara, Japan

The Essential
Ananda K. Coomaraswamy

Edited by

Rama P. Coomaraswamy

Foreword by
Arvind Sharma

Prologue by
Marco Pallis

World Wisdom

The Essential Ananda K. Coomaraswamy
English Language Edition © 2004 World Wisdom, Inc.

For complete bibliographic information on the articles
in this anthology, please refer to the page of Bibliographical References
placed at the back of the book.

Library of Congress Cataloging-in-Publication Data

Coomaraswamy, Ananda Kentish, 1877-1947.
    The essential Ananda K. Coomaraswamy / edited by Rama P. Coomaraswamy;
    foreword by Arvind Sharma ; prologue by Marco Pallis.
        p. cm. – (The perennial philosophy series)
Includes bibliographical references and index.
    ISBN 0-941532-46-1 (pbk. : alk. paper)
    1. Religion–Philosophy. 2. Philosophy and religion. I.
Coomaraswamy, Rama P. II. Title. III. Series. BL51 .C655 2004 082–dc22
                                                              2003026493

Printed on acid-free paper in China

For information address World Wisdom, Inc.
P.O. Box 2682, Bloomington, Indiana 47402-2682

www.worldwisdom.com

Table of Contents

List of Color Illustrations

List of Black-and-White Illustrations

List of Abbreviations

No attempt has been made to achieve total stylistic consistency in the citation of the most frequently referenced works by Ananda K. Coomaraswamy. References may be cited in full or in abbreviated form (e.g. Rig Veda, or RV).

A	Anguttara-Nikâya
AA	Aitareya Âranyaka
AB	Aitareya Brâhmana
Ait. Up.	Aitareya Upanishad
AV	Atharva Veda
BG	Bhagavad Gîtâ
BU	Brihadâranyaka Upanishad
CU	Chandogya Upanishad
D	Dîgha-Nikâya
Dh	Dhammapada
DhA	Dhammapada Atthakathâ
HJAS	Harvard Journal of Asiatic Studies
IC	Indian Culture
IHQ	Indian Historical Quarterly
J	Jâtaka
JAOS	Journal of the American Oriental Society
JB	Jaimanîya Brâhmana
JIH	Journal of Indian History
JUB	Jaiminîya Upanishad Brâhmana
KB	Kausîtaki Brahmana
KU	Katha Upanishad
Kaus. Up.	Kausîtaki Upanishad
Lib.	*Libellus* (Hermes Trismegistus)
Mand. Up.	Mandûkya Upanishad
Mil.	Milinda Pañho
MU	Maitri Upanishad
Mund.	Mundaka Upanishad
PB	Pañcavimsa Brâhmana
Pras. Up.	Prasna Upanishad
RV	Rig Veda
S	Samyutta-Nikâya
SA	Sânkhâyana Âranyaka
SB	Satapatha Brâhmana

Sn	Sutta-Nipâta
Svet. Up.	Svetâsvatara Upanishad
Sum. Theol.	Summa Theologica (St. Thomas Aquinas)
TA	Taittirîya Âranyaka
TB	Taittarîya Brâhmana
TS	Taittirîya Samhitâ
TU	Taittirîya Upanishad
VS	Vâjasaneyi Samhitâ

Ananda Coomaraswamy in the 1940s

Foreword

The name of Ananda K. Coomaraswamy has become synonymous with an entire approach to art and of the civilization of which it is an expression. Coomaraswamy's genius lay not only in presenting it to the modern Western world but also in demonstrating that this civilizational art and artistic civilization was contrapuntal and not necessarily antithetical to the modern West, as ears less gifted than his to hearing celestial harmonies might have proposed. His multi-splendored genius expressed itself in over a thousand published items. One might say that Coomaraswamy wrote more than many people read in the course of one life.

The publication of his seminal contributions in the form of the compendium of his essential writings that you hold in your hands is therefore to be greatly welcomed. It conveys to us the flavor of his thought, as water collected in a small shell on the shore conveys the flavor of the entire ocean. Of course it cannot convey a sense of the ocean's magnitude, but it earns our gratitude in conveying a sense of its taste; of how the divine dialectic of the transformation of religion into art and art into religion might hold the key to the rejuvenation of both life and art in the modern world.

Our contemporary world is trying to rejuvenate itself not through God but through religion, thereby creating for itself the problem of fundamentalism, an outcome which would not have surprised Coomaraswamy, who insisted that the modern world must rejuvenate itself through God rather than religion, and bring its wasteland to life by irrigating it with the waters of Tradition. This Tradition offers perennial answers to contemporary questions whereas modernity has only been able, if at all, to offer contemporary (and fugitive) answers to perennial questions. It is not merely an accident then that while that great work of the Enlightenment, Voltaire's *Candide*, ends with Dr. Pangloss cultivating his garden living in the best of all possible worlds, Coomaraswamy, when he sensed that his life was about to run its course, chose to leave his body in the manner of a Hindu renunciate, also in a garden, symbolizing the fact that he brought to us from all possible worlds the spiritual fragrance of humanity, fresh from the exquisite gardens of its various religions. And they are various. For none of the great expositors of the perennial philosophy—not Coomaraswamy in any case—made the mistake, to which some are prone, of imagining that just because all the religions say more or less the same thing that they are therefore all the same. Thus Coomaraswamy has rightly been hailed as a bridge-builder at a time when the West was acting like a steamroller in the rest of the world.

All the reader need do to verify what I have said, lest he or she be inclined to consider the thoughts and emotions I have just shared as too encomiastic or enthusiastic, is to read this book.

Arvind Sharma
McGill University

Introduction

Some years ago when giving a talk at the University of Hawaii, I was approached by a young man who had wished to do his Ph.D thesis on Ananda Coomaraswamy.[1] His request was denied because, as his advisor said, "Coomaraswamy never said anything original!" I think my father would have been delighted, for if there is anything characteristic of his work, it is the absence of self-indulgence or originality. This of course does not mean that he lacked the consummate skill of an artist in re-stating what had been said from all times, for to quote him, "the beauty of a well turned phrase is the *splendor veritatis.*"

How is it possible to situate a person who was a recognized scholar in many areas, whose total literary output numbered well over 1000 items, the value of which has not diminished with time?[2] He once said that he wrote to clarify his own thoughts and that if his efforts helped others, he was delighted. He also considered his scholarship and literary output as the fulfillment of his dharma and a karma-yoga—the way of works by which one perfects one's soul—for him the Benedictine principle that *laborare est orare* truly applied. How can we best situate this individual? There are several ways to consider this.

Perhaps most importantly he is a spokesperson for what has been called the Traditional view of life, or for the Philosophia Perennis (Sanatana Dharma in Hindu terms). He is one of several which the present age has brought forth. He is often linked with René Guénon, and Frithjof Schuon, though the names of several others might well be included. Attempts are sometimes made to determine which of them influenced the other—a futile endeavor—for each of them elucidated a slightly different aspect of the truth which is far too

1. Referred to as AKC for reasons of brevity.
2. A definitive Bibliography, itself the product of some twenty years of work by James Crouch, has recently been published by the Indira Gandhi National Center for the Arts (IGNCA), New Delhi, India.

"many splendored" for any single individual to encompass it totally. Thus it is that in many ways they complement each other.

It is of some value to consider his life. This is difficult to do as he was extremely reticent about personal matters. Indeed, he felt that autobiography in general was *aswarga*, or against the very principles that he had made his own and was expounding. At the same time his life was a pilgrimage and a constant growth towards the center and in its course traversed many and varied bypasses with which many of us are familiar. It is therefore of some value to review what little is known.

The family, Tamil in origin, must have originally come from the Indian subcontinent as connections were maintained with a temple in Allahabad. They, however, for several generations were established in Jafna, the northern part of Ceylon, and with the advent of British control, became increasingly prominent on the political scene. They belonged to the Velella caste which has been called the "fifth" caste, and is best situated as being between Brahmins and Kshatriyas. His father, Sir Mutu, who was the first Hindu to be called to the English bar, was actually a member of the British parliament. He was a close friend of Disraeli and is probably the "Indian gentleman" described in Disraeli's book *Coningsby*. He married Lady Elizabeth Bibi, one of the ladies in waiting on Queen Victoria and returned to Ceylon where AKC was born. Unfortunately Sir Mutu died shortly thereafter of Bright's Disease, or what is now referred to as renal failure due to glomerulonephritis. Lady Bibi then returned to England with the three-year-old child, who as soon as he was of age was sent to Wycliffe College, a private boarding school at Shroud (Stonehouse), Gloucestershire. As was common in the England of that period, there was very little parental influence, which was perhaps a blessing in disguise as his mother became involved in the fashionable spiritualistic practices of the day.

Wycliffe was in many ways a blessing. Not only did it inculcate a knowledge of Latin, Greek and French, but it gave him the opportunity to explore other languages. He taught himself Icelandic and the family has a copy of his translation of an Icelandic Saga which at the age of 14 he sent to the professor of Icelandic at Oxford for correction and received instead congratulations. Many years later when a gentleman from Iceland visited, he was able to carry on an evening's conversation with him in his native tongue. This linguistic ability remained with him throughout his life. I once asked him for

involved in the independence movement. He was listed among the 400 and while he disengaged himself from such activities, our home was on occasion visited by former revolutionary colleagues. For a brief period he spent time in Madras and was acquainted with Annie Besant but was never directly involved in the Theosophical movement. Traveling more to the north he also spent time at Shantiniketan with the Tagores who were attempting to revive Indian painting and culture. He collected an enormous amount of Indian art at a time when no one was particularly interested in such material, and then offered it to the British government in India if they would build a museum to house it. His offer was rejected and so he brought it back to England in order to preserve it from destruction.

His writings in the field of art reversed the negative opinion of western critics about the value and nature of Indian art and it is in this area that he is best known in India—indeed, he has been called the "Father of Indian Art" and, as such, allowed Indians to become proud of their heritage. This is rather unfortunate in so far as the majority of Indians are completely unaware of his sociological and exegetical writings both of which they are in dire need of absorbing. While in northern India he received the *yajnopavite* or sacred thread, which in essence affiliated him formerly into the Hindu tradition.

He returned to England around 1914 and established his residence at Norman Chapel, a run down Norman ruin which he converted into a home (and which subsequently became a national monument) where he continued his studies and publishing. It was here that he produced *The Arts and Crafts of India and Ceylon, Mediaeval Singhalese Art*, as well as his book on *Rajput Paintings*. This is but to touch upon some of the more significant publications. In 1917 he was asked to join the British Army and refused on the grounds that India was not an independent nation. This led to his being exiled from the British Commonwealth. Arrangements were made for him to move to America and he was allowed to take his art collection with him, which today fills the halls of many American museums. Because of his expertise in the field of oriental art, he was given the position of "Keeper of Indian and Mohammedan Art" at the Boston Museum of Fine Arts, a position he held until his death in 1947.

This of course allowed him to continue both his studies and his publishing. In 1918 he published a collection of essays under the title of *The Dance of Siva* and thereafter followed innumerable texts dealing with Indian Art including his monumental *The History of Indian and Indonesian Art*. His life during the late 20s was complicated by a series of personal and family problems as well as by the loss of his personal fortune in the crash of 1929. At the same time however, and perhaps not unrelated, he deepened his approach to the arts and sought to penetrate their meaning and purpose, much as he had done with regard to vocational craftsmanship in an earlier period. In doing so, he not only turned to the traditional eastern authorities, but penetrated deeply into the Platonic and Christian sources. We begin to see the production of what can be considered his major work. In 1934 he published *A New Approach to the Vedas* which was an essay in translation and exegesis, and shortly thereafter *The Transformation of Nature in Art, The Darker Side of Dawn, Angel and Titan*, and the *Rg Veda as Land-Nama Bok*.

There is speculation as to whether some acute episode precipitated the change of emphasis which can be detected in his work. However, a closer familiarity with his literary output would indicate that there is a continuity throughout, and a progressive deepening of his understanding as he searched the Scriptures (his own phrase) of all the orthodox traditions in order to penetrate the unanimity of their teachings. This resulted in the production of his most significant and lasting works such as *The Christian and Oriental or True Philosophy of Art, Why Exhibit Works of Art?, Am I My Brother's Keeper, Spiritual Authority and Temporal Power in the Indian Theory of Government, Hinduism and Buddhism,*[3] *Time and Eternity,*[4] *Figures of Speech or Figures of Thought, The Living Thoughts of Gotama the Buddha,* and the two volumes of *Selected Papers* published by Princeton University Press. During this period of his life he also carried on an extensive correspondence with scholars and friends throughout the world, and many of these letters have been published in *Selected Letters* (temporarily out of print), which serves as an excellent introduction to his works.

3. Forthcoming, World Wisdom, 2005.
4. Forthcoming, World Wisdom, 2006.

politicians and the mass-media alike; the progressivist psychosis needs a rather naive optimism for its complement, as has been shown again and again. The warnings of a Coomaraswamy do not fall gratefully on such ears.

While I myself was working with Arnold Dolmetsch, Coomaraswamy's name had occasionally cropped up in conversation, but at the time its mention struck no particular chord in my consciousness. Awareness of what he really stood for came indirectly, after one of my fellow-students had introduced me to the writings of René Guénon, a French author who was then creating a stir among the reading public of his own country by his frontal attack on all basic assumptions and valuations on which the modern Western civilization rested, including the belief in "progress"; these ideas he contrasted with the traditional principles and values still current in the East and especially in India. A French periodical to which Guénon was a frequent contributor and to which, for that reason, I hastened to subscribe, was found to contain a continual stream of articles from Coomaraswamy's pen which, as I soon perceived, matched those of Guénon both on the critical side of things and in their most telling exposition of metaphysical doctrine, in which Gita and Upanishads, Plato and Meister Eckhart complemented one another in a never ending synthesis. Such was the intellectual food on which my eager mind was nourished during those formative years; looking back now, it is difficult to imagine what later life might have become but for these timely influences.

It can perhaps be said, however, that the seed thus sown did not fall on ground altogether unprepared for its reception. Discovery of Guénon and Coomaraswamy came to me less as a fresh illumination than as an adequately documented and reasoned confirmation of something I had believed ever since I was a small child, namely that the West enjoyed no innate superiority versus the East, rather did the balance of evidence lean, for me, the other way. I did not have to go outside my family circle to discover this; my parents (both of whom were Greek) had spent many happy years in India and the tales they told me about their life out there coupled with the no less telling evidence afforded by objects of Indian craftsmanship to be found in our home had left my childish mind convinced that the Indian ideal was the one for me. The colonialist claims and arguments which my English teachers, when I went to school, wove into the history lesson only drove me to exasperation; by the time I was ten *purna svaraj* for the Indians had become an article of faith, though everybody around me said this could never happen. Given this pre-existing tilt in my thinking and feeling, the reading of Coomaraswamy and Guénon was just what I needed in order to bring my ideas into focus by showing, apart from the particular case of India, that there was an essential rightness attaching to a traditional mode of life, whether found in Europe, Asia or elsewhere, as compared with the secularist, progressive, bigotedly "tolerant" liberal society in which I had grown up. Occasional contributions to Mahatma Gandhi's funds marked my youthful enthusiasm for the Indian cause; the danger that India herself might, under pressure of events, get caught up in the secularist ideology after the departure of her former colonial masters did not at that time cloud the horizon of my hopes to any serious extent.

To return to Guénon and Coomaraswamy: in terms of their respective dialectical styles contrast between these two authors could hardly have been greater; if they agreed about their main conclusions, as indeed they did, one can yet describe them as temperamentally poles apart. In the Frenchman, with his Latin scholastic formation under Jesuit guidance, we meet a mind of phenomenal lucidity of a type one can best describe as "mathematical" in its apparent detachment from anything savoring of aesthetic and even moral justifications; his criteria of what was right and what was inadmissible remained wholly intellectual ones needing no considerations drawn from a different order of reality to re-enforce them—their own self-evidence sufficed. Guénon was in fact a mathematician of no small parts, as can be gathered from a brief treatise he wrote on the *Infinitesimal Calculus* where the subject is expressly related to transcendent principles; a science describable as traditional will always take stock of this possibility, where a profanely conceived science will ignore it; all the tragedy of modern science is bound up with this cause.

To a mind like Guénon's abstract thinking comes all too easily; it was to his great credit that he all along stressed the need, side by side with a theoretical grasp of any given doctrine, for its concrete— one can also say its ontological—realization failing which one cannot properly speak of knowledge; for academic philosophizing Guénon had nothing but contempt. His insistence on the essential part to be played by an initiatic transmission, from guru to disciple, took many people by surprise at the time when his first books

which continued with ever increasing frequency and intimacy during the years that followed. With the outbreak of war in the autumn of 1939 I found myself caught up in local activities of various kinds which, however, left me some time for writing. I and my friend Richard Nicholson, who shared my principal interests and had taken part in the Indian expeditions mentioned above, decided to use our leisure time in translating two of Guénon's most important treatises the *Introduction to the Study of the Hindu Doctrines* and his supreme masterpiece, *Man and his Becoming according to the Vedanta*; they were eventually published by Luzac, London, as part of a series covering much of Guénon's work.*

Each of these books presented a problem which touched us personally in the shape of a chapter concerning Buddhism, which Guénon summarily dismissed as little more than a heretical development within the Hindu world itself; there was no evidence to show that Guénon before arriving at this negative conclusion had consulted any authoritative Buddhist texts as a check upon any hostile criticisms he might quote from already prejudiced sources, an omission of which Coomaraswamy would have been incapable. What were we then, as translators, to do? Should we simply render the text just as it stood or should we, before doing so, risk an appeal to the author in the hopes that he might reconsider some of the things he had said on the subject? For him to think of doing so, however, some fresh and convincing evidence was indispensable: how could the personal experience of two young men carry any weight with a man of the eminence of René Guénon? Only one person seemed qualified to make him think again: this was Coomaraswamy both because of the high respect in which Guénon held him and also as a scholar able to produce concrete evidence of an irrefutable kind. A letter was hastily sent to Boston asking for support in the form of authoritative quotations coupled with permission to use his name.

Coomaraswamy willingly acceded to our request; a letter from him soon followed containing incontrovertible evidence proving that Guénon had made a number of mis-statements of fact in regard to what Buddhism actually teaches; it was left to us, however, to mar-

* Editor's Note: The publishers Sophia Perennis of Ghent, New York are in the process of completing the publication of *The Collected Works of René Guénon* (in 24 volumes).

shal the arguments in logical succession on the basis of the fresh material thus supplied to us, to which we now were able to add some observations of our own, based on what we had seen and heard during our intercourse with Buddhist authorities in Sikkim, Ladak and other places. This letter was then sent off to Cairo where Guénon was then living: in fact he spent all the rest of life in that city.

We were not left to wait long for a reply, which went beyond our fondest hopes in its completeness. Guénon directed that the two offending chapters be suppressed, promising also to replace them by others composed on quite different lines. Indeed, he went further, since he directed us, by anticipation, to make similar corrections in other texts of his if and when we came to translate them; for this purpose he supplied a number of re-worded passages, mostly not of great length, but sufficient to meet our various objections. For this comforting result we have to thank Coomaraswamy to a large extent, even though the initiative came from us; Guénon's intellectual integrity in bowing before the evidence also deserves grateful acknowledgment.

What perhaps also comes out of this episode is the fact that, in judging the authenticity of a tradition, there are other ways besides the scrutiny of texts, important though this obviously is; an intelligent perception of beauty can provide no less valid criteria. Could anyone really look on the paintings to be found at Ajanta and in countless Japanese or Tibetan temples and still believe that the impulse behind these things stemmed from a basic error? The same argument would apply to the art of the Christian and Islamic, as well as of countless tribal, traditions existing all over the world until recent times, to say nothing of Hindu art in all its exuberant glories. Contrariwise, the sheer ugliness of the modern civilization as displayed in its most typical products bespeaks an underlying error; this evidence of the senses, which Guénon largely ignored, was crucial for Coomaraswamy, being complementary to whatever his reason for its part could show him. So should it be for ourselves, though not many today think or feel in this manner. If they did so, the world would be a very different place.

The end of the war sent our thoughts speeding in an easterly direction, with Tibet as our ultimate goal. Some time previously we had received the joyful news that Ananda Coomaraswamy, his wife and their son Rama were about to transfer their home to India, where they hoped to find some quiet spot, in the Kumaon hills per-

With Coomaraswamy the intellectual balance was held more evenly: though his own paternal ancestry imparted a characteristically Indian trend to his thinking his commentaries on Christian and Platonic themes displayed a sympathetic insight not less than when he was handling Hindu or Buddhist subjects. His bridge was designed to carry a two-way traffic without particular bias in one or other direction. This does not mean, however, that he was any less severe than Guénon in condemning the West for the harm it had wrought in all those Asian and African countries that had, during the colonial era, come under its sway; he singled out for particular blame that alien system of education with which the name of Macaulay is associated in India as well as the industrialism which, all over the world, has deprived the multitude of simple men and women of that sacred motivation which is the true satisfaction of the human need to work; but at the same time he was also forever reminding Western people of the precious spiritual and artistic heritage it still could claim to possess, if only it would re-read the signs of its own history.

Since the years when Guénon and Coomaraswamy were both writing, the climate of Western thought and feeling has undergone a noticeable change, of which those who are watching events from an easterly vantage-point might profitably take stock. Though the official ideology in Europe and America is still geared to the dogma of "progress," that is to say of an optimistically slanted evolutionary process with Utopia (or shall we say the reign of Antichrist?) at the end of the road, many of the previously confident assumptions that go with such an ideology are now being seriously called in question by a thoughtful minority and more especially among the young. Doubts concerning the long range viability, not of such and such a socio-political institution, but of the modern civilization in its entirety are to be heard with increasing frequency in the "liberal" countries—in places under Marxist control to express such opinions might well land a man in Solzhenitsin's "Gulag Archipelago." Where free criticism on the subject is still forthcoming, it often takes the concrete form of small-scale attempts to opt out of the prevailing system, for example by going in for a hard life of subsistence farming in a remote corner of the country—its very hardness is welcomed as an ascesis—or else by embracing a handicraft like weaving or pottery; one such highly successful craft has been the making of musical instruments according to ancient models, by way of supplying a growing demand consequent upon the revival of early music inaugurated by my own teacher, Arnold Dolmetsch. Individual experiments apart, the Gandhian ideal of moderation, affecting human appetites as well as possessions, has certainly gained a lot of ground in the West, not merely because people think this will make for greater happiness in the long run, but also as offering them a somewhat better chance of survival if and when the catastrophe many are now fearing comes to pass.

Yet another sign of weakening belief in the modern way of life and its hitherto accepted valuations is the wish, evinced by many people, to come to proper terms with Nature instead of treating her together with all her progeny as a field for limitless exploitation or else as a potential enemy to be brought to heel; phrases like the "conquest" of Everest or of the Moon no longer win the passive acquiescence of some time ago; in many ears they strike a sacrilegious note. People nowadays are apt to feel uncomfortable when they hear it said, across the official media, that lions or tigers are to be saved from extermination to serve as "big game" or that rare plants should be scheduled for protection as being "of scientific interest." The need to safeguard some beautiful mountain area does not spring from the fact that this provides an attraction for tourists (not to mention their money); for this sort of argument the present generation of Nature-lovers has no use. As for the pollution of which we hear so much today—the gradual poisoning of land, sea, the very air we breathe by the accumulated by-products of industrial expansion—this is now seen by many as the reflex of a no less widespread pollution of the mind: without a prior cleansing of the mind to the point of revising all its demands both material, moral and intellectual, how dare one hope to escape the consequences of past heedlessness?—this question is also being asked today.

All these various forms of self-questioning are converging towards an awareness of the fact that man's place in this world, if it confers privileges on the one hand, comprises grave responsibilities on the other both in regard to how we view and treat our fellow-creatures great and small (including even those we term "inanimate," a questionable term in itself) and also in regard to how we shall acknowledge, through our own conduct, the global sacredness of Nature in her capacity of cosmic theophany, in which each kind of manifested being, including ourselves, has its appointed place

the sage advice to be had there was Whitall N. Perry, now living in Switzerland.* Somewhere in his writings the great Doctor had expressed the opinion that, with the way things are tending, a day might soon come when a man of culture would be expected to familiarize himself with more than just what the Greek and Latin languages had offered hitherto: Sanskrit and Chinese, Tibetan and Arabic would all contribute to the intellectual nourishment of such a person, failing which he would remain hopelessly provincial in his outlook. In this same connection Coomaraswamy had mentioned the need for someone to compile an encyclopedia of the great traditions of the world, both Eastern and Western, to serve as a general book of references for those seeking corroboration of their own faith in the parallel experience of men of other orientations; he also spoke of "paths that lead to the same summit" as the common ideal which, if sincerely realized might yet rescue mankind from the worst disaster. But to assemble such an anthology—here was a task to daunt even a brave and assiduous mind! Could anyone be found to undertake it?

The task itself found its man in Whitall Perry. For some seventeen years he labored in selfless dedication, combing the spiritual literature of the world, past and present, East and West together. The outcome of all this was a complex mosaic of quotations arranged in such a way as to illuminate, and by their contrast heighten, one another's meaning. Highly informative but concise comments precede each section and sub-section of this monumental compilation, while an ingenious system of cross-references is there to enable students of particular subjects to unearth additional material to be found elsewhere. At the end of it all, the author did me the honor of asking me to contribute a preface, which I did all the more gladly since this enabled me to pay, if indirectly, a concrete tribute to Coomaraswamy himself as originator of the idea of an encyclopedic work laid out on this scale. The title chosen for it was *A Treasury of Traditional Wisdom*: would that the man who inspired this project had lived to see his expressed wish realized so amply!

By natural disposition Ananda K. Coomaraswamy was nothing if not a *karma-yogin*. Assuredly a metaphysical flair like his does not go

* Editor's Note: Whitall N. Perry has subsequently relocated to America, where he currently resides in Bloomington, Indiana.

without a strongly contemplative bent; nevertheless he remained primarily a man of action, a warrior for *dharma* with pen and word. This impression of the man moreover provides a cue for us in this, his centenary year. What better homage to his memory can one find than to join him in striking a blow or two in the battle of Kurukshetra, which is ever with us? No need to look far afield for opportunities; one's daily occupations, one's home with its furnishings, how one spends one's leisure time, what one chooses to wear or not to wear and for what reason, all these things together contribute a field of battle adequate to the powers of any normal person, to say nothing of various public causes.

If all these matters of human choice and conduct belong by definition to *samsara* as generator of distinctions and contrasts continually varied and renewed, it is well to remember that this unremitting round of birth and death, terrible as such, yet offers us who are involved in it one compensating advantage inasmuch as it also provides a constant and inescapable reminder of *nirvana*; but for the variety of experience thus made available, what motive would anyone have for thinking of *moksha*, let alone realizing it actively? To quote another master of the Perennial Philosophy, Frithjof Schuon, "do what it may to affirm itself, *samsara* is condemned to unveil *nirvana*": could anyone have put the intrinsic message of existence more succinctly?

I venture to believe that Coomaraswamy, were he with us again today, facing a world that seems to be decomposing before our eyes, would express himself in similar terms: hopefully therefore, in function of those very vicissitudes which, for the man of profane disposition, drive him to despair.

1

A Figure of Speech or a Figure of Thought?[1]

"Egô de technên ou kalô, ho an ê alogon pragma."
Plato, *Gorgias* 465A[2]

We are peculiar people. I say this with reference to the fact that whereas almost all other peoples have called their theory of art or expression a "rhetoric" and have thought of art as a kind of knowledge, we have invented an "aesthetic" and think of art as a kind of feeling.

The Greek original of the word "aesthetic" means perception by the senses, especially by feeling. Aesthetic experience is a faculty that we share with animals and vegetables, and is irrational. The "aesthetic soul" is that part of our psychic makeup that "senses" things and reacts to them: in other words, the "sentimental" part of us. To identify our approach to art with the pursuit of these reactions is not to make art "fine" but to apply it only to the life of pleasure and to disconnect it from the active and contemplative lives.

Our word "aesthetic," then, takes for granted what is now commonly assumed, viz. that art is evoked by, and has for its end to express and again evoke, emotions. In this connection, Alfred North Whitehead has remarked that "it was a tremendous discovery, how to excite emotions for their own sake."[3] We have gone on to invent a science of our likes and dislikes, a "science of the soul," psychology, and have substituted psychological explanations for the traditional conception of art as an intellectual virtue and of beauty as pertaining to knowledge.[4] Our current resentment of meaning in art is as strong as the word "aesthetic" implies. When we speak of a work of art as "significant" we try to forget that this word can only be used with a following "of," that expression can be significant only *of* some thesis that was to be expressed, and we overlook that whatever does not mean something is literally *in-significant*. If, indeed, the whole end of art were "to express emotion," then the degree of our emotional reaction would be the measure of beauty and all

21

judgment would be subjective, for there can be no disputing about tastes. It should be remembered that a reaction is an "affection," and every affection a passion, that is, something passively suffered or undergone, and not—as in the operation of judgment—an activity on our part.[5] To equate the love of art with a love of fine sensations is to make of works of art a kind of aphrodisiac. The words "disinterested aesthetic contemplation" are a contradiction in terms and a pure non-sense.

"Rhetoric," of which the Greek original means skill in public speaking, implies, on the other hand, a theory of art as the effective expression of theses. There is a very wide difference between what is said for effect, and what is said or made to be *effective*, and must *work*, or would not have been worth saying or making. It is true that there is a so-called rhetoric of the production of "effects," just as there is a so-called poetry that consists only of emotive words, and a sort of painting that is merely spectacular; but this kind of eloquence that makes use of figures for their own sake, or merely to display the artist, or to betray the truth in courts of law, is not properly a rhetoric, but a sophistic, or art of flattery. By "rhetoric" we mean, with Plato and Aristotle, "the art of giving effectiveness to truth."[6] My thesis will be, then, that if we propose to use or understand any works of art (with the possible exception of contemporary works, which may be "unintelligible"[7]), we ought to abandon the term "aesthetic" in its present application and return to "rhetoric," Quintilian's "bene dicendi scientia."

It may be objected by those for whom art is not a language but a spectacle that rhetoric has primarily to do with verbal eloquence and not with the life of works of art in general. I am not sure that even such objectors would really agree to describe their own works as dumb or ineloquent. But however this may be, we must affirm that the principles of art are not altered by the variety of the material in which the artist works—materials such as vibrant air in the case of music or poetry, human flesh on the stage, or stone, metal, clay in architecture, sculpture, and pottery. Nor can one material be called more beautiful than another; you cannot make a better sword of gold than of steel. Indeed, the material as such, being relatively formless, is relatively ugly. Art implies a transformation of the material, the impression of a new form on material that had been more or less formless; and it is precisely in this sense that the creation of the world from a completely formless matter is called a "work of adornment."

There are good reasons for the fact that the theory of art has generally been stated in terms of the spoken (or secondarily, written) word. It is, in the first place, "by a word conceived in intellect" that the artist, whether human or divine, works.[8] Again, those whose own art was, like mine, verbal, naturally discussed the art of verbal expression, while those who worked in other materials were not also necessarily expert in "logical" formulation. And finally, the art of speaking can be better understood by all than could the art of, let us say, the potter, because all men make use of speech (whether rhetorically, to communicate a meaning, or sophistically, to exhibit themselves), while relatively few are workers in clay.

All our sources are conscious of the fundamental identity of all the arts. Plato, for example, remarks that "the expert, who is intent upon the best when he speaks, will surely not speak at random, but with an end in view; he is just like all those other artists, the painters, builders, ship-wrights, etc.";[9] and again, "the productions of all arts are kinds of poetry, and their craftsmen are all poets,"[10] in the broad sense of the word. "Demiurge" (*dêmiourgos*) and "technician" (*technitês*) are the ordinary Greek words for "artist" (*artifex*), and under these headings Plato includes not only poets, painters, and musicians, but also archers, weavers, embroiderers, potters, carpenters, sculptors, farmers, doctors, hunters, and above all those whose art is government, only making a distinction between creation (*dêmiourgia*) and mere labor (*cheirourgia*), art (*technê*) and artless industry (*atechnos tribê*).[11] All these artists, insofar as they are really makers and not merely industrious, insofar as they are musical and therefore wise and good, and insofar as they are in possession of their art (*entechnos*, cf. *entheos*) and governed by it, are infallible.[12] The primary meaning of the word *sophia*, "wisdom," is that of "skill," just as Sanskrit *kausalam* is "skill" of any kind, whether in making, doing, or knowing.

Now what are all these arts for? Always and only to supply a real or an imagined need or deficiency on the part of the human patron, for whom as the collective consumer the artist works.[13] When he is working for himself, the artist as a human being is also a consumer. The necessities to be served by art may appear to be material *or* spiritual, but as Plato insists, it is one and the same art— or a combination of both arts, practical and philosophical—that must serve both body and soul if it is to be admitted in the ideal

City.[14] We shall see presently that to propose to serve the two ends separately is the peculiar symptom of our modern "heartlessness." Our distinction of "fine" from "applied" art (ridiculous, because the fine art itself is applied to giving pleasure) is as though "not by bread alone"[15] had meant "by cake" for the elite that go to exhibitions and "bread alone" for the majority and usually for all. Plato's music and gymnastics, which correspond to what we seem to intend by "fine" and "applied" art (since one is for the soul and the other for the body), are never divorced in his theory of education; to follow one alone leads to effeminacy, to follow only the other, to brutality; the tender artist is no more a man than the tough athlete; music must be realized in bodily graces, and physical power should be exercised only in measured, not in violent motions.[16]

It would be superfluous to explain what are the material necessities to be served by art: we need only remember that a censorship of what ought or ought not to be made at all should correspond to our knowledge of what is good or bad for us. It is clear that a wise government, even a government of the free by the free, cannot permit the manufacture and sale of products that are necessarily injurious, however profitable such manufacture may be to those whose interest it is to sell, but must insist upon those standards of living to secure which was once the function of the guilds and of the individual artist "inclined by justice, which rectifies the will, to do his work faithfully."[17]

As for the spiritual ends of the arts, what Plato says is that we are endowed by the gods with vision and hearing, and harmony "was given by the Muses to him that can use them intellectually (*meta nou*), not as an aid to irrational pleasure (*hêdonê alogos*), as is nowadays supposed, but to assist the soul's interior revolution, to restore it to order and concord with itself. And because of the want of measure and lack of graces in most of us, rhythm was given us by the same gods for the same ends";[18] and that while the passion (*pathê*) evoked by a composition of sounds "furnishes a pleasure-of-the-senses (*hêdonê*) to the unintelligent, it (the composition) bestows on the intelligent that hearts ease that is induced by the imitation of the divine harmony produced in mortal motions."[19] This last delight or gladness that is experienced when we partake of the feast of reason, which is also a communion, is not a passion but an ecstasy, a going out of ourselves and being in the spirit: a condition insusceptible of analysis in terms of the pleasure or pain that can be felt by sensitive bodies or souls.

The soulful or sentimental self enjoys itself in the aesthetic surfaces of natural or artificial things, to which it is akin; the intellectual or spiritual self enjoys their order and is nourished by what in them is akin to it. The spirit is much rather a fastidious than a sensitive entity; it is not the physical qualities of things, but what is called their scent or flavor, for example "the picture not in the colors," or "the unheard music," not a sensible shape but an intelligible form, that it tastes. Plato's "hearts ease" is the same as that "intellectual beatitude" which Indian rhetoric sees in the "tasting of the flavor" of a work of art, an immediate experience, and congeneric with the tasting of God.[20]

This is, then, by no means an aesthetic or psychological experience but implies what Plato and Aristotle call a *katharsis*, and a "defeat of the sensations of pleasure" or pain.[21] *Katharsis* is a sacrificial purgation and purification "consisting in a separation, as far as that is possible, of the soul from the body"; it is, in other words, a kind of dying, that kind of dying to which the philosopher's life is dedicated.[22] The Platonic *katharsis* implies an ecstasy, or "standing aside" of the energetic, spiritual, and imperturbable self from the passive, aesthetic, and natural self, a "being out of oneself" that is a being "in one's right mind" and real Self, that "in-sistence" that Plato has in mind when he "would be born again in beauty inwardly," and calls this a sufficient prayer.[23]

Plato rebukes his much-beloved Homer for attributing to the gods and heroes all-too-human passions, and for the skillful imitations of these passions that are so well calculated to arouse our own "sym-pathies."[24] The *katharsis* of Plato's City is to be effected not by such exhibitions as this, but by the banishment of artists who allow themselves to imitate all sorts of things, however shameful. Our own novelists and biographers would have been the first to go, while among modern poets it is not easy to think of any but William Morris of whom Plato could have heartily approved.

The *katharsis* of the City parallels that of the individual; the emotions are traditionally connected with the organs of evacuation, precisely because the emotions are waste products. It is difficult to be sure of the exact meaning of Aristotle's better-known definition, in which tragedy "by its imitation of pity and fear effects a *katharsis* from these and like passions,"[25] though it is clear that for him too the purification is *from* the passions (*pathêmata*); we must bear in mind that, for Aristotle, tragedy is still essentially a representation of actions, and not of character. It is certainly not a periodical "outlet" of—that is to say, indulgence in—our "pent-up" emotions that can bring about an emancipation from them; such an outlet, like a drunkard's bout, can be only a temporary satiation.[26] In what Plato calls with approval the "more austere" kind of poetry, we are presumed to be enjoying a feast of reason rather than a "break-fast" of sensations. His *katharsis* is an ecstasy or liberation of the "immortal soul" from the affections of the "mortal," a conception of emancipation that is closely paralleled in the Indian texts in which liberation is realized by a process of "shaking off one's bodies."[27] The reader or spectator of the imitation of a "myth" is to be rapt away from his habitual and passible personality and, just as in all other sacrificial rituals, becomes a god for the duration of the rite and only returns to himself when the rite is relinquished, when the epiphany is at an end and the curtain falls. We must remember that all artistic operations were originally rites, and that the purpose of the rite (as the word *teletê* implies) is to sacrifice the old and to bring into being a new and more perfect man.]

We can well imagine, then, what Plato, stating a philosophy of art that is not "his own" but intrinsic to the Philosophia Perennis, would have thought of our aesthetic interpretations and of our contention that the last end of art is simply to please. For, as he says, "ornament, painting, and music made only to give pleasure" are just "toys."[28] The "lover of art," in other words, is a "playboy." It is admitted that a majority of men judge works of art by the pleasure they afford; but rather than sink to such a level, Socrates says no, "not even if all the oxen and horses and animals in the world, by their pursuit of pleasure, proclaim that such is the criterion."[29] The kind of music of which he approves is not a multifarious and changeable but a canonical music;[30] not the sound of "poly-harmonic" instruments, but the simple music (*haplotês*) of the lyre accompanied by chanting "deliberately designed to produce in the soul that symphony of which we have been speaking";[31] not the music of Marsyas the Satyr, but that of Apollo.[32]

All the arts, without exception, are imitative. The work of art can only be judged as such (and independently of its "value") by the degree to which the model has been correctly represented. The beauty of the work is proportionate to its accuracy (*orthotês* = *integri-*

tas sive perfectio), or truth (*alêtheia* = *veritas*). In other words, the artist's judgment of his own work by the criterion of art is a criticism based upon the proportion of essential to actual form, paradigm to image. "Imitation" (*mimêsis*), a word that can be as easily misunderstood as St. Thomas Aquinas's "Art is the imitation of Nature in her manner of operation,"[33] can be mistaken to mean that that is the best art that is "truest to nature," as we now use the word in its most limited sense, with reference not to "Mother Nature," Natura naturans, Creatrix Universalis, Deus, but to whatever is presented by our own immediate and natural environment, whether visually or otherwise accessible to observation (*aisthêsis*). In this connection it is important not to overlook that the delineation of character (*êthos*) in literature and painting is, just as much as the representation of the looking-glass image of a physiognomy, an empirical and realistic procedure, dependent on observation. St. Thomas's "Nature," on the other hand, is that Nature "to find which," as Meister Eckhart says, "all her forms must be shattered."

The imitation or "re-presentation" of a model (even a "presented" model) involves, indeed, a likeness (*homoia, similitudo*, Skr. *sâdrsya*), but hardly what we usually mean by "verisimilitude" (*homoiotês*). What is traditionally meant by "likeness" is not a copy but an image akin (*sungenês*) and "equal" (*isos*) to its model; in other words, a natural and "ad-equate" symbol of its referent. The representation of a man, for example, must really correspond to the idea of the man, but must not look so like him as to deceive the eye; for the work of art, as regards its form, is a mind-made thing and aims at the mind, but an illusion is no more intelligible than the natural object it mimics. The plaster cast of a man will not be a work of art, but the representation of a man on wheels where verisimilitude would have required feet may be an entirely adequate "imitation" well and *truly* made.[34]

It is with perfect right that the mathematician speaks of a "beautiful equation" and feels for it what we feel about "art."[35] The beauty of the admirable equation is the attractive aspect of its simplicity. It is a single form that is the form of many different things. In the same way Beauty absolutely is the equation that is the single form of all things, which are themselves beautiful to the extent that they participate in the simplicity of their source. "The beauty of the straight line and the circle, and the plane and solid figures formed from these ... is not, like that of other things, relative, but always

27

absolutely beautiful."[36] Now we know that Plato, who says this, is always praising what is ancient and deprecating innovations (of which the causes are, in the strictest and worst sense of the word, aesthetic), and that he ranks the formal and canonical arts of Egypt far above the humanistic Greek art that he saw coming into fashion.[37] The kind of art that Plato endorsed was, then, precisely what we know as Greek Geometric art. We must not think that it would have been primarily for its decorative values that Plato must have admired this kind of "primitive" art, but for its truth or accuracy, *because* of which it has the kind of beauty that is universal and invariable, its equations being "akin" to the First Principles of which the myths and mysteries, related or enacted, are imitations in other kinds of material. The forms of the simplest and severest kinds of art, the synoptic kind of art that we call "primitive," are the natural language of all traditional philosophy; and it is for this very reason that Plato's dialectic makes continual use of *figures* of speech, which are really figures of thought.

Plato knew as well as the Scholastic philosophers that the artist as such has no moral responsibilities, and can sin as an artist only if he fails to consider the sole good of the work to be done, whatever it may be.[38] But, like Cicero, Plato also knows that "though he is an artist, he is nevertheless a man"[39] and, if a free man, responsible as such for whatever it may be that he undertakes to make; a man who, if he represents what ought not to be represented and brings into being things unworthy of free men, should be punished, or at the least restrained or exiled like any other criminal or madman. It is precisely those poets or other artists who imitate anything and everything, and are not ashamed to represent or even "idealize" things essentially base, that Plato, without respect for their abilities, however great, would banish from the society of rational men, "lest from the imitation of shameful things men should imbibe their actuality,"[40] that is to say, for the same reasons that we in moments of sanity (*sôphrosunê*) see fit to condemn the exhibition of gangster films in which the villain is made a hero, or agree to forbid the manufacture of even the most skillfully adulterated foods.

If we dare not ask with Plato "imitations of what sort of life?" and "whether of the appearance or the reality, the phantasm or the truth?"[41] it is because we are no longer sure what kind of life it is that we ought for our own good and happiness to imitate, and are for the most part convinced that no one knows or can know the final truth about anything: we only know what we "approve" of, i.e., what we *like* to do or think, and we desire a freedom to do and think what we like more than we desire a freedom from error. Our educational systems are chaotic because we are not agreed for what to educate, if not for self-expression. But all tradition is agreed as to what kind of models are to be imitated: "The city can never otherwise be happy unless it is designed by those painters who follow a divine original";[42] "The crafts such as building and carpentry ... take their principles from that realm and from the thinking there";[43] "Lo, make all things in accordance with the pattern that was shown thee upon the mount";[44] "It is in imitation (*anukrti*) of the divine forms that any human form (*silpa*) is invented here";[45] "There is this divine harp, to be sure; this human harp comes into being in its likeness" (*tad anukrti*);[46] "We must do what the Gods did first."[47] *This* is the "imitation of Nature in her manner of operation," and, like the first creation, the imitation of an intelligible, not a perceptible model.

But such an imitation of the divine principles is only possible if we have known them "as they are," for if we have not ourselves seen them, our mimetic iconography, based upon opinion, will be at fault; we cannot know the reflection of anything unless we know itself.[48] It is the basis of Plato's criticism of naturalistic poets and painters that they know nothing of the reality but only the appearances of things, for which their vision is overkeen; their imitations are not of the divine originals, but are only copies of copies.[49] And seeing that God alone is truly beautiful, and all other beauty is by participation, it is only a work of art that has been wrought, in its kind (*idea*) and its significance (*dunamis*), after an eternal model, that can be called beautiful.[50] And since the eternal and intelligible models are supersensual and invisible, it is evidently "not by observation" but in contemplation that they must be known.[51] Two acts, then, one of contemplation and one of operation, are necessary to the production of any work of art.[52]

And now as to the judgment of the work of art, first by the criterion of art, and second with respect to its human value. As we have already seen, it is not by our reactions, pleasurable or otherwise, but by its perfect accuracy, beauty, or perfection, or truth—in other words, by the equality or proportion of the image to its model—that a work of art can be judged as such. That is to consider only the good of the work to be done, the business of the artist. But we have also to consider the good of the man for whom the work is done, whether this "consumer" (*chrômenos*) be the artist himself or some other patron.[53] This man judges in another way, not, or not only, by this truth or accuracy, but by the artifact's utility or aptitude (*ôpheleia*) to serve the purpose of its original intention (*boulêsis*), viz. the need (*endeia*) that was the first and is also the last cause of the work. Accuracy and aptitude together make the "wholesomeness" (*hugieinon*) of the work that is its ultimate-rightness (*orthotês*).[54] The distinction of beauty from utility is logical, not real (*in re*).

So when taste has been rejected as a criterion in art, Plato's Stranger sums up thus, "The judge of anything that has been made (*poiêma*) must know its essence—what its intention (*boulêsis*) is and what the real thing of which it is an image—or else will hardly be able to diagnose whether it hits or misses the mark of its intention." And again, "The expert critic of any image, whether in painting, music, or any other art, must know three things, what was the archetype, and in each case whether it was correctly and whether well made ... whether the representation was good (*kalon*) or not."[55] The complete judgment, made by the whole man, is as to whether the thing under consideration has been both truly *and* well made. It is only "by the mob that the beautiful and the just are rent apart,"[56] by the mob, shall we say, of "aesthetes," the men who "know what they like"?

Of the two judgments, respectively by art and by value, the first only establishes the existence of the object as a true work of art and not a falsification (*pseudos*) of its archetype: it is a judgment normally made by the artist before he can allow the work to leave his shop, and so a judgment that is really presupposed when we as patrons or consumers propose to evaluate the work. It is only under certain conditions, and typically those of modern manufacture and salesmanship, that it becomes necessary for the patron or consumer to ask whether the object he has commissioned or proposes to buy is really a true work of art. Under normal conditions, where making is a vocation and the artist is disposed *and free* to consider nothing but the good of the work to be done, it is superfluous to ask, Is this a "true" work of art? When, however, the question must be asked, or if we wish to ask it in order to understand completely the genesis of the work, then the grounds of our judgment in this respect will be the same as for the original artist; we must know of what the work is intended to remind us, and whether it is equal to (is an "adequate symbol" of) this content, or by want of truth betrays its paradigm. In any case, when this judgment has been made, or is taken for granted, we can proceed to ask whether or not the work has a value for us, to ask whether it will serve our needs. If we are whole men, not such as live by bread alone, the question will be asked with respect to spiritual and physical needs to be satisfied together; we shall ask whether the model has been well chosen, and whether it has been applied to the material in such a way as to serve our immediate need; in other words, What does it say? and Will it work? If we have asked for a bread that will support the whole man, and receive however fine a stone, we are not morally, though we may be legally, bound to "pay the piper." All our efforts to obey the Devil and "command this stone that it be made bread" are doomed to failure.

It is one of Plato's virtues, and that of all traditional doctrine about art, that "value" is never taken to mean an exclusively spiritual or exclusively physical value. It is neither advantageous, nor altogether possible, to separate these values, making some things sacred and others profane: the highest wisdom must be "mixed"[57] with practical knowledge, the contemplative life combined with the active. The pleasures that pertain to these lives are altogether legitimate, and it is only those pleasures that are irrational, bestial, and in the worst sense of the words seductive and distracting that are to be excluded. Plato's music and gymnastics, which correspond to our culture and physical training, are not alternative curricula, but essential parts of one and the same education.[58] Philosophy is the highest form of music (culture), but the philosopher who has escaped from the cave must return to it to participate in the everyday life of the world and, quite literally, play the game.[59] Plato's criterion of "wholesomeness" implies that nothing ought to be made, nothing can be really worth having, that is not at the same time correct or true or formal or beautiful (whichever word you prefer) *and* adapted to good use.

For, to state the Platonic doctrine in more familiar words, "It is written that man shall not live by bread alone, but by every word of God, ... that bread which came down from heaven,"[60] that is, not by mere utilities but also by those "divine realities" and "causal beauty" with which the wholesome works of art are informed, so that they also live and speak. It is just to the extent that we try to live by bread alone and by all the other in-significant utilities that "bread alone" includes—good as utilities, but bad as *mere* utilities—that our contemporary civilization can be rightly called inhuman and must be unfavorably compared with the "primitive" cultures in which, as the anthropologists assure us, "the needs of the body and soul are satisfied together."[61] Manufacture for the needs of the body alone is the curse of modern civilization.

Should we propose to raise our standard of living to the savage level, on which there is no distinction of fine from applied or sacred from profane art, it need not imply the sacrifice of any of the necessities or even conveniences of life, but only of luxuries, only of such utilities as are not at the same time useful *and* significant. If such a proposal to return to primitive levels of culture should seem to be utopian and impracticable, it is only because a manufacture of significant utilities would have to be a manufacture for use, the use of the whole man, and not for the salesman's profit. The price to be paid for putting back into the market place, where they belong, such things as are now to be seen only in museums would be that of economic revolution. It may be doubted whether our boasted love of art extends so far.

It has sometimes been asked whether the "artist" can survive under modern conditions. In the sense in which the word is used by those who ask the question, one does not see how he can or why he should survive. For, just as the modern artist is neither a useful or significant, but only an ornamental member of society, so the modern workman is nothing but a useful member and is neither significant nor ornamental. It is certain that we shall have to go on working, but not so certain that we could not live, and handsomely, without the exhibitionists of our studios, galleries, and playing fields. We cannot do without art, because art is the knowledge of how things ought to be made, art is the principle of manufacture (*recta ratio factibilium*), and while an artless play may be innocent, an artless manufacture is merely brutish labor and a sin against the wholesomeness of human nature; we *can* do without "fine" artists, whose art does not "apply" to anything, and whose organized manufacture of art in studios is the inverse of the laborer's artless manufacture in factories; and we *ought* to be able to do without the base mechanics "whose souls are bowed and mutilated by their vulgar occupations even as their bodies are marred by their mechanical arts."[62]

Plato himself discusses, in connection with all the arts, whether of potter, painter, poet, or "craftsman of civic liberty," the relation between the practice of an art and the earning of a livelihood.[63] He points out that the practice of an art and the wage-earning capacity are two different things; that the artist (in Plato's sense and that of the Christian and Oriental social philosophies) does not earn wages by his art. He *works by* his art, and is only accidentally a trader if he sells what he makes. Being a vocation, his art is most intimately his own and pertains to his own nature, and the pleasure that he takes in it perfects the operation. There is nothing he would rather work (or "play") at than his making; to him the leisure state would be an abomination of boredom. This situation, in which each man does what is naturally (*kata phusin* = Skr. *svabhâvatas*) his to do (*to heautou prattein* = Skr. *svadharma, svakarma*), not only is the type of Justice,[64] but furthermore, under these conditions (i.e., when the maker loves to work), "more is done, and better done, and with more ease, than in any other way."[65] Artists are not trades men. "They know how to make, but not how to hoard."[66] Under these conditions the worker and maker is not a hireling, but one whose salary enables him to go on doing and making. He is just like any other member of a feudal society, in which none are "hired" men, but all enfeoffed and all possessed of a hereditary standing, that of a professional whose reward is by gift or endowment and not "at so much an hour."

The separation of the creative from the profit motive not only leaves the artist free to put the good of the work above his own good, but at the same time abstracts from manufacture the stain of simony, or "traffic in things sacred"; and this conclusion, which rings strangely in our ears, for whom work and play are alike secular activities, is actually in complete agreement with the traditional order, in which the artist's operation is not a meaningless labor, but quite literally a significant and sacred rite, and quite as much as the product itself an adequate symbol of a spiritual reality. It is therefore a way, or rather *the* way, by which the artist, whether potter or painter, poet or king, can best erect or edify (*exorthoô*) *himself* at the same time that he "trues" or cor-rects (*orthoô*) his work.[67] It is, indeed, only by the "true" workman that "true" work can be done; like engenders like.

When Plato lays it down that the arts shall "care for the bodies and souls of your citizens," and that only things that are sane and free and not any shameful things unbecoming free men (*aneleuthera*)[68] are to be represented, it is as much as to say that the true artist in whatever material must be a free man, meaning by this not an "emancipated artist" in the vulgar sense of one having no obligation or commitment of any kind, but a man emancipated from the despotism of the salesman. Whoever is to "imitate the actions of gods and heroes, the intellections and revolutions of the All," the very selves and divine paradigms or ideas of our useful inventions, must have known these realities "themselves (*auta*) and as they really are (*hoia estin*)": for "what we have not and know not we can neither give to another nor teach our neighbor."[69]

In other words, an act of "imagination," in which the idea to be represented is first clothed in the imitable form or image of the thing to be made, must precede the operation in which this form is impressed upon the actual material. The first of these acts, in the terms of Scholastic philosophy, is free, the second servile. It is only if the first be omitted that the word "servile" acquires a dishonorable connotation; then we can speak only of labor, and not of art. It need hardly be argued that our methods of manufacture are, in this shameful sense, servile, nor be denied that the industrial system, for which these methods are needed, is an abomination "unfit for free men." A system of manufacture governed by money values presupposes that there shall be two different kinds of makers, privileged artists who may be "inspired," and underprivileged laborers, unimaginative by hypothesis, since they are required only to make what other men have imagined, or more often only to copy what other men have already made. It has often been claimed that the productions of "fine" art are useless; it would seem to be a mockery to speak of a society as "free" where it is only the makers of useless things who are supposedly free.

Inspiration is defined in Webster as "a supernatural influence which qualifies men to receive and communicate divine truth." This is stated in the word itself, which implies the presence of a guiding "spirit" distinguished from but nevertheless "within" the agent who is in-spired, but is certainly not inspired if "expressing himself." Before continuing, we must clear the air by showing how the word "inspire" has been scabrously abused by modern authors. We have found it said that "a poet or other artist may let the rain inspire him."[70] Such misuse of words debar the student from ever learning what the ancient writers may have really meant. We say "misuse" because neither is the rain, or anything perceptible to sense, *in* us; nor is the rain a kind of *spirit*. The rationalist has a right to disbelieve in inspiration and to leave it out of his account, as he very easily can if he is considering art only from the aesthetic (sensational) point of view, but he has no right to pretend that one can be "inspired" by a sense perception, by which, in fact, one can only be "affected," and to which one can only "react." On the other hand, Meister Eckhart's phrase "inspired by his art" is quite correct, since art is a kind of knowledge, not anything that can be seen, but akin to the soul and prior to the body and the world.[71] We can properly say that not only "Love" but "Art" and "Law" are names of the Spirit.

Here we are concerned not with the rationalist's point of view, but only with the sources from which we can learn how the artist's operation is explained in a tradition that we must understand if we are to understand its products. Here it is always by the Spirit that a man is thought of as inspired (*entheos*, sc. *upo tou erôtos*). "The Genius breathed into my heart (*enepneuse phresi daimôn*) to weave," Penelope says.[72] Hesiod tells us that the Muses "breathed into me a divine voice (*enepneusan de moi audên thespin*)... and bade me sing the race of the blessed Gods."[73] Christ, "through whom all things were made," does not bear witness of (express) himself, but says "I do nothing of myself, but as my Father taught me, I speak."[74] Dante writes, I am "one who when Love (Amor, Eros) inspires me (*mi spira*), attend, and go setting it forth in such wise as He dictates within me."[75] For "there is no real speaking that does not lay hold upon the Truth."[76] And who is it ("What self?") that speaks the "Truth that cannot be refuted"? Not this man, So-and-so, Dante, or Socrates, or "I," but the Synteresis, the Immanent Spirit, Socrates' and Plato's Daimon, he "who lives in every one of us"[77] and "cares for nothing but the Truth."[78] It is the "God himself that speaks" when we are not thinking our own thoughts but are His exponents, or priests.

And so as Plato, the father of European wisdom, asks, "Do we not know that as regards the practice of the arts (*tên tôn technôn dêmiourgian*) the man who has this God for his teacher will be renowned and as it were a beacon light, but one whom Love has not possessed will be obscure?"[79] This is with particular reference to the divine originators of archery, medicine, and oracles, music, metalwork, weaving, and piloting, each of whom was "Love's disciple." He means, of course, the "cosmic Love" that harmonizes opposite forces, the Love that acts for the sake of what it has and to beget itself, not the profane love that lacks and desires. So the maker of anything, if he is to be called a creator, is at his best the servant of an immanent Genius; he must not be called "a genius," but "*ingenious*"; he is not working of or for himself, but by and for another energy, that of the Immanent Eros, Sanctus Spiritus, the source of all "gifts." "All that is true, by whomsoever it has been said, has its origin in the Spirit."[80]

We can now, perhaps, consider, with less danger of misunderstanding, Plato's longest passage on inspiration. "It is a divine power that moves (*theia de dunamis, hê ... kinei*) "[81] even the rhapsodist or literary critic, insofar as he speaks well, though he is only the exponent of an exponent. The original maker and exponent, if he is to be an imitator of realities and not of mere appearances, "is God-indwelt and possessed (*entheos, katechomenos*) ... an airy, winged and sacred substance (*hieron*, Skr. *brahma-*); unable ever to indite until he has been born again of the God within him (*prin an entheos te genêtai*)[82] and is out of his own wits (*ekphrôn*), and his own mind (*nous*) is no longer in him;[83] for every man, so long as he retains *that* property is powerless to make (*poiein*) or to incant (*chrêsmôdein*, Skr. *mantrakr*) ... The men whom he dements God uses as his ministers (*hupêretai*) ... but it is the God[84] himself (*ho theos autos*) that speaks, and through them enlightens (*phthengetai*) us ... The makers are but His exponents (*hermênês*) according to the way in which they are possessed."[85] It is only when he returns to himself from what is really a sacrificial operation that the maker exercises his own powers of judgment; and then primarily to "try the spirits, whether they be of God," and secondarily to try his work, whether it agrees with the vision or audition.

The most immediately significant point that emerges from this profound analysis of the nature of inspiration is that of the artist's priestly or ministerial function. The original intention of intelligible forms was not to entertain us, but literally to "re-mind" us. The chant is not for the approval of the ear,[86] nor the picture for that of the eye (although these senses can be taught to approve the splendor of truth, and can be trusted when they have been trained), but to effect such a transformation of our being as is the purpose of all ritual acts. It is, in fact, the ritual arts that are the most "artistic," because the most "correct," as they must be if they are to be effectual.

The heavens declare the glory of God: their interpretation in science or art—and *ars sine scientia nihil*—is not in order to flatter or

merely "interest" us, but "in order that we may follow up the intellections and revolutions of the All, not those revolutions that are in
our own heads and were distorted at our birth, but correcting (*exor-
thounta*) these by studying the harmonies and revolutions of the All:
so that by an assimilation of the knower to the to-be-known (*tô
katanooumenô to katanooun exomoiôsai*),[87] the archetypal Nature, and
coming to be in *that* likeness,[88] we may attain at last to a part in that
'life's best' that has been appointed by the gods to men for this time
being and hereafter."[89]

This is what is spoken of in India as a "metrical self-integration"
(*candobhir âtimânam samskarana*), or "edification of another man"
(*anyam âtmânam*), to be achieved by an imitation (*anukarana*) of the
divine forms (*daivyâni silpâni*).[90] The final reference to a good to be
realized here *and* hereafter brings us back again to the "wholesomeness" of art, defined in terms of its simultaneous application to
practical necessities and spiritual meanings, back to that fulfillment
of the needs of the body and soul together that is characteristic of
the arts of the uncivilized peoples and the "folk" but foreign to our
industrial life. For in that life the arts are *either* for use *or* for pleasure, but are never spiritually significant and very rarely intelligible.

Such an application of the arts as Plato prescribes for his City of
God, arts that as he says "will care for the bodies and the souls of
your citizens,"[91] survives for so long as forms and symbols are
employed to express a meaning, for so long as "ornament" means
"equipment,"[92] and until what were originally imitations of the reality, not the appearance, of things become (as they were already rap-
idly becoming in Plato's time) merely "art forms, more and more
emptied of significance on their way down to us"[93]—no longer figures of thought, but only figures of speech.

We have so far made use of Oriental sources only incidentally,
and chiefly to remind ourselves that the true philosophy of art is
always and everywhere the same. But since we are dealing with the
distinction between the arts of flattery and those of ministration, we
propose to refer briefly to some of the Indian texts in which the
"whole end of the expressive faculty" is discussed. This natural faculty is that of the "Voice": not the audibly spoken word, but the the
organon by which a concept is communicated. The relation of this
maternal Voice to the paternal Intellect is that of our feminine
"nature" to our masculine "essence"; their begotten child is the
Logos of theology and the spoken myth of anthropology. The work

of art is expressly the artist's child, the child of both his natures, human and divine: stillborn if he has not at his command the art of delivery (rhetoric), a bastard if the Voice has been seduced, but a valid concept if born in lawful marriage.

The Voice is at once the daughter, bride, messenger, and instrument of the Intellect.[94] Possessed of him, the immanent deity, she brings forth his image (reflection, imitation, similitude, *pratirûpa*, child).[95] She is the power and the glory,[96] without whom the Sacrifice itself could not proceed.[97] But if he, the divine Intellect, Brahmâ or Prajâpati, "does not precede and direct her, then it is only a gibberish in which she expresses herself."[98] Translated into the terms of the art of government, this means that if the Regnum acts on its own initiative, unadvised by the Sacerdotium, it will not be Law, but only regulations that it promulgates.

The conflict of Apollo with Marsyas the Satyr, to which Plato alludes,[99] is the same as that of Prajâpati (the Progenitor) with Death,[100] and the same as the contention of the Gandharvas, the gods of Love and Science, with the mundane deities, the sense powers, for the hand of the Voice, the Mother of the Word, the wife of the Sacerdotium.[101] This is, in fact, the debate of the Sacerdotium and the Regnum with which we are most familiar in terms of an opposition of sacred and profane, eternal and secular, an opposition that must be present wherever the needs of the soul and the body are *not* satisfied together.

Now what was chanted and enacted by the Progenitor in his sacrificial contest with Death was "calculated" (*samkhyânam*)[102] and "immortal," and what by Death "uncalculated" and "mortal"; and that deadly music played by Death is now our secular art of the "parlor" (*patnisâlâ*), "whatever people sing to the harp, or dance, or do to please themselves (*vrthâ*)," or even more literally, "do heretically," for the words "*vrthâ*" and "heresy" derive from a common root that means to "choose for oneself," to "know what one likes and to grasp at it." Death's informal and irregular music is disintegrating. On the other hand, the Progenitor "puts himself together," composes or synthesizes himself, "by means of the meters"; the Sacrificer "perfects himself so as to be metrically constituted,"[103] and makes of the measures the wings of his ascension.[104] The distinctions made here between a quickening art and one that adds to the sum of our mortality are those that underlie Plato's *katharsis* and all true puritanism and fastidiousness. There is no disparagement of the Voice (Sophia) herself, or of music or dancing or any other art as such. Whatever disparagement there is, is not of the instrument; there can be no good use without art.

The contest of the Gandharvas, the high gods of Love and Music (in Plato's broad sense of that word), is with the unregenerate powers of the soul, whose natural inclination is the pursuit of pleasures. What the Gandharvas offer to the Voice is their sacred science, the thesis of their incantation; what the mundane deities offer is "to please her." The Gandharvas' is a holy conversation (*brahmodaya*), that of the mundane deities an appetizing colloquy (*prakâmodaya*). Only too often the Voice, the expressive power, is seduced by the mundane deities to lend herself to the representation of whatever may best please them and be most flattering to herself; and it is when she thus prefers the pleasant falsehoods to the splendor of the sometimes bitter truth that the high gods have to fear lest she in turn seduce their legitimate spokesman, the Sacrificer himself; to fear, that is to say, a secularization of the sacred symbols and the hieratic language, the depletion of meaning that we are only too familiar with in the history of art, as it descends from formality to figuration, just as language develops from an original precision to what are ultimately hardly more than blurred emotive values.

It was not for this, as Plato said, that powers of vision and hearing are ours. In language as nearly as may be identical with his, and in terms of the universal philosophy wherever we find it, the Indian texts define the "whole end of the Voice" (*krtsnam vâgârtham*). We have already called the voice an "organ," to be taken in the musical as well as the organic sense. It is very evidently not the reason of an organ to play of itself, but to be played upon, just as it is not for the clay to determine the form of the vessel, but to receive it.

"Now there is this divine harp: the human harp is in its likeness ... and just as the harp struck by a skilled player fulfills the whole reason of the harp, so the Voice moved by a skilled speaker fulfills its whole reason."[105] "Skill in any performance is a yoking, as of steeds together,"[106] or, in other words, implies a marriage of the master and the means. The product of the marriage of the player, Intellect, with the instrument, the Voice, is Truth (*satyam*) or Science (*vidyâ*),[107] not that approximate, hypothetical, and statistical truth that we refer to as science, but philosophy in Plato's

sense,[108] and that "meaning of the Vedas" by which, if we understand it, "all good" (*sakalam bhadram*) is attainable, here and hereafter.[109]

The *raison d'être* of the Voice is to incarnate in a communicable
form the concept of Truth; the formal beauty of the precise expression is that of the *splendor veritatis*. The player and the instrument
are both essential here. We, in our somatic individuality, are the
instrument, of which the "strings" or "senses" are to be regulated, so
as to be neither slack nor overstrained; we are the organ, the inor-
ganic God within us the organist. We are the organism, He its energy. It is not for us to play our own tunes, but to sing His songs, who
is both the Person in the Sun (Apollo) and our own Person (as distinguished from our "personality"). When "those who sing here to
the harp sing Him,"[110] then all desires are attainable, here and hereafter.

There is, then, a distinction to be drawn between a significant
(*padârthâbhinaya*) and liberating (*vimuktida*) art, the art of those
who in their performances are celebrating God, the Golden Person,
in both His natures, immanent and transcendent, and the *in-significant* art that is "colored by worldly passion" (*lokânurañjaka*) and
"dependent on the moods" (*bhâvâsraya*). The former is the "highway" (*mârga, hodos*) art that leads directly to the end of the road, the
latter a "pagan" (*desî, agrios*) and eccentric art that wanders off in all
directions, imitating anything and everything.[111]

If now the orthodox doctrines reported by Plato and the East
are not convincing, this is because our sentimental generation, in
which the power of the intellect has been so perverted by the power
of observation that we can no longer distinguish the reality from the
phenomenon, the Person in the Sun from his sightly body, or the
untreated from electric light, will not be persuaded "though one
rose from the dead." Yet I hope to have shown, in a way that may be
ignored but cannot be refuted, that our use of the term "aesthetic"
forbids us also to speak of art as pertaining to the "higher things of
life" or the immortal part of us; that the distinction of "fine" from
"applied" art, and corresponding manufacture of art in studios and
artless industry in factories, takes it for granted that neither the
artist nor the artisan shall be a whole man; that our freedom to work
or starve is not a responsible freedom but only a legal fiction that
conceals an actual servitude; that our hankering after a leisure state,

or state of pleasure, to be attained by a multiplication of labor-saving devices, is born of the fact that most of us are doing forced labor, working at jobs to which we could never have been "called" by any other master than the salesman; that the very few, the happy few of us whose work is a vocation, and whose status is relatively secure, like nothing better than our work and can hardly be dragged away from it; that our division of labor, Plato's "fractioning of human faculty," makes the workman a part of the machine, unable ever to make or to co-operate responsibly in the making of any whole thing; that in the last analysis the so-called "emancipation of the artist"[112] is nothing but his final release from any obligation whatever to the God within him, and his opportunity to imitate himself or any other common clay at its worst; that all willful self-expression is autoerotic, narcissistic, and satanic, and the more its essentially paranoiac quality develops, suicidal; that while our invention of innumerable conveniences has made our unnatural manner of living in great cities so endurable that we cannot imagine what it would be like to do without them, yet the fact remains that not even the multimillionaire is rich enough to commission such works of art as are preserved in our museums but were originally made for men of relatively moderate means or, under the patronage of the church, for God and all men, and the fact remains that the multimillionaire can no longer send to the ends of the earth for the products of other courts or the humbler works of the folk, for all these things have been destroyed and their makers reduced to being the providers of raw materials for our factories, wherever our civilizing influence has been felt; and so, in short, that while the operation that we call a "progress" has been very successful, man the patient has succumbed.

Let us, then, admit that the greater part of what is taught in the fine arts departments of our universities, all of the psychologies of art, all the obscurities of modern aesthetics, are only so much verbiage, only a kind of defense that stands in the way of our understanding of the wholesome art, at the same time iconographically true and practically useful, that was once to be had in the marketplace or from any good artist; and that whereas the rhetoric that cares for nothing but the truth is the rule and method of the intellectual arts, our aesthetic is nothing but a false rhetoric, and a flattery of human weakness by which we can account only for the arts that have no other purpose than to please.

The whole intention of our own art may be aesthetic, and we may wish to have it so. But however this may be, we also pretend to a scientific and objective discipline of the history and appreciation of art, in which we take account not only of contemporary or very recent art but also of the whole of art from the beginning until now. It is in this arena that I shall throw down a minimum challenge: put it to you that it is not by our aesthetic, but only by their rhetoric, that we can hope to understand and interpret the arts of other peoples and other ages than our own. I put it to you that our present university courses in this field embody a pathetic fallacy, and are anything but scientific in any sense.

And now, finally, in case you should complain that I have been drawing upon very antiquated sources (and what else could I do, seeing that we are all "so young" and "do not possess a single belief that is ancient and derived from old tradition, nor yet one science that is hoary with age"[113]) let me conclude with a very modern echo of this ancient wisdom, and say with Thomas Mann that I like to think—yes, I feel sure—that a future is coming in which we shall condemn as black magic, as the brainless, irresponsible product of instinct, all art which is not controlled by the intellect."[114]

Notes

1. Quintilian IX.4.117, "Figura? Quae? cum orationis, turn etiam sententiae?" Cf. Plato, *Republic* 601B.

2. "I cannot fairly give the name of 'art' to anything irrational." Cf. *Laws* 890D, "Law and art are children of the intellect" (*nous*). Sensation (*aisthêsis*) and pleasure (*hêdonê*) are irrational (*alogos*, see *Timaeus* 28A, 47D, 69D). In the *Gorgias*, the irrational is that which cannot give an account of itself, that which is unreasonable, has no *raison d'être*. See also Philo, *Legum Allegoriarum* I.48, "For as grass is the food of irrational beings, so has the sensibly-perceptible (*to aisthêton*) been assigned to the irrational part of the soul." *Aisthêsis* is just what the biologist now calls "irritability."

3. Quoted with approval by Herbert Read, *Art and Society* (New York, 1937), p. 84, from Alfred North Whitehead, *Religion in the Making* (New York, 1926).

4. *Sum. Theol.* I-II.57.3c (art is an intellectual virtue); I.5.4 ad 1 (beauty pertains to the cognitive, not the appetitive faculty).

5. "Pathology ... 2. The study of the passions or emotions" (*The Oxford English Dictionary*, 1933, VII, 554). The "psychology of art" is not a science of art but of the way in which we are affected by works of art. An affection (*pathêma*) is passive; making or doing (*poiêma, ergon*) is an activity.

6. See Charles Sears Baldwin, *Medieval Rhetoric and Poetic* (New York, 1928), p. 3. "A real art of speaking which does not lay hold upon the truth does not exist and never will" (*Phaedrus* 260E; cf. *Gorgias* 463-465, 513D, 517A, 527C, *Laws* 937E).

7. See E. F. Rothschild, *The Meaning* of *Unintelligibility in Modern Art* (Chicago, 1934), p. 98. "The course of artistic achievement was the change from the visual as a means of comprehending the non-visual to the visual as an end in itself and the abstract structure of physical forms as the purely artistic transcendence of the visual ... *a transcendence utterly alien and unintelligible* to the average [sc. normal] man" (F. de W. Bolman, criticizing E. Kahler's *Man the Measure*, in *Journal* of *Philosophy*, XLI, 1944, 134-135; italics mine).

8. *Sum. Theol.* I.45.6c, "Artifex autem per verbum in intellectu conceptum et per amorem suae voluntatis ad aliquid relatum, operatur"; I.14.8c, "Artifex operatur per suum intellectum"; I.45.7c "Forma artificiati est ex conceptione artificis." See also St. Bonaventura, *Il Sententiarum* I-I.I.I ad 3 and 4, "Agens per intellectum producit per formas." Informality is ugliness.

9. *Gorgias* 503E.

10. *Symposium* 205C.

11. See, for example, *Statesman* 259E, *Phaedrus* 260E, *Laws* 938A. The word *tribê* literally means "a rubbing," and is an exact equivalent of our modern expression "a grind." (Cf. Hippocrates, *Fractures* 772, "shameful and artless," and Ruskin's "industry without art is brutality.") "For all well-governed peoples there is a work enjoined upon each man which he must perform" (*Republic* 406C). "Leisure" is the opportunity to do this work without interference (*Republic* 370C). A "work for leisure" is one requiring undivided attention (Euripides, *Andromache* 552). Plato's view of work in no way differs from that of Hesiod, who says that work is no reproach but the best gift of the gods to men (*Works and Days* 295-296). Whenever Plato disparages the mechanical arts, it is with reference to the kinds of work that provide for the well-being of the body only, and do not at the same time provide spiritual food; he does not connect culture with idleness.

12. *Republic* 342BC. What is made by art is correctly made (*Alcibiades* 1.108B). It will follow that those who are in possession of and governed by their art and not by their own irrational impulses, which yearn for innovations, will operate in the same way (*Republic* 349-350, *Laws* 660B). "Art has fixed ends and ascertained means of operation" (*Sum. Theol.* II-II.47.4 ad 2, 49.5 *ad* 2). It is in the same way that an oracle, speaking *ex cathedra*, is infallible, but not so the man when speaking for himself. This is similarly true in the case of a guru.

13. *Republic* 369BC, *Statesman* 279CD, *Epinomis* 975C.

14. *Republic* 398A, 401B, 605-607; *Laws* 656C.

15. Deut. 8:3, Luke 4:4.

16. *Republic* 376E, 410A-412A, 521E-522A, *Laws* 673A. Plato always has in view an attainment of the "best" for both the body and the soul, "since for any single kind to be left by itself pure and isolated is not good, nor altogether possible" (*Philebus* 63B; cf. *Republic* 409-410). "The one means of salvation from these evils is neither to exercise the soul without the body nor the body without the soul" (*Timaeus* 88B).

17. *Sum. Theol.* I-II.57.3 ad 2 (based on Plato's view of justice, which assigns to every man the work for which he is naturally fitted). None of the arts pursues its own

good, but only the patron's (*Republic* 342B, 347A), which lies in the excellence of the product.

18. *Timaeus* 47DE; cf. *Laws* 659E, on the chant.

19. *Timaeus* 80B, echoed in Quintilian IX.117, "docti rationem componendi intelligunt, etiam indocti voluptatem." Cf. *Timaeus* 47, 90D.

20. *Sâhitya Darpana* III.2–3; cf. Coomaraswamy, *The Transformation of Nature in Art,* 1934, pp. 48-51.

21. *Laws* 840C.c. On *katharsis,* see Plato, *Sophist* 226-227, *Phaedrus* 243AB, *Phaedo* 66-67, 82B, *Republic* 399E; Aristotle, *Poetics* VI.2.1449b.

22. *Phaedo* 67DE.

23. *Phaedrus* 279BC; *so* also Hermes, *Lib.* XIII.3, 4, "I have passed forth out of myself," and Chuang-tzu, ch. 2, "Today I buried myself." Cf. Coomaraswamy, "On Being in One's Right Mind," 1942.

24. *Republic* 389-398.

25. Aristotle, *Poetics* VI.2.1449b.

26. The aesthetic man is "one who is too weak to stand up against pleasure and pain" (*Republic* 556c). If we think of impassibility (*apatheia*), not what we mean by "apathy" but a being superior to the pulls of pleasure and pain; cf. BG II.56) with horror, it is because we should be "unwilling to live without hunger and thirst and the like, if we could not also *suffer* (*paschô,* Skr. *bâdh*) the natural consequences of these passions," the pleasures of eating and drinking and enjoying fine colors and sounds (*Philebus* 54E, 55B). Our attitude to pleasures and pains is always passive, if not, indeed, masochistic. Cf. Coomaraswamy, *Time and Eternity,* 1947, p. 73 and notes.

It is very clear from *Republic* 606 that the enjoyment of an emotional storm is just what Plato does not mean by a *katharsis;* such an indulgence merely fosters the very feelings that we are trying to suppress. A perfect parallel is found in the *Milinda Pañho* (Mil, p. 76); it is asked, of tears shed for the death of a mother or shed for love of the Truth, which can be called a "cure" (*bhesajjam*)—i.e. for man's mortality—and it is pointed out that the former are fevered, the latter cool, and that it is what cools that cures.

27. JUB III.30.2 and 39.2; BU III.7.3-4; CU VIII.13; Svet. Up. V.14. Cf. *Phaedo* 65-69.

28. *Statesman* 288C.

29. *Philebus* 67B.

30. *Republic* 399-404; cf. *Laws* 656E, 660, 797-799.

31. *Laws* 659E; see also note 86, below.

32. *Republic* 399E; cf. Dante, *Paradiso* 1.13-21.

33. Aristotle, *Physics* II.2.194a 20, *hê technê mimeitai tên phusin*—both employing suitable means toward a known end.

34. Art is iconography, the making of images or copies of some model (*paradeigma*), whether visible (presented) or invisible (contemplated); see Plato, *Republic* 373B, 377E, 392-397, 402, *Laws* 667-669, *Statesman* 306D, *Cratylus* 439A, *Timaeus* 28AB, 52BC, *Sophist* 234C, 236C; Aristotle, *Poetics* I.1-2. In the same way, Indian works of art are called counterfeits or commensurations (*anukrti, tadâkâratâ, pratikrti, pratibimba, pratimâna*), and likeness (*sârûpya, sâdrsya*) is

demanded. This does not mean that it is a likeness in all respects that is needed to evoke the original, but an equality as to the whichness (*tosouton, hoson*) and what-ness (*toiouton, hoion*)—or form (*idea*) and force (*dunamis*)—of the archetype. It is this "real equality" or "adequacy" (*auto to ison*) that is the truth and the beauty of the work (*Laws* 667-668, *Timaeus* 28AB, *Phaedo* 74-75). We have shown elsewhere that the Indian *sâdrsya* does not imply an illusion but only a real equivalence. It is clear from *Timaeus* 28-29 that by "equality" and "likeness" Plato also means a real kinship (*sungeneia*) and analogy (*analogia*), and that it is these qualities that make it possible for an image to "interpret" or "deduce" (*exêgeomai*, cf. Skr. *ânî*) its arche-type. For example, words are *eidôla* of things (*Sophist* 234C), "true names'" are not correct by accident (*Cratylus* 387D, 439A), the body is an *eidôlon* of the soul (*Laws* 959B), and these images are at the same time like and yet unlike their referents. In other words, what Plato means by "imitation" and by "art" is an "adequate symbol-ism"; cf. distinction of image from duplicate, *Cratylus* 432.

35. "The mathematician's patterns, like the painter's or the poet's, must be *beauti-ful*" (G. H. Hardy, *A Mathematician's Apology*, Cambridge, 1940, p. 85); cf. Coomaraswamy, *Why Exhibit Works of Art?*, 1943, ch. 9.

36. *Philebus* 51C. For beauty by participation, see *Phaedo* 100D; cf. *Republic* 476; St. Augustine, *Confessions* X.34; Dionysius, *De divinis nominibus* IV.5.

37. *Laws* 657AB, 665C, 700C.

38. *Laws* 670E; *Sum. Theol.* I.91.3, I-II.57.3 ad 2.

39. Cicero, *Pro quinctio* XXV.78.

40. *Republic* 395C; cf. 395-401, esp. 401BC, 605-607, and *Laws* 656C.

41. *Republic* 400A, 598B; cf. *Timaeus* 29C.

42. *Republic* 500E.

43. Plotinus, *Enneads* V.9.II, like Plato, *Timaeus* 28AB.

44. Exod. 25:40.

45. AB VI.27.

46. SA VIII.9.

47. SB VII.2.1.4; cf. III.3.3.16, XIV.1.2.26, and TS V.5.4.4. Whenever the Sacrificers are at a loss, they are required to contemplate (*cetayadhvam*), and the required form thus seen becomes their model. Cf. Philo, *Moses* II.74-76.

48. *Republic* 377, 402, *Laws* 667-668, *Timaeus* 28AB, *Phaedrus* 243AB (on *hamartia peri muthologian*), *Republic* 382BC (misuse of words is a symptom of sickness in the soul).

49. See *Republic* 601, for example. Porphyry tells us that Plotinus refused to have his portrait painted, objecting, "Must I consent to leave, as a desirable spectacle for posterity, an image of an image?" Cf. Asterius, bishop of Amasea, ca. A.D. 340: "Paint not Christ: for the one humility of his incarnation suffices him" (Migne, *Patrologia graeca* XI.167). The real basis of the Semitic objection to graven images, and of all other iconoclasm, is not an objection to art (adequate symbolism), but an objection to a realism that implies an essentially idolatrous worship of nature. The figuration of the Ark according to the pattern that was seen upon the mount (Exod. 25:40) is not "that kind of imagery with reference to which the prohibition was given" (Tertullian, *Contra Marcionem* II.22).

50. *Timaeus* 28AB; cf. note 34, above. The symbols that are rightly sanctioned by a hieratic art are not conventionally but *naturally* correct (*orthotêta phusei parechomena, Laws* 657A). One distinguishes, accordingly, between *le symbolisme qui sait* and *le symbolisme qui cherche*. It is the former that the iconographer can and must understand, but he will hardly be able to do so unless he is himself accustomed to thinking in these precise terms.

51. The realities are seen "by the eye of the soul" (*Republic* 533D), "the soul alone and by itself" (*Theaetetus* 186A, 187A), "gazing ever on what is authentic" (*pros to kata tauta echon blepôn aei, Timaeus* 28A; cf. *pros ton theon blepein, Phaedrus* 253A), and thus "by inwit (intuition) of what really is" (*peri to on ontôs ennoiais, Philebus* 59D). Just so in India, it is only when the senses have been withdrawn from their objects, only when the eye has been turned round (*aâvrtta caksus*), and with the eye of Gnosis (*jñâna caksus*), that the reality can be apprehended.

52. The contemplative *actus primus* (*theôria*, Skr. *dhî, dhyâna*) and operative *actus secundus* (*apergasia*, Skr. *karma*) of the Scholastic philosophers.

53. "One man is able to beget the productions of art, but the ability to judge of their utility (*ôphelia*) or harmfulness to their users belongs to another" (*Phaedrus* 274E). The two men are united in the whole man and complete connoisseur, as they are in the Divine Architect whose "judgments" are recorded in Gen. 1:25 and 31.

54. *Laws* 667; for a need as first and last cause, see *Republic* 369BC. As to "wholesomeness," cf. Richard Bernheimer, in *Art: A Bryn Mawr Symposium* (Bryn Mawr, 1940), pp. 28-29: "There should be a deep ethical purpose in all of art, of which the classical aesthetic was fully aware ... To have forgotten this purpose before the mirage of absolute patterns and designs is perhaps the fundamental fallacy of the abstract movement in art." The modern abstractionist forgets that the Neolithic formalist was not an interior decorator but a metaphysical man who had to live by his wits.

The indivisibility of beauty and use is affirmed in Xenophon, *Memorabilia* III.8.8, "that the same house is both beautiful and useful was a lesson in the art of building houses as they ought to be" (cf. IV.6.9). "Omnis enim artifex intendit producere opus pulcrum et utile et stabile ... Scientia reddit opus pulcrum, voluntas reddit utile, perseverantia reddit stabile." (St. Bonaventura, *De reductione artium ad theologiam* 13; tr. de Vinck: "Every maker intends to produce a beautiful, useful, and enduring object ... Knowledge makes a work beautiful, the will makes it useful, and perseverance makes it enduring.") So for St. Augustine, the stylus is "et in suo genere pulcher, et ad usum nostrum accommodatus" (*De vera religione* 39). Philo defines art as "a system of concepts co-ordinated towards some useful end" (*Congr.* 141). Only those whose notion of utility is solely with reference to bodily needs, or on the other hand, the pseudomystics who despise the body rather than use it, vaunt the "uselessness" of art: so Gautier, "Il n'y a de vraiment beau que ce qui ne peut servir à rien; tout ce qui est utile est laid" (quoted by Dorothy Richardson, "Saintsbury and Art for Art's Sake in England," PMLA, XLIX, 1944, 245), and Paul Valéry (see Coomaraswamy, *Why Exhibit Works of Art?* 1943, p. 95). Gautier's cynical "tout ce qui est utile est laid" adequately illustrates Ruskin's "industry without art is brutality"; a more scathing judgment of the modern world in which utilities are really ugly could hardly be imagined. As H. J. Massingham said, "The combination of use and beauty is part of what used to be called 'the natural law' and is indispensable for self-preservation," and it is because of the neglect of this principle that civilization "is perishing" (*This Plot of Earth*, London, 1944, p. 176). The modern world is dying of its own squalor just because *its* concept of practical utility is limited to that which "can be used directly for the destruction of human life or for accentuating the present inequalities in the distribution of wealth" (Hardy, *A Mathematician's Apology*, p. 120, note), and it is only under these unprecedented conditions that it could have been propounded by the escapists that the useful and the beautiful are opposites.

55. *Laws* 668C, 669AB, 670E.

56. *Laws* 860C.

57. *Philebus* 61B-D.

58. *Republic* 376E, 410-412, 521E-522A.

59. *Republic* 519-520, 539E, *Laws* 644, and 803 in conjunction with 807. Cf. BG III.I-25; also Coomaraswamy, "Lîlâ," 1941, and "Play and Seriousness," 1942.

60. Deut. 8:3, Luke 4:4, John 6:58.

61. R. R. Schmidt, *Dawn of the Human Mind* (*Der Geist der Forzeit*), tr. R.A.S. Macalister (London, 1936), p. 167.

62. *Republic* 495E; cf. 522B, 611D, *Theaetetus* 173AB. That "industry without art is brutality" is hardly flattering to those whose admiration of the industrial system is equal to their interest in it. Aristotle defines as "slaves" those who have nothing but their bodies to offer (*Politics* I.5.1254b 18). It is on the work of such "slaves," or literally "prostitutes," that the industrial system of production for profit ultimately rests. Their political freedom does not make of assembly-line workers and other "base mechanics" what Plato means by "free men."

63. *Republic* 395B, 500D. Cf. Philo, *De opificio mundi* 78.

64. *Republic* 433B, 443C.

65. *Republic* 370C; cf. 347E, 374BC, 406C. Paul Shorey had the naïveté to see in Plato's conception of a vocational society an anticipation of Adam Smith's division of labor; see *The Republic*, tr. and ed. P. Shorey (LCL, 1935), I, 150-151, note b. Actually, no two conceptions could be more contrary. In Plato's division of labor it is taken for granted not that the artist is a special kind of man but that every man is a special kind of artist; his specialization is for the good of all concerned, producer and consumer alike. Adam Smith's division benefits no one but the manufacturer and salesman. Plato, who detested any "fractioning of human faculty" (*Republic* 395B), could hardly have seen in *our* division of labor a type of justice. Modern research has rediscovered that "workers are *not* governed primarily by economic motives" (see Stuart Chase, "What Makes the Worker Like to Work?" *Reader's Digest*, February 1941, p. 19).

66. Chuang-tzu, as quoted by Arthur Waley, *Three Ways of Thought in Ancient China* (London, 1939), p. 62. It is not true to say that "the artist is a mercenary living by the sale of his own works" (F. J. Mather, *Concerning Beauty*, Princeton, 1935, p. 240). He is not working in order to make money but accepts money (or its equivalent) in order to be able to go on working at his living—and I say "working at his *living*" because the man *is* what he does.

67. "A man attains perfection by devotion to his own work ... by his own work praising Him who wove this all ... Whoever does the work appointed by his own nature incurs no sin" (BG XVIII.45-46).

68. *Republic* 395C. See Aristotle on "leisure," *Nicomachean Ethics* X.7.5-7.1177b.

69. *Republic* 377E, Symposium 196E.

70. H. J. Rose, *A Handbook of Greek Mythology* (2d ed., London, 1933), p. 11. Clement Greenberg (in *The Nation*, April 19, 1941, p. 481) tells us that the "modern painter derives his inspiration from the very physical materials he works with." Both critics forget the customary distinction of spirit from matter. What their statements actually mean is that the modern artist may be excited, but is not inspired.

71. Eckhart, Evans ed., II, 211; cf. *Laws* 892BC.

72. Homer, *Odyssey* XIX.138

73. *Theogony* 31-32.

74. John 8:28; cf. 5:19 and 30, 7:16 and 18 ("He that speaketh from himself seeketh his own glory"). A column in *Parnassus*, XIII (May 1941), 189, comments on the female nude as Maillol's "exclusive inspiration." That is mere hot air; Renoir was not afraid to call a spade a spade when he said with what brush he painted.

75. *Purgatorio* XXIV.52-54.

76. *Phaedrus* 260E; *Symposium* 201C (on the irrefutable truth).

77. *Timaeus* 69C, 90A.

78. *Hippias Major* 288D.

79. *Symposium* 197A.

80. Ambrose on I Cor. 12:3, cited in *Sum. Theol.* I-II.109.1. Note that "a quocumque dicatur" contradicts the claim that it is only Christian truth that is "revealed."

81. *Ion* 533D. For the passage on inspiration, see *Ion* 533D-536D. Plato's doctrine of inspiration is not "mechanical" but "dynamic"; in a later theology it became a matter for debate in which of these two ways the Spirit actuates the interpreter.

82. *Ion* 533E, 534B. *gignomai* here is used in the radical sense of "coming into a new state of being." Cf. *Phaedrus* 279B, *kalô genesthai tandothen*, "May I be born in beauty inwardly," i.e., born of the immanent deity (*d' en hêmin theiô, Timaeus* 90D), authentic and divine beauty (*auto to theion kalon, Symposium* 211E:). The New Testament equivalents are "in the Spirit" and "born again of the Spirit."

83. *Ion* 534B. "The madness that comes of God is superior to the sanity which is of human origin" (*Phaedrus* 244D, 245A). Cf. *Timaeus* 71D-72B, *Laws* 719C; and MU VI.34.7, "When one attains to mindlessness, that is the last step." The subject needs a longer explanation; briefly, the supralogical is superior to the logical, the logical to the illogical.

84. "The God" is the Immanent Spirit, Daimon, Eros. "He is a maker (*poiêtês*) so really wise (*sophos*) that he is the cause of making in others" (*Symposium* 196E). The voice is "enigmatic" (*Timaeus* 72B), and poetry, therefore, "naturally enigmatic" (*Alcibiades* II 147B), so that in "revelation" (scripture, Skr. *sruti*, "what was heard") we see "through a glass darkly" (*en ainigmati*, I Cor. 13:12). Because divination is of a Truth that cannot (with human faculties) be seen directly (Skr. *sâksât*), the soothsayer must speak in symbols (whether verbal or visual), which are reflections of the Truth; it is for us to understand and use the symbols as supports of contemplation

and with a view to "recollection." It is because the symbols are things seen "through a glass" that contemplation is "speculation."

85. See *Ion* 534, 535. Related passages have been cited in notes 82-84, above. The last words refer to the diversity of the gifts of the spirit; see I Cor. 12:4-11.

86. "What we call 'chants' ... are evidently in reality 'incantations' seriously designated to produce in souls that harmony of which we have been speaking" (*Laws* 659E; cf. 665C, 656E, 660B, 668-669, 812C, *Republic* 399, 424). Such incantations are called *mantras* in Sanskrit.

87. *Timaeus* 90D. The whole purpose of contemplation and yoga is to reach that state of being in which there is no longer any distinction of knower from known, or being from knowing. It is just from this point of view that while all the arts are imitative, it matters so much *what* is imitated, a reality or an effect, for we become like what we think most about. "One comes to be of just such stuff as that on which the mind is set" (MU VI.34).

88. "To become like God (*homoiôsis theô*), so far as that is possible, is to 'escape'" (*Theaetetus* 176B; *phugê* here = *lusis* = Skr. *moksa*). "But we all, with open face beholding as in a glass the glory of the Lord, are changed into the same image ... looking not at the things which are seen, but at the things which are not seen ... the things which ... *are* eternal" (II Cor. 3:18, 4:18). "This likeness begins now again to be formed in us" (St. Augustine, *De spiritu et littera* 37). Cf. Coomaraswamy, "The Traditional Conception of Ideal Portraiture," in *Why Exhibit Works o f Art?*, 1943.

89. *Timaeus* 90D.

90. AB VI.27

91. *Republic* 409-410.

92. See Coomaraswamy, "Ornament."

93. Walter Andrae, *Die ionische Säule* (Berlin, 1933), p. 65. The same scholar writes, with reference to pottery, especially that of the Stone Age and with reference to Assyrian glazing, "Ceramic art in the service of Wisdom, the wisdom that activates knowledge to the level of the spiritual, indeed the divine, as science does to earthbound things of all kinds. Service is here a voluntary, entirely self-sacrificing and entirely conscious dedication of the personality ... as it is and should be in true divine worship. Only this service is worthy of art, of ceramic art. To make the primordial truth intelligible, to make the unheard audible, to enunciate the primordial word, to illustrate the primordial image—such is the task of art, or it is not art." ("Keramik im Dienste der Weisheit," *Berichte der deutschen keramischen Gesellschaft*, XVII,12 [1936], 623.) Cf. *Timaeus* 28AB.

94. SB VIII,1.2.8; AB V.23; TS II.5.II.5; JUB I.33.4 (*karoty eva vâcâ ... gamayati manasa*). Vâc is the Muse, and as the Muses are the daughters of Zeus, so is Vâc the daughter of the Progenitor, of Intellect (*Manas, nous*)—i.e., *intellectus vel spiritus*, "the habit of First Principles." As Sarasvatî she bears the lute and is seated on the Sunbird as vehicle.

95. "This the 'Beatitude' (*ânanda*) of Brahmâ, that by means of Intellect (*Manas, nous*), his highest form, he betakes himself to 'the Woman' (Vâc); a son like himself is born of her" (BU IV.1.6). The son is Agni, *brhad uktha*, the Logos.

96. RV X.31.2 (*sreyânsam daksam manasâ jagrbhyât*); BD II.84. The governing authority is always masculine, the power feminine.

97. AB V.33, etc. Srî as brahmavâdinî is "Theologia."

98. SB III.2.4.11; cf. "the Asura's gibberish" (SB III.2.1.23). It is because of the dual possibility of an application of the Voice to the statement of truth or falsehood that she is called the "double-faced"—i.e., "two-tongued" (SB III.2.4.16). These two possibilities correspond to Plato's distinction of the Uranian from the Pandemic (*Pandêmos*) and disordered (*ataktos*) Aphrodite, one the mother of the Uranian or Cosmic Eros, the other, the "Queen of Various Song" (*Polumnia*) and mother of the Pandemic Eros (*Symposium* 180DE, 187E, *Laws* 840E).

99. *Republic* 399E.

100. JB II.69, 70, and 73.

101. JB III.2.4.1-6 and 16-22; cf. III.2.1.19-23.

102. *Samkhyânam* is "reckoning" or "calculation" and corresponds in more senses than one to Plato's *logismos*. We have seen that accuracy (*orthotês, integritas*) is the first requirement for good art, and that this amounts to saying that art is essentially iconography, to be distinguished by its *logic* from merely emotional and instinctive expression. It is precisely the precision of "classical" and "canonical" art that modern feeling most resents; we demand organic forms adapted to an "in-feeling" (*Einfühlung*) rather than the measured forms that require "in-sight" (*Einsehen*).

A good example of this can be cited in Lars-Ivar Ringbom's "Entstehung und Entwicklung der Spiralornamentik," in *Acta Archaeologica*, IV (1933), 151—200. Ringbom demonstrates first the extraordinary perfection of early spiral ornament and shows how even its most complicated forms must have been produced with the aid of simple *tools*. But he resents this "measured" perfection, as of something "known and deliberately made, the work of the intellect rather than a psychic expression" ("sie ist bewusst und willkürlich gemacht, mehr Verstandesarbeit als seelischer Ausdruck") and admires the later "forms of freer growth, approximating more to those of Nature." These organic ("organisch-gewachsen") forms are the "psychological expression of man's instinctive powers, that drive him more and more to representation and figuration." Ringbom could hardly have better described the kind of art that Plato would have called unworthy of free men; the free man is not "driven by forces of instinct." What Plato admired was precisely not the organic and figurative art that was coming into fashion in his time, but the formal and canonical art of Egypt that remained constant for what he thought had been ten thousand years, for there it had been possible "for those modes that are by nature correct to be canonized and held forever sacred" (*Laws* 656-657; cf. 798AB, 799A). There "art ... was not for the delectation ... of the senses" (Earl Baldwin Smith, *Egyptian Architecture*, New York, 1938, p. 27).

103. AÂ III.2.6, *sa candobhir âtmânam samâdadhât*; AB VI.27, *candomayam ... âtmânam samskurute.*

104. For what Plato means by wings, see *Phaedrus* 246-256 and *Ion* 534B. "It is as a bird that the Sacrificer reaches the world of heaven" (PB V.3.5). *Phaedrus* 247BC corresponds to PB XIV.1.12-13, "Those who reach the top of the great tree, how do they fare thereafter? Those who have wings fly forth, those that are wingless fall down"; the former are the "wise," the latter the "foolish" (cf. *Phaedrus* 249C, "It is only the philosopher's discriminating mind that is winged"). For the Gandharva (Eros) as a winged "maker" and as such the archetype of human poets, see RV

X.177.2 and JUB III.36. For "metrical wings," see PB X.4.5 and XIX.11.8; JUB III.13.10; AV VIII.9.12. The meters are "birds" (TS VI.1.6.1; PB XIX.11.8).

105. SA VIII.10.

106. BG II.50, *yogah karmasu kausalam.* If yoga is also the "renunciation" (*samnyâsa*) of works (BG V.1 and VI.2), this is only another way of saying the same thing, since this renunciation is essentially the abandonment of the notion "I am the doer" and a reference of the works to their real author whose skill is infallible: {The Father that dwelleth in me, he doeth the works} (John 14:10).

107. SA VII.5 and 7; cf. *Phaedo* 61AB.

108. What is meant by *vidyâ* as opposed to *avidyâ* is explicit in *Phaedrus* 247C—E, "All true knowledge is concerned with what is colorless, formless and intangible (Skr. *avarna, arûpa, agrahya*)" "not such knowledge as has a beginning and varies as it is associated with one or another of the things that we now call realities, but that which is really real (Skr. *satyasya satyam*)." Cf. CU VII.16.1 and 17.1, with commentary; also *Philebus* 58A.

109. SA XIV.2.

110. CU 1.7.6-7. Cf. Coomaraswamy, "The Sun-kiss," 1940, p. 49, n. 11.

111. For all the statements in this paragraph, see CU 1.6-9; *Sâhitya Darpana* 1.4-6; and Dasarûpa 1.12-14.

112. See John D. Wild, *Plato's Theory of Man* (Cambridge, Mass., 1946), p. 84.

113. *Timaeus* 22BC.

114. In *The Nation* (December 10, 1938). Cf. Socrates' dictum at the head of this chapter.

2

The Bugbear of Literacy

It was possible for Aristotle,[1] starting from the premise that a man, being actually cultured, may *also* become literate, to ask whether there is a necessary or merely an accidental connection of literacy with culture. Such a question can hardly arise for us, to whom illiteracy implies, as a matter of course, ignorance, backwardness, unfitness for self-government: for us, unlettered peoples are uncivilized peoples, and vice versa—as a recent publisher's blurb expresses it: "The greatest force in civilization is the collective wisdom of a literate people."

There are reasons for this point of view; they inhere in the distinction of a people, or folk, from a proletariat, that of a social organism from a human ant heap. For a proletariat, literacy is a practical and cultural necessity. We may remark in passing that necessities are not always goods in themselves, out of their context; some, like wooden legs, are advantageous only to men already maimed. However that may be, it remains that literacy is a necessity *for us*, and from both points of view; (1) because our industrial system can only be operated and profits can only be made by men provided with at least an elementary knowledge of the "three R's"; and (2) because, where there is no longer any necessary connection between one's "skill" (now a timesaving "economy of motion" rather than a control of the product) and one's "wisdom," the possibility of culture depends so much on our ability to read the best books. We say "possibility" here because, whereas the literacy actually produced by compulsory mass education often involves little or no more than an ability and the will to read the newspapers and advertisements, an actually cultured man under these conditions will be one who has studied many books in many languages, and this is not a kind of knowledge that can be handed out to everyone under "compulsion" (even if *any* nation could afford the needed quantity and quality of teachers) or that could be acquired by everyone, however ambitious.

We have allowed that in industrial societies, where it is assumed that man is made for commerce and where men are cultured, if at all, in spite of rather than because of their environment, literacy is a necessary skill. It will naturally follow that if, on the principle that misery loves company, we are planning to industrialize the rest of the world, we are also in duty bound to train it in Basic English, or words to that effect—American is already a language of exclusively external relationships, a tradesman's tongue—lest the other peoples should be unable to compete effectively with us. Competition is the life of trade, and gangsters must have rivals.

In the present article we are concerned with something else, viz., the assumption that, even for societies not yet industrialized, literacy is "an unqualified good and an indispensible condition of culture."[2] The vast majority of the world's population is still unindustrialized and unlettered, and there are peoples still "unspoiled" (in the interior of Borneo): but the average American who knows of no other way of living than his own, judges that "unlettered" means "uncultured," *as if* this majority consisted only of a depressed class in the context of his own environment. It is because of this, as well as for some meaner reasons, not unrelated to "imperial" interests, that when we propose not merely to exploit but also to educate "the lesser breeds without the [i.e. *our*] law" we inflict upon them profound, and often lethal, injuries. We say "lethal" rather than "fatal" here because it is precisely a destruction of their *memories* that is involved. We overlook that "education" is never creative, but a two-edged weapon, always destructive; whether of ignorance or of knowledge depending upon the educator's wisdom or folly. Too often fools rush in where angels might fear to tread.

As against the complacent prejudice we shall essay to show (1) that there is no necessary connection of literacy with culture, and (2) that to impose our literacy (and our contemporary "literature") upon a cultured but illiterate people is to destroy their culture in the name of our own. For the sake of brevity we shall assume without argument that "culture" implies an ideal quality and a good form that can be realized by all men irrespective of condition: and, since we are treating of culture chiefly as expressed in words, we shall identify culture with "poetry"; not having in view the kind of poetry that nowadays babbles of green fields or that merely reflects social behavior or our private reactions to passing events, but with reference to that whole class of prophetic literature that includes the Bible, the Vedas, the Edda, the great epics, and in general the world's "best books," and the most philosophical if we agree with Plato that "wonder is the beginning of philosophy." Of these "books" many existed long before they were written down, many have never been written down, and others have been or will be lost.

We shall have now to make some quotations from the works of men whose "culture" cannot be called in question; for while the merely literate are often very proud of their literacy, such as it is, it is only by men who are "not only literate but also cultured" that it has been widely recognized that "letters" at their best are only a means to an end and never an end in themselves, or, indeed, that "the letter kills." A "literary" man, if ever there was one, the late Professor G. L. Kittredge writes:[3] "It requires a combined effort of the reason and the imagination to conceive a poet as a person who cannot write, singing or reciting his verses to an audience that cannot read ... The ability of oral tradition to transmit great masses of verse for hundreds of years is proved and admitted ... To this oral literature, as the French call it, education is no friend. Culture destroys it, sometimes with amazing rapidity. *When a nation begins to read ... what was once the possession of the folk as a whole, becomes the heritage of the illiterate only, and soon, unless it is gathered up by the antiquary, vanishes altogether.*" Mark, too, that this oral literature once belonged "to the whole people ... the community whose intellectual interests are the same from the top of the social structure to the bottom," while in the reading society it is accessible only to antiquaries, and is no longer bound up with everyday life. A point of further importance is this: that the traditional oral literatures interested not only all *classes*, but also all *ages* of the population; while the books that are nowadays written expressly "for children" are such as no mature mind could tolerate; it is now only the comic strips that appeal alike to children who have been given nothing better and at the same time to "adults" who have never grown up.

It is in just the same way that music is thrown away; folk songs are lost to the people at the same time that they are collected and "put in a bag"; and in the same way that the "preservation" of a people's art in folk museums is a funeral rite, for preservatives are only necessary when the patient has already died. Nor must we suppose that "community singing" can take the place of folk song; its level can be no higher than that of the Basic English in which our undergraduates must be similarly drilled, if they are to understand even the language of their elementary textbooks.

In other words, "Universal compulsory education, of the type introduced at the end of the last century, has not fulfilled expectations by producing happier and more effective citizens; on the contrary, it has created readers of the yellow press and cinemagoers" (Karl Otten). A master who can himself not only read, but also *write* good classical Latin and Greek, remarks that "there is no doubt of the quantitative increase in literacy of a kind, and amid the general satisfaction that something is being multiplied it escapes enquiry whether the something is profit or deficit." He is discussing only the "worst effects" of enforced literacy, and concludes: "Learning and wisdom have often been divided; perhaps the clearest result of modern literacy has been to maintain and enlarge the gulf."

Douglas Hyde remarks that "in vain have disinterested visitors opened wide eyes of astonishment at schoolmasters who knew no Irish being appointed to teach pupils who knew no English ... Intelligent children endowed with a vocabulary in every day use of about three thousand words enter the Schools of the Chief Commissioner, to come out at the end with their natural vivacity gone, their intelligence almost completely sapped, their splendid command of their native language lost forever, and a vocabulary of five or six hundred English words, badly pronounced and barbarously employed, substituted for it ... Story, lay, poem, song, aphorism, proverb, and the unique stock in trade of an Irish speaker's mind, is gone forever, *and replaced by nothing* ... The children are taught, if nothing else, to be ashamed of their own parents, ashamed of their own nationality, ashamed of their own names ... It is a remarkable system of 'education'"[4]—this system that you, "civilized and literate" Americans, have inflicted upon your own Amerindians, and that all imperial races are still inflicting upon their subjected peoples, and would like to impose upon their allies—the Chinese, for example.

The problem involved is both of languages and what is said in them. As for language, let us bear in mind, in the first place, that no such thing as a "primitive language," in the sense of one having a limited vocabulary fitted only to express the simplest external relationships, is known. Much rather, that is a condition to which, under certain circumstances and as the result of "nothing-morist" philosophies, languages tend, rather than one from which they originate; for example, 90 per cent of our American "literacy" is a two-syllabled affair.[5]

In the seventeenth century Robert Knox said of the Sinhalese that "their ordinary Plow-men and Husbandmen do speak elegantly, and are full of complement. And there is no difference of ability and speech of a Country-man and a Courtier."[6] Abundant testimony to the like effect could be cited from all over the world. Thus of Gaelic, J. F. Campbell wrote, "I am inclined to think that dialect the best which is spoken by the most illiterate in the islands ...men with clear heads and wonderful memories, generally very poor and old, living in remote corners of remote islands, and speaking only Gaelic,"[7] and he quotes Hector Maclean, who says that the loss of their oral literature is due "partly to reading ... partly to bigoted religious ideas, and partly to narrow utilitarian views"—which are, precisely, the three typical forms in which modern civilization impresses itself upon the older cultures. Alexander Carmichael says that "the people of Lews, like the people of the Highlands and Islands generally, carry the Scriptures in their minds and apply them in their speech ... Perhaps no people had a fuller ritual of song and story, of secular rite and religious ceremony ... than the ill-understood and so-called illiterate Highlanders of Scotland."[8]

St. Barbe Baker tells us that in Central Africa "my trusted friend and companion was an old man who could not read or write, though well versed in stories of the past ... The old chiefs listened enthralled ... Under the present system of education there is grave risk that much of this may be lost."[9] W. G. Archer points out that "unlike the English system in which one could pass one's life without coming into contact with poetry, the Uraon tribal system uses poetry as a vital appendix to dancing, marriages and the cultivation of a crop—functions in which all Uraons join as a part of their tribal life," adding that "if we have to single out the factor which caused the decline of English village culture, we should have to say it was literacy."[10] In an older England, as Prior and Gardner remind us, "even the ignorant and unlettered man could read the meaning of sculptures that now only trained archeologists can interpret."[11]

The anthropologist Paul Radin points out that "the distortion in our whole psychic life and in our whole apperception of the external realities produced by the invention of the alphabet, the whole tendency of which has been to elevate thought and thinking to the rank of the exclusive proof of all verities, never occurred among primitive peoples," adding that "it must be explicitly recognized that in temperament and in capacity for logical and symbolical thought, there is no difference between civilized and primitive man," and as to "progress," that none in ethnology will ever be achieved "until scholars rid themselves, once and for all, of the curious notion that everything possesses an evolutionary history; until they realize that certain ideas and certain concepts are as ultimate for man"[12] as his physical constitution. "The distinction of peoples in a state of nature from civilized peoples can no longer be maintained."[13]

We have so far considered only the dicta of literary men. A really "savage" situation and point of view are recorded by Tom Harrisson, from the New Hebrides. "The children are educated by listening and watching ... Without writing, memory is perfect, tradition exact. The growing child is taught all that is known ... Intangible things cooperate in every effort of making, from conception to canoe-building ... Songs are a form of story-telling ... The lay-out and content in the thousand myths which every child learns (often word perfect, and one story may last for hours) are a whole library ... the hearers are held in a web of spun words"; they converse together "with that accuracy and pattern of beauty in words that we have lost." And what do they think of us? "The natives easily learn to write after white impact. They regard it as a curious and useless performance. They say: 'Cannot a man remember and speak?'"[14] They consider us "mad," and may be right.

When we set out to "educate" the South Sea Islanders it is generally in order to make them more useful to ourselves (this was admittedly the beginning of "English education" in India), or to "convert" them to our way of thinking; not having in view to introduce them to Plato. But if we or they should happen upon Plato, it might startle both to find that their protest, "Cannot a man *remember*?" is also his.[15] "For," he says, "this invention [of letters] will produce forgetfulness in the minds of those who learn to use it, because they will not exercise their memory. Their trust in writing, produced by external characters which are no part of themselves, will discourage the use of their own memory within them. You have invented an elixir *not of memory, but of reminding*; and you offer your pupils the appearance of wisdom, not true wisdom, for they will read many things without teaching, and will therefore seem to know many things [Professor E. K. Rand's "more and more of less and less"], when they are for the most part ignorant and hard to get along with, since they are not wise but only wiseacres." He goes on to say that there is another kind of "word," of higher origin and greater power than the written (or as we should say, the printed word) and maintains that the wise man, "*when in earnest,* will not write in ink" dead words that cannot teach the truth effectively, but will sow the seeds of wisdom in souls that are able to receive them and so "to pass them on forever."

There is nothing strange or peculiar in Plato's point of view; it is one, for example, with which every cultured Indian unaffected by modern European influences would agree wholly. It will suffice to cite that great scholar of Indian languages, Sir George A. Grierson, who says that "the ancient Indian system by which literature is recorded not on paper but on the memory, and carried down from generation to generation of teachers and pupils, is still [1920] in complete survival in Kashmir. Such fleshly tables of the heart are often more trustworthy than birch bark or paper manuscripts. The reciters, even when learned Pandits, take every care to deliver the messages word for word," and records taken down from professional storytellers are thus "in some respects more valuable than any written manuscript."[16]

From the Indian point of view a man can only be said to *know* what he knows *by heart*; what he must go to a book to be reminded of, he merely knows of. There are hundreds of thousands of Indians even now who daily repeat from knowledge by heart either the whole or some large part of the *Bhagavad Gîtâ*; others more learned can recite hundreds of thousands of verses of longer texts. It was from a traveling village singer in Kashmir that I first heard sung the Odes of the classical Persian poet, Jalâlu'd-Dîn Rûmî. From the earliest times, Indians have thought of the learned man, not as one who has read much, but as one who has been profoundly taught. It is much rather from a master than from any book that wisdom can be learned.

We come now to the last part of our problem, which has to do with the characteristic preoccupations of the oral and the written literature; for although no hard and fast line can be drawn between them, there is a qualitative and thematic distinction, as between literatures that were originally oral and those that are created, so to speak, on paper—"In the beginning was the WORD." The distinction is largely of poetry from prose and myth from fact. The quality of oral literature is essentially poetical, its content essentially mythical, and its preoccupation with the spiritual adventures of heroes: the quality of originally written literature is essentially prosaic, its content literal, and its preoccupation with secular events and with personalities. In saying "poetical" we mean to imply "mantic," and are naturally taking for granted that the "poetic" is a literary *quality*, and not merely a literary (versified) form. Contemporary poetry is essentially and inevitably of the same caliber as modern prose; both are equally opinionated, and the best in either embodies a few "happy thoughts" rather than any certainty. As a famous gloss expresses it, "Unbelief is for the mob." We who can call an art "significant," knowing not of what, are also proud to "progress," we know not whither.

Plato maintains that one who is *in earnest* will not write, but teach; and that if the wise man writes at all, it will be either only for amusement—mere "belles lettres"—or to provide reminders for himself when his memory is weakened by old age. We know exactly what Plato means by the words "in earnest"; it is not about human affairs or personalities, but about the eternal verities, the nature of real being, and the nourishment of our immortal part, that the wise man will be in earnest. Our mortal part can survive "by bread alone," but it is by the Myth that our Inner Man is fed; or, if we substitute for the true myths the propagandist myths of "race," "uplift," "progress," and "civilizing mission," the Inner Man starves. The written text, as Plato says, can serve those whose memories have been weakened by old age. Thus it is that in the senility of culture we have found it necessary to "preserve" the masterpieces of art in museums, and at the same time to record in writing and so also to "preserve" (if only for scholars) as much as can be "collected" of oral literatures that would otherwise be lost forever; and this must be done before it is *too late*.

All serious students of human societies are agreed that agriculture and handicraft are essential foundations of any civilization; the primary meaning of the word being that of making a home for oneself. But, as Albert Schweitzer says, "We proceed as if not agriculture and handicraft, but reading and writing were the beginning of civilization," and, "from schools which are mere copies of those of Europe they ["natives"] are turned out as 'educated' persons, that is, who think themselves superior to manual work, and want to follow only commercial or intellectual callings those who go through the schools are mostly lost to agriculture and handicraft."[17] As that great missionary, Charles Johnson of Zululand, also said, "the central idea [of the mission schools] was to prize individuals off the mass of the national life."

Our literary figures of thought, for example, the notions of "culture" (analogous to agriculture), "wisdom" (originally "skill"), and "asceticism" (originally "hard work"), are derived from the productive and constructive arts; for, as St. Bonaventura says, ("There is nothing therein which does not bespeak a true wisdom, and it is for this reason that Holy Scripture very properly makes use of such similes.")[18] In normal societies, the necessary labors of production and construction are no mere "jobs," but also rites, and the poetry and music that are associated with them are a kind of liturgy. The "lesser mysteries" of the crafts are a natural preparation for the greater "mysteries of the kingdom of heaven." But for us, who can no longer think in terms of Plato's divine "justice" of which the social aspect is vocational, that Christ was a carpenter and the son of a carpenter was only an historical accident; we read, but do not understand that where we speak of primary matter as "wood," we must also speak of Him "through whom all things were made" as a "carpenter." At the best, we interpret the classical figures of thought, not in their universality but as figures of speech invented by individual authors. Where literacy becomes an only skill, "the collective wisdom of a literate people" may be only a collective ignorance— while "backward communities are the oral libraries of the world's ancient cultures."[19]

The purpose of our educational activities abroad is to assimilate our pupils to our ways of thinking and living. It is not easy for any foreign teacher to acknowledge Ruskin's truth, that there is one way only to help others, and that that is, not to train them in our way of living (however bigoted our faith in it may be), but to find out what they have been trying to do, and were doing before we came, and if possible help them to do it better. Some Jesuit missionaries in China are actually sent to remote villages and required to earn their living there by the practice of an indigenous craft for at least two years before they are allowed to teach at all. Some such condition as this ought to be imposed upon all foreign teachers, whether in mission or government schools. How dare we forget that we are dealing with peoples "whose intellectual interests are the same from the top of the social structure to the bottom," and for whom our unfortunate distinctions of religious from secular learning, fine from applied art, and significance from use have not yet been made? When we have introduced these distinctions and have divided an "educated" from a still "illiterate" class, it is to the latter that we must turn if we want to study the language, the poetry, and the whole culture of these peoples, "before it is too late."

In speaking of a "proselytizing fury" in a former article I had not only in view the activities of professed missionaries but more generally those of everyone bent by the weight of the white man's burden and anxious to confer the "blessings" of our civilization upon others. What lies below this fury, of which our punitive expeditions and "wars of pacification" are only more evident manifestations? It would not be too much to say that our educational activities abroad (a word that must be taken to include the American Indian reservations) are motivated by an *intention* to destroy existing cultures. And that is not only, I think, because of our conviction of the absolute superiority of our *Kultur*, and consequent contempt and hatred for whatever else we have not understood all those for whom the economic motive is not decisive, but grounded in an unconscious and deep-rooted envy of the serenity and leisure that we cannot help but recognize in people whom we call "unspoiled." It irks us that these others, who are neither, as we are, industrialized nor, as we are, "democratic," should nevertheless be *contented*; we feel bound to discontent them, and especially to discontent their women, who might learn from us to work in factories or to find careers. I used the word *Kultur* deliberately just now, because there is not much real difference between the Germans' will to enforce their culture upon the backward races of the rest of Europe and our determination to enforce our own upon the rest of the world; the methods employed in their case may be more evidently brutal, but the kind of will involved is the same.[20] As I implied above, that "misery loves company" is the true and unacknowledged basis of our will to create a brave new world of uniformly literate mechanics. This was recently repeated to a group of young American workmen, one of whom responded, "And *are* we miserable!"

But however we may be whistling in the dark when we pride ourselves upon "the collective wisdom of a literate people," regardless of what is read by the "literates," the primary concern of the present essay is not with the limitations and defects of modern Western education *in situ*, but with the spread of an education of this type elsewhere. Our real concern is with the fallacy involved in the attachment of an absolute value to literacy, and the very dangerous consequences that are involved in the setting up of "literacy" as a standard by which to measure the cultures of unlettered peoples. Our blind faith in literacy not only obscures for us the significance of other skills, so that we care not under what subhuman conditions a man may have to learn his living, if only he can read, no matter what, in his hours of leisure; it is also one of the fundamental grounds of inter-racial prejudice and becomes a prime factor in the spiritual impoverishment of all the "backward" people whom we propose to "civilize."

Notes

1. *Metaphysics*, VI: 2, 4, and XI: 8, 12. "Reading, for a man devoid of prior-understanding, is like a blind man's looking in a mirror" (*Garuda Purâna*, XVI: 82).

2. Walter Shewring, "Literacy," in the *Dictionary of World Literature*, 1943. "We are becoming culturally illiterate faster than all these agencies are managing to make us literate in the use of the potentialities of the culture" (Robert S. Lynd, in *Knowledge for What?*). Professor John U. Nef of Chicago, speaking at Hamline University in 1944, remarked: "In spite of the alleged great spread of literacy [in America] ... the proportion of the population who can communicate with each other on a relatively high level of discourse is very much smaller than it was." A recent study sponsored by the Carnegie Foundation for the Advancement of Teaching found that "the average senior in six colleges recognized only 61 out of 100 words in familiar use by educated people"! In view of all the facts, it is indeed astonishing to find Lord Raglan saying: "By savage I mean illiterate" (in the *Rationalist Annual*, 1946, p. 43). There was a time, indeed, when the English bourgeoisie thought of the Gaelic Highlanders as "savages"; but from an anthropologist one would expect a refutation of such "myths," rather than their revival!

3. F. G. Childe, *English and Scottish Popular Ballads*, Introduction by G. L. Kittredge. Cf. W. W. Comfort, *Chrétien de Troyes* (Everyman's Library), Introduction: Chrétien's poetry "was intended for a society that was still homogeneous, and to it at the outset doubtless all classes of the population listened with equal interest." Nothing of this kind is or can be achieved by the organized and compulsory education of today—"a province of its own, detached from life" with its "atmosphere of intense boredom that damps the vitality of the young" and of which "the result is: the young people do not know anything really well," or as "it would be more exact to say, they do not know what knowledge is," which "explains the dangerous gullibility which propaganda exploits" (Erich Meissner, *Germany in Peril*, 1942, pp. 47, 48).

4. Douglas Hyde, *Literary History of Ireland*, 1903, p. 633.

5. American is already "a one-dimensional public language, a language oriented to the description of external aspects of behavior, weak in overtones ... our words lack ... the formal precision which comes from awareness of past and different usage" (Margaret Mead, *And Keep Your Powder Dry*, 1942, p.82). Any author who uses words precisely is liable to be misunderstood.

"Perhaps at no other time have men been so knowing and yet so unaware, so burdened with purposes and so purposeless, so disillusioned and so completely the victims of illusion. This strange contradiction pervades our entire modern culture, our science and our philosophy, our literature and our art" (W. M. Urban, *The Intelligible World*, 1929, p. 172). Under such conditions, ability to read a printed page becomes a mere trick, and is no guarantee whatever of power to grasp or to communicate ideas.

6. Robert Knox, *An Historical Relation of Ceylon*, 1681 (1911 ed., p.168).

7. J. F. Campbell, *Popular Tales of the West Highlands* (1890 ed., pp. v, xxiii, cxxii).

8. Alexander Carmichael, *Carmina Gadelica*, Vol. I, 1900, pp. xxiii, xxix. Cf. J. G. Mackay, *More West Highland Tales*, 1940, General Preface: "The poorest classes generally speak the language admirably ... Some recited thousands of lines of ancient heroic poems ... Another cause of the fragmentary character of some tales is the obliterating effect of modern civilization"; and J. Watson, *ibid.*, Introduction: "This intellectual inheritance ... this ancient culture extended over all the north and northerly midlands of Scotland. The people who possessed this culture may have been, and usually were, unlettered. They were far from being uneducated. It is sad to think that its decay has been partly due to the schools and the Church!" It is, in fact, precisely by "the schools and the Church" that the decay of cultures all over the world has been hastened in the last hundred years.

H. J. Massingham in *This Plot of Earth* (1944, p. 233) tells of "the old man, Seonardh Coinbeul, who could neither read nor write and carried 4500 lines of his own bardic composition in his head, together with all manner of songs and stories."

A. Solonylsin in the *Asiatic Review* (NS. XLI, Jan., 1945, p. 86) remarks that the recording of the Kirghiz epic is still incomplete, although over 1,100,000 lines have already been taken down by the Kirghiz Research Institute—"Bards who recite the 'Manas'—or 'Manaschi'—have phenomenal memories in addition to poetic talent. Only this can explain the fact that hundreds of thousands of verses have been handed down orally." A writer reviewing *Manas, Kirghiski Narodni Epos* in the *Journal of American Folklore*, 58, 1945, p. 65, observes that "general education has already done much to remove the raison d'être of the minstrel's position in tribal life ... With acculturation becoming a rolling Juggernaut it is not surprising that what remains of epic singing may soon degenerate into an artificial and ostentatiously national publicity device."

9. R. St. Barbe Baker, *Africa Drums*, 1942, p. 145.

10. W. G. Archer, *The Blue Grove*, 1940, Preface; and in JBORS, Vol. XXIX, p. 68.

11. Edward Schröder Prior and Arthur Gardner, *An Account of Medieval Figure-Sculpture in England*, 1912, p. 25.

12. Paul Radin, *Primitive Man as Philosopher*, 1927.

13. J. Strzygowski, *Spüren indogermanische Glaubens in der bildenden Kunst*, 1936, p. 344.

14. Tom Harrisson, *Savage Civilization*, 1937, pp. 45, 344, 351, 353.

15. Plato, *Phaedrus*, 275 f. Cf. H. Gauss, *Plato's Conception of Philosophy*, 1937, pp. 262–5.

16. Sir George A. Grierson, *Lallâ Vâkyâni*, 1920, p. 3.

17. Albert Schweitzer, *On the Edge of the Primeval Forest.*

18. *De reductione artium ad theologiam*, 14.

19. N. K. Chadwick, *Poetry and Prophecy*, 1942, Preface, further, "The experience of exclusively literate communities is too narrow." "Ever learning, and never able to come to the knowledge of the truth" (II Timothy 3:7)!

20. Modern "education" imposed upon traditional cultures (e.g. Gaelic, Indian, Polynesian, American Indian) is only less deliberately, not less actually, destructive than the Nazi destruction of Polish libraries, which was intended to wipe out their racial memories; the Germans acted consciously, but we who Anglicize or Americanize or Frenchify are driven by a rancor that we do not recognize and could not confess. This rancor is, in fact, our reaction to a superiority that we resent and therefore would like to destroy.

3

On the Pertinence of Philosophy

"Wisdom uncreate, the same now as it ever was, and the same to be for evermore." St. Augustine, *Confessions*, IX. 10.

"Primordial and present Witness."
Prakâsânanda, *Siddhântamuktâvali*, 44

I. Definition and Status of Philosophy, or Wisdom

To discuss the "problems of philosophy" presupposes a definition of "philosophy." It will not be contested that "philosophy" implies rather the love of wisdom than the love of knowledge, nor secondarily that from the "love of wisdom," philosophy has come by a natural transition to mean the doctrine of those who love wisdom and are called philosophers.[1]

Now knowledge as such is not the mere report of the senses (the reflection of anything in the retinal mirror may be perfect, in an animal or idiot, and yet is not knowledge), nor the mere act of recognition (names being merely a means of alluding to the aforesaid reports), but is an abstraction from these reports, in which abstraction the names of the things are used as convenient substitutes for the things themselves. Knowledge is not then of individual presentations, but of types of presentation; in other words, of things in their intelligible aspect, i.e. of the being that things have in the mind of the knower, as principles, genera and species. In so far as knowledge is directed to the attainment of ends it is called practical; in so far as it remains in the knower, theoretical or speculative. Finally, we cannot say that a man knows wisely, but that he knows well; wisdom takes knowledge for granted and governs the movement of the will with respect to things known; or we may say that wisdom is the criterion of value, according to which a decision is made to act or not to act in any given case or universally. Which will apply not merely to external acts, but also to contemplative or theoretical acts.

Philosophy, accordingly, is a wisdom about knowledge, a *correction du savoir-penser*. In general, philosophy (2)[2] has been held to embrace what we have referred to above as theoretical or speculative knowledge, for example, logic, ethics, psychology, aesthetic, theology, ontology; and in this sense the problems of philosophy are evidently those of rationalization, the purpose of philosophy being so to correlate the data of empirical experience as to "make sense" of them, which is accomplished for the most part by a reduction of particulars to universals (deduction). And thus defined, the function of philosophy contrasts with that of practical science, of which the proper function is that of predicting the particular from the universal (induction). Beyond this, however, philosophy (1) has been held to mean a wisdom not so much about particular kinds of thought, as a wisdom about thinking, and an analysis of what it means to think, and an enquiry as to what may be the nature of the ultimate reference of thought. In this sense the problems of philosophy are with respect to the ultimate nature of reality, actuality or experience; meaning by reality whatever is in act and not merely potential. We may ask, for example, what are truth, goodness and beauty (considered as concepts abstracted from experience), or we may ask whether these or any other concepts abstracted from experience have actually any being of their own; which is the matter in debate as between nominalists on the one hand and realists, or idealists, on the other.[3] It may be noted that, since in all these applications philosophy means "wisdom," if or when we speak of philosophies in the plural, we shall mean not different kinds of wisdom, but wisdom with respect to different kinds of things. The wisdom may be more or less, but still one and the same order of wisdom.

As to this order, if knowledge is by abstraction, and wisdom about knowledge, it follows that this wisdom, pertaining to things known or knowable, and attained by a process of reasoning or dialectic from experimental data, and neither being nor claiming to be a revealed or gnostic doctrine, in no way transcends thought, but is rather the best kind of thought, or, let us say, the truest science. It is, indeed, an excellent wisdom, and assuming a good will, one of great value to man.[4] But let us not forget that because of its experimental, that is to say statistical basis, and even supposing an infallible operation of the reason such as may be granted to mathematics, this wisdom can never establish absolute certainties, and can predict only with very great probability of success; the "laws" of science, however useful, do nothing more than resume past experience. Furthermore, philosophy in the second of the above senses, or human wisdom about things known or knowable, must be systematic, since it is required by hypothesis that its perfection will consist in an accounting for everything, in a perfect fitting together of all the parts of the puzzle to make one logical whole; and the system must be a *closed* system, one namely limited to the field of time and space, cause and effect, for it is by hypothesis about knowable and determinate things, all of which are presented to the cognitive faculty in the guise of effects, for which causes are sought.[5] For example, space being of indefinite and not infinite extent,[6] the wisdom about determinate things cannot have any application to whatever "reality" may or may not belong to non-spatial, or immaterial, modes, or similarly, to a non-temporal mode, for if there be a "now" we have no sensible experience of any such thing, nor can we conceive it in terms of logic. If it were attempted by means of the human wisdom to overstep the natural limits of its operation, the most that could be said would be that the reference "indefinite magnitude" (mathematical infinity) presents a certain analogy to the reference "essential infinity" as postulated in religion and metaphysics, but nothing could be affirmed or denied with respect to the "isness" (*esse*) of this infinite in essence.

If the human wisdom, depending upon itself alone ("rationalism"), proposes a religion, this will be what is called a "natural religion," having for its deity that referent of which the operation is seen everywhere, and yet is most refractory to analysis, viz. "life" or "energy." And this natural religion will be a pantheism or monism, postulating a soul (*anima*, "animation") of the universe, everywhere known by its effects perceptible in the movements of things; amongst which things any distinction of animate and inanimate will be out of place, inasmuch as animation can be defined rationally only as "that which is expressed in, or is the cause of, motion." Or if not a pantheism, then a polytheism or pluralism in which a variety of animations ("forces") is postulated as underlying and "explaining" a corresponding variety of motions.[7] But nothing can be affirmed or denied as regards the proposition that such animation or animations may be merely determinate and contingent aspects of a "reality" indeterminate in itself. Expressed more technically, pantheism and polytheism are essentially profane conceptions, and if recognizable in a given religious or metaphysical doctrine, are there interpolations of the reason, not essential to the religious or metaphysical doctrine in itself.[8]

On the other hand, the human wisdom, not relying on itself alone, may be applied to a partial, viz., analogical, exposition of the religious or metaphysical wisdoms, these being taken as prior to itself. For although the two wisdoms (philosophy (2) and philosophy (1)) are different in kind, there can be a formal coincidence, and in this sense what is called a "reconciliation of science and religion." Each is then dependent on the other, although in different ways; the sciences depending on revealed truth for their formal correction, and revealed truth relying upon the sciences for its demonstration by analogy, "not as though it stood in need of them, but only to make its teaching clearer."

In either case, the final end of human wisdom is a good or happiness that shall accrue either to the philosopher himself, or to his neighbors, or to humanity at large, but necessarily in terms of material well-being. The kind of good envisaged may or may not be a moral good.[9] For example, if we assume a good will, i.e. a natural sense of justice, the natural religion will be expressed in ethics in a sanction of such laws of conduct as most conduce to the common good, and he may be admired who sacrifices even life for the sake of this. In aesthetic (art being *circa factibilia*) the natural religion, given a good will, will justify the manufacture of such goods as are apt for human well-being, whether as physical necessities or as sources of sensible pleasure. All this belongs to "humanism" and is very far from despicable. But in case there is not a good will, the natural religion may equally be employed to justify the proposition "might is right" or "devil take the hindmost," and in manufacture the production of goods either by methods which are injurious to the common good, or which in themselves are immediately adapted to ends injurious to the common good; as in the case of child-labor and the manufacture of poison gas. Revealed truth, on the contrary, demands a good will *a priori*, adding that the aid of the rational philosophy, as science or art, is required in order that the good will may be made effective.[10]

There is then another kind of philosophy (1), viz., that to which we have alluded as "revealed truth," which though it covers the whole ground of philosophy (2), does so in another way, while beyond this it treats confidently of "realities" which may indeed be immanent in time and space tissue, and are not wholly incapable of rational demonstration, but are nevertheless said to be transcendent with respect to this tissue, i.e. by no means wholly contained within it nor given by it, nor wholly amenable to demonstration. The First Philosophy, for example, affirms the actuality of a "now" independent of the flux of time; while experience is only of a past and future. Again, the procedure of the First Philosophy is no longer in the first place deductive and secondarily inductive, but inductive from first to last, its logic proceeding invariably from the transcendental to the universal, and thence as before to the particular. This First Philosophy, indeed, taking for granted the principle "as above, so below" and vice-versa,[11] is able to find in every microcosmic fact the trace or symbol of a macrocosmic actuality, and accordingly resorts to "proof" by analogy; but this apparently deductive procedure is here employed by way of demonstration, and not by way of proof, where logical proof is out of the question, and its place is taken either by faith (Augustine's *credo ut intelligam*) or by the evidence of immediate experience (*alaukikapratyaksa*).[12]

Our first problem in connection with the highest wisdom, considered as a doctrine known by revelation (whether through ear or symbolic transmission), consistent but unsystematic, and intelligible in itself although it treats in part of unintelligible things, is to distinguish without dividing religion from metaphysics, philosophy (2) from philosophy (1). This is a distinction without a difference, like that of attribute from essence, and yet a distinction of fundamental importance if we are to grasp the true meaning of any given spiritual act.

We proceed therefore first to emphasize the distinctions that can be drawn as between religion and metaphysics with respect to a wisdom that is one in itself and in any case primarily directed to immaterial, or rationally speaking, "unreal" things.[13] Broadly speaking, the distinction is that of Christianity from Gnosticism, Sunni from Shi'a doctrine, Râmânuja from Sankarâcârya, of the will from the intellect, participation (*bhakti*) from gnosis (*jñâna*), or knowledge-of (*avidyâ*) from knowledge-as (*vidyâ*). As regards the Way, the distinction is one of consecration from initiation, and of passive from active integration; and as regards the End, of assimilation (*tadâkâratâ*) from identification (*tadbhâva*). Religion requires of its adherents to be perfected; metaphysics that they realize their own perfection that has never been infringed (even Satan is still virtually Lucifer, being fallen in grace and not in nature). Sin, from the standpoint of religion, is moral; from that of metaphysics, intellectual (mortal sin in metaphysics being a conviction or assertion of independent self-subsistence, as in Satan's case, or envy of the spiritual attainments of others, as in Indra's).

Religion, in general, proceeds from the being in act (*kâryâvasthâ*) of the First Principle, without regard to its being in potentiality (*kâranâvasthâ*);[14] while metaphysics treats of the Supreme Identity as an indisseverable unity of potentiality and act, darkness and light, holding that these can also and must also be considered apart when we attempt to understand their operation in identity in It or Him. And so religion assumes an aspect of duality,[15] viz., when it postulates a "primary matter," "potentiality" or "non-being" far removed from the actuality of God, and does not take account of the principal presence of this "primary matter" in, or rather "of" the First, as its "nature."[16]

Religions may and must be many, each being an "arrangement of God," and stylistically differentiated, inasmuch as the thing known can only be in the knower according to the mode of the knower, and hence as we say in India, "He takes the forms that are imagined by His worshippers," or as Eckhart expresses it, "I am the cause that God is God."[17] And this is why religious beliefs, as much as they have united men, have also divided men against each other, as Christian or heathen, orthodox or heretical.[18] So that if we are to consider what may be the most urgent practical problem to be resolved by the philosopher, we can only answer that this is to be recognized in a control and revision of the principles of comparative religion, the true end of which science, judged by the best wisdom (and judgment is the proper function of applied wisdom), should be to demonstrate the common metaphysical basis of all religions and that diverse cultures are fundamentally related to one another as being the dialects of a common spiritual and intellectual language; for whoever recognizes this, will no longer wish to assert that "My religion is best," but only that it is the "best for me."[19] In other words, the purpose of religious controversy should be, not to "convert" the opponent, but to persuade him that his religion is essentially the same as our own. To cite a case in point, it is not long since we received a communication from a Catholic friend in which he said "I've been ashamed for years at the superficiality and cheapness of my attempt to state a difference between Christians and

Hindus." It is noteworthy that a pronouncement such as this will assuredly strike a majority of European readers with a sense of horror. We recognize in fact that religious controversy has still generally in view to convince the opponent of error rather than of correctness in our eyes; and one even detects in modern propagandist writing an undertone of fear, as though it would be a disaster that might upset our own faith, were we to discover essential truth in the opponent; a fear which is occasioned by the very fact that with increasing knowledge and understanding, it is becoming more and more difficult to establish fundamental differences as between one religion and another. It is one of the functions of the First Philosophy to dissipate such fears. Nor is there any other ground whatever upon which all men can be in absolute agreement, excepting that of metaphysics, which we assert is the basis and norm of all religious formulations. Once such a common ground is recognized, it becomes a simple matter to agree to disagree in matters of detail, for it will be seen that the various dogmatic formulations are no more than paraphrases of one and the same principle.[20]

Few will deny that at the present day Western civilization is faced with the imminent possibility of total functional failure nor that at the same time this civilization has long acted and still continues to act as a powerful agent of disorder and oppression throughout the rest of the world. We dare say that both of these conditions are referable in the last analysis to that impotence and arrogance which have found a perfect expression in the dictum "East is East and West is West, and never the twain shall meet," a proposition to which only the most abysmal ignorance and deepest discouragement could have given rise. On the other hand, we recognize that the only possible ground upon which an effective entente of East and West can be accomplished is that of the purely intellectual wisdom that is one and the same at all times and for all men, and is independent of all environmental idiosyncrasy.[21]

We had intended to discuss at greater length the differentia of religion and metaphysics, but shall rather conclude the present section by an assertion of their ultimate identity. Both, considered as Ways, or praxis, are means of accomplishing the rectification, regeneration and reintegration of the aberrant and fragmented individual consciousness, both conceive of man's last end (*purusârtha*) as consisting in a realization by the individual of all the possibilities inherent in his own being, or may go farther, and see in

73

a realization of all the possibilities of being in any mode and also in possibilities of non-being, a final goal. For the Neo-Platonists and Augustine, and again for Erigena, Eckhart and Dante, and for such as Rûmî, Ibn 'Arabî, Sankarâcârya, and many others in Asia, religious and intellectual experience are too closely interwoven ever to be wholly divided;[22] who for example would have suspected that the words "How can That, which the Comprehending call the Eye of all things, the Intellect of intellects, the Light of lights, and numinous Omnipresence, be other than man's last end," and "Thou hast been touched and taken! long has Thou dwelt apart from me, but now that I have found Thee, I shall never let Thee go," are taken, not from a "theistic" source, but from purely Vedântic hymns addressed to the Essence (âtman) and to the "impersonal" Brahman!

II. How Diverse Wisdoms have considered Immortality

Let us consider the application of different kinds of wisdom to a particular problem of general significance. The pertinence of philosophy to the problem of immortality is evident, inasmuch as wisdom is primarily concerned with immaterial things, and it is evident that material things are not immortal as such (in *esse per se*) nor even from one moment to another, but are continually in flux, and this is undeniable, regardless of whether there may or may not be in such perpetually becoming things some immortal principle. Or to regard the matter from another angle, we may say that whatever, if anything, there may be immortal in phenomenal things must have been so since time began, for to speak of an immortal principle as having become mortal is the same thing as to say it was always mortal.

It needs no argument to demonstrate that human wisdom, rationalism, our philosophy (2), will understand by "immortality," not an everlasting life on earth, but an after-death persistence of individual consciousness and memory and character, such as in our experience survives from day to day across the nightly intervals of death-like sleep. Rational wisdom then will take up either one of two positions. It may in the first place argue that we have no experience of nor can conceive of the functioning of consciousness apart from the actual physical bases on which the functioning seems to rest, if indeed consciousness be in itself anything whatever more than a function of matter in motion, that is to say of physical existence; and will not therefore conceive the possibility of any other than an immortality in history, viz., in the memories of other mortal beings. In this sense there can also be postulated the possibility of a kind of resurrection, as when memory is refreshed by the discovery of documentary proofs of the existence of some individual or people whose very names had been forgotten it may be for millennia. Or human wisdom may maintain, rightly or wrongly, that evidences have been found of the "survival of personality," viz., in communications from the "other world," of such sort as to prove either by reference to facts unknown to the observer, but which are afterwards verified, or by "manifestations" of one sort or another, a continuity of memory and persistence of individual character in the deceased who is assumed to be in communication with the observer. If it is then attempted to rationalize the evidence thus accepted, it is argued that there may be kinds of matter other and subtler than those perceptible to our present physical senses, and that these other modalities of matter may very well serve as the suppositum of consciousness functioning on other planes of being.

It will be readily seen that no spiritual or intellectual distinction can be drawn between the two rationalistic interpretations, the only difference between them being as regards the amount or kind of time in which the continuity of individual character and consciousness can be maintained in a dimensioned space and on a material basis, theories of "fourth dimensions" or of "subtle matter" changing nothing in principle. Both of the rationalistic interpretations are rejected *in toto*, equally by religion and metaphysics.

Not that the possibility of an indefinite perdurance of individual consciousness upon indefinitely numerous or various platforms of being and various temporal modes is by any means denied in religion or in metaphysics (it being rather assumed that individual consciousness even now functions on other levels than those of our present terrestrial experience),[23] but that a persistence in such modes of being is not, strictly speaking, an immortality, this being taken to mean an immutability of being without development or change and wholly uneventful; while that which is thus presumed to subsist apart from contingency, viz. the soul, form or noumenal principle (*nâma*) of the individual, by which it is *what* it is, must be distinguished alike from the subtle and the gross bodies (*sûksma* and *sthûla sarîra*) which are equally phenomenal (*rûpa*), as being wholly intellectual and immaterial.[24]

For example, "things belonging to the state of glory are not under the sun" (St. Thomas, *Sum. Theol.* III, Supp. q. I, a. I), i.e. not in any mode of time or space; rather, "it is through the midst of the Sun that one escapes altogether" (*atimucyate, Jaiminîya Up. Brâhmana* I.3), where the sun is the "gateway of the worlds" (*loka-dvâra*), (*Chând. Up.* VIII.6.6), Eckhart's "gate through which all things return perfectly free to their supreme felicity (*pûrnânan-da*)...*free* as the Godhead in its non-existence" (*asat*), the "Door" of John X, "Heaven's gate that Agni opens" (*svargasya lokasya dvâram avrnot*), (*Aitareya Brâhmana,* III.42).[25] It is true that here again we shall inevitably meet with a certain and by no means negligible distinction of the religious from the metaphysical formulation. The religious concept of supreme felicity culminates as we have already seen in the assimilation of the soul to Deity in act; the soul's own act being one of adoration rather than of union. Likewise, and without inconsistency, since it is assumed that the individual soul remains numerically distinct alike from God and from other substances, religion offers to mortal consciousness the consolatory promise of finding there in Heaven, not only God, but those whom it loved on earth, and may remember and recognize.

Nor will metaphysics deny that even in a "Heaven," on the farther side of time, there may be, at least until the "Last Judgment," a knowledge-of (*avidyâ*) rather than a knowledge-as (*vidyâ*), though it will not think of him whose modality is still in knowledge-of as wholly Comprehending (*vidvân*) nor as absolutely Enlarged (*atimukta*). Metaphysics will allow, and here in formal agreement with religion, that there may or even must be states of being by no means wholly in time, nor yet in eternity (the timeless now), but aeviternal, "aeviternity" (Vedic *amrtatva*) being defined as a mean between eternity and time;[26] the Angels for example, as conscious intellectual substances, partaking of eternity as to their immutable nature and understanding, but of time as regards their accidental awareness of before and after, the changeability of their affections (liability to fall from grace, etc.), and inasmuch as the angelic independence of local motion (because of which Angels are represented as winged, and spoken of as "birds"),[27] whereby they can be anywhere, is other than the immanence of the First, which implies an equal presence everywhere. Nor is it denied by religion that "Certain men even in this state of life are greater than certain angels, not actually, but virtually" (St. Thomas, *Sum. Theol.,* I, q. 117, a. 2, *ad* 3), whence it naturally follows that "Some men are taken up into the highest angelic orders" (Gregory, *Hom. in Ev.* XXXIV), thus partaking of an aeviternal being; all of which corresponds to what is implied by the familiar Hindu expression *devo bhûtvâ,* equivalent to "dead and gone to Heaven." Precisely this point of view is more technically expressed in the critical text, *Brhadâranyaka Up.* III.2.12, "When a man dies, what does not forsake (*na jahâti*) him is his 'soul' (*nâma*),[28] the soul is without end (*ananta,* "aeviternal"), without end is what the Several Angels are, so then he wins the world everlasting" (*anantam lokam*). Cf. Rûmî (XII in Nicholson's *Shams-i-Tabrîz*), "Every shape you see has its archetype in the placeless world, and if the shape perished, no matter, since its original is everlasting" (*lâmkân-ast*); and St. Thomas, *Sum. Theol.* II-I, q. 67, a. 2C, "as regards the intelligible species, which are in the *possible* intellect, the intellectual virtues remain," viz. when the body is corrupted. This was also expounded by Philo, for whom "Le lieu de cette vie immortelle est le monde intelligible,"[29] that is to say the same as the "Intellectual Realm" of Plotinus, *passim.* If we now consider the implications of these dicta in connection with Boehme's answer to the scholar who enquires, "Whither goeth the soul when the body dieth?" viz. that "There is no necessity for it to *go* anywither... For... whichsoever of the two (that is either heaven or hell) is manifested in it (now), in that the soul standeth (then)...the judgment is, indeed, immediately at the departure of the body"[30] and in the light of *Brhadâranyaka Up.,* IV.4.5-6, "As is his will...so is his lot" (*yat kâmam...tat sampadyate*) and "He whose mind is attached (to mundane things)...returns again to this world...but he whose desire is the Essence (*âtman*), his life (*prânâh*) does not leave him, but he goes as Brahman unto Brahman," it will be apparent that although the soul or intellect (Vedic manas) is immortal by nature (i.e. an individual potentiality that cannot be annihilated, whatever its "fate"), nevertheless the actual "fate" of an individual consciousness, whether it be destined to be "saved" or "liberated" (*devayâna*), or to enter into time again (*pitryâna*), or to be "lost" (*nirrtha*), depends upon itself. And therefore we are told to "Lay up treasure in Heaven, where neither moth nor rust corrupt"; for evidently, if the conscious life of the individual be even now established intellectually (or in religious phraseology, "spiritually"), and the intellectual or spiritual world be aeviternal (as follows from the consideration that ideas have neither place nor date), this conscious life cannot be infringed by the death of the body, which changes nothing in this respect. Or if the consciousness be still attached to and involved in ends (whether good or evil) such as can only be accomplished in time and space, but have not yet been accomplished when the body dies, then evidently such a consciousness will find its way back into those conditions, viz., of space and time, in which the desired ends can be accomplished.[31] Or finally, if conscious life has been led altogether in the flesh, it must be thought of as cut off when its sole support is destroyed; that is, it must be thought of as "backsliding" into a mere potentiality or hell.

Space will not permit us to discuss the theory of "reincarnation" at any length. The fundamentals are given in the *Rg Veda*, where it is primarily a matter of recurring manifestation, in this sense for example, Mitra *jâyate punah* (X.85.19) and Usas is *punahpunar jâyamâna* (I.19.10). An individual application in the spirit of "Thy will be done" is found in V.46.1, "As a comprehending (*vidvân*) horse I yoke myself unto the pole (of the chariot of the year)...seeking neither a release nor to come back again (*na asyâh vimucam na âvrttam punah*), may He (*Agni*) as Comprehender (*vidvân*) and our Waywise Guide lead us aright." The individual, indeed, "is born according to the measure of his understanding" (*Aitareya Âranyaka*, II.3.2), and just as "the world itself is pregnant with the causes of unborn things" (Augustine, *De Trin.* III.9), so is the individual pregnant with the accidents that must befall him; as St. Thomas expresses it, "fate is in the created causes themselves" (*Sum. Theol.* I. q. 116, 2), or Plotinus, "the law is given in the entities upon whom it falls,... it prevails because it is within them...and sets up in them a painful longing to enter the realm to which they are bidden from within" (*Enneads*, IV.3.15); and similarly Ibn 'Arabî, who says that while being is from God, modality is not directly from Him, "for He only wills what they have it in them to become" (Nicholson, *Studies in Islamic Mysticism*, 1921, p.151). On the other hand, it may be taken as certain that the Buddhist and still more the modern Theosophical interpretations of causality (*karma*) or fate (*adrsta*), which assert the necessity of a return (except for one who is mukta or has "reached" *nirvâna*) to the very same conditions that have been left behind at death, involve a metaphysical antinomy; "You would not step twice into the same waters, for other waters are ever flowing in upon you" (Heracleitus). What is really contemplated in Vedic and other traditional doctrines is the necessity of a recurrent manifestation in aeon after aeon, though not again within one and the same temporal cycle,[32] of all those individual potentialities or forces in which the desire to "prolong their line" is still effective; every Patriarch (*pitr*) being, like Prajâpati himself, *prajâ-kâmya*, and therefore willingly committed to the "Patriarchal Way" (*pitryâna*).

What is then from the standpoint of metaphysics the whole course of an individual potentiality, from the "time" that it first awakens in the primordial ocean of universal possibility until the "time" it reaches the last harbor? It is a return into the source and well-spring of life, from which life originates, and thus a passage from one "drowning" to another; but with a distinction, valid from the standpoint of the individual in himself so long as he is a Wayfarer and not a Comprehender, for, seen as a process, it is a passage from a merely possible perfection through actual imperfection to an actual perfection, from potentiality to act, from slumber (*abodhya*) to a full awakening (*sambodhi*). Ignoring now the Patriarchal Way as being a "round about" course, and considering only the straight Angelic Way (*devayâna*), with which the *Rg Veda* is primarily and the individual *mumukṣu* specifically concerned, we may say that this Way is one at first of a diminishing and afterwards of an increasing realization of all the possibilities intrinsic to the fact of being in a given mode (the human, for example), and ultimately leads to the realization of all the possibilities of being in any or every mode, and over and beyond this of those of being not in any mode whatever. We cannot do more than allude here to the part that is taken by what is called "initiation" in this connection; only saying that the intention of initiation is to communicate from one to another a spiritual or rather intellectual impulse that has been continuously transmitted in *guru-paramparâ-krama* from the beginning and is ultimately of non-human origin, and whereby the contracted and disintegrated individual is awakened to the possibility of a re-integration (*samskarana*);[33] and that metaphysical rites, or "mysteries" (which are in imitation of the means employed by the Father to accomplish His own re-integration, the necessity for which is occasioned by the incontinence of the creative act), are, like the analogous traditional scriptures, intended to provide the individual with the necessary preparatory education in and means of intellectual operation; but the "Great Work," that of accomplishing the reunion of essence with Essence, must be done by himself within himself.

We have so far followed the Wayfarer's course by the Angelic Way to the spiritual or intellectual realm; and here, from the religious point of view, lies his immortality, for indeed "the duration of aeviternity is infinite" (St. Thomas, *Sum. Theol.* I, q. 10, a. 5, ad 4). But it will be maintained in metaphysics, or even in a religion or by an individual mystic such as Eckhart (in so far as the religious experience is both devotional and intellectual in the deepest sense of both words) that an aeviternal station (*pada*), such as is implied in the concept of being in a heaven, is not the end, nor by any means a full return (*nivrtti*), but only a resting place (*visrâma*).[34] And likewise, it will be maintained that to conceive of the intellectual realm itself as a place of memories would be a derogation, for as Plotinus says of its natives, "if they neither seek nor doubt, and never learn, nothing being at any time absent from their knowledge ... what reasonings, what processes of rational investigation, can take place in them? In other words, they have seen God and they do not recollect? Ah, no...such reminiscence is only for souls that have forgotten" (*Enneads*, IV.4.6);[35] and still more must we say respecting mundane memories (*vâsanâ*) that "when the soul's act is directed to another order, it must utterly reject the memory of such things, over and done with now" (*ibid*, IV.4.4.8).

The metaphysical concept of Perfection, indeed, envisages a state of being that is, not inhuman since it is maintained that such a state is always and everywhere accessible to whoever will press inwards to the central point of consciousness and being on any ground or plane of being, nor "heartless" unless we mean by "heart" the seat of soulfulness and sentimentality; but assuredly non-human. For example, in *Chândogya Up.* V.10.2 it is precisely as *amânava purusa*, "non-human person," that the Son and aeviternal *avatâra*, Agni,[36] is said to lead onward the Comprehending one who has found his way through the Supernal Sun to the farther side of the worlds, and this is the "pathway of the Angels" (*devayâna*) as contrasted with that of the Patriarchs (*pitryâna*) which does not lead beyond the Sun but to re-embodiment in a human mode of being. And it is foreseen that this *devayâna* must lead, whether sooner or later, to what is expressed in doctrinal mysticism as a "final death of the soul," or "drowning," the Sufi *al-fanâ 'an al-fanâ*; by which is implied a passage beyond even consciousness in deity as act, to a Supreme (Skt. *para, parâtpara*) beyond all trace or even an exemplary multiplicity, nor in any way "intelligible." And there, so far that is from any possible "reminiscence" of any that have been known or loved in otherness, in the words of Eckhart, "No one will ask me whence I came or whither I went," or in Rumi's, "None has knowledge of each who enters that he is so-and-so or so-and-so."[37]

If this appears to be a denial of ultimate significance to human love, the position has been altogether misunderstood. For all metaphysical formulations, assuming that an infallible analogy relates every plane of being to every other, have seen in human love an image of divine felicity (*pûrnânanda*), imagined not as a contradiction of but as transformation (*parâvrtti*) of sensual experience. This is the theory of "Platonic love," according to which, as Ibn Fârid expresses it, "the charm of every fair youth or lovely girl is lent to them from Her beauty"; a point of view implicit too in Erigena's conception of the world as a theophany, and in the Scholastic doctrine of the *vestigium pedis*, the trace or footprint of divinity in time, which has its equivalent in Vedic and Zen symbolisms. What this means in actual tradition is that the beloved on earth is to be realized *there* not as she is in herself but as she is in God,[38] and so it is in the case of Dante and Beatrice, Ibn 'Arabî and an-Nizâm[39] and in that of Chandîdâs and Râmî.[40] The beauty of the Beloved *there* is no longer as it is here contingent and merely a participation or reflection, but that of the Supernal Wisdom, that of the One Madonna, that of the intrinsic being of the Bride, which "rains down flames of fire" (*Convivio*) and as claritas illuminates and guides the pure intellect. In that last and hidden station (*guhyam padam*), nature and essence, Apsaras and Gandharva, are one and indivisible, knowing nothing of a within or a without (*na bâhyam kimcana veda nântaram, Brhadâranyaka Up.* IV.321), and that is their supreme felicity, and that of every liberated consciousness.

All this can only be described in terms of negation, in terms of what it is not, and therefore we say again that metaphysics can in no way be thought of as a doctrine offering consolations to a suffering humanity. What metaphysics understands by immortality and by eternity implies and demands of every man a total and uncompromising denial of himself and a final mortification, to be dead and buried in the Godhead. "Whoever realizes this, avoids contingent death (*punar mrtyu*), death gets him not, for Death becomes his essence, and of all these Angels he becomes the One" (*Brhadâranyaka Up.* I.2.7). For the Supreme Identity is no less a Death and a Darkness than a Life and a Light, no less Asura than

81

Deva: "His overshadowing is both Aeviternity and Death" (*yasya châyâ amrta, yasya mrtyuh, Rg Veda,* X. 121.2).[41] And this is what we understand to be the final purport of the First Philosophy.

Notes

1. It is not pretended to lay down a final definition of philosophy.

2. Our numbering of the philosophies in inverse order as (2) and (1) is because Aristotle's First Philosophy, viz. Metaphysics, is actually prior in logical order of thought, which proceeds from within outwards.

3. This is, for example, the matter in debate as between Buddhist and Brahmanical philosophers. For the nominalist, the ultimate forms, ideas, images or reasons are merely names of the counters of thought and valid only as means of communication; for the realist (idealist) the ultimate forms are "realities" dependent upon and inherent in being, i.e. real in their being and nominal only in the sense "only logically distinguishable."

4. Common sense is an admirable thing, as is also instinct, but neither of these is the same as reason, nor the same as the wisdom that is not about human affairs, but "speculative," i.e. known in the mirror of the pure intellect.

5. When a cause is discovered, this is called an explanation. But each cause was once an effect, and so on indefinitely, so that our picture of reality takes the form of a series of causes extending backward into the past, and of effects expected in the future, but we have no empirical experience of a now, nor can we explain empirically how causes produce effects, the assumption *post hoc propter hoc* being always an act of faith.

6. As is very elegantly demonstrated by St. Thomas, *Sum. Theol.* I, q. 7, a. 3, cf. q. 14, a. 12, *ad* 3; his "relatively infinite" being our "indefinite" (*ananta*), incalculable (*asamkhya*) but not placeless (*adesa*) nor wholly timeless (*akâla*).

7. Science differs from animism only in this respect, that while science assumes forces in the sense of blind wills, animism (which is also a kind of philosophy) personifies these forces and endows them with a free will.

8. Pantheism is more commonly predicated of a given doctrine merely by imputation, either with unconsciously dishonest intention or by customary usage uncritically perpetuated. In every case the observer presumed to be impartial should consider the doctrine itself, and not what is said of it by hostile critics. On the general impropriety of the term "pantheism" in connection with the Vedanta, see Lacombe, Avant-propos to René Grousset, *Les Philosophies Indiennes*, p. xiv, note 1, and Whitby, Preface to René Guénon, *Man and his Becoming according to the Vedânta*, 1945, p. ix.

9. St. Thomas, *Sum. Theol.* I, q. 1, a. 6, ad 2.

10. Prudence is defined as *recta ratio agibilium*, art as *recta ratio factibilium*.

11. E.g. *Aitareya Brâhmana*, VIII.2.

12. "Metaphysics can dispute with one who denies its principles, if only the opponent will make some concession; but if he concede nothing, it can have no dispute with him... If our opponent believes nothing of divine revelation, there is no longer

any means of proving the articles of faith by reasoning" (St. Thomas, *Sum. Theol.* I, q. 1, a. 8 c.); and ibid. q. 46, a. 2: "The articles of faith cannot be proved demonstratively."

Similarly in India it is repeatedly and explicitly asserted that the truth of Vedic doctrine cannot be demonstrated but only experienced. "By what should one know the Knower of knowing" (*Brhadâranyaka Up.* IV. 5.15).

13. Throughout the present essay it is assumed that sensibility means the perception of things by the senses, not a cognition but a reaction; reason, the activity of the intelligence with respect to the causal series of accidents, sometimes called the chain of fate, or in other words an intelligence with respect to things phenomenally known in time and space and called "material"; and intellect, the habit of first principles.

14. Thus *Chândogya Up.* VI.2.1 asserts a religious point of view, as distinct from the metaphysical point of view that prevails in the Upanisads generally, e.g. *Taittiriya Up.* II.7. Christian philosophy maintains that God is "wholly in act." Metaphysics concurs in the definition of perfection as a realization of all the possibilities of being, but would rather say of God that "He does not proceed from potentiality to act" than that He is without potentiality.

15. Duality, as of "spirit and matter," "act and potentiality," "form and substance," "good and evil." This is avoided in Christianity metaphysically, when it is shown that evil is not a self-subsistent nature, but merely a privation, and can be known to the First Intellect only as a goodness or perfection *in potentia*. It is avoided in Sufi metaphysic by considering good and evil as merely reflections in time and space of His essential attributes of Mercy and Majesty.

16. "Matter" here must not be confused with the "solid matter" of everyday parlance; in Christian philosophy, "primary matter" is precisely that "nothing" with respect to which it is said *ex nihilo fit*. Such "matter" is said to be "insatiable for form," and the same is implied when in the *Jaiminiya Up. Brâhmana*, 1.56, it is said that "In the beginning, the woman (= Urvasî, Apsaras) went about in the flood seeking a master (*icchantl salile patim*).

17. The physical analogy is represented in the assertion of the anthropologist that "God is man-made"; a proposition perfectly valid within the conditions of its own level of reference.

18. That is mainly, of course, in Europe from the thirteenth century onwards. In Hinduism, a man is regarded as a true teacher who gives to any individual a better access to that individual's own scriptures; for "the path men take from every side is Mine" (*Bhagavad Gîtâ*, IV.11). Clement of Alexandria allows that "There was always a natural manifestation of the one Almighty God amongst all right-thinking men" (*Misc.*, V); Eckhart says almost in the words of the *Bhagavad Gîtâ* cited above, "In whatever way you find God best, that way pursue"; Dante will not exclude all the pagan philosophers from Heaven; in the Grail tradition, Malory says that "Merlyn made the round table in tokenyng of the roundenes of the world for by the round table is the world sygnifyed by ryghte. For all the world crysten and hethen repayren unto the round table" (*Mort d'Arthur*, XIV.2); these may be contrasted with the position taken in the Song of Roland where, when Saragossa has been taken, "A thousand Franks enter the synagogues and mosques, whose every wall with mallet and axe they shatter...the heathen folk are driven in crowds to the baptismal font, to take Christ's yoke upon them."

19. The "best for me" need not be "truest absolutely" as judged by absolute metaphysical standards. Nevertheless, the metaphysician will not suggest that the follower of a "second best" religion should abandon it for another (cf. *Bhagavad Gîtâ*, III.26, *na buddhibhedam janayed ajnânam*), but rather that he go farther in where he already is, and thus verify as "true" his own images, not by those of another pattern, but rather by the prior form that is common to both.

20. "Diverse dogmatic formulations," i.e. *dharma-paryâya* as this expression is employed in the *Saddharma Pundarika.*

21. In this context the reader is recommended to René Guénon, *L'Orient et l'Occident*, 1932.

22. Cf. Erigena, *De div. naturae*, 1, 66, *Ambo siquidem ex una fonte, divina scilicet sapientia, manare dubium non est*, and *Bhagavad Gîtâ*, V.4-5, "it is the children of this world, and not the men of learning who think of gnosis and works as different...He sees in truth who sees that gnosis and works are one" (for Sâmkhya and Yoga as meaning gnosis and works respectively, see *ibid*, III.3). That the Way of Gnosis and the Way of Participation have one and the same end becomes evident when we consider that love and knowledge can only be conceived of as perfected in an identity of lover and beloved, knower and known.

23. "Even we ourselves as mentally tasting something eternal, are not in this world." St. Augustine, *De Trin.* IV.20.

24. Therefore incapable of "proof," whether the phenomena adduced be "scientific" or "spiritualistic."

25. While it is shown here how the formulations of different religions may express the same conceptions in almost verbal agreement, it must not be supposed that we therefore advocate any kind of eclecticism, or conceive the possibility of a new religion compounded of all existing religions. Eclecticism in religion results only in confusion and caricature, of which a good example can be cited in "Theosophy."

26. St. Thomas, *Sum. Theol.* I, q. 10, a. 5. He says "states of being" in the plural deliberately (cf. René Guénon, *Les États multiples de l'Être*, 1932), although for purposes of generalization it has been necessary to speak only of three, viz. the human, angelic and divine, that is those to which the literal, metaphorical and analogical understandings pertain respectively.

With the Christian "aeviternity," Indian *amrtatva*, and the traditional concept of "humanity" and "Perfect Man" (e.g. Islamic *insanu'l kamil*), cf. Jung, *Modern Man in Search of a Soul*, p. 215: "If it were permissible to personify the unconscious, we might call it a collective human being combining the characteristics of both sexes, transcending youth and age, birth and death, and from having at its command a human experience of one or two million years, almost immortal. If such a being existed, he would be exalted above all temporal change...he would have lived countless times over the life of the individual, or the family, tribe and people, and he would possess the living sense of the rhythm of growth, flowering and decay. It would be positively grotesque for us to call this immense system of the experience of the unconscious psyche an illusion." Here it may be noted that "unconscious" presents an analogy with "Deep-Sleep" (*susupti* = *samâdhi* = *excessus* or *raptus*); on the other hand, the use of the word "collective" betrays a purely scientific, and not a metaphysical conception.

27. "Intellect is the swiftest of birds" (*manah javistam patayatsu anah, Rg. Veda*,

VI.9.5). It is as birds that the Angels "celebrate in the Tree of Life their share of aeviternity" (*yatra suparnâ amrtasya bhâgam...abhi svaranti, ibid.*, 1.164.21). The traditional expression "language of birds" (which survives in "a little bird told me") refers to angelic communications.

28. *Nâma* is the correlative of *rûpa*, being the noumenal or intelligible part and efficient cause of the integration *nâma-rupa*, viz. the individual as he is in himself; and therefore to be rendered not by "name" (for this is not a nominalist but a realist doctrine), but by "idea," "archetype," "form" or "soul" (as when it is said "the soul is the form of the body"); *âtman* on the other hand being "essence" rather than "soul" (*essentia*, that by which a substance has *esse* in whatever mode).

29. Bréhier, *Les Idées philosophiques et religieuses de Philon d'Alexandrie*, 1925, p.240.

30. Boehme, *On Heaven and Hell* (in Everyman's Library, volume entitled *Signatura Rerum*, etc.).

31. It is the good purpose, for example, which operates in the return of a Bodhisattva, who is otherwise fit for Nirvâna.

32. In *Bhagavad Gîtâ*, VI.41, for example, *sâsvatî samâ* is very far from implying "forthwith." We doubt very much whether any passage from the Upanishads could be cited as implying a re-embodiment otherwise than at the dawn of a new cycle, and then only as the growth of a seed sown in the previous aeon, or as a tendency with which the new age can be said to be pregnant.

33. See *Aitareya Âranyaka*, III.2.6; *Aitareya Brâhmana*, VI.27; *Satapatha Brâhmana*, VII.1.2.1 and *passim*. Cf. also Guénon, "L'Initiation et les Métiers," *Le Voile d'Isis*, No. 172, 1934.

34. *Saddharma Pundarika*, V.74. Similarly, the true end of the ritual acts and appointed sacrifices of the Veda is not the attainment of a temporary heaven, but the awakening of a desire to know the Essence (*âtman*) (*Siddhântamuktâvalî*, XXXII, with Venis' note "Paradise is as it were but the half-way house").

35. Similarly in Dante, *Paradiso*, XXIX, 79-81, "there sight is never intercepted by any new perception, and so there is no need of memory, for thought has not been cleft."

36. Agni (-Prajâpati), who in the Vedas is the Herdsman of the Spheres (*gopâ bhuvanasya*), Waywise Leader (*vidvân pathah puraeta*), Messenger and Herald (*dûta, arati*), and stands as the Pillar of Life at the Parting of the Ways (*dyor ha skambha... pathâm visarge, Rg Veda*, X.5.6) in cosmic crucifixion (*dharunesu sthitah, ibid.*), corresponding to the "dogmatic" Buddha, Christ as distinguished from Jesus, and to the "Idea of Muhammad.".

37. Nicholson, *Shams-i-Tabriz*, p. 61.

38. Cf. *Tarjumân al-Ashwâq*, XL.2, "She was exalted in majesty above time" and Rûmî, "'Tis love and the lover that live to all eternity" (XIII, in Nicholson, *Shams-i-Tabriz*). Another example could be cited in the Shepherd of Hermas.

39. Whom Ibn 'Arabî met at Mecca in 1201, see Nicholson, *Tarjumân al-Ashwâq*, 1911.

40. Cf. "Sahaja" in our *Dance of Siva*, 1917.

41. Similarly, *Satapatha Brâhmana*, X.4.3.1-3 *Esa vai mrtyur yat samvatsarah...prajâpatih*, "He, the Father, who is the Year and likewise Death."

The Darkness and Light, belonging to His *asuratva* and *devatva* respectively, remain in Him, who is both *asura* and *deva*, Titan and angel, *sarpa* and *âditya*; at the same time that from the Wayfarer's point of view their reflections in time and space are evil and good. In Hinduism, "the Darkness in Him is called Rudra" (*Maitri Up.* VI.2), and is represented in the names and hues of Kâlî and Krsna; in Christian yoga, the Dark Ray or Divine Darkness, Eckhart's "sable stillness" and "motionless dark that no one knows but He in whom it reigns" (cf. the "Clouds and thick darkness" of Deut. 4: 11), is spoken of already in the *Codex Brucianus* and by Dionysius, and becomes the subject of the contemplatio in caligine. Regarding the propriety of the expression "Christian yoga," we need only point out that St. Bernard's *consideratio, contemplatio,* and *excessus* or *raptus* correspond exactly to *dhârana, dhyâna* and *samâdhi.*

4

Eastern Wisdom and Western Knowledge

East and West, The Crisis of the Modern World, Introduction to the Study of the Hindu Doctrines, and *Man and His Becoming* (Luzac, London, 1941-46) are the first of a series in which the majority of René Guénon's works already published in French will appear in English. Another version of *Man and His Becoming* had appeared earlier.[1] M. René Guénon is not an "Orientalist" but what the Hindus would call a "master," formerly resident in Paris, and now for many years in Egypt, where his affiliations are Islamic. His *Introduction générale à l'étude des doctrines hindoues* appeared in 1921.[2] As a preliminary to his further expositions of the traditional philosophy, sometimes called the *Philosophia Perennis* (*et Universalis* must be understood, for this "philosophy" has been the common inheritance of all mankind without exception), Guénon cleared the ground of all possible misconception in two large and rather tedious, but by no means unnecessary, volumes, *L'Erreur spirite* (i.e. "Fallacy of Spiritualism," a work for which *Bhagavad Gîtâ*, XVII, 4, "Men of darkness are they who make a cult of the departed and of spirits," might have served as a motto),[3] and *Le Théosophisme, histoire d'une pseudo-religion.*[4] These are followed by *L'Homme et son devenir selon le Vedanta* and *L'Esotérisme de Dante,*[5] *Le roi du monde,*[6] *St. Bernard,*[7] *Orient et Occident* and *Autorité spirituelle et pouvoir temporel,*[8] *Le symbolisme de la croix,*[9] *Les états multiples de l'être,*[10] and *La métaphysique orientale.*[11] More recently M. Guénon has published in mimeographed, and subsequently printed, editions *Le règne de la quantité et les signes des temps*[12] and *Les principes du calcul infinitésimal.*[13]

In the meantime important articles from Guénon's pen appeared monthly in *Le Voile d'Isis,* later *Études Traditionnelles,* a journal of which the appearance was interrupted by the war, but which has been continued as from September-October, 1945. *Études Traditionnelles* is devoted to "La Tradition Perpétuelle et Unanime, révélée tant par les dogmes et les rites des religions orthodoxes que par la langue universelle des symboles initiatiques." Of articles that have appeared elsewhere attention may be called to "L'Esotérisme Islamique" in *Cahiers du Sud*.[14] Excerpts from Guénon's writings, with some comment, have appeared in *Triveni* (1935) and in the *Visvabharatî Quarterly* (1935, 1938). A work by L. de Gaigneron entitled *Vers la connaissance interdite*[15] is closely connected with Guénon's; it is presented in the form of a discussion in which the Âtman (Spiritus), Mentalité ("Reason," in the current, not the Platonic, sense), and a Roman abbé take part; the "forbidden knowledge" is that of the gnosis which the modern Church and the rationalist alike reject, though for very different reasons—the former because it cannot tolerate a point of view which considers Christianity only as one amongst other orthodox religions and the latter because, as a great Orientalist (Professor A. B. Keith) has remarked, ("such knowledge as is not empirical is meaningless to us and should not be described as knowledge")[16]—an almost classical confession of the limitations of the "scientific" position.

Guénon's French is at once precise and limpid, and inevitably loses in translation; his subject matter is of absorbing interest, at least to anyone who cares for what Plato calls the really serious things.[17] Nevertheless it has often been found unpalatable; partly for reasons already given, but also for reasons that have been stated, paradoxically enough, by a reviewer of Blakney's *Meister Eckhart* in the *Harvard Divinity School Bulletin*,[18] who says that "To an age which believes in personality and personalism, the impersonality of mysticism is baffling; and to an age which is trying to quicken its insight into history the indifference of the mystics to events in time is disconcerting." As for history, Guénon's "he who cannot escape from the standpoint of temporal succession so as to see all things in their simultaneity is incapable of the least conception of the metaphysical order"[19] adequately complements Jacob Behmen's designation of the "history that was once brought to pass" as "merely the (outward) form of Christianity."[20] For the Hindu, the events of the Rg Veda are nowever and dateless, and the Krishna Lîlâ "not an historical event"; and the reliance of Christianity upon supposedly historical "facts" seems to be its greatest weakness. The value of literary history for doxography is very little, and it is for this reason that so many orthodox Hindus have thought of Western scholarship as a "crime": *their* interest is not in "what men have believed," but in the truth. A further difficulty is presented by Guénon's uncompromising language; "Western civilization is an anomaly, not to say a monstrosity."

Of this a reviewer[21] has remarked that "such sweeping remarks cannot be shared even by critics of Western achievements." I should have thought that now that its denouement is before our eyes, the truth of such a statement might have been recognized by every unprejudiced European; at any rate Sir George Birdwood in 1915 described modern Western civilization as "secular, joyless, inane, and self-destructive" and Professor La Piana has said that "what we call our civilization is but a murderous machine with no conscience and no ideals"[22] and might well have said suicidal as well as murderous. It would be very easy to cite innumerable criticisms of the same kind; Sir S. Radhakrishnan holds, for example, that "civilization is not worth saving if it continues on its present foundations,"[23] and this it would be hard to deny; Professor A. N. Whitehead has spoken quite as forcibly—"There remains the show of civilization, without any of its realities."[24]

In any case, if we are to read Guénon at all, we must have outgrown the temporally provincial view that has for so long and so complacently envisaged a continuous progress of humanity culminating in the twentieth century and be willing at least to ask ourselves whether there has not been rather a continued decline, "from the stone age until now," as one of the most learned men in the U.S.A. once put it to me. It is not by "science" that we can be saved: "the possession of the sciences as a whole, if it does not include the best, will in some few cases aid but more often harm the owner."[25] "We are obliged to admit that our European culture is a culture of the mind and senses only";[26] "The prostitution of science may lead to world catastrophe";[27] "Our dignity and our interests require that we shall be the directors and not the victims of technical and scientific advance";[28] "Few will deny that the twentieth century thus far has brought us bitter disappointment."[29] "We are now faced with the prospect of complete bankruptcy in every department of life."[30] Eric Gill speaks of the "monstrous inhumanity" of industrialism, and of the modern way of life, as "neither human nor normal nor Christian ... It is our way of thinking that is odd and unnatural."[31] This sense of frustration is perhaps the most encouraging sign of the times. We have laid stress on these things because it is only to those who feel this frustration, and not to those who still believe in progress, that Guénon addresses himself; to those who are complacent everything that he has to say will seem to be preposterous.

The reactions of Roman Catholics to Guénon are illuminating. One has pointed out that he is a "serious metaphysician," i.e. one convinced of the truth he expounds and eager to show the unanimity of the Eastern and scholastic traditions, and observes that "in such matters belief and understanding must go together."[32] *Crede ut intelligas* is a piece of advice that modern scholars would, indeed, do well to consider; it is, perhaps, just because we have not believed that we have not yet understood the East. The same author writes of *East and West,* "Rene Guénon is one of the few writers of our time whose work is really of importance ... he stands for the primacy of pure metaphysics over all other forms of knowledge, and presents himself as the exponent of a major tradition of thought, predominantly Eastern, but shared in the Middle Ages by the scholastics of the West ... clearly Guénon's position is not that of Christian orthodoxy, but many, perhaps most, of his theses are, in fact, better in accord with authentic Thomist doctrine than are many opinions of devout but ill-instructed Christians."[33] We should do well to remember that even St. Thomas Aquinas did not disdain to make use of "intrinsic and probable proofs" derived from the "pagan" philosophers.

Gerald Vann, on the other hand, makes the mistake which the title of his review, "René Guénon's Orientalism,"[34] announces; for this is not another "ism," nor a geographical antithesis, but one of modern empiricism and traditional theory. Vann springs to the defense of the very Christianity in which Guénon himself sees almost the only possibility of salvation for the West; only possibility, not because there is no other body of truth, but because the mentality of the West is adapted to and needs a religion of just this sort. But if Christianity should fail, it is just because its intellectual aspects have been submerged, and it has become a code of ethics rather than a doctrine from which all other applications can and should be derived; hardly two consecutive sentences of some of Meister Eckhart's sermons would be intelligible to an average modern congregation, which does not expect doctrine, and only expects to be told how to behave. If Guénon wants the West to turn to Eastern metaphysics, it is not because they are Eastern but because this is metaphysics. If "Eastern" metaphysics differed from a "Western" metaphysics—as true philosophy differs from what is often so called in our modern universities—one or the other would not be metaphysics. It is from metaphysics that the West has turned away in its desperate endeavor to live by bread alone, an endeavor of which the Dead Sea fruits are before our eyes. It is only because this metaphysics still survives as a living power in Eastern societies, in so far as they have not been corrupted by the withering touch of Western, or rather, *modern* civilization (for the contrast is not of East or West as such, but of "those paths that the rest of mankind follows as a matter of course" with those post-Renaissance paths that have brought us to our present impasse), and not to Orientalize the West, but to bring back the West to a consciousness of the roots of her own life and of values that have been transvalued in the most sinister sense, that Guénon asks us to turn to the East. He does not mean, and makes it very clear that he does not mean, that Europeans ought to become Hindus or Buddhists, but much rather that they, who are getting nowhere by the study of "the Bible as literature," or that of Dante "as a poet," should rediscover Christianity, or what amounts to the same thing, Plato ("that great priest," as Meister Eckhart calls him). I often marvel at men's immunity to the *Apology* and *Phaedo* or the seventh chapter of the *Republic;* I suppose it is because they would not hear, "though one rose from the dead."

The issue of "East and West" is not merely a theoretical (we must remind the modern reader that from the standpoint of the traditional philosophy, "theoretical" is anything but a term of disparagement) but also an urgent practical problem. Pearl Buck asks, "Why should prejudices be so strong at this moment? The answer it seems to me is simple. Physical conveyance and other circumstances have forced parts of the world once remote from each other into actual intimacy for which peoples are *not mentally or spiritually prepared* ... It is not necessary to believe that this initial stage must continue. If those prepared to act as interpreters will do their proper work, we may find that within another generation or two, or even sooner, dislike and prejudice may be gone. This is only possible if prompt and strong measures are taken by peoples to keep step mentally with the increasing closeness to which the war is compelling us."[35] But if this is to happen, the West will have to abandon what Guénon calls its "proselytizing fury," an expression that must *not* be taken to refer only to the activities of Christian missionaries, regrettable as these often are, but to those of all the distributors of modern "civilization" and those of practically all those "educators" who feel that they have more to give than to learn from what are often called the "backward" or "unprogressive" peoples; to whom it does not occur that one may not wish or need to "progress" if one has reached a state of equilibrium that already provides for the realization of what one regards as the greatest purposes of life. It is as an expression of good will and of the best intentions that this proselytizing fury takes on its most dangerous aspects. To many this "fury" can only suggest the fable of the fox that lost its tail, and persuaded the other foxes to cut off theirs. An industrialization of the East may be inevitable, but do not let us call it a blessing that a folk should be reduced to the level of a proletariat, or assume that materially higher standards of living necessarily make for greater happiness. The West is only just discovering, to its great astonishment, that "material inducements, that is, money or the things that money can buy" are by no means so cogent a force as has been supposed; "Beyond the subsistence level, the theory that this incentive is decisive is largely an illusion."[36] As for the East, as Guénon says, "The only impression that, for example, mechanical inventions make on most Orientals is one of deep repulsion; certainly it all seems to them far more harmful than beneficial, and if they find themselves obliged to accept certain things which the present epoch has made necessary, they do so in the hope of future riddance ... what the people of the West call 'rising' would be called by some 'sinking'; that is what all true Orientals think."[37] It must not be supposed that because so many Eastern peoples have imitated us in self-defense that they have therefore accepted our values; on the contrary, it is just because the conservative East still challenges all the presuppositions on which our illusion of progress rests, that it deserves our most serious consideration.

There is nothing in economic intimacies that is likely to reduce prejudice or promote mutual understandings automatically. Even when Europeans live amongst Orientals, "*economic* contact between the Eastern and Western groups is practically the only contact there is. There is very little social or religious give and take between the two. Each lives in a world almost entirely closed to the other—and by 'closed' we mean not only 'unknown' but more: incomprehensible and unattainable."[38] That is an inhuman relationship, by which both parties are degraded.

Neither must it be assumed that the Orient thinks it important that the masses should learn to read and write. Literacy is a practical necessity in an industrial society, where the keeping of accounts is all important. But in India, in so far as Western methods of education have not been imposed from without, all higher education is imparted orally, and to have *heard* is far more important than to have *read*. At the same time the peasant, prevented by his illiteracy and poverty from devouring the newspapers and magazines that form the daily and almost the only reading of the vast majority of Western "literates," is, like Hesiod's Boeotian farmers, and still more like the Gaelic-speaking Highlanders before the era of the board schools, thoroughly familiar with an epic literature of profound spiritual significance and a body of poetry and music of incalculable value; and one can only regret the spread of an "education" that involves the destruction of all these things, or only preserves them as curiosities within the covers of books. For cultural purposes it is not important that the masses should be literate; it is not necessary that anyone should be literate; it is only necessary that there should be amongst the people philosophers (in the traditional, not the modern sense of the word), and that there should be preserved deep respect on the part of laymen for true learning that is the antithesis of the American attitude to a "professor." In these respects the whole East is still far in advance of the West, and hence the learning of the elite exerts a far profounder influence upon society as a whole than the Western specialist "thinker" can ever hope to wield.

It is not, however, primarily with a protection of the East against the subversive inroads of Western "culture" that Guénon is concerned, but rather with the question, What possibility of regeneration, if any, can be envisaged for the West? The possibility exists only in the event of a return to first principles and to the normal ways of living that proceed from the application of first principles to contingent circumstances; and as it is only in the East that these things are still alive, it is to the East that the West must turn. "It is the West that must take the initiative, but she must be prepared really to go towards the East, not merely seeking to draw the East towards herself, as she has tried to do so far. There is no reason why the East should take this initiative, and there would still be none, even if the Western world were not in such a state as to make any effort in this direction useless ... It now remains for us to show how the West might attempt to approach the East."[39]

He proceeds to show that the work is to be done in the two fields of metaphysics and religion, and that it can only be carried out on the highest intellectual levels, where agreement on first principles can be reached and apart from any propaganda on behalf of or even apology for "Western civilization."

The work must be undertaken, therefore, by an "elite." And as it is here more than anywhere that Guénon's meaning is likely to be willfully misinterpreted, we must understand clearly what he means by such an elite. The divergence of the West and East being only "accidental," "the bringing of these two portions of mankind together and the return of the West to a normal civilization are really just one and the same thing." An elite will necessarily work in the first place "for itself, since its members will naturally reap from their own development an immediate and altogether unfailing benefit." An indirect result—"indirect," because on this intellectual level one does not think of "doing good" to others, or in terms of "service," but seeks truth because one needs it oneself—would, or might under favorable conditions, bring about "a return of the West to a traditional civilization," i.e. one in which "everything is seen as the application and extension of a doctrine whose essence is purely intellectual and metaphysical."[40]

It is emphasized again and again that such an elite does not mean a body of specialists or scholars who would absorb and put over on the West the forms of an alien culture, nor even persuade the West to return to such a traditional civilization as existed in the Middle Ages. Traditional cultures develop by the application of principles to conditions; the principles, indeed, are unchangeable and universal, but just as nothing can be known except in the mode of the knower, so nothing valid can be accomplished socially without taking into account the character of those concerned and the particular circumstances of the period in which they live. There is no "fusion" of cultures to be hoped for; it would be nothing like an "eclecticism" or "syncretism" that an elite would have in view. Neither would such an elite be organized in any way so as to exercise such a direct influence as that which, for example, the Technocrats would like to exercise for the good of mankind. If such an elite ever came into being, the vast majority of Western men would never know of it; it would operate only as a sort of leaven, and certainly on behalf of rather than against whatever survives of traditional essence in, for example, the Greek Orthodox and Roman Catholic domains. It is, indeed, a curious fact that some of the most powerful defenders of Christian dogma are to be found amongst Orientals who are not themselves Christians, or ever likely to become Christians, but recognize in the Christian tradition an embodiment of the universal truth to which God has never nor anywhere left himself without a witness.

In the meantime, M. Guénon asks, "Is this really 'the beginning of an end' for the modern civilization? ... At least there are many signs which should give food for reflection to those who are still capable of it; will the West be able to regain control of herself in time?" Few would deny that we are faced with the possibility of a total disintegration of culture. We are at war with ourselves, and *therefore* at war with one another. Western man is unbalanced, and the question, Can he recover himself? is a very real one. No one to whom the question presents itself can afford to ignore the writings of the leading living exponent of a traditional wisdom that is no more essentially Oriental than it is Occidental, though it may be only in the uttermost parts of the earth that it is still remembered and must be sought.

Notes

1. London, Rider, 1928.
2. Paris, 2nd ed., 1932.
3. Paris, 1923, 2nd ed., 1930.
4. Paris, 1921, 2nd ed., 1930.
5. Both Paris, 1925.
6. Paris, 1927.
7. Marseille, 1929.
8. Both Paris, 1930.
9. Paris, 1931.
10. Paris, 1932.
11. Paris, 1939—a lecture delivered at the Sorbonne in 1925; 2nd ed., 1946.
12. Cairo, 1943, and London, 1944.
13. Cairo, 1943.- Printed Paris, 1946.
14. 22me année, 1935.
15. Paris, 1935.
16. *Aitareya Âranyaka*, Oxford, 1909, p. 42.
17. *Laws*, 803 B, C; *Philebus*, 58 A; *Republic*, 521 C, D; *Timaeus*, 47 B, etc.
18. XXXIX, 1942, p. 107.
19. *La métaphysique orientale*, p.17.
20. *Signatura rerum*, XV, 24.
21. Betty Heiman in *BSOAS.*, X, 1942, p. 1048.
22. *Harvard Divinity School Bulletin*, XXVII, 27.
23. *Eastern Religions and Western Thought*, p.257.
24. *Adventures of Ideas*, 1933, p.358.

25. Plato, *Alcibiades*, II, 144 D.

26. Worrington, *Form in Gothic*, p. 75.

27. Leroy Waterman in *JAOS*, LVIII, 410.

28. Rt. Hon. Herbert Morison in the British Association Report, *Science and World Order*, January, 1942, p. 33.

29. Professor J. M. Mecklin in *Passing of the Saint*, p.197.

30. Lionel Giles in *Luzac's Oriental List.*

31. *Autobiography*, pp. 145, 174, 279.

32. Walter Shewring in the *Weekly Review*, January, 1939.

33. *Weekly Review*, August 28, 1941.

34. In the *New English Weekly*, September, 1941.

35. *Asia*, March, 1942, italics mine.

36. National Research Council, *Fatigue of Workers*, 1942, p. 143.

37. *East and West*, pp. 44, 71.

38. J. H. Bocke, *Structure of Netherlands Indian Economy*, 1942, p. 68.

39. *East and West*, p. 162.

40. *East and West*, p. 241.

5

Beauty and Truth

"Ex divina pulchritudine esse omnium derivatur."
St. Thomas Aquinas, *De Pulchro*

It is affirmed that "beauty relates to the cognitive faculty" (St. Thomas Aquinas, *Sum. Theol.*, I, 5, 4 ad 1) being the cause of knowledge, for, "since knowledge is by assimilation, and similitude is with respect to form, beauty properly belongs to the nature of a formal cause" (*ibid.*). Again, St. Thomas endorses the definition of beauty as a cause, in *Sum. Theol.*, III, 88, 3, he says that "God is the cause of all things by his knowledge" and this again emphasizes the connection of beauty with wisdom. "It is knowledge that makes the work beautiful" (St. Bonaventura, *De reductione artium ad theologiam*, 13). It is of course, by its quality of lucidity or illumination (*claritas*), which Ulrich of Strassburg explains as the "shining of the formal light upon what is formed or proportioned," that beauty is identified with intelligibility: brilliance of expression being unthinkable apart from perspicacity. Vagueness of any sort, as being a privation of due form is necessarily a defect of beauty. Hence it is that in medieval rhetoric so much stress is laid on the communicative nature of art, which must be always explicit.

It is precisely this communicative character that distinguished Christian from late classical art, in which style is pursued for its own sake, and content valued only as a point of departure; and in the same way, from the greater part of modern art, which endeavors to eliminate subject (*gravitas*). Augustine made a clean break with sophism, which he defines as follows: "Even though not quibbling, a speech seeking verbal ornament (Skr. *alamkâra*) beyond the bounds of responsibility to its burden (*gravitas*) is called sophistic" (*De doctrina christiana*, II, 31). Augustine's own rhetoric "goes back over centuries of the lore of personal triumph to the ancient idea of moving men to truth" (Baldwin, *Medieval Rhetoric and Poetic*, p. 51), to Plato's position when he asks: "About what does the sophist make

97

a man more eloquent?" (*Protagoras*, 312), and Aristotle's, whose theory of rhetoric was one of the "energizing of knowledge, the bringing of truth to bear upon men ... Rhetoric is conceived by Aristotle as the art of giving effectiveness to truth; it is conceived by the earlier and the later sophists as the art of giving effectiveness as to the speaker" (Baldwin, *loc. cit.*, p. 3). We must not think of this as having an application only to oratory or literature; what is said applies to any art, as Plato makes explicit in the *Gorgias*, 503, where again he deals with the problem of what is to be said—"the good man, who is intent on the best when he speaks ... is just like any other craftsman ...You have only to look, for example, at the painters, the builders ..." The scholastic position is, then, as remote from the modern as it is from the late classic: for just as in sophism, so in the greater part of modern art, the intention is either to please others or to express oneself. Whereas the art of pleasing, or as Plato calls it, "flattery" (*Gorgias*), is not for the Middle Ages the purpose of art, but an accessory (and for great minds not even an indispensable) means, so that as Augustine says, "I am not now treating of how to please; I am speaking of how they are to be taught who desire instruction" (*ibid.*, IV, 10). And whereas in the greater part of modern art one cannot fail to recognize an exhibitionism in which the artist rather exploits himself than demonstrates a truth, and modern individualism frankly justifies this self-expressionism, the medieval artist is characteristically anonymous and of "unobtrusive demeanor," and it is not who speaks, but what is said that matters.

No distinction can be drawn between the principles of medieval plastic and figurative art and symbolic "ornament" and those of contemporary "sermons" and "tracts," of which an indication may be cited in the designation "Biblia pauperum" as applied to a pictorial relation of scriptural themes. As Professor Morey remarks, "The cathedral ... is as much an exposition of medieval Christianity as the *Summa* of Thomas Aquinas" (*Christian Art*, 1935, p. 49); and Baldwin, "The cathedrals still exhibit in sculpture and glass what came in words from their pulpits ... Such preaching shows the same preoccupations as the symbolic windows of the cathedrals, their carved capitals, above all the thronged but harmonized groups of their great porches" (*Medieval Rhetoric and Poetic*, pp. 239, 244). It is therefore entirely pertinent to note that according to Augustine, who may be said to have defined once for all the principles of Christian art (*De doctrina christiana*, book IV, a treatise that "has historical significance out of all proportion to its size," Baldwin, *op. cit.*, p. 51), the business of Christian eloquence is "to teach, in order to instruct; to please, in order to hold; and also, assuredly, to move, in order to convince" (IV, 12-13); the formula *docere, delectare, flectere,* or alternatively *probare, delectare, movere,* deriving from Cicero; *probare* means the demonstration of *quod est probandum,* the theme or burden of the work.[1] The meaning of "pleasure" (*delectatio*) is explained by St. Augustine when he says "one is pleasing (*gratus*) when he clears up matters that need to be made understood" (IV, 25). But in the present context Augustine is thinking rather of pleasure given by "charm of diction" (*suavitas dictionis*) by means of which the truth to be communicated is at it were made palatable by the addition of a "seasoning" which, for the sake of weak minds, ought not to be neglected but is not essential if we are considering only those who are so eager for the truth that they care not how inelegantly (*inculte*) it may have been expressed, since "it is the fine characteristic of great minds (*bonorum ingeniorum*) that they love the truth that is in the words, rather than the words themselves" (IV, 11). And with reference to what we should call, perhaps, the severity of "primitive" art, Augustine's words are very pertinent: "O eloquence, so much the more terrible as it is so unadorned; and as it is so genuine, so much the more powerful: O truly, an axe hewing the rock!" (IV, 14).

Perspicacity is the first consideration; such language must therefore be used as will be intelligible to those who are addressed. If necessary, even "correctness" (*integritas*)[2] of expression may be sacrificed, if the matter itself can be taught and understood "correctly" (*integre*) thereby (IV, 10). In other words, the syntax and vocabulary are for the sake of the demonstration (*evidentia: quod ostendere intendit*), and not the theme for the sake of the style (as modern aestheticians appear to believe). The argument is directed against a mechanical adhesion to a pedantic or academic "accuracy," and arises in connection with the problem of addressing a somewhat uncultivated audience. It amounts to this, that in actual teaching, one should employ the vernacular of those who are taught, provided that this is for the good of the thing to be taught, or as the *Lankâvatâra Sûtra,* II, 114, expresses it, "the doctrine is communicated only indirectly by means of the picture: and whatever is not adapted to such and such persons as are to be taught, cannot be called teaching." The end is not to be confused with the means, nor are those good means which may seem to be good in themselves, but those which are good in the given application. It is of the greatest interest to observe that these principles amount to a recognition and sanction of such "distortions" or "departures from academic perfection" as are represented by what are called "architectural refinements." In the case of *entasis*, for example, the end in view is probably that the column may be understood to be perpendicular and straight-sided, the desired result being obtained by an actual divergence from straight-sidedness. At the same time, the accommodation is not made for aesthetic but for intellectual reasons; it is in this way that the "idea" of perpendicularity is best communicated, and if the resulting "effect" is also visually satisfying, this is rather a matter of grace than the immediate purpose of the modification. In the same way with the composition of any work, this composition is determined by the logic of the theme to be communicated, and not for the comfort of the eye, and if the eye is satisfied, it is because a physical order in the organ of perception corresponds to the rational order present in whatever is intelligible, and not because the work of art was for the sake of the eye or ear alone. Another way in which "correctness," in this case "archeological accuracy," can properly be sacrificed to the higher end of intelligibility can be cited in the customary medieval treatment of Biblical themes as if they had been enacted in the actual environment of those who depicted them, and with consequent anachronism. It hardly needs to be pointed out that a treatment which represents a mystical event as if a current event communicates its theme not less but more vividly, and in this sense more "correctly," than one which by a pedantic regard for archeological precision rather separates the event from the spectator's "now" and makes it a thing of the past.

Augustine's principles are nowhere better exemplified than in the case of the *Divina Commedia*, which we now persist in regarding as an example of "poetry" or *belles-lettres*, notwithstanding that Dante says of it himself that "the whole work was undertaken not for a speculative but a practical end ... the purpose of the whole is to remove those who are living in this life from the state of wretchedness, and to lead them to the state of blessedness" (*Ep. ad Can. Grand.*, §§ 16 and 15). Current criticism similarly misinterprets the Rig Veda, insisting on its "lyrical" qualities, although those who are in and of, and not merely students of, the Vedic tradition are well assured of the primarily injunctive function of its verses, and have regard not so much to their artistry as to their truth, which is the source of their moving power. The same confusions are repeated in our conceptions of "decorative art" and the "history of ornament." It is tacitly ignored that all that we call ornament or decoration in ancient and medieval and, it may be added, in folk art, had originally, and for the most part still has there, an altogether other value than that which we impute to it when we nowadays plagiarize its forms in what is really "interior decoration" and nothing more; and this we call a scientific approach!

In Europe, the now despised doctrine of a necessary intelligibility reappears at a comparatively late date in a musical connection. Not only had Josquin des Prés in the fifteenth century argued that music must not only sound well but mean something, but it is about this very point that the struggle between plainsong and counterpoint centered in the sixteenth century. The Church demanded that the words of the Mass should be "clearly distinguishable through the web of counterpoint which embroidered the plainsong." Record is preserved of a bishop of Ruremonde "who states that after giving the closest attention he had been unable to distinguish one word sung by the choir" (Z. K. Pyne, *Palestrina, his Life and Times*, London, 1922, pp. 31 and 48). It was only when the popes and the Council of Trent had been convinced by the work of Palestrina that the new and more intricate musical forms were not actually incompatible with lucidity, that the position of the figured music was made secure.

Bearing in mind what has already been said on the invariably occasional character of art, together with what has been cited as to intelligibility, it is sufficiently evident that from a Christian point of view, the work of art is always a means, and never an end in itself. Being a means, it is ordered to a given end, without which it has no *raison d'être*, and can only be treated as bric-à-brac. The current approach may be compared to that of a traveler who, when he finds a signpost, proceeds to admire its elegance, to ask who made it, and finally cuts it down and decides to use it as a mantelpiece ornament. That may be all very well, but can hardly be called an understanding of the work; for unless the end be apparent to ourselves, as it was to the artist, how can we pretend to have understood, or how can we judge his operation?

If indeed we divert the work of art to some other than its original use, then, in the first place, its beauty will be correspondingly diminished, for, as St. Thomas says above, "if they are applied to another use or end, their harmony and therefore their beauty is no longer maintained," and, in the second place, even though we may derive a certain pleasure from the work that has been torn out of its context, to rest in this pleasure will be a sin in terms of Augustine's definitions "to enjoy what we should use" (*De Trinitate*, X, 10), or a "madness," as he elsewhere calls the view that art has no other function than to please (*De doc. christ.*, IV, 14). The sin, insofar as it has to do with conduct and ignores the ultimate function of the work, which is to convince and instigate (*movere*), is one of luxury; but since we are here concerned rather with aesthetic than with moral default, let us say in order to avoid the exclusively moralistic implications now almost inseparable from the idea of sin, that to be content only with the pleasure that can be derived from a work of art without respect to its context or significance will be an aesthetic solecism, and that it is thus that the aesthete and the art "depart from the order to the end." Whereas, "if the spectator could enter into these images, approaching them on the fiery chariot (Skr. *jyoti-ratha*) of contemplative thought (Skr. *dhyâna, dhî*) ... then would he arise from the grave, then would he meet the Lord in the air, and then he would be happy "(Blake), which is more than to be merely pleased.

Notes

1. St. Bonaventura *De reductione artium ad theologiam*, (17, 18), *ad exprimendum, ad erudiendum et ad movendem*, "to express, instruct and persuade," viz., to express by means of a likeness, to instruct by a clear light, and to persuade by means of power. It may be noted that "clear light" is *lumen arguens*, and that our word "argument" is etymologically and originally "clarification" or "making bright."

2. St. Augustine's *locutionis integritas* corresponds to Cicero's *sermonis integritas* (*Brut.* 35. 132) and means "correctness of expression." Similarly in St. Thomas, *Sum. Theol.*, I, 39, 8 *integritas sive perfection*, as a necessary condition of beauty, *integritas* is "accuracy" rather than "integrity" or "integration." Bearing in mind that all expression is by means of some likeness, what this means is "adequate symbolism," i. e., correctness of the iconography. We too often overlook that in speech just as much as in the visual arts, expression is by means of *images*.

6

The Interpretation of Symbols

The scholar of symbols is often accused of "reading meanings" into the verbal or visual emblems of which he proposes an exegesis. On the other hand, the aesthetician and art historian, himself preoccupied with stylistic peculiarities rather than with iconographic necessities, generally avoids the problem altogether; in some cases perhaps, because an iconographic analysis would exceed his capacities. We conceive, however, that the most significant element in a given work of art is precisely that aspect of it which may, and often does, persist unchanged throughout millennia and in widely separated areas; and the least significant, those accidental variations of style by which we are enabled to date a given work or even in some cases to attribute it to an individual artist. No explanation of a work of art can be called complete which does not account for its composition or constitution, which we may call its "constant" as distinguished from its "variable." In other words, no "art history" can be considered complete which merely regards the decorative usage and values as a motif, and ignores the *raison d'être* of its component parts, and the logic of their relationship in the composition. It is begging the question to attribute the precise and minute particulars of a traditional iconography merely to the operation of an "aesthetic instinct"; we have still to explain why the formal cause has been imagined as it was, and for this we cannot supply the answer until we have understood the final cause in response to which the formal image arose in a given mentality.

Naturally, we are not discussing the reading of subjective or "fancied" meanings in iconographic formulae, but only a reading of the meaning of such formulae. It is not in doubt that those who made use of the symbols (as distinguished from ourselves who merely look at them, and generally speaking consider only their aesthetic surfaces) as means of communication expected from their audiences something more than an appreciation of rhetorical ornaments, and something more than a recognition of meanings literally expressed.

As regards the ornaments, we may say with Clement, who points out that the style of Scripture is parabolic, and has been so from antiquity, that "prophecy does not employ figurative forms in the expressions for the sake of beauty of diction" (*Misc.* VI.15);[1] and point out that the iconolater's attitude is to regard the colors and the art, not as worthy of honor for their own sake, but as pointers to the archetype which is the final cause of the work (Hermeneia of Athos, 445). On the other hand, it is the iconoclast who assumes that the symbol is literally worshiped as such; as it really is worshiped by the aesthetician, who goes so far as to say that the whole significance and value of the symbol are contained in its aesthetic surfaces, and completely ignores the "picture that is not in the colors" (*Lankâvatâra Sûtra*, II.117). As regards the "more than literal meanings" we need only point out that it has been universally assumed that "Many meanings underlie the same Holy Writ"; the distinction of literal from ultimate meanings, or of signs from symbols, presupposing that "whereas in every other science things are signified by words, this science has the property that the things signified by the words have themselves also a signification" (St. Thomas, *Sum Theol.* III, App. 1.2.5.ad 3 and 1.10.10C).[2] We find in fact that those who themselves speak "parabolically," for which manner of speaking there are more adequate reasons than can be dealt with on the present occasion, invariably take it for granted that there will be some who are and others who are not qualified to understand what has been said: for example, Matt. 13:13-15: "I speak to them in parables; because they seeing, see not; and hearing, they hear not, neither do they understand ... For this people's ... ears are dull of hearing, and their eyes they have closed; lest at any time they should see" etc. (cf Mark, 8:15-21). In the same way Dante, who assures us that the whole of the *Commedia* was written with a practical purpose, and applies to his own work the Scholastic principle of fourfold interpretation, asks us to marvel, not at his art, but "at the teaching that conceals itself beneath the veil of the strange verses."

The Indian rhetorician, too, assumes that the essential value of a poetic dictum lies not so much in what is said as in what is suggested or implied.[3] To put it plainly, "A literal significance is grasped even by brutes; horses and elephants pull at the word of command. But the wise man (*panditah* = doctor) understands even what is unsaid; the enlightened, the full content of what has been communicated only by a hint." We have said enough, perhaps, to convince the reader that there are meanings immanent and causative in verbal and visual symbols, which must be read in them, and not, as we have said above, read into them, before we can pretend to have understood their reason, Tertullian's *rationem artis.*[5]

The graduate, whose eyes have been closed and heart hardened by a course of university instruction in the Fine Arts or Literature is actually debarred from the complete understanding of a work of art. If a given form has for him a merely decorative and aesthetic value, it is far easier and far more comfortable for him to assume that it never had any other than a sensational value, than it would be for him to undertake the *self-denying* task of entering into and consenting to the mentality in which the form was first conceived. It is nevertheless just this task that the professional honor of the art historian requires of him; at any rate, it is this task that he undertakes nominally, however great a part of it he may neglect in fact.

The question of how far an ancient author or artist has understood his material also arises. In a given literary or plastic work the iconography may be at fault, by defect of knowledge in the artist; or a text may have been distorted by the carelessness or ignorance of a scribe. It is evident that we cannot pass a valid judgment in such cases from the standpoint of our own accidental knowledge or ignorance of the matiére. How often one sees an emendation suggested by the philologist, which may be unimpeachable grammatically, but shows a total lack of understanding of what could have been meant originally! How often the technically skilled restorer can make a picture look well, not knowing that he has introduced insoluble contradictions!

In many cases, however, the ancient author or artist has not in fact misunderstood his material, and nothing but our own historical interpretation is at fault. We suppose, for example, that in the great epics, the miraculous elements have been "introduced" by an "imaginative" poet to enhance his effects, and nothing is more usual than to attempt to arrive at a kernel of "fact" by eliminating all incomprehensible symbolic matter from an epic or gospel. What are really technicalities in the work of such authors as Homer, Dante, or Valmiki, for example, we speak of as literary ornaments, to be accredited to the poet's imagination, and to be praised or condemned in the measure of their appeal.[6] On the contrary: the work of the prophetic poet, the texts for example of the *Rg Veda* or of *Genesis,* or the *logoi* of a Messiah, are only "beautiful" in the same sense that the mathematician speaks of an equation as "elegant"; by which we mean to imply the very opposite of a disparagement of their "beauty." From the point of view of an older and more learned aesthetic, beauty is not a mere effect, but, properly belongs to the nature of a formal cause; the beautiful is not the final cause of the work to be done, but "adds to the good an ordering to the cognitive faculty by which the good is known as such";[7] the "appeal" of beauty is not *to* the senses, but *through* the senses, to the intellect.[8]

Let us realize that "symbolism" is not a personal affair, but as Emile Mâle expressed it in connection with Christian art, a calculus. The semantics of visible symbols is at least as much an exact science as the semantics of verbal symbols, or "words." Distinguishing "symbolism" accordingly, from the making of behavioristic signs, we may say that however unintelligently a symbol may have been used on a given occasion, it can never, so long as it remains recognizable, be called unintelligible: intelligibility is essential to the idea of a symbol, while intelligence in the observer is accidental. Admitting the possibility and the actual frequency of a degeneration from a significant to a merely decorative and ornamental use of symbols, we must point out that merely to state the problem in these terms is to confirm the dictum of a well-known Assyriologist, that "When we sound the archetype, the ultimate origin of the form, then we find that it is anchored in the highest, not the lowest."[9]

What all this implies is of particular significance to the student, not merely of such hieratic arts as those of India or the Middle Ages, but of folk and savage art, and of fairy tales and popular rites; since it is precisely in all these arts that the parabolic or symbolic style has best survived in our otherwise self-expressive environment. Archeologists are indeed beginning to realize this. Strzygowski, for example, discussing the conservation of ancient motifs in modern Chinese peasant embroideries, endorses the dictum that "the thought of many so-called primitive peoples is far more spiritualized than that of many so-called civilized peoples," adding that "in any case, it is clear that in matters of religion we shall have to drop the distinction between primitive and civilized peoples."[10] The art historian is being left behind in his own field by the archeologist, who is nowadays in a fair way to offer a far more complete explanation of the work of art than the aesthetician who judges all things by his own standards. The archeologist and anthropologist are impressed, in spite of themselves, by the antiquity and ubiquity of formal cultures by no means inferior to our own, except in the extent of their material resources.

It is mainly our infatuation with the idea of "progress" and the conception of ourselves as "civilized" and of former ages and other cultures as being "barbarous"[11] that has made it so difficult for the historian of art—despite his recognition of the fact that all "art cycles" are in fact descents from the levels attained by the "primitives," if not indeed descents from the sublime to the ridiculous—to accept the proposition that an "art form" is already a defunct and derelict form, and strictly speaking a "superstition," i.e. a "stand over" from a more intellectual humanity than our own; in other words, exceedingly difficult for him to accept the proposition that what is for us a "decorative motif" and a sort of upholstery is really the vestige of a more abstract mentality than our own, a mentality that used less means to mean more, and that made use of symbols primarily for their intellectual values, and not as we do, sentimentally.[12] We say here "sentimentally," rather than "aesthetically," reflecting that both words are the same in their literal significance, and both equivalent to "materialistic"; *aesthesis* being "feeling," sense the means of feeling, and "matter" what is felt. To speak of an aesthetic experience as "disinterested" really involves an antinomy; it is only a noetic or cognitive experience that can be disinterested. For the complete appreciation or experiencing of a work of traditional art (we do not deny that there are modern works of art that only appeal to the feelings) we need at least as much to *eindenken* as to *einfühlen*, to "think-in" and "think-with" at least as much as to "feel-in" and "feel-with."

The aesthetician will object that we are ignoring both the question of artistic quality, and that of the distinction of a noble from a decadent style. By no means. We merely take it for granted that every serious student is equipped by temperament and training to distinguish good from bad workmanship. And if there are noble and decadent periods of art, despite the fact that workmanship may be as skillful or even more skillful in the decadent than in the noble period, we say that the decadence is by no means the fault of the artist as such (the "maker by art"), but of the man, who in the decadent period has so much more to say, and means so much less. More to say, the less to mean—this is a matter, not of formal, but of final causes, implying defect, not in the artist, but in the patron.[13]

We say, then, that the "scientific" art historian, whose standards of explanation are altogether too facile and too merely sensitive and psychological, need feel no qualms about the "reading of meanings into" given formulae. When meanings, which are also *raisons d'être*, have been forgotten, it is indispensable that those who can remember them, and can demonstrate by reference to chapter and verse the validity of their "memory," should re-read meanings into forms from which the meaning has been ignorantly "read out," whether recently or long ago. For in no other way can the art historian be said to have fulfilled his task of fully explaining and accounting for the form, which he has not invented himself, and only knows of as an inherited "superstition." It is not as such that the reading of meanings into works of art can be criticized, but only as regards the precision with which the work is done; the scholar being always, of course, subject to the possibility of self-correction or of correction by his peers, in matters of detail, though we may add that in case the iconographer is really in possession of his art, the possibilities of fundamental error are rather small. For the rest, with such "aesthetic" mentalities as ours, we are in little danger of proposing over-intellectual interpretations of ancient works of art.

Notes

1. Cf. the Hasidic Anthology, p. 509: "let us now hear you talk of your doctrine; you speak so beautifully." "May I be struck dumb ere I speak beautifully." As Plato demanded, "*About what* is the sophist so eloquent?" a question that might be put to many modern artists.

2. We need hardly say that nothing in principle, but only in the material, distinguishes the use of verbal from visual images, and that in the foregoing citation, "representations" may be substituted for "words."

3. *Pancatantra*, I.44.

4. Edgerton, Fr., "Indirect suggestion in poetry: a Hindu theory of literary aesthetics." *Proceedings of the American Philological Society* LXXVI. 1936. pp. 687 f.

5. Tertullian, *Docti rationem artis intelligunt, indocti voluptatem.*

6. As remarked by Victor-Emile Michelet, *Le Secret de la Chevalerie*, 1930, p. 78 "L'enseignment vulgaire considère que le poème épique, en vertu de sa tradition et de la technique du genre, renforce le récit des exploits guerriers par des inventions d'un merveilleux plus ou moins conventionnel destiné à servir d'agrément et d'élément décoratif."

7. St. Thomas, *Summa Theol.* I.5.4 ad 1, and Comm. on Dionysius, *De Div. Nom.* V.

8. And thus, as recognized by Herbert Spinden (*Brooklyn Museum Quarterly*, Oct. 1935), "Our first reaction is one of wonder, but our second should be an effort to understand. Nor should we accept a pleasurable effect upon our unintelligent nerve ends as an index of understanding."

9. Andrae, W., *Die ionische Säule*, 1933, p. 65. The reader is strongly recommended to the whole of Andrae's "Schlusswort." Cf. Zoltan de Takacs, *Francis Hopp Memorial Exhibition*, 1933 (Budapest, 1933), p. 47; "The older and more generally understood a symbol is, the more perfect and self-expressive it is" and p. 34: "the value of art forms in (the) prehistoric ages was, therefore, determined, not simply by the delight of the eyes, but by the purity of traditional notions conjured by the representation itself."

10. Strzygowski, J., *Spuren indogermanischen Glaubens in der bildenden Kunst*, 1936, p. 334.

11. Gleizes, A., *Vie et Mort de l'occident chrétien*, Sablons (1936), p. 60: "Deux mots, *barbarie et civilisation*, sont à la base de tout dévelopement historique. Ils donnent à la notion de progrès la continuité qu'on lui désire sur tous les terrains particuliers en éveillant l'idée d'infériorité et de supériorité. Ils nous débarrassent de tout souci d'avenir, la barbarie étant derrière nous et la civilisation s'améliorant chaque jour." [translated by Aristide Messinesi as *Life and Death of the Christian West*, London, 1947.] I cite these remarks not so much in confirmation, as to call attention to the works of M. Gleizes, himself a painter, but who says of himself "Mon art je l'ai voulu métier ... Ainsi, je pense ne pas être humainement inutile." M. Gleizes' most considerable work is *La Forme et l'Histoire: vers une Conscience Plastique*, Paris, 1932.

12. Despite the recognition of a typical "descent," the notion of a meliorative "progress" is so attractive and so comfortably supports an optimistic view of the future that one still and in face of all the evidence to the contrary fancies that primitive man and savage races "drew like that" because they "could not" represent natural effects as we represent them; and in this way it becomes possible to treat all "early" forms of art as striving towards and preparing the way for a more "mature" development; to envisage the supercession of form by figure as a favorable "evolution." In fact, however, the primitive "drew like that" because he imagined like that, and like all artists, wished to draw as he imagined; he did not in our sense "observe," because he had not in view the statement of singular facts; he "imitated" nature, not in her effects, but in her manner of operation. Our "advance" has been from the sublime to the ridiculous. To complain that primitive symbols do not look like their referents is as naïve as it would be to complain of a mathematical equation, that it does not resemble the locus it represents.

13. It is extraneous to the business of the art historian or curator, as such, to distinguish noble from decadent styles; the business of these persons as such is to know what is good of its kind, exhibit, and explain it. At the same time, it is not enough to be merely an art historian or merely a curator; it is also the business of man as patron, to distinguish a hierarchy of values in what has been made, just as it is his business to decide what it is worth while to make now.

7

Why Exhibit Works of Art?

What is an Art Museum for? As the word "Curator" implies, the first and most essential function of such a Museum is to take care of ancient or unique works of art which are no longer in their original places or no longer used as was originally intended, and are therefore in danger of destruction by neglect or otherwise. This care of works of art does not necessarily involve their exhibition.

If we ask, why should the protected works of art be exhibited and made accessible and explained to the public, the answer will be made, that this is to be done with an educational purpose. But before we proceed to a consideration of this purpose, before we ask, Education in or for what? a distinction must be made between the exhibition of the works of living artists and that of ancient or relatively ancient or exotic works of art. It is unnecessary for Museums to exhibit the works of living artists, which are not in imminent danger of destruction; or at least, if such works are exhibited, it should be clearly understood that the Museum is really advertising the artist and acting on behalf of the art dealer or middleman whose business it is to find a market for the artist; the only difference being that while the Museum does the same sort of work as the dealer, it makes no profit. On the other hand, that a living artist should wish to be "hung" or "shown" in a Museum can be only due to his need or his vanity. For things are made normally for certain purposes and certain places to which they are appropriate, and not simply "for exhibition"; and because whatever is thus custom-made, i.e., made by an artist for a consumer, is controlled by certain requirements and kept in order. Whereas, as Mr. Steinfels has recently remarked, "Art which is only intended to be hung on the walls of a Museum is one kind of art that need not consider its relationship to its ultimate surroundings. The artist can paint anything he wishes, any way he wishes, and if the Curators and Trustees like it well enough they will line it up on the wall with all the other curiosities."

We are left with the real problem, Why exhibit? as it applies to the relatively ancient or foreign works of art which, because of their fragility and because they no longer correspond to any needs of our own of which we are actively conscious, are preserved in our Museums, where they form the bulk of the collections. If we are to exhibit these objects for educational reasons, and not as mere curios, it is evident that we are proposing to make such use of them as is possible without an actual handling. It will be imaginatively and not actually that we must use the medieval reliquary, or lie on the Egyptian bed, or make our offering to some ancient deity. The educational ends that an exhibition can serve demand, accordingly, the services not of a Curator only, who prepares the exhibition, but of a Docent who explains the original patron's needs and the original artists' methods; for it is because of what these patrons and artists were that the works before us are what they are. If the exhibition is to be anything more than a show of curiosities and an entertaining spectacle it will not suffice to be satisfied with our own reactions to the objects; to know why they are what they are we must know the men that made them. It will not be "educational" to interpret such objects by our likes or dislikes, or to assume that these men thought of art in our fashion, or that they had aesthetic motives, or were "expressing themselves." We must examine *their* theory of art, first of all in order to understand the things that they made by art, and secondly in order to ask whether their view of art, if it is found to differ from ours, may not have been a truer one.

Let us assume that we are considering an exhibition of Greek objects, and call upon Plato to act as our Docent. He knows nothing of our distinction of fine from applied arts. For him painting and agriculture, music and carpentry and pottery are all equally kinds of poetry or making. And as Plotinus, following Plato, tells us, the arts such as music and carpentry are not based on human wisdom but on the thinking "there."

Whenever Plato speaks disparagingly of the "base mechanical arts" and of mere "labor" as distinguished from the "fine work" of making things, it is with reference to kinds of manufacture that provide for the needs of the body alone. The kind of art that he calls wholesome and will admit to his ideal state must be not only useful but also true to rightly chosen models and therefore beautiful, and this art, he says, will provide at the same time "for the souls and bodies of your citizens." His "music" stands for all that we mean by "culture," and his "gymnastics" for all that we mean by physical training and well-being; he insists that these ends of culture and physique must never be separately pursued; the tender artist and the brutal athlete are equally contemptible. We, on the other hand are accustomed to think of music, and culture in general, as useless, but still valuable. We forget that music, traditionally, is never something only for the ear, something only to be heard, but always the accompaniment of some kind of action. Our own conceptions of culture are typically negative. I believe that Professor Dewey is right in calling our cultural values snobbish. The lessons of the Museum must be applied to our life.

Because we are not going to handle the exhibited objects, we shall take their aptitude for use, that is to say their efficiency, for granted, and rather ask in what sense they are also true or significant; for if these objects can no longer serve our bodily needs, perhaps they can still serve those of our soul, or if you prefer the word, our reason. What Plato means by "true" is "iconographically correct." For all the arts, without exception, are representations or likenesses of a model; which does not mean that they are such as to tell us what the model looks like, which would be impossible seeing that the forms of traditional art are typically imitative of invisible things, which have no looks, but that they are such adequate analogies as to be able to remind us, i.e., put us in mind again, of their archetypes. Works of art are reminders; in other words, supports of contemplation. Now since the contemplation and understanding of these works is to serve the needs of the soul, that is to say in Plato's own words, to attune our own distorted modes of thought to cosmic harmonies, "so that by an assimilation of the knower to the to-be-known, the archetypal nature, and coming to be in that likeness, we may attain at last to a part in that 'life's best' that has been appointed by the Gods to man for this time being and hereafter," or stated in Indian terms, to effect our own metrical reintegration through the imitation of divine forms; and because, as the Upanishad reminds us, "one comes to be of just such stuff as that on which the mind is set," it follows that it is not only requisite that the shapes of art should be adequate reminders of their paradigms, but that the nature of these paradigms themselves must be of the utmost importance, if we are thinking of a cultural value of art in any serious sense of the word "culture." The *what* of art is far more important than the how; it should, indeed, be the what that determines the how, as form determines shape. Plato has always in view the representation of invisible and intelligible forms. The imitation of anything and everything is despicable; it is the actions of Gods and Heroes, not the artist's feelings or the natures of men who are all too human like himself, that are the legitimate theme of art. If a poet cannot imitate the eternal realities, but only the vagaries of human character, there can be no place for him in an ideal society, however true or intriguing his representations may be. The Assyriologist Andrae is speaking in perfect accord with Plato when he says, in connection with pottery, that "It is the business of art to grasp the primordial truth, to make the inaudible audible, to enunciate the primordial word, to reproduce the primordial images-or it is not art." In other words, a real art is one of symbolic and significant representation; a representation of things that cannot be seen except by the intellect. In this sense art is the antithesis of what we mean by visual education, for this has in view to tell us what things that we do not see, but might see, look like. It is the natural instinct of a child to work from within outwards; "First I think, and then I draw my think." What wasted efforts we make to teach the child to stop thinking, and only to observe! Instead of training the child to think, and how to think and of what, we make him "correct" his drawing by what he sees. It is clear that the Museum at its best must be the sworn enemy of the methods of instruction currently prevailing in our Schools of Art.

It was anything but "the Greek miracle" in art that Plato admired; what he praised was the canonical art of Egypt in which "these modes (of representation) that are by nature correct had been held for ever sacred." The point of view is identical with that of the Scholastic philosophers, for whom "art has fixed ends and ascertained means of operation." New songs, yes; but never new kinds of music, for these may destroy our whole civilization. It is the irrational impulses that yearn for innovation. Our sentimental or aesthetic culture—sentimental, aesthetic and materialistic are virtually synonyms—prefers instinctive expression to the formal beauty of rational art. But Plato could not have seen any difference between the mathematician thrilled by a "beautiful equation" and the artist thrilled by his formal vision. For he asked us to stand up like men against our instinctive reactions to what is pleasant or unpleasant, and to admire in works of art, not their aesthetic surfaces but the logic or right reason of their composition. And so naturally he points out that "The beauty of the straight line and the circle, and the plane and the solid figures formed from these ... is

not, like other things, relative, but always absolutely beautiful."
Taken together with all that he has to say elsewhere of the humanistic art that was coming into fashion in his own time and with what
he has to say of Egyptian Art, this amounts to an endorsement of
Greek Archaic and Greek Geometric Art—the arts that really correspond to the content of those myths and fairy tales that he held
in such high respect and so often quotes. Translated into more
familiar terms, this means that from this intellectual point of view
the art of the American Indian sand painting is superior in kind to
any painting that has been done in Europe or white America within the last several centuries. As the Director of one of the five greatest museums in our Eastern States has more than once remarked to
me, From the Stone Age until now, what a decline! He meant, of
course, a decline in intellectuality, not in comfort. It should be one
of the functions of a well organized Museum exhibition to deflate
the illusion of progress.

At this point I must digress to correct a widespread confusion.
There exists a general impression that modern abstract art is in
some way like and related to, or even "inspired" by the formality of
primitive art. The likeness is altogether superficial. Our abstraction
is nothing but a mannerism. Neolithic art is abstract, or rather algebraic, because it is only an algebraical form that can be the single
form of very different things. The forms of early Greek are what
they are because it is only in such forms that the polar balance of
physical and metaphysical can be maintained. "To have forgotten,"
as Bernheimer recently said, "this purpose before the mirage of
absolute patterns and designs is perhaps the fundamental fallacy of
the abstract movement in art." The modern abstractionist forgets
that the Neolithic formalist was not an interior decorator, but a
metaphysical man who saw life whole and had to live by his wits; one
who did not, as we seek to, live by bread alone, for as the anthropologists assure us, primitive cultures provided for the needs of the
soul and the body at one and the same time. The Museum exhibition should amount to an exhortation to return to these savage levels of culture.

A natural effect of the Museum exhibition will be to lead the
public to enquire why it is that objects of "museum quality" are to
be found only in Museums and are not in daily use and readily
obtainable. For the Museum objects, on the whole, were not originally "treasures" made to be seen in glass cases, but rather common

objects of the market place that could have been bought and used by anyone. What underlies the deterioration in the quality of our environment? Why should we have to depend as much as we do upon "antiques"? The only possible answer will again reveal the essential opposition of the Museum to the world. For this answer will be that the Museum objects were custom made and made for use, while the things that are made in our factories are made primarily for sale. The word "manufacturer" itself, meaning one who makes things by hand, has come to mean a salesman who gets things made for him by machinery. The museum objects were humanly made by responsible men, for whom their means of livelihood was a vocation and a profession. The museum objects were made by free men. Have those in our department stores been made by free men? Let us not take the answer for granted.

When Plato lays it down that the arts shall "care for the bodies and souls of your citizens," and that only things that are sane and free, and not any shameful things unbecoming free men, are to be made, it is as much as to say that the artist in whatever material must be a free man; not meaning thereby an "emancipated artist" in the vulgar sense of one having no obligation or commitment of any kind, but a man emancipated from the despotism of the salesman. If the artist is to represent the eternal realities, he must have known them as they are. In other words an act of imagination in which the idea to be represented is first clothed in an imitable form must have preceded the operation in which this form is to be embodied in the actual material. The first of these acts is called "free," the latter "servile." But it is only if the first be omitted that the word servile acquires a dishonorable connotation. It hardly needs demonstration that our methods of manufacture are, in this shameful sense, servile, or can be denied that the industrial system, for which these methods are indispensable, is unfit for free men. A system of "manufacture," or rather of quantity production dominated by money values, presupposes that there shall be two different kinds of makers, privileged "artists" who may be "inspired," and under-privileged laborers, unimaginative by hypothesis, since they are asked only to make what other men have imagined. As Eric Gill put it, "On the one hand we have the artist concerned solely to express himself; on the other is the workman deprived of any self to express." It has often been claimed that the productions of "fine" art are useless; it would seem to be a mockery to speak of a society as free, where it is only the makers of useless things, and not the makers of utilities, that can be called free, except in the sense that we are all free to work or starve.

It is, then, by the notion of a vocational making, as distinguished from earning one's living by working at a job, regardless of what it may be, that the difference between the museum objects and those in the department store can be best explained. Under these conditions, which have been those of all non-industrial societies, that is to say when each man makes one kind of thing, doing only that kind of work for which he is fitted by his own nature and for which he is therefore destined, Plato reminds us that "more will be done, and better done than in any other way." Under these conditions a man at work is doing what he likes best, and the pleasure that he takes in his work perfects the operation. We see the evidence of this pleasure in the Museum objects, but not in the products of chain-belt operation, which are more like those of the chain-gang than like those of men who enjoy their work. Our hankering for a state of leisure or leisure state is the proof of the fact that most of us are working at a task to which we could never have been called by anyone but a salesman, certainly not by God or by our own natures. Traditional craftsmen whom I have known in the East cannot be dragged away from their work, and will work overtime to their own pecuniary loss.

We have gone so far as to divorce work from culture, and to think of culture as something to be acquired in hours of leisure; but there can be only a hothouse and unreal culture where work itself is not its means; if culture does not show itself in all we make we are not cultured. We ourselves have lost this vocational way of living, the way that Plato made his type of justice; and there can be no better proof of the depth of our loss than the fact that we have destroyed the cultures of all other peoples whom the withering touch of our civilization has reached.

In order to understand the works of art that we are asked to look at it will not do to explain them in the terms of our own psychology and our aesthetics; to do so would be a pathetic fallacy. We shall not have understood these arts until we can think about them as their authors did. The Docent will have to instruct us in the elements of what will seem a strange language; though we know its terms, it is with very different meanings that we nowadays employ them. The meaning of such terms as art, nature, inspiration, form, ornament and aesthetic will have to be explained to our public in words of two syllables. For none of these terms are used in the traditional philosophy as we use them today. We shall have to begin by discarding the term *aesthetic* altogether. For these arts were not produced for the delectation of the senses. The Greek original of this modern word means nothing but sensation or reaction to external stimuli; the sensibility implied by the word *aisthesis* is present in plants, animals, and man; it is what the biologist calls "irritability." These sensations, which are the passions or emotions of the psychologist, are the driving forces of instinct. Plato asks us to stand up like men against the pulls of pleasure and pain. For these, as the word passion implies, are pleasant and unpleasant experiences to which we are subjected; they are not acts on our part, but things done to us; only the judgment and appreciation of art is an activity. Aesthetic experience is of the skin you love to touch, or the fruit you love to taste. "Disinterested aesthetic contemplation" is a contradiction in terms and a pure non-sense. Art is an intellectual, not a physical virtue; beauty has to do with knowledge and goodness, of which it is precisely the attractive aspect; and since it is by its beauty that we are attracted to a work, its beauty is evidently a means to an end, and not itself the end of art; the purpose of art is always one of effective communication. The man of action, then, will not be content to substitute the knowledge of what he likes for an understanding judgment; he will not merely enjoy what he should use (those who merely enjoy we call "aesthetes" rightly); it is not the aesthetic surfaces of works of art but the right reason or logic of the composition that will concern him. Now the composition of such works as we are exhibiting is not for aesthetic but for expressive reasons. The fundamental judgment is of the degree of the artist's success in giving clear expression to the theme of his work. In order to answer the question, Has the thing been well said? it will evidently be necessary for us to know what it was that was to be said. It is for this reason that in every discussion of works of art we must begin with their subject matter.

We take account, in other words, of the *form* of the work. "Form" in the traditional philosophy does not mean tangible shape, but is synonymous with idea and even with soul; the soul, for example, is called the form of the body.[1] If there be a real unity of form and matter such as we expect in a work of art, the shape of its body will express its form, which is that of the pattern in the artist's mind, to which pattern or image he moulds the material shape. The degree of his success in this imitative operation is the measure of the work's perfection. So God is said to have called his creation good because it conformed to the intelligible pattern according to which he had worked; it is in the same way that the human workman still speaks of "trueing" his work. The formality of a work is its beauty, its informality its ugliness. If it is uninformed it will be shapeless. Everything must be in good form.

In the same way *art* is nothing tangible. We cannot call a painting "art." As the words "artifact" and "artificial" imply, the thing made is a work of art, made by art, but not itself art; the art remains in the artist and is the knowledge by which things are made. What is made according to the art is correct; what one makes as one likes may very well be awkward. We must not confuse taste with judgment, or loveliness with beauty, for as Augustine says, some people like deformities.

Works of art are generally *ornamental* or in some way ornamented. The Docent will sometimes discuss the history of ornament. In doing so he will explain that all the words that mean ornament or decoration in the four languages with which we are chiefly concerned, and probably in all languages, originally meant equipment; just as furnishing originally meant tables and chairs for use and not an interior decoration designed to keep up with the Joneses or to display our connoisseurship. We must not think of ornament as something added to an object which might have been ugly without it. The beauty of anything unadorned is not increased by ornament, but made more effective by it. Ornament is characterization; ornaments are attributes. We are often told, and not quite incorrectly, that primitive ornament had a magical value; it would be truer to say a metaphysical value, since it is generally by means of what we now call its decoration that a thing is ritually transformed and made to function spiritually as well as physically. The use of solar symbols in harness, for example, makes the steed the Sun in a likeness; solar patterns are appropriate to buttons because the Sun himself is the primordial fastening to which all things are attached by the thread of the Spirit; the egg and dart pattern was originally what it still is in India, a lotus petal molding symbolic of a solid foundation. It is only when the symbolic values of ornament have been lost, that decoration becomes a sophistry, irresponsible to the content of the work. For Socrates, the distinction of beauty from use is logical, but not real, not objective; a thing can only be beautiful in the context for which it is designed.

Critics nowadays speak of an artist as *inspired* by external objects, or even by his material. This is a misuse of language that makes it impossible for the student to understand the earlier literature or art. "Inspiration" can never mean anything but the working of some spiritual force within you; the word is properly defined by Webster as a "supernatural divine influence." The Docent, if a rationalist, may wish to deny the possibility of inspiration; but he must not obscure the fact that from Homer onwards the word has been used always with one exact meaning, that of Dante, when he says that Love, that is to say the Holy Ghost, "inspires" him, and that he goes "setting the matter forth even as He dictates within me."

Nature, for example in the statement "Art imitates nature in her manner of operation," does not refer to any visible part of our environment; and when Plato says "according to nature," he does not mean "as things behave," but as they should behave, not "sinning against nature." The traditional Nature is Mother Nature, that principle by which things are "natured," by which, for example, a horse is horsey and by which a man is human. Art is an imitation of the nature of things, not of their appearances.

In these ways we shall prepare our public to understand the pertinence of ancient works of art. If, on the other hand, we ignore the evidence and decide that the appreciation of art is merely an aesthetic experience, we shall evidently arrange our exhibition to appeal to the public's sensibilities. This is to assume that the public must be taught to feel. But the view that the public is a hard-hearted animal is strangely at variance with the evidence afforded by the kind of art that the public chooses for itself, without the help of museums. For we perceive that this public already knows what it likes. It likes fine colors and sounds and whatever is spectacular or personal or anecdotal or that flatters its faith in progress. This public loves its comfort. If we believe that the appreciation of art is an aesthetic experience we shall give the public what it wants.

But it is not the function of a museum or of any educator to flatter and amuse the public. If the exhibition of works of art, like the reading of books, is to have a cultural value, i.e., if it is to nourish and make the best part of us grow, as plants are nourished and grow in suitable soils, it is to the understanding and not to fine feelings that an appeal must be made. In one respect the public is right; it always wants to know what a work of art is "about." "About what," as Plato asked, "does the sophist make us so eloquent?" Let us tell them what these works of art are about and not merely tell them things about these works of art. Let us tell them the painful truth, that most of these works of art are about God, whom we never mention in polite society. Let us admit that if we are to offer an education in agreement with the innermost nature and eloquence of the exhibits themselves, that this will not be an education in sensibility, but an education in philosophy, in Plato's and Aristotle's sense of the word, for whom it means ontology and theology and the map of life, and a wisdom to be applied to everyday matters. Let us recognize that nothing will have been accomplished unless men's lives are affected and their values changed by what we have to show. Taking this point of view, we shall break down the social and economic distinction of fine from applied art; we shall no longer divorce anthropology from art, but recognize that the anthropological approach to art is a much closer approach than the aesthetician's; we shall no longer pretend that the content of the folk arts is anything but metaphysical. We shall teach our public to demand above all things lucidity in works of art.

For example, we shall place a painted Neolithic potsherd or Indian punch-marked coin side by side with a Medieval representation of the Seven gifts of the Spirit, and make it clear by means of labels or Docents or both that the reason of all these compositions is to state the universal doctrine of the "Seven Rays of the Sun." We shall put together an Egyptian representation of the Sun-door guarded by the Sun himself and the figure of the Pantokrator in the oculus of a Byzantine dome, and explain that these doors by which one breaks out of the universe are the same as the hole in the roof by which an American Indian enters or leaves his *hogan*, the same as the hole in the center of a Chinese *pi*, the same as the luffer of the Siberian Shaman's *yurt*, and the same as the foramen of the roof above the altar of Jupiter Terminus; explaining that all these constructions are reminders of the Door-god, of One who could say "I am the door." Our study of the history of architecture will make it clear that "harmony" was first of all a carpenter's word meaning "joinery," and that it was inevitable, equally in the Greek and the Indian traditions that the Father and the Son should have been "carpenters," and show that this must have been a doctrine of Neolithic, or rather "Hylic," antiquity. We shall sharply distinguish the "visual education" that only tells us what things look like (leaving us to *react* as we must) from the iconograph of things that are themselves invisible (but by which we can be guided how to *act*).

It may be that the understanding of the ancient works of art and of the conditions under which they were produced will undermine our loyalty to contemporary art and contemporary methods of manufacture. This will be the proof of our success as educators; we must not shrink from the truth that all education implies revaluation. Whatever is made only to give pleasure is, as Plato put it, a toy, for the delectation of that part of us that passively submits to emotional storms; whereas the education to be derived from works of art should be an education in the love of what is ordered and the dislike of what is disordered. We have proposed to educate the public to ask first of all these two questions of a work of art, Is it true? or beautiful? (whichever word you prefer) and what good use does it serve? We shall hope to have demonstrated by our exhibition that the human value of anything made is determined by the coincidence in it of beauty and utility, significance and aptitude; that artifacts of this sort can only be made by free and responsible workmen, free to consider only the good of the work to be done and individually responsible for its quality: and that the manufacture of "art" in studios coupled with an artless "manufacture" in factories represents a reduction of the standard of living to subhuman levels.

These are not personal opinions, but only the logical deductions of a lifetime spent in the handling of works of art, the observation of men at work, and the study of the universal philosophy of art from which philosophy our own "aesthetic" is only a temporally provincial aberration. It is for the museum militant to maintain with Plato that "we cannot give the name of art to anything irrational."

Notes

1. Accordingly, the following sentence (taken from the *Journal of Aesthetics*, I, p. 29), "Walter Pater here seems to be in the right when he maintains that it is the sensuous element of art that is essentially artistic, from which follows his thesis that music, the most formal of the arts, is also the measure of all the arts" propounds a shocking *non sequitur* and can only confuse the unhappy student.

8

The Christian and Oriental,
or True, Philosophy of Art

"Cum artifex ... um vir."
Cicero, *Pro Quintio*, XXV. 78.

I

I have called this lecture the "Christian and Oriental" philoso-phy of art because we are considering a catholic or universal doc-trine, with which the humanistic philosophies of art can neither be compared nor reconciled, but only contrasted; and "True" philoso-phy both because of its authority and because of its consistency. It will not be out of place to say that I believe what I have to expound: for the study of any subject can live only to the extent that the stu-dent himself stands or falls by the life of the subject studied; the interdependence of faith and understanding[1] applying as much to the theory of art as to any other doctrine. In the text of what follows I shall not distinguish Christian from Oriental, nor cite authorities by chapter and verse: I have done this elsewhere, and am hardly afraid that anyone will imagine that I am propounding any views that I regard as my own except in the sense that I have made them my own. It is not the personal view of anyone that I shall try to explain, but that doctrine of art which is intrinsic to the Philosophia Perennis and can be recognized wherever it has not been forgotten that "culture" originates in work and not in play. If I use the lan-guage of Scholasticism rather than a Sanskrit vocabulary, it is because I am talking English, and must use that kind of English in which ideas can be clearly expressed.

Man's activity consists in either a making or a doing. Both of these aspects of the active life depend for their correction upon the contemplative life. The making of things is governed by art, the doing of things by prudence.[2] An absolute distinction of art from prudence is made for purposes of logical understanding:[3] but while we make this distinction, we must not forget that the man is a whole man, and cannot be justified as such merely by what he makes; the artist works "by art and *willingly*."[4] Even supposing that he avoids artistic sin, it is still essential to him as a man to have had a right will, and so to have avoided moral sin.[5] We cannot absolve the artist from this moral responsibility by laying it upon the patron, or only if the artist be in some way compelled; for the artist is normally either his own patron, deciding what is to be made, or formally and freely consents to the will of the patron, which becomes his own as soon as the commission has been accepted, after which the artist is only concerned with the good of the work to be done:[6] if any other motive affects him in his work he has no longer any proper place in the social order. Manufacture is for use and not for profit. The artist is not a special kind of man, but every man who is not an artist in some field, every man without a vocation, is an idler. The kind of artist that a man should be, carpenter, painter, lawyer, farmer or priest, is determined by his own nature, in other words by his nativity. The only man who has a right to abstain from all constructive activities is the monk who has also surrendered all those uses that depend on things that can be made and is no longer a member of society. No man has a right to any social status who is not an artist.

We are thus introduced at the outset to the problem of the use of art and the worth of the artist to a serious society. This use is in general the good of man, the good of society, and in particular the occasional good of an individual requirement. All of these goods correspond to the desires of men: so that what is actually made in a given society is a key to the governing conception of the purpose of life in that society, which can be judged by its works in that sense, and better than in any other way. There can be no doubt about the purpose of art in a traditional society: when it has been decided that such and such a thing should be made, it is *by art* that it can be properly made. There can be no good use without art:[7] that is, no good use if things are not properly made. The artist is producing a utility, something to be used. Mere pleasure is not a use from this point of view. An illustration can be given in our taste for Shaker or other simple furniture, or for Chinese bronzes or other abstract arts of exotic origin, which are not foods but sauces to our palate.

Our "aesthetic" appreciation, essentially sentimental because it is just what the word "aesthetic" means, a kind of feeling rather than an understanding, has little or nothing to do with their *raison d'être*.

If they please our taste and are fashionable, this only means that we have over-eaten of other foods, not that we are such as those who made these things and made "good use" of them. To "enjoy" what does not correspond to any vital needs of our own and what we have not verified in our own life can only be described as an indulgence. It is luxurious to make mantelpiece ornaments of the artifacts of what we term uncivilized or superstitious peoples, whose culture we think of as much inferior to our own, and which our touch has destroyed: the attitude, however ignorant, of those who used to call these things "abominations" and "beastly devices of the heathen," was a much healthier one. It is the same if we read the scriptures of any tradition, or authors such as Dante or Ashvaghosha who tell us frankly that they wrote with other than "aesthetic" ends in view; or if we listen to sacrificial music for the ears' sake only. We have a right to be pleased by these things only through our understanding use of them. We have goods enough of our own "perceptible to the senses": if the nature of our civilization be such that we lack a sufficiency of "intelligible goods," we had better remake ourselves than divert the intelligible goods of others to the multiplication of our own aesthetic satisfactions.

In the philosophy that we are considering, only the contemplative and active lives are reckoned human. The life of pleasure only, one of which the end is pleasure, is subhuman ; every animal "knows what it likes," and seeks for it. This is not an exclusion of pleasure from life as if pleasure were wrong in itself, it is an exclusion of the pursuit of pleasure thought of as a "diversion," and apart from "life." It is in life itself, in "proper operation," that pleasure arises naturally, and this very pleasure is said to "perfect the operation" itself.[8] In the same way in the case of the pleasures of use or the understanding of use.

We need hardly say that from the traditional point of view there could hardly be found a stronger condemnation of the present social order than in the fact that the man at work is no longer doing what he likes best, but rather what he must, and in the general belief that a man can only be really happy when he "gets away" and is at play. For even if we mean by "happy" to enjoy the "higher things of life," it is a cruel error to pretend that this can be done at leisure if it has not been done at work. For "the man devoted to his own vocation finds perfection ... That man whose prayer and praise of God are in the doing of his own work perfects himself."[9] It is this way of life that our civilization denies to the vast majority of men, and in this respect that it is notably inferior to even the most primitive or savage societies with which it can be contrasted.

Manufacture, the practise of an art, is thus not only the production of utilities but in the highest possible sense the education of men. It can never be, unless for the sentimentalist who lives for pleasure, an "art for art's sake," that is to say a production of "fine" or useless objects only that we may be delighted by "fine colors and sounds"; neither can we speak of our traditional art as a "decorative" art, for to think of decoration as its essence would be the same as to think of millinery as the essence of costume or of upholstery as the essence of furniture. The greater part of our boasted "love of art" is nothing but the enjoyment of comfortable feelings. One had better be an artist than go about "loving art": just as one had better be a botanist than go about "loving the pines."

In our traditional view of art, in folk-art, Christian and Oriental art, there is no essential distinction of a fine and useless art from a utilitarian craftsmanship.[10] There is no distinction in principle of orator from carpenter,[11] but only a distinction of things well and truly made from things not so made and of what is beautiful from what is ugly in terms of formality and informality. But, you may object, do not some things serve the uses of the spirit or intellect, and others those of the body; is not a symphony nobler than a bomb, an icon than a fireplace? Let us first of all beware of confusing art with ethics. "Noble" is an ethical value, and pertains to the *a priori* censorship of what ought or ought not to be made at all. The judgment of works of art from this point of view is not merely legitimate, but essential to a good life and the welfare of humanity. But it is not a judgment of the work of art as such. The bomb, for example, is only bad as a work of art if it fails to destroy and kill to the required extent. The distinction of artistic from moral sin which is so sharply drawn in Christian philosophy can be recognized again in Confucius, who speaks of a Succession Dance as being "at the same time perfect beauty and perfect goodness," and of the War Dance as being "perfect beauty but not perfect goodness."[12] It will be obvious that there can be no moral judgment of art itself, since it is not an act but a kind of knowledge or power by which things can be well made, whether for good or evil use: the art by which utilities are produced cannot be judged morally, because it is not a kind of willing but a kind of knowing.

Beauty in this philosophy is the attractive power of perfection.[13] There are perfections or beauties of different kinds of things or in different contexts, but we cannot arrange these beauties in a hierarchy, as we can the things themselves: we can no more say that a cathedral as such is "better" than a barn as such than we can say that a rose as such is "better" than a skunk cabbage as such; each is beautiful to the extent that it is what it purports to be, and in the same proportion good.[14] To say that a perfect cathedral is a greater work of art than a perfect barn is either to assume that there can be degrees of perfection, or to assume that the artist who made the barn was really trying to make a cathedral. We see that this is absurd; and yet it is just in this way that whoever believes that art "progresses" contrasts the most primitive with the most advanced (or decadent) styles of art, as though the primitive had been trying to do what we try to do, and had drawn like that while really trying to draw as we draw; and that is to impute artistic sin to the primitive (any sin being defined as a departure from the order to the end). So far from this, the only test of excellence in a work of art is the measure of the artist's actual success in making what was intended.

One of the most important implications of this position is that beauty is objective, residing in the artifact and not in the spectator, who may or may not be qualified to recognize it.[15] The work of art is good of its kind, or not good at all; its excellence is as independent of our reactions to its aesthetic surfaces as it is of our moral reaction to its thesis. Just as the artist conceives the form of the thing to be made only after he has consented to the patron's will, so we, if we are to judge as the artist could, must already have consented to the existence of the object before we can be free to compare its actual shape with its prototype in the artist. We must not condescend to "primitive" works by saying "That was before they knew anything about anatomy, or perspective," or call their work "unnatural" because of its formality: we must have learnt that these primitives did not feel our kind of interest in anatomy, nor intend to tell us what things are like; we must have learnt that it is because they had something definite to say that their art is more abstract, more intellectual, and less than our own a matter of mere reminiscence or emotion. If the medieval artist's constructions corresponded to a certain way of thinking, it is certain that we cannot understand them except to the extent that we can identify ourselves with this way of thinking. "The greater the ignorance of modern times, the deeper grows the darkness of the Middle Ages."[16] The Middle Ages and the East are mysterious to us only because we know, not what to think, but what we like to think. As humanists and individualists it flatters us to think that art is an expression of personal feelings and sentiments, preference and free choice, unfettered by the sciences of mathematics and cosmology. But medieval art was not like ours "free" to ignore truth. For them, *Ars sine scientia nihil*.[17] by "science," we mean of course, the reference of all particulars to unifying principles, not the "laws" of statistical prediction.

The perfection of the object is something of which the critic cannot judge, its beauty something that he cannot feel, if he has not like the original artist made himself such as the thing itself should be; it is in this way that "criticism is reproduction," and "judgment the perfection of art." The "appreciation of art" must not be confused with a psycho-analysis of our likes and dislikes, dignified by the name of "aesthetic reactions": "aesthetic pathology is an excrescence upon a genuine interest in art which seems to be peculiar to civilized peoples."[18] The study of art, if it is to have any cultural value will demand two far more difficult operations than this, in the first place an understanding and acceptance of the whole point of view from which the necessity for the work arose, and in the second place a bringing to life in ourselves of the form in which the artist conceived the work and by which he judged it. The student of art, if he is to do more than accumulate facts, must also sacrifice himself: the wider the scope of his study in time and space, the more must he cease to be a provincial, the more he must universalize himself, whatever may be his own temperament and training. He must assimilate whole cultures that seem strange to him, and must also be able to elevate his own levels of reference from those of observation to that of the vision of ideal forms. He must rather love than be curious about the subject of his study. It is just because so much is demanded that the study of "art" can have a cultural value, that is to say may become a means of growth. How often our college courses require of the student much less than this!

A need, or "indigence" as Plato calls it, is thus the first cause of the production of a work of art. We spoke of spiritual and physical needs, and said that works of art could *not* be classified accordingly. If this is difficult for us to admit, it is because we have forgotten what we are, what "man" in this philosophy denotes, a spiritual as well as a psychophysical being. We are therefore well contented with a functional art, good of its kind insofar as goodness does not interfere with profitable saleability, and can hardly understand how things to be used can also have a meaning. It is true that what we have come to understand by "man," viz., "the reasoning and mortal animal,"[19] can live by "bread alone," and that bread alone, make no mistake about it, is therefore a good; to function is the very least that can be expected of any work of art. "Bread alone" is the same thing as a "merely functional art." But when it is said that man does not live by bread alone but "by every word that proceedeth out of the mouth of God,"[20] it is the whole man that is meant. The "words of God" are precisely those ideas and principles that can be expressed whether verbally or visually by art; the words or visual forms in which they are expressed are not merely sensible but also significant. To separate as we do the functional from the significant art, applied from a so-called fine art, is to require of the vast majority of men to live by the merely functional art, a "bread alone" that is nothing but the "husks that the swine did eat." The insincerity and inconsistency of the whole position is to be seen in the fact that we do not expect of the "significant" art that it be significant *of* anything, nor from the "fine" art anything but an "aesthetic" pleasure; if the artist himself declares that his work is charged with meaning and exists for the sake of this meaning, we call it an irrelevance, but decide that he may have been an artist in spite of it.[21] In other words, if the merely functional arts are the husks, the fine arts are the tinsel of life, and art for us has no significance whatever.

Primitive man, despite the pressure of his struggle for existence, knew nothing of such merely functional arts. The whole man is naturally a metaphysician, and only later on a philosopher and psychologist, a systematist. His reasoning is by analogy, or in other words by means of an "adequate symbolism." As a person rather than an animal he knows immortal through mortal things.[22]

That the "invisible things of God" (that is to say, the ideas or eternal reasons of things, by which we know what they ought to be like) are to be seen in "the things that are made"[23] applied for him not only to the things that God had made but to those that he made himself. He could not have thought of meaning as something that might or might not be added to useful objects at will. Primitive man made no real distinction of sacred from secular: his weapons, clothing, vehicles and house were all of them imitations of divine prototypes, and were to him even more what they meant than what they were in themselves; he made them this "more" by incantation and by rites.[24] Thus he fought with thunderbolts, put on celestial garments, rode in a chariot of fire, saw in his roof the starry sky, and in himself more than "this man" So-and-so. All these things belonged to the "Lesser Mysteries" of the crafts, and to the knowledge of "Companions." Nothing of it remains to us but the transformation of the bread in sacrificial rites, and in the reference to its prototype of the honor paid to an icon.

The Indian actor prepares for his performance by prayer. The Indian architect is often spoken of as visiting heaven and there making notes of the prevailing forms of architecture, which he imitates here below. All traditional architecture, in fact, follows a cosmic pattern?[25] Those who think of their house as only a "machine to live in" should judge their point of view by that of Neolithic man, who also lived in a house, but a house that embodied a cosmology. We are more than sufficiently provided with overheating systems: we should have found his house uncomfortable; but let us not forget that he identified the column of smoke that rose from his hearth to disappear from view through a hole in the roof with the Axis of the Universe, saw in this luffer an image of the Heavenly Door, and in his hearth the Navel of the Earth, formulae that we at the present day are hardly capable of understanding; we, for whom "such knowledge as is not empirical is meaningless."[26] Most of the things that Plato called "ideas" are only "superstitions" to us.

To have seen in his artifacts nothing but the things themselves, and in the myth a mere anecdote would have been a mortal sin, for this would have been the same as to see in oneself nothing but the "reasoning and mortal animal," to recognize only "this man," and never the "form of humanity." It is just insofar as we do now see only the things as they are in themselves, and only ourselves as we are in ourselves, that we have killed the metaphysical man and shut ourselves up in the dismal cave of functional and economic determinism. Do you begin to see now what I meant by saying that works of art consistent with the Philosophia Perennis cannot be divided into the categories of the utilitarian and the spiritual, but pertain to both worlds, functional and significant, physical and metaphysical?[27]

Hindu

The Muktesvara Temple at Bhubaneswar, Orissa, India
late 9th century

I

Shiva, as Lord Nataraj, performing his Cosmic Dance
of dissolution and renewal of creation
Tamil Nadu, India, 12th century

II

Shiva and his consort Parvati
Tamil Nadu, India, 11th century

III

Hindu

The Cosmic Dance (*Rasamandala*): Krishna with the encircling Gopis
Jaipur, India, late 18th century

Hindu

Krishna and Radha
Kangra valley, India, 18th century

V

Gautama Buddha
Sarnath, near Varanasi, India, 5th century

Buddhist

The Bodhisattva Padmapati, the "Lotus Born"
Ajanta caves, India, 6th century

VII

Buddhist

Thangka of Green Tara
Central Tibet, late 12th century

VIII

Thangka of the "Wheel of Life" (*Bhavachakramudra*)
Tibet

Christian

Page from *The Book of Kells*
8th century

X

Christian

Icon of the Transfiguration
c. 1200, Constantinople

XI

Christian

Romanesque Madonna

XII

Christian

Church of Saint-Nectaire, Auvergne, France
12th century

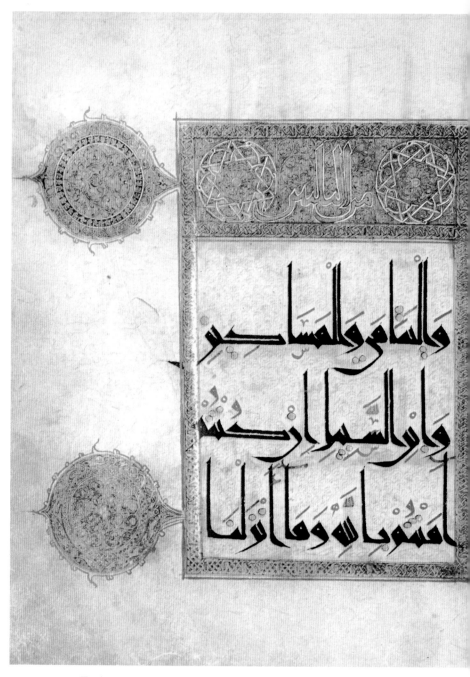

Facing pages from a Koran in Eastern Kufic style
Iraq/Persia, 11th century

The mihrab of the Great Mosque of Córdoba
Spain, 9th century

II

The artist has now accepted his commission and is expected to practicse his art. It is by this art that he knows both what the thing should be like, and how to impress this form upon the available material, so that it may be informed with what is actually alive in himself. His operation will be twofold, "free" and "servile," theoretical and operative, inventive and imitative. It is in terms of the freely invented formal cause that we can best explain how the pattern of the thing to be made or arranged, this essay or this house for example, is known. It is this cause by which the actual shape of the thing can best be understood; because "similitude is with respect to the form"[28] of the thing to be made, and not with respect to the shape or appearance of some other and already existing thing: so that in saying "imitative" we are by no means saying "naturalistic." "Art imitates nature in her manner of operation,"[29] that is to say God in his manner of creation, in which he does not repeat himself or exhibit deceptive illusions in which the species of things are confused.

How is the form of the thing to be made evoked? This is the kernel of our doctrine, and the answer can be made in a great many different ways. The art of God is the Son "through whom all things are made";[30] in the same way the art in the human artist is his child through which some one thing is to be made. The intuition-expression of an imitable form is an intellectual conception born of the artist's wisdom, just as the eternal reasons are born of the Eternal Wisdom. [31] The image arises naturally in his spirit, not by way of an aimless inspiration, but in purposeful and vital operation, "by a word *conceived* in intellect."[32] It is this filial image, and not a retinal reflection or the memory of a retinal reflection, that he imitates in the material, just as at the creation of the world "God's will beheld that beauteous world and imitated it,"[33] that is to say impressed on primary matter a "world-picture" already "painted by the spirit on the canvas of the spirit."[34]All things are to be seen in this eternal mirror better than in any other way:[35] for there the artist's models are all alive and more alive than those that are posed when we are taught in schools of art to draw "from life." If shapes of natural origin often enter into the artist's compositions, this does not mean that they pertain to his art, but they are the material in which the form is clothed; just as the poet uses sounds, which are not his thesis, but only means. The artist's spirals are the forms of life, and not only of this or that life; the form of the crosier was not suggested by that of a fern frond. The superficial resemblances of art to "nature" are accidental; and when they are deliberately sought, the art is already in its anecdotage. It is not by the looks of existing things, but as Augustine says, by their ideas, that we know what we proposed to make should be like.[36] He who does not see more vividly and clearly than this perishing mortal eye can see, does not see creatively at all;[37] "The city can never otherwise be happy unless it is drawn by those painters who follow a divine original."[38]

What do we mean by "invention"? The entertainment of ideas; the intuition of things as they are on higher than empirical levels of reference. We must digress to explain that in using the terms intuition and expression as the equivalents of conception or generation, we are not thinking either of Bergson or of Croce. By "intuition" we mean with Augustine an intellection extending beyond the range of dialectic to that of the eternal reasons[39]—a contemplation, therefore, rather than a thinking: by "expression" we mean with Bonaventura a begotten rather than a calculated likeness.[40]

It may be asked, How can the artist's primary act of imagination be spoken of as "free" if in fact he is working to some formula, specification or iconographic prescription, or even drawing from nature? If in fact a man is blindly copying a shape defined in words or already visibly existing, he is not a free agent, but only performing a servile operation. This is the case in quantitative production; here the craftsman's work, however skillful, can be called mechanical rather than artistic, and it is only in this sense that the phrase "mere craftsmanship" acquired a meaning. It would be the same with the performance of any rite,[41] to the extent that performance becomes a habit, unenlivened by any recollection. The mechanical product may still be a work of art: but the art was not the workman's, nor the workman an artist, but a hireling; and this is one of the many ways in which an "Industry without art is brutality."

The artist's theoretical or imaginative act is said to be "free" because it is *not* assumed or admitted that he is blindly copying any model extrinsic to himself, but expressing himself, even in adhering to a prescription or responding to requirements that may remain essentially the same for millennia. It is true that to be properly expressed a thing must proceed from within, moved by its form:[42] and yet it is not true that in practicing an art that has "fixed ends and ascertained means of operation"[43] the artist's freedom is denied; it is only the academician and the hireling whose work is under constraint. It is true that if the artist has not conformed *himself* to the pattern of the thing to be made he has not really known it and cannot work originally.[44] But if he has thus conformed himself he will be in fact expressing *himself* in bringing it forth.[45] Not indeed expressing his "personality," himself as "this man" So-and-so, but himself *sub specie aeternitatis*, and apart from individual idiosyncrasy. The idea of the thing to be made is brought to life in him, and it will be from this supra-individual life of the artist himself that the vitality of the finished work will be derived.[46] "It is not the tongue, but our very life that sings the new song."[47] In this way too the human operation reflects the manner of operation *in divinis*: "All things that were made were life in Him."[48]

"Through the mouth of Hermes the divine Eros began to speak."[49] We must not conclude from the form of the words that the artist is a passive instrument, like a stenographer. "He" is much rather actively and consciously making use of "himself" as an instrument. Body and mind are not the man, but only his instrument and vehicle. The man is passive only when he identifies himself with the psychophysical ego letting it take him where it will: but in act when he directs it. Inspiration and aspiration are not exclusive alternatives, but one and the same; because the spirit to which both words refer cannot work in the man except to the extent that *he* is "in the spirit." It is only when the form of the thing to be made has been known that the artist returns to "himself," performing the servile operation with good will, a will directed solely to the good of the thing to be made. He is willing to make "what was shown him upon the Mount." The man incapable of contemplation cannot be an artist, but only a skillful workman; it is demanded of the artist to be both a contemplative and a good workman. Best of all if, like the angels, he need not in his activity "lose the delights of inward contemplation."

What is implied by contemplation is to raise our level of reference from the empirical to the ideal, from observation to vision, from any auditory sensation to audition; the imager (or worshiper, for no distinction can be made here) "taking ideal form under the action of the vision, while remaining only potentially 'himself'."[50] "I am one," says Dante, accounting for his *dolce stil nuovo*, "who when Love inspires me take note, and go setting it forth in such wise as He dictates within me."[51] "Lo, make all things in accordance with

133

the pattern that was shown thee on the mount."[52] "It is in imitation of angelic works of art that any work of art is wrought here":[53] the "crafts such as building and carpentry take their principles from that realm and from the thinking there."[54] It is in agreement with these traditional dicta that Blake equated with Christianity itself "the divine arts of imagination" and asked "Is the Holy Ghost any other than an intellectual fountain?" and that Emerson said, "The intellect searches out the absolute order of things as they stand in the mind of God, and without the colors of affection." Where we see "genius" as a peculiarly developed "personality" to be exploited, traditional philosophy sees the immanent Spirit, beside which the individual personality is relatively nil: "Thou madest," as Augustine says, "that *ingenium* whereby the artificer may take his art, and may see within what he has to do without."[55] It is the light of this Spirit that becomes "the light of a mechanical art." What Augustine calls *ingenium* corresponds to Philo's Hegemon, the Sanskrit "Inner Controller," and to what is called in medieval theology the Synteresis, the immanent Spirit thought of equally as an artistic, moral and speculative conscience, both as we use the word and in its older sense of "consciousness." Augustine's *ingenium* corresponds to Greek *daimon*, but not to what we mean to-day by "genius." No man, considered as So-and-so, can *be* a genius: but all men *have* a genius, to be served or disobeyed at their own peril. There can be no property in ideas, because these are gifts of the Spirit, and not to be confused with talents: ideas are never made, but can only be "invented," that is "found," and entertained. No matter how many times they may already have been "applied" by others, whoever conforms himself to an idea and so makes it his own, will be working originally, but not so if he is expressing only his own ideals or opinions.

To "think for oneself" is always to think of oneself; what is called "free thought" is therefore the natural expression of a humanistic philosophy. We are at the mercy of our thoughts and corresponding desires. Free thought is a passion; it is much rather the thoughts than ourselves that are free. We cannot too much emphasize that contemplation is not a passion but an act: and that where modern psychology sees in "inspiration" the uprush of an instinctive and *sub*conscious will, the orthodox philosophy sees an elevation of the artist's being to *super*conscious and *supra*-individual levels. Where

134

the psychologist invokes a demon, the metaphysician invokes a daemon: what is for the one the "libido" is for the other "the divine
Eros."[56]

There is also a sense in which the man as an individual "expresses himself," whether he will or no. This is inevitable, only because
nothing can be known or done except in accordance with the mode
of the knower. So the man himself, as he is in himself, appears in
style and handling, and can be recognized accordingly. The uses
and significance of works of art may remain the same for millennia,
and yet we can often date and place a work at first glance. Human
idiosyncrasy is thus the explanation of style and of stylistic
sequences: "style is the man." Styles are the basis of our histories of
art, which are written like other histories to flatter our human vanity. But the artist whom we have in view is innocent of history and
unaware of the existence of stylistic sequences. Styles are the accident and by no means the essence of art; the free man is not trying
to express himself, but that which was to be expressed. Our conception of art as essentially the expression of a personality, our
whole view of genius, our impertinent curiosities about the artist's
private life, all these things are the products of a perverted individualism and prevent our understanding of the nature of medieval
and oriental art. The modern mania for attribution is the expression of Renaissance conceit and nineteenth century humanism; it
has nothing to do with the nature of medieval art, and becomes a
pathetic fallacy when applied to it.[57]

In all respects the traditional artist devotes himself to the good
of the work to be done.[57a] The operation is a rite, the celebrant neither intentionally nor even consciously expressing himself. It is by
no accident of time, but in accordance with a governing concept of
the meaning of life, of which the goal is implied in St. Paul's *Vivo
autem jam non ego*, that works of traditional art, whether Christian,
Oriental or folk art, are hardly ever signed: the artist is anonymous,
or if a name has survived, we know little or nothing of the man. This
is true as much for literary as for plastic artifacts. In traditional arts
it is never Who said? but only What was said? that concerns us: for
"all that is true, by whomsoever it has been said, has its origin in the
Spirit."[58]

So the first sane questions that can be asked about a work of art
are, What was it for? and What does it mean? We have seen already
that whatever, and however humble, the functional purpose of the

work of art may have been, it had always a spiritual meaning, by no means an arbitrary meaning, but one that the function itself expresses adequately by analogy. Function and meaning cannot be forced apart; the meaning of the work of art is its intrinsic form as much as the soul is the form of the body. Meaning is even historically prior to utilitarian application. Forms such as that of the dome, arch and circle have not been "evolved," but only applied: the circle can no more have been suggested by the wheel than a myth by a mimetic rite. The ontology of useful inventions parallels that of the world: in both "creations" the Sun is the single form of many different things; that this is actually so in the case of human production by art will be realised by everyone who is sufficiently familiar with the solar significance of almost every known type of circular or annular artifact or part of an artifact. I will only cite by way of example the eye of a needle, and remark that there is a metaphysics of embroidery and weaving, for a detailed exposition of which a whole volume might be required. It is in the same way by no accident that the Crusader's sword was also a cross, at once the means of physical and symbol of spiritual victory. There is no traditional game or any form of athletics, nor any kind of fairy-tale properly to be so called (excepting, that is to say, those which merely reflect the fancies of individual littérateurs, a purely modern phenomenon) nor any sort of traditional jugglery, that is not at the same time an entertainment, the embodiment of a metaphysical doctrine. The meaning is literally the "spirit" of the performance or the anecdote. Iconography, in other words, is art: that art by which the actual forms of things are determined; and the final problem of research in the field of art is to understand the iconographic form of whatever composition it may be that we are studying. It is only when we have understood the *raisons d'être* of iconography that we can be said to have gone back to first principles; and that is what we mean by the "Reduction of Art to Theology."[59] The student understands the logic of the composition; the illiterate only its aesthetic value.[60]

The anonymity of the artist belongs to a type of culture dominated by the longing to be liberated from oneself. All the force of this philosophy is directed against the delusion "I am the doer." "I" am not in fact the doer, but the instrument; human individuality is not an end but only a means. The supreme achievement of individual consciousness is to lose or find (both words mean the same) itself in what is both its first beginning and its last end:

"Whoever would save his *psyche*, let him lose it."[61] All that is required of the instrument is efficiency and obedience; it is not for the subject to aspire to the throne; the constitution of man is not a democracy, but the hierarchy of body, soul and spirit. Is it for the Christian to consider any work "his own," when even Christ has said that "I do nothing of myself"?[62] or for the Hindu, when Krishna has said that "The Comprehensor cannot form the concept 'I am the doer'"?[63] or the Buddhist, for whom it has been said that "To wish that it may be made known that 'I was the author' is the thought of a man not yet adult"?[64] It hardly occurred to the individual artist to sign his works, unless for practical purposes of distinction; and we find the same conditions prevailing in the scarcely yet defunct community of the Shakers, who made perfection of workmanship a part of their religion, but made it a rule that works should not be signed.[65] It is under such conditions that a really living art, unlike what Plato calls the arts of flattery, flourishes; and where the artist exploits his own personality and becomes an exhibitionist that art declines.

There is another aspect of the question that has to do with the patron rather than the artist; this too must be understood, if we are not to mistake the intentions of traditional art. It will have been observed that in traditional arts, the effigy of an individual, for whatever purpose it may have been made, is very rarely a likeness in the sense that we conceive a likeness, but much rather the representation of a type.[66] The man is represented by his function rather than by his appearance; the effigy is of the king, the soldier, the merchant or the smith, rather than of So-and-so. The ultimate reasons for this have nothing to do with any technical inabilities or lack of the power of observation in the artist, but are hard to explain to ourselves whose pre-occupations are so different and whose faith in the eternal values of "personality" is so naive; hard to explain to ourselves, who shrink from the saying that a man must "hate" himself "if he would be My disciple."[67] The whole position is bound up with a traditional view that also finds expression in the doctrine of the hereditary transmission of character and function, because of which the man can die in peace, knowing that his work will be carried on by another representative. As So-and-so, the man is reborn in his descendants, each of whom occupies in turn what was much rather an office than a person. For in what we call personality, tradition sees only a temporal function "which you hold in lease." The very person of the king, surviving death, may be manifested in some way in some other ensemble of possibilities than these; but the royal personality descends from generation to generation, by hereditary and ritual delegation; and so we say, The king is dead, long live the king. It is the same if the man has been a merchant or craftsman; if the son to whom his personality has been transmitted is not also, for example, a blacksmith, the blacksmith of a given community, the family line is at an end; and if personal functions are not in this way transmitted from generation to generation, the social order itself has come to an end, and chaos supervenes.

We find accordingly that if an ancestral image or tomb effigy is to be set up for reasons bound up with what is rather loosely called "ancestor worship," this image has two peculiarities, (1) it is identified as the image of the deceased by the insignia and costume of his vocation and the inscription of his name, and (2) for the rest, it is an individually indeterminate type, or what is called an "ideal" likeness. In this way both selves of the man are represented; the one that is to be inherited, and that which corresponds to an intrinsic and regenerated form that he should have built up for himself in the course of life itself, considered as a sacrificial operation terminating at death. The whole purpose of life has been that this man should realise himself in this other and essential form, in which alone the form of divinity can be thought of as adequately reflected. As St. Augustine expresses it, "*This* likeness begins now to be formed again in us."[68] It is not surprising that even in life a man would rather be represented thus, not as he is, but as he ought to be, impassibly superior to the accidents of temporal manifestation. It is characteristic of ancestral images in many parts of the East, that they cannot be recognized, except by their legends, as the portraits of individuals; there is nothing else to distinguish them from the form of the divinity to whom the spirit had been returned when the man "gave up the ghost"; almost in the same way an angelic serenity and the absence of human imperfection, and of the signs of age, are characteristic of the Christian effigy before the thirteenth century, when the study of death-masks came back into fashion and modern portraiture was born in the charnel house. The traditional image is of the man as he would be at the Resurrection, in an ageless body of glory, not as he was accidentally: "I would go down unto Annihilation and Eternal Death, lest the Last Judgment come and find me Unannihilate, and I be seiz'd and giv'n into the hands of my own Selfhood." Let us not forget that it is only the intellectual virtues, and by no means our individual affections, that are thought of as surviving death.

The same holds good for the heroes of epic and romance; for modern criticism, these are "unreal types," and there is no "psychological analysis." We ought to have realised that if this is not a humanistic art, this may have been its essential virtue. We ought to have known that this was a typal art by right of long inheritance; the romance is still essentially an epic, the epic essentially a myth; and that it is just because the hero exhibits universal qualities, without individual peculiarity or limitations, that he can be a pattern imitable by every man alike in accordance with his own possibilities whatever these may be. In the last analysis the hero is always God, whose only idiosyncrasy is being, and to whom it would be absurd to attribute individual characteristics. It is only when the artist, whatever his subject may be, is chiefly concerned to exhibit himself, and when we descend to the level of the psychological novel, that the study and analysis of individuality acquires an importance. Then only portraiture in our sense takes the place of what was once an iconographic portrayal.

All these things apply only so much the more if we are to consider the deliberate portrayal of a divinity, the fundamental thesis of all traditional arts. An adequate knowledge of theology and cosmology is then indispensable to an understanding of the history of art, insofar as the actual shapes and structures of works of art are determined by their real content. Christian art, for example, begins with the representation of deity by abstract symbols, which may be geometrical, vegetable or theriomorphic, and are devoid of any sentimental appeal whatever. An anthropomorphic symbol follows, but this is still a form and not a figuration; not made as though to function biologically or as if to illustrate a text book of anatomy or of dramatic expression. Still later, the form is sentimentalised; the features of the crucified are made to exhibit human suffering, the type is completely humanised, and where we began with the shape of humanity as an analogical representation of the idea of God, we end with the portrait of the artist's mistress posing as the Madonna and the representation of an all-too-human baby; the Christ is no longer a man-God, but the sort of man that we can approve of. With what extraordinary prescience St. Thomas Aquinas commends the use of the lower rather than the nobler forms of existence as divine symbols, "especially for those who can think of nothing nobler than bodies"![69]

The course of art reflects the course of thought. The artist, asserting a specious liberty, expresses himself; our age commends the man who thinks for himself, and therefore of himself. We can see in the hero only an imperfectly remembered historical figure, around which there have gathered mythical and miraculous accretions; the hero's manhood interests us more than his divinity, and this applies as much to our conception of Christ or Krishna or Buddha as it does to our conceptions of Cuchullain or Sigurd or Gilgamesh. We treat the mythical elements of the story, which are its essence, as its accidents, and substitute anecdote for meaning. The secularisation of art and the rationalisation of religion are inseparably connected, however unaware of it we may be. It follows that for any man who can still believe in the eternal birth of any avatar ("Before Abraham was, I am")[70] the content of works of art cannot be a matter of indifference; the artistic humanisation of the Son or of the Mother of God is as much a denial of Christian truth as any form of verbal rationalism or other heretical position. The vulgarity of humanism appears nakedly and unashamed in all euhemerism.

It is by no accident that it should have been discovered only comparatively recently that art is essentially an "aesthetic" activity. No real distinction can be drawn between aesthetic and materialistic; *aisthesis* being sensation, and matter what can be sensed. So we regard the lack of interest in anatomy as a defect of art, the absence of psychological analysis as evidence of undeveloped character; we deprecate the representation of the Bambino as a little man rather than as a child, and think of the frontality of the imagery as due to an inability to realise the three-dimensional mass of existing things; in place of the abstract light that corresponds to the gnomic aorists of the legend itself we demand the cast shadows that belong to momentary effects. We speak of a want of scientific perspective, forgetting that perspective in art is a kind of visual syntax and only a means to an end. We forget that while our perspective serves the purposes of representation in which we are primarily interested, there are other perspectives that are more intelligible and better adapted to the communicative purposes of the traditional arts.

In deprecating the secularisation of art we are not confusing religion with art, but seeking to understand the content of art at different times with a view to unbiased judgment. In speaking of the decadence of art, it is really the decadence of man from intellectual to sentimental interests that we mean. For the artist's skill may remain the same throughout: he is able to do what he intends. It is the mental image to which he works that changes : that "art has fixed ends" is no longer true as soon as we know what we like instead of liking what we know. Our point is that without an understanding of the change, the integrity of even a supposedly objective historical study is destroyed; we judge the traditional works, not by their actual accomplishment, but by our own intentions, and so inevitably come to believe in a progress of art, as we do in the progress of man.

Ignorant of the traditional philosophy and of its formulae we often think of the artist as having been trying to do just what he may have been consciously avoiding. For example, if Damascene says that Christ from the moment of his conception possessed a "rational and intellectual soul,"[71] if as St. Thomas Aquinas says "his body was perfectly formed and assumed in the first instant,"[72] if the Buddha is said to have spoken in the womb, and to have taken seven strides at birth, from one end to the other of the universe, could the artist have intended to represent either of the newborn children as a puling infant? If we are disturbed by what we call the "vacancy" of a Buddha's expression, ought we not to bear in mind that he is thought of as the Eye in the World, the impassible spectator of things as they really are, and that it would have been impertinent to have given him features molded by human curiosity or passion ? If it was an artistic canon that veins and bones should not be made apparent, can we blame the Indian artist as an artist for not displaying such a knowledge of anatomy as might have evoked *our* admiration? If we know from authoritative literary sources that the lotus on which the Buddha sits or stands is not a botanical specimen, but the universal ground of existence inflorescent in the waters of its indefinite possibilities, how inappropriate it would have been to represent him in the solid flesh precariously balanced on the surface of a real and fragile flower! The same considerations will apply to all our reading of mythology and fairy tale, and to all our judgments of primitive, savage or folk art: the anthropologist whose interest is in a culture is a better historian of such arts than is the critic whose only interest is in the aesthetic surfaces of the artifacts themselves.

In the traditional philosophy, as we cannot too often repeat, "art has to do with cognition";[73] beauty is the attractive power of a perfect expression. This we can only judge and only really enjoy as an "intelligible good, which is the good of reason"[74] if we have really known what it was that was to be expressed. If sophistry be "ornament more than is appropriate to the thesis of the work,"[75] can we judge of what is or is not sophistry if we ourselves remain indifferent to this content? Evidently not. One might as well attempt the study of Christian or Buddhist art without a knowledge of the corresponding philosophies as attempt the study of a mathematical papyrus without the knowledge of mathematics.

III

Let us conclude with a discussion of the problems of voluntary poverty and of iconoclasm. In cultures molded by the traditional philosophy we find that two contrasting positions are maintained, either at any one time or alternately: the work of art, both as a utility and in its significance is on the one hand a good, and on the other an evil.

The ideal of voluntary poverty, which rejects utilities, can be readily understood. It is easy to see that an indefinite multiplication of utilities, the means of life, may end in an identification of culture with comfort, and the substitution of means for ends; to multiply wants is to multiply man's servitude to his own machinery. I do not say that this has not already taken place. On the other hand, the man is most self-sufficient, autochthonous and free who is least dependent upon possessions. We all recognize to some extent the value of living simply. But the question of possessions is a matter relative to the individual's vocation; the workman needs his tools and the soldier his weapons, but the contemplative is the nearer to his goal the fewer his needs. It was not until after the Fall that Adam and Eve had occasion to practice the tailor's art: they had no images of a God with whom they daily conversed. The angels, also, "have fewer ideas and useless means than men."[76] Possessions are a necessity to the extent that we can use them; it is altogether legitimate to enjoy what we do use, but equally inordinate to enjoy what we cannot use or to use what cannot be enjoyed. All possessions not at the same time beautiful and useful are an affront to human dignity. Ours is perhaps the first society to find it natural that some things should be beautiful and others useful. To be voluntarily poor is to have rejected what we cannot both admire and use; this definition can be applied alike to the case of the millionaire and to that of the monk.

The reference of iconoclasm is more particularly to the use of images as supports of contemplation. The same rule will apply. There are those, the great majority, whose contemplation requires such supports, and others, the minority, whose vision of God is immediate. For the latter to think of God in terms of any verbal or visual concept would be the same as to forget him.[77] "We cannot make one rule apply to both cases. The professional iconoclast is such either because he does not understand the nature of images and rites, or because he does not trust the understanding of those who practice iconolatry or follow rites. To call the other man an idolater or superstitious is, generally speaking, only a manner of asserting our own superiority. Idolatry is the misuse of symbols, a definition needing no further qualifications. The traditional philosophy has nothing to say against the use of symbols and rites; though there is much that the most orthodox can have to say against their misuse. It may be emphasized that the danger of treating verbal formulae as absolutes is generally greater than that of misusing plastic images.

We shall consider only the *use* of symbols, and their rejection when their utility is at an end. A clear understanding of the principles involved is absolutely necessary if we are not to be confused by the iconoclastic controversies that play so large a part in the histories of every art. It is inasmuch as he "knows immortal things by the mortal" that the man as a veritable person is distinguished from the human animal, who knows only the things as they are in themselves and is guided only by this estimative knowledge. The unmanifested can be known by analogy; His silence by His utterance. That "the invisible things of Him" can be seen through "the things which are made" will apply not only to God's works but also to things made by hands, if they have been made by such an art as we have tried to describe: "In these outlines, my son, I have drawn a likeness of God for you, as far as that is possible; and if you gaze upon this likeness with the eyes of your heart ... the sight itself will guide you on your way."[78] This point of view Christianity inherited from Neoplatonism: and therefore, as Dante says, "doth the Scripture condescend to your capacity, assigning foot and hand to God, with other meaning."

We have no other language whatever except the symbolic in which to speak of ultimate reality: the only alternative is silence; in the meantime, "The ray of divine revelation is not extinguished by the sensible imagery wherewith it is veiled."[79]

"Revelation" itself implies a veiling rather than a disclosure: a symbol is a " mystery."[80] "Half reveal and half conceal" fitly describes the parabolic style of the scriptures and of all conceptual images of being in itself, which cannot disclose itself to our physical senses. Because of this Augustine could say that in the last analysis "All scripture is vain." For "If any one in seeing God conceives something in his mind, this is not God, but one of God's effects":[81] "We have no means for considering how God is, but rather how he is not";[82] there are "things which our intellect cannot behold ... we cannot understand what they are except by denying things of them."[83] Dicta to this effect could be cited from innumerable sources, both Christian and Oriental.

It does not follow that the spiritual tradition is at war with itself with respect to the use of conceptual images. The controversy that plays so large a part in the history of art is maintained only by human partisans of limited points of view. As we said before, the question is really one of utility only: it parallels that of works and faith. Conceptual images and works alike, art and prudence equally, are means that must not be mistaken for ends; the end is one of beatific contemplation, not requiring any operation. One who proposes to cross a river needs a boat; "but let him no longer use the Law as a means of arrival when he has arrived."[84] Religious art is simply a visual theology: Christian and Oriental theology alike are means to an end, but not to be confused with the end. Both alike involve a dual method, that of the *via affirmativa* and of the *via negativa*; on the one hand affirming things of God by way of praise, and on the other denying every one of these limiting descriptive affirmations, for though the worship is dispositive to immediate vision, God is not and never can be "what men worship here."[85] The two ways are far from mutually exclusive; they are complementary. Because they are so well known to the student of Christian theology I shall only cite from an Upanishad, where it is a question of the use of certain types of concepts of deity regarded as supports of contemplation. Which of these is the best? That depends upon individual faculties. But in any case, these are pre-eminent aspects of the incorporeal deity; "These one should contemplate and praise, but then deny. For with these one rises from higher to higher states of being. But when all these forms are resolved, then he attains to the unity of the Person."[86]

To resume: the normal view of art that we have described above, starting from the position that "Though he is an artist, the artist is nevertheless a man," is not the private property of any philosopher, or time, or place: we can only say that there are certain times, and notably our own, at which it has been forgotten. We have emphasized that art is for the man, and not the man for art: that whatever is made only to give pleasure is a luxury and that the love of art under these conditions becomes a mortal sin;[87] that in traditional art function and meaning are inseparable goods; that it holds in both respects that there can be no good use without art; and that all good uses involve the corresponding pleasures. We have shown that the traditional artist is not expressing himself, but a thesis: that it is in this sense that both human and divine art are expressions, but only to be spoken of as "self expressions" if it has been clearly understood what "self" is meant. We have shown that the traditional artist is normally anonymous, the individual as such being only the instrument of the "self" that finds expression. We have shown that art is essentially symbolic, and only accidentally illustrative or historical; and finally that art, even the highest, is only the means to an end, that even the scriptural art is only a manner of "seeing through a glass, darkly," and that although this is far better than not to see at all, the utility of iconography must come to an end when vision is "face to face."[88]

Notes

1. *Credo ut intelligas, intellige ut credas.* "Through faith we understand" (*Jas.* V. 15). "The nature of faith ... consists in knowledge alone" (St. Thomas Aquinas, *Sum. Theol.* II-II.47.13 ad 2).

2. *Ars nihil quod recta ratio factibilium. Omnis applicatio rationis rectae ad aliquid factibile pertinet ad artem; sed ad prudentiam non pertinet nisi applicatio rationis rectae ad ca de quibuis est consilium. Prudentia est recta ratio agibilium.* (St. Thomas Aquinas, *Sum. Theol.* I-II.57.5; II-II.47.2; IV.3.7 and 8. Aristotle Ethic. VI.5).

3. Cf. Plotinus, *Enneads* IV.3.7.

4. *Per artem et ex voluntate* (St. Thomas Aquinas, *Sum. Theol.* I.45.6, cf. I.14. 8c).

5. St. Thomas Aquinas, *Sum. Theol.* I-II.57.5; II-II.21.2 ad 2; 47.8; 167.2; and 16q. 2 ad 4.

6. *Ibid.* I.91.3; and I-II.57.3 ad 2 ("It is evident that a craftsman is inclined by justice, which rectifies his will, to do his work faithfully").

7. *Ibid.* I-II.57.3. ad 1.

8. *Ibid.* I-II.33. 4.

9. *Bhagavad Gîtâ,* XVIII.45-46, *sve sve karmany-abhiratah samsiddham labhate narah,* etc. "And if man takes upon him in all its fullness the proper office of his own vocation (*curam propriam diligentiae suae*), it is brought about that both he and the world are the means of right order to one another ... For since the world is God's handiwork, he who maintains and heightens its beauty by his tendance (*diligentia*) is cooperating with the will of God, when he by the aid of his bodily strength, and by his work and his administration (*opere curaque*) composes any figure that he forms in accordance with the divine intention (*cum speciem, quam ille intentione formavit ... componit*). What shall be his reward? ... that when we are retired from office (*emeritos*) ... God will restore us to the nature of our better part, that is divine" (Hermetica, *Asclepius*, I.10, 12). In this magnificent definition of the artist's function, it may be noted that *cura propria* corresponds to the *svakarma* of the *Bhagavad Gîtâ*, and that *diligentia* (from *diligo*, to love) becomes "tendance in precisely the same way that *ratah* (from *ram*, to take delight in) becomes "intent upon" or "devoted to." It is the man who while at work is doing what he likes best that can be called "cultured."

10. *Nec oportet, si liberales artes sunt nobiliores, quod magis eis conveniat ratio artis* (St. Thomas Aquinas, *Sum. Theol.* I-II.57.3 ad 3). "The productions of all arts are kinds of poetry and their craftsmen are all poets" (Plato, *Symposium*, 205C).

11. Plato, *Gorgias*, 503. In Rigveda IX.112 the work of the carpenter, doctor, fletcher and sacrificial priest are all alike treated as ritual "operations," or "rites" (*vrata*).

12. *Analects*, III.25.

13. Plato, *Cratylus*, 416C; Dionysius Areopagiticus, *De div. nom.* IV.5; Ulrich of Strassburg, *De pulchro; Lantkâvatâra Sûtra*, II.118-9, etc.

14. *Ens et bonum convertuntur.*

15. Witelo, *Perspectiva*, IV.148-9. Baeumker, *Witelo*, p. 639, fails to see that Witelo's recognition of the subjectivity of taste in no way contradicts his enunciation of the objectivity of beauty. Taste is a matter of the affections; beauty one of judgment, which is "the perfection of art" (St. Thomas Aquinas, *Sum. Theol.* II-II.47.8.), where there is no room for preferences, art being comparable to science in its certainty, and differing from science only in being ordered to operation.

16. Hasak, M. , *Kirchenbau des Mittelalters*, 2nd ed., Leipzig, 1913, p. 268.

17. Said by the Parisian Master Jean Mignot in connection with the building of the cathedral of Milan in 1398, in answer to the opinion *scientia est unum et ars aliud. Scientia reddit opus pulchrum.* St. Bonaventura, *De reductione artium ad theologiam* 13. *Nam qui canil quod non sapil, diffinitur bestia ... Non verum facil ars cantorem, sed documentum*, Guido d'Arezzo. The actual distinction of science from art is drawn by St. Thomas Aquinas in *Sum. Theol.* I.14.8 and I-II.57.3 ad 3: both have to do with cognition, but whereas science has in view a knowledge only, art is ordered to an external operation. It will be seen that the greater part of modern science is what the medieval philosopher would have called an art, the engineer, for example, being essentially an artist, despite the fact that "without science art would be nothing"-but guesswork. "The antithesis between science and art is a false one, maintained only

by the incurably, if enjoyably, sentimental" (Professor Crane Brinton, in *The American Scholar*, 1938, p. 152).

18. Firth, R., *Art and life in New Guinea*, 1936, p. 9.

19. Boethius, *De consol.* I.6.45.

20. Matt. 4:4.

21. Dante, *Ep. ad Can. Grand.* 15, 16: "The whole work was undertaken not for a speculative but a practical end. The purpose of the whole is to remove those who are living in this life from the state of wretchedness and to lead them to the state of blessedness." Ashvaghosha, *Saundârananda*, colophon: "This poem, pregnant with the burden of Liberation, has been composed by me in the poetic manner, not for the sake of giving pleasure, but for the sake of giving peace, and to win over other-minded hearers. If I have dealt in it with subjects other than that of Liberation, that pertains to what is proper to poetry, to make it tasty, just as when honey is mixed with a sour medicinal herb to make it drinkable. Since I beheld the world for the most part given over to objects of sense and disliking to consider Liberation, I have spoken here of the Principle in the garb of poetry, holding that Liberation is the primary value. Whoever understands this, let him retain what is set forth, and not the play of fancy, just as only the gold is cared for when it has been separated from the ore and dross." "Dante and Milton claimed to be didactic; we consider the claim a curious weakness in masters of style whose true but unconscious mission was to regale us with 'aesthetic emotion'." (Walter Shewring in *Integration*, II. 2, Oct. -Nov., 1938, p. 11).

Dante's "practical purpose" is precisely what Guido d'Arezzo means by *usus* in the lines,

Musicorum et cantorum magna est distancia:
Isti dicunt, illi sciunt quae componit musica.
Nam qui canit quod non sapit, diffinitur bestia;
Bestia non cantor qui non canit arte, sed usu;
Non verum facit ars cantorem, sed documentum.

I.e. "Between the 'virtuosi' and the 'singers' the difference is very great: the former merely vocalize, the latter understand the music's composition. He who sings of what he savors not is termed a 'brute'; no 'brute' is he who sings, not merely artfully, but usefully; it is not art alone, but the theme that makes the real 'singer'."

Professor Lang, in his *Music and Western Civilization*, p. 87, misunderstands the penultimate line, which he renders by "A brute by rote and not by art produces melody," a version that ignores the double negative and misinterprets *usu*, which is not "by habit" but "usefully" or "profitably," *ôphélimôs*. The thought is like St. Augustine's, "not to enjoy what we should use," and Plato's, for whom the Muses are given us "that we may use them intellectually (*metà noû*), not as a source of irrational pleasure (*eph' êdonên á 'logon*) but as an aid to the revolution of the soul within us, of which the harmony was lost at birth, to help in restoring it to order and consent with its Self" (*Timaeus* 47D, cf. 90D). The words *sciunt quae componit musica are reminiscent* of Quintillian's *Docti rationem componendi intelligunt, etiam indocti voluptatem* (IX.4.116), based on and almost a literal translation of Plato, *Timaeus* 80B. *Sapit*, as in *sapientia*, "scientia cum amore."

22. *Aitareya Âranyaka*, II.3.2; *Aitareya Brâhmana*, VII.10; *Katha Upanishad*, II.10b.

23. Rom. I:20. Aquinas repeatedly compares the human and divine architects:

God's knowledge is to his creation as is the artist's knowledge of art to the things made by art (*Sum. Theol.* I.14.8; 1.17.1; 1.22.2; 1.45.6; I-II.13.2 ad 3).

24. Cf. "Le symbolisme de l'epée" in *Études Traditionelles* 43, Jan. 1938.

25. Lethaby, W. R., *Architecture, Mysticism and Myth*, London, 1892: my "Symbolism of the Dome," *Indian Historical Qtly.* XVI, 1938, pp. 1-56.

26. Keith, A. B., *Aitareya Âranyaka*, p. 42. "The first principle of democracy ... is that no one knows the final truth about anything" (W. H. Auden, in the *Nation*, March 25, 1939, p. 353). "For there is a rancor that is contemptuous of immortality, and will not let us recognize what is divine in us" (Hermetica, *Asclepius*, I.12 b).

27. "To make the primordial truth intelligible, to make the unheard audible, to enunciate the primordial word, to represent the archetype, such is the task of art, or it is not art" (Andrae, W., "Keramik im Dienste der Weisheit" in *Berichte de Deutschen Keramischen Gesellschaft*, XVII, Dec., 1936, p. 623): but "The sensible forms, in which there was at first a polar balance of the physical and metaphysical, have been more and more voided of content on their way down to us, and so we say 'This is an ornament'" (Andrae, W., *Die ionische Saüle, Bauform oder Symbol?* 1933, p. 65).

28. St. Thomas Aquinas, *Sum. Theol.*, I.5.4: St. Basil, *De Spir. Sanct.* XVIII. 45. "The first perfection of a thing consists in its very form, from which it receives its species" (St. Thomas Aquinas, *ibid.* III.29.2c). The form that is the perfection of the thing (its exemplary form) is the standard by which the actual form of the thing itself is judged: in other words, it is by their ideas that we know what things ought to be like (St. Augustine, *De Trin.*, IX.6,11), and not by any observation or recollection of already existing things. Our authors commonly speak of the arch as an illustration of an exemplary form; thus St. Augustine, *ibid.*, and St. Bonaventura, II *Sent.*, d.1, p. 11, a.1, q ad 3, 4 *Agens per intellectum producit per formas, quae sunt aliquid rei, sed idea in mente sicut artifex producit arcam.*

29. *Natura naturans, Creatrix Universalis, Deus,* from whom all natured things derive their specific aspect.

30. "The perfect Word, not wanting in anything, and, so to speak, the art of God" (St. Augustine, *De Trin.* VI.10). "Der sun ist ein verstentnisse des vaters und ist bildner (architect) aller dinge in sinem vater" (Eckhart, Pfeiffer, p. 391). "Through him all things were made" (John 1:3).

31. *Omnes enim rationes exemplares concipuntur ab aeterno in vulva aeternae sapientiae seu utero,* St. Bonaventura, *In Hexaem,* coll, 20, n.5. The conception of an imitable form is a "vital operation," that is to say, a generation.

32. *Per verbum in intellectu conceptum,* St. Thomas Aquinas, *Sum. Theol.*, I.45.6c.

33. Hermetica, *Lib.* I.86, cf. Boethius, *De consol.* III, "Holding the world in His mind, and forming it into His image." "The divine essence, whereby the divine intellect understands, is a sufficient likeness of all things that are" (St. Thomas Aquinas, *Sum. Theol.*, I.14.12c). Cf. my "Vedic Exemplarism" in Harvard Journal of Asiatic Studies, I, April, 1936.

34. Sankarâcârya, *Svâtmanirûpana,* 95. On the world-picture as an actual form see Vimuktatman, as cited by Dasgupta, *History of Indian Philosophy*, II.203. The perfection of judgment is represented in Genesis 1:31, "God saw everything that he had made, and behold it was very good." This judgment can only have been with respect to the ideal pattern pre-existent in the divine intellect, not with reference

to any external standard.

35. St. Augustine, as cited by Bonaventura, *I Sent.* d. 35, a. unic., q. 1, fund. 3 see Bissen, *L'exemplarisme divin selon St. Bonaventure*, 1929, p. 39.

36. St. Augustine, *De Trin.* IX.6, 11; see Gilson, *Introduction à l'étude de St. Augustin*, 1931, p. 121.

37. William Blake.

38. Plato, *Republic*, 500E.

39. Gilson, *loc. cit.*, p. 121, note 2.

40. For St. Bonaventura's "expressionism" see Bissen *loc. cit.*, pp. 92-93.

41. Every mimetic rite is by nature a work of art; in the traditional philosophy of art the artist's operation is also always a rite, and thus essentially a religious activity.

42. Meister Eckhart.

43. St. Thomas Aquinas, *Sum. Theol.*, II-II.47.4 ad 2.

44. Dante, *Convito*, Canzone III.53-54 and IV.10.106. Plotinus, *Enneads*, IV.4.2. My "Intellectual operation in Indian art," *Journ. Indian Society of Oriental Art*, III, 1935, p. 6 note 5.

45. Since in this case "Diu künste sint meister in dem meister" (Eckhart, Pfeiffer, p. 390).

46. St. Bonaventura *I Sent.*, d.36, a.2q.1 ad 4 citing St. Augustine, *res factae ... in artifice creato dicuntur vivere.*

47. St. Augustine, *Enarratio in Ps. XXXII*: cf. in Ps. CXLVI *Vis ergo psallere? Non solum vox tua sonet laudes Dei, sed opera tua concordent cum voce tua.* It is by no means necessary to exclude from "opera" here whatever is made *per artem et ex voluntate.*

48. John 1:3, as cited by Sts. Augustine, Bonaventura, Aquinas, etc., see M. d'Asbeck, *La mystique de Ruysbroeck l'Admirable*, 1930, p. 159.

49. Hermetica, *Asclepius*, prologue.

50. Plotinus, *Enneads*, IV.4.2.

51. *Purgatorio*, XXIV. 52-54. "In the making of things by art, do we not know that a man who has this God for his leader achieves a brilliant success, whereas he on whom Love has laid no hold is obscure?" (Plato, *Symposium*, 197A). "My doctrine is not mine, but his that sent me ... He that speaketh of himself seeketh his own glory," John 7:16, 18.

52. Exodus, 25:40.

53. *Aitareya Brâhmana*, VI.27. Cf. *Sâṅkhâyana Âranyaka*, VIII.9. "There is this celestial harp: this human harp is a likeness of it."

54. Plotinus, *Enneads*, V.9.11. The builder and carpenter are then doing the will of God "on earth as it is done in heaven."

55. Conf. XI.5.

56. "As regards the most lordly part of our soul, we must conceive of it in this wise: we declare that God has given to each of us, as his daemon, that kind of soul which is housed in the top of our body and which raises us—seeing that we are not an earthly but a heavenly plant—up from earth towards our kindred in heaven" (Plato, *Timaeus*, 90A).

57. "The artist in Viking times is not to be thought of as an individual, as would be

the case today ... It is a creative art" (Strzygowski, *Early Church Art in Northern Europe*, 1928, pp. 159-160): "It is in the very nature of Medieval Art that very few names of artists have been transmitted to us ... The entire mania for connecting the few names preserved by tradition with well-known masterpieces,—all this is characteristic of the nineteenth century's cult of individualism, based upon ideals of the Renaissance" (H. Swarzenski, in *Journal of the Walters Art Gallery*, I, 1938, p. 55). "The academic styles that have succeeded each other since the seventeenth century, as a consequence of this curious divorce of beauty from truth, can hardly be classified as Christian art, since they recognize no inspiration higher than the human mind" (C. R. Morey, *Christian Art*, 1935).

57a. Plato, *Republic*, 342BC.

58. St. Ambrose on 1 Cor. 12:3, cited by St. Thomas Aquinas, *Sum. Theol.*, I-II.109.1 ad 1.

59. The title of a work by St. Bonaventura.

60. Quintillian, IX.4.

61. Luke, 17:33. Hence the repeated question of the Upanishads, "By which self is the *summum bonum* attainable?" and the traditional "Know thyself."

62. John, 8:28.

63. *Bhagavad Gîtâ*, III.27; V.8. Cf. *Jaiminîya Upanishad Brâhmana*, I.5.2; *Udâna* 70.

64. *Dhammapada*, 74.

65. E. D. and F. Andrews, *Shaker Furniture*, 1937, p.44.

66. See Jitta-Zadoks, *Ancestral Portraiture in Rome*, 1932, pp. 87, 92 f. Tomb effigies about 1200 "represented the deceased not as he actually appeared after death but as he hoped and trusted to be on the Day of Judgment. This is apparent in the pure and happy expression of all the equally youthful and equally beautiful faces, which have lost every trace of individuality. But towards the end of the XIIIth ... century not how they perhaps appear one day but how they had actually been in life was considered important ... As the last consequence of this demand for exact likeness the death mask, taken from the actual features, made its appearance ... rationalism and realism appearing at the same time." Cf. my *Transformation of Nature in Art*, p. 91 and note 64, and "The traditional conception of ideal portraiture," *Twice a Year*, No. 3/4 (Autumn, 1939).

67. Luke, 14:26.

68. *De spiritu et littera*, 37.

69. *Sum. Theol.*, I.1.9.

70. John 8:58. Cf. *Bhagavad Gîtâ* IV.1, 4, 5; *Saddharma Pundarîka*, XIV.44 and XV.1.

71. *De fid. orthod.* III.

72. *Sum. Theol.*, III.33.1.

73. *Ibid.* I.5.4 ad 1.

74. *Ibid.* I-II.30.1c. Cf. Witelo, *Lib. de intelligentiis*, XVIII, XIX.

74. St. Augustine, *De doc. christ.*, II.31.

75. Eckhart.

77. Plotinus, *Enneads*, IV.4.6, "In other words, they have seen God and they do not remember? Ah, no: it is that they see God still and always, and that as long as they see, they cannot tell themselves they have had the vision; such reminiscence is for

souls that have lost it." Nicolas of Cusa, *De vis. Dei*, Ch. XVI: "What satisfies the intellect is not what it understands." *Kena Upanishad*, 30, "The thought of God is his by whom it is unthought, or if he thinks the thought, it is that he does not understand." *Vajracchedika Sutra*, f. 38 XXVI, "Those who see me in any form, or think of me in words, their way of thinking is false, they do not see me at all. The Beneficent Ones are to be seen in the Law, theirs is a Law-body: the Buddha is rightly to be understood as being of the nature of the Law, he cannot be understood by any means."

78. Hermetica, *Lib.* IV.11b.

79. St. Thomas Aquinas, *Sum. Theol.*, I.1.9.

80. Clement of Alexandria, *Protr.* II.15. Cf. René Guénon, "Mythes, Mystères et Symboles," in *Voile d'Isis* (*Études Traditionelles*) 40, 1935. That "revelation" means a "displaying" depends upon the fact that an exhibition of the principle in a likeness, and as it were clothed in the veil of analogy, though it is not an exhibition of the principle in its naked essence, is relatively to what would otherwise be the obscurity of a total ignorance, a true "demonstration."

81. St. Thomas Aquinas, *Sum. Theol.*, III.92.1 ad 4.

82. *Ibid.* I.3.1. Cf. *Brhadâranyaka Upanishad*, IV.4.22; *Maitri Upanishad* IV.5, etc.

83. Dante, *Convito*, III.15. Nicolas of Cusa, *De fil. Dei*, "Deus, cum non possit nisi negative, extra intellectualem regionem, attingi." Eckhart, "Wilta komen in die kuntschaft der verborgenen heimelicheit gotes, so muostu übergan alles, daz dich gehindern mac an luterr bekentnisse, daz du begrifem maht mit verstentnisse" (Pfeiffer, p. 505).

84. Parable of the raft, *Majjhima Nikâya*, I.135; St. Augustine, *De spir. et lit.*, 16.

85. *Kena Upanishad*, 2-8.

86. *Maitri Upanishad*, IV.5.

87. For the conditions under which ornamentation becomes a sin, see St. Thomas Aquinas, *Sum. Theol.*, II-II.167.2 and 169.2 ad 4. Cf. my "On the relation of beauty to truth" in *Art Bulletin*, XX, pp. 72-77, and "ornament," *d.* XXI.

88. I Cor. 13 :12.

9

Is Art a Superstition, or a Way of Life?

By a superstition we mean something that "stands over" from a former time, and which we no longer understand and no longer have any use for. By a way of life, we mean a habit conducive to man's good, and in particular to the attainment of man's last and present end of happiness.

It seems to be a matter of general agreement at the present day that "Art" is a part of the higher things of life, to be enjoyed in hours of leisure earned by other hours of inartistic "Work." We find accordingly as one of the most obvious characteristics of our culture a class division of artists from workmen, of those for example who paint on canvas from those who paint the walls of houses, and of those who handle the pen from those who handle the hammer. We are certainly not denying here that there is a distinction of the contemplative from the active life, nor of free from servile operation: but mean to say that in our civilization we have in the first place made an absolute divorce of the contemplative from the active life, and in the second place substituted for the contemplative life an aesthetic life,—or as the term implies, a life of pleasure. We shall return to this point. In any case we have come to think of art and work as incompatible, or at least independent, categories and have for the first time in history created an industry without art.

Individualists and humanists as we are, we attach an inordinate value to personal opinion and personal experience, and feel an insatiable interest in the personal experiences of others; the work of art has come to be for us a sort of autobiography of the artist. Art having been abstracted from the general activity of making things for human use, material or spiritual, has come to mean for us the projection in a visible form of the feelings or reactions of the peculiarly-endowed personality of the artist, and especially of those most peculiarly-endowed personalities which we think of as "inspired" or describe in terms of genius. Because the artistic genius is mysterious we, who accept the humbler status of the workman, have been only too willing to call the artist a "prophet," and in return for his "vision" to allow him many privileges that a common man might hesitate to exercise. Above all we congratulate ourselves that the artist has been "emancipated" from what was once his position as the servant of church or state, believing that his mysterious imagination can operate best at random; if an artist like Blake still respects a traditional iconography we say that he is an artist in spite of it, and if as in Russia or Germany the state presumes to conscript the artist, it is even more the principle involved than the nature of the state itself that disturbs us. If we ourselves exercise a censorship necessitated by the moral inconvenience of certain types of art, we feel it needful at least to make apologies. Whereas it was once the highest purpose of life to achieve a freedom *from* oneself, it is now our will to secure the greatest possible measure of freedom *for* oneself, no matter from what.

Despite the evidence of our environment, with its exaggerated standards of living, and equally depreciated standards of life, our conception of history is optimistically based on the idea of "progress"; we designate cultures of the past or those of other peoples as relatively "barbaric" and our own as relatively "civilized," never reflecting that such prejudgments, which are really wish-fulfillments, may be very far from fact. The student of the history of art discovers, indeed, in every art cycle a decline from a primitive power to a refinement of sentimentality or cynicism. But being a sentimentalist, materialist, cynic, or more briefly a humanist himself, he is able to think what he likes, and to argue that the primitive or savage artist "drew like that" because he knew no better; because he (whose knowledge of nature was so much greater and more intimate than that of the "civilized" or "city" man) had not learnt to see things as they are, was not acquainted with anatomy or perspective, and therefore drew like a child! We are indeed careful to explain when we speak of an imitation of nature or study of nature we do not mean a "photographic" imitation, but rather an imitation of nature as experienced by the individual artist, or finally a representation of the nature of the artist as experienced by himself. Art is then "self-expression," but still an imitation of nature as effect, and essentially figurative rather than formal.

On the other hand we have said to ourselves that in the greatest works of art there is always a quality of abstraction, and have invoked the Platonic endorsement of a geometrical beauty; we have said, Go to, let us also make use of abstract formulae. It was over-looked here that the abstract formulae of ancient art were its natural vehicle, and not a personal or even local invention but the common language of the world. The result of the modern interest in abstraction as such, and apart from questions of content and communicability, has been indeed to eliminate recognizability in art, but scarcely to modify its still essentially representative purpose. Personal symbolisms have been evolved which are not based on any natural correspondences of things to principles, but rather on private associations of ideas. The consequence is that every abstract artist must be individually "explained": the art is not communicative of ideas, but like the remainder of contemporary art, only serves to provoke reactions.

What is then the peculiar endowment of the artist, so much valued? It is evidently, and by general consent, a special sensibility, and it is just for this reason that the modern terms "aesthetic" and "empathy" have been found so appropriate. By sensibility we mean of course an emotional sensibility; *aisthesis* in Hellenistic usage implying physical affectability as distinguished from mental operations. We speak of a work of art as "felt" and never of its "truth," or only of its truth to nature or natural feeling; "appreciation" is a "feeling into" the work. Now an emotional reaction is evoked by whatever we like (or dislike, but as we do not think of works of art as intended to provoke disgust, we need only consider them here as sources of pleasure): what we like, we call beautiful, admitting at the same time that matters of taste are not subject to law. The purpose of art is then to reveal a beauty that we like or can be taught to like; the purpose of art is to give pleasure; the work of art as the source of pleasure is its own end; art is for art's sake. We value the work for the pleasure to be derived from the sight, sound, or touch of its aesthetic surfaces; our conception of beauty is literally skin-deep; questions of utility and intelligibility rarely arise, and if they arise are dismissed as irrelevant. If we propose to dissect the pleasure derived from a work of art, it becomes a matter of psychoanalysis, and ultimately a sort of science of affections and behaviors. If we nevertheless sometimes make use of such high-sounding expressions as "significant form," we do so ignoring that nothing can properly be called a "sign" that is not significant of something other than itself, and for the sake of which it exists. We think of "composition" as an arrangement of masses designed for visual comfort, rather than as determined by the logic of a given content. Our theoretical knowledge of the material and technical bases of art, and of its actual forms, is encyclopedic; but we are either indifferent to its *raison d'être* and final cause, or find this ultimate reason and justification for the very existence of the work in the pleasure to be derived from its beauty by the patron. We say the patron; but under present conditions, it is oftener for his own than for the patron's pleasure that the artist works; the perfect patron being nowadays, not the man who knows what he wants, but the man who is willing to commission the artist to do whatever he likes, and thus as we express it, "respects the freedom of the artist." The consumer, the man, is at the mercy of the manufacturer for pleasure (the "artist") and manufacturer for profit (the "exploiter") and these two are more nearly the same than we suspect.

To say that art is essentially a matter of feeling is to say that its sufficient purpose is to please; the work of art is then a luxury, accessory to the life of pleasure. It may be enquired, Are not pleasures legitimate? Do not the office worker and factory hand deserve and need more pleasures than are normally afforded by the colorless routine of wage-earning tasks? Assuredly. But there is a profound distinction between the deliberate pursuit of pleasure and the enjoyment of pleasures proper to the active or contemplative life. It is one of the greatest counts against our civilization that the pleasures afforded by art, whether in the making or of subsequent appreciation, are not enjoyed or even supposed to be enjoyed by the workman at work. It is taken for granted that while at work we are doing what we like least, and while at play what we should wish to be doing all the time. And this is a part of what we meant by speaking of our depreciated standards of life: it is not so shocking that the workman should be underpaid, as that he should not be able to delight as much in what he does for hire as in what he does by free choice. As Meister Eckhart says, "the craftsman likes talking of his handicraft"; but, the factory worker likes talking of the ball game! It is an inevitable consequence of production under such conditions that quality is sacrificed to quantity: an industry without art provides a necessary apparatus of existence, houses, clothing, frying pans, and so forth, but an apparatus lacking the essential characteristics of things made by art, the characteristics, viz., of beauty and significance. Hence we say that the life that we call civilized is more nearly an animal and mechanical life than a human life; and that in all these respects it contrasts unfavorably with the life of savages, of American Indians for example, to whom it had never occurred that manufacture, the activity of making things for use, could ever be made an artless activity.

Most of us take for granted the conception of art and artists outlined above and so completely that we not only accept its consequences for ourselves, but misinterpret the art and artists of former ages and other cultures in terms that are only appropriate to our own historically provincial point of view. Undisturbed by our own environment, we assume that the artist has always been a peculiar person, that artist and patron have always been at cross purposes, and that work has always been thought of as a necessary evil. But let us now consider what we have often called the "normal view of art," meaning by "normal" a theory not merely hitherto and elsewhere universally accepted as basic to the structure of society, but also a correct or upright doctrine of art. We shall find that this normal, traditional, and orthodox view of art contradicts in almost every particular the aesthetic doctrines of our time, and shall imply that the common wisdom of the world may have been superior to our own, adding that a thorough understanding of the traditional meaning of "art" and theory of "beauty" are indispensable for the serious student of the history of art, whose business it is to explain the genesis of works of art produced for patrons with whose purposes and interests we are no longer familiar.

To begin with, then, the active life of a man consists on the one hand in doing, and on the other in making or arranging things with a view to efficient doing: broadly speaking, man as doer is the patron, and man as maker the artist. The patron knows what purpose is to be served, for example, he needs shelter. The artist knows how to construct what is required, namely a house. Everyone is naturally a doer, patron, and consumer; and at the same time an artist, that is to say a maker by art, in some specialized sense, for example, either a painter, carpenter, or farmer. There is a division of labor, and for whatever a man does not make for himself he commissions another professional, the shoemaker, for example, when he needs shoes, or the author when he needs a book. In any case, in such relatively unanimous societies as we are considering, societies whose form is predetermined by traditional conceptions of order and meaning, there can hardly arise an opposition of interest as between patron and artist; both require the same kind of shoes, or worship at the same shrines, fashions changing only slowly and imperceptibly, so that under these conditions it has been truly said that "Art has fixed ends, and ascertained means of operation."

In the normal society as envisaged by Plato, or realized in a feudal social order or caste system, occupation is vocational, and usually hereditary; it is intended at least that every man shall be engaged in the useful occupation for which he is best fitted by nature, and in which therefore he can best serve the society to which he belongs and at the same time realize his own perfection. As everyone makes use of things that are made artfully, as the designation "artifact" implies, and everyone possesses an art of some sort, whether of painting, sculpture, blacksmithing, weaving, cookery or agriculture, no necessity is felt to explain the nature of art in general, but only to communicate a knowledge of particular arts to those who are to practice them; which knowledge is regularly passed on from master to apprentice, without there being any necessity for "schools of art." An integrated society of this sort can function harmoniously for millennia, in the absence of external interference. On the other hand, the contentment of innumerable peoples can be destroyed in a generation by the withering touch of our civilization; the local market is flooded by a production in quantity with which the responsible maker by art cannot compete; the vocational structure of society, with all its guild organization and standards of workmanship, is undermined; the artist is robbed of his art and forced to find himself a "job"; until finally the ancient society is industrialized and reduced to the level of such societies as ours, in which business takes precedence of life. Can one wonder that western nations are feared and hated by other peoples, not alone for obvious political or economic reasons, but even more profoundly and instinctively for spiritual reasons?

What is art, or rather what was art? In the first place the property of the artist, a kind of knowledge and skill by which he knows, not what ought to be made, but how to imagine the form of the thing that is to be made, and how to embody this form in suitable material, so that the resulting artifact may be used. The shipbuilder builds, not for aesthetic reasons, but in order that men may be able to sail on the water; it is a matter of fact that the well-built ship will be beautiful, but it is not for the sake of making something beautiful that the shipbuilder goes to work; it is a matter of fact that a well made icon will be beautiful, in other words that it will please when seen by those for whose use it was made, but the imager is casting his bronze primarily for use and not as a mantelpiece ornament or for the museum showcase.

Art can then be defined as the embodiment in material of a pre-conceived form. The artist's operation is dual, in the first place intellectual or "free" and in the second place manual and "servile." "To be properly expressed," as Eckhart says, "a thing must proceed from within, moved by its form." It is just as necessary that the idea of the work to be done should first of all be imagined in an imitable form as that the workman should command the technique by which this mental image can be imitated in the available material. "It is," as Augustine says, "by their ideas that we judge of what things ought to be like." A private property in ideas in inconceivable, since ideas have no existence apart from the intellect that entertains them and of which they are the forms; there cannot be an authorship of ideas, but only an entertainment, whether by one or many intellects is immaterial. It is not then in the ideas to be expressed in art, or to speak more simply not in the themes of his work, that an artist's intellectual operation is spoken of as "free"; the nature of the ideas to be expressed in art is predetermined by a traditional doctrine, ultimately of superhuman origin, and through the authority of which the necessity of a clear and repeated expression of such and such ideas has come to be accepted without question. As Aristotle expresses it, the general end of art is the good of man. This is a matter of religious art only in this sense, that in a traditional society there is little or nothing that can properly be called secular; whatever the material uses of artifacts, we find that what we (who scarcely distinguish in principle art from millinery), describe as their ornamentation or decoration, has always a precise significance; no distinction can be drawn between the ideas expressed in the humblest peasant art of a given period and those expressed in the actually hieratic arts of the same period. We cannot too often repeat that the art of a traditional society expresses throughout its range the governing ideology of the group; art has fixed ends and ascertained means of operation; art is a conscience about form, precisely as prudence is a conscience about conduct,—a conscience in both senses of the word, i.e., both as rule and as awareness. Hence it is that we can speak of a conformity or non-conformity in art, just as we can of regular and irregular, orderly and disorderly in conduct. Good art is no more a matter of moods than good conduct a matter of inclination; both are habits; it is the recollected man, and not the excited man, who can either make or do well.

On the other hand, nothing can be known or stated except in some way; the way of the individual knower. Whatever may be known to you and me in common can only be stated by either of us each in our own way. At any given moment these ways of different individuals will be and are so much alike as to be pleasing and intelligible to all concerned; but in proportion as the psychology and somatology of the group changes with time, so will the ways of knowing and idiom of expression; an iconography may not vary for millennia, and yet the style of every century will be distinct and recognizable at a glance. It is in this respect that the intellectual operation is called free; the style is the man, and that in which the style of one individual or period differs from that of another is the infallible trace of the artist's personal nature; not a deliberate, but an unconscious self-expression of the free man.

The orator whose sermon is not the expression of a private opinion or philosophy, but the exposition of a traditional doctrine, is speaking with perfect freedom, and originality; the doctrine is his, not as having invented it, but by conformation (*adaequatio rei et intellectus*). Even in direct citation he is not a parrot, but giving out of himself a recreated theme. The artist is the servant of the work to be done; and it is as true here as in the realm of conduct that "My service is perfect freedom." It is only a lip-service that can be called slavish; only when an inherited formula has become an "art form," or "ornament," to be imitated as such without any understanding of its significance, that the artist, no longer a traditional craftsman but an academician, can properly be called a forger or plagiarist. Our repetition of classic forms in modern architecture is generally a forgery in this sense; the manufacturer of "brummagem idols" is both a forger and a prostitute; but the hereditary craftsman, who may be repeating formulae inherited from the stone age, remains an original artist until he is forced by economic pressure to accept the status of a parasite supplying the demand of the ignorant tourist in search of drawing-room ornaments and what he calls "the mysterious East."

Where an idea to be expressed remains the same throughout long sequences of stylistic variation, it is evident that this idea remains the motif or motivating power behind the work; the artist has worked throughout for the sake of the idea to be expressed, although expressing this idea always in his own way. The primary necessity is that he should really have entertained the idea and always visualized it in an imitable form; and this, implying an intellectual activity that must be ever renewed, is what we mean by originality as distinguished from novelty, and by power as distinguished from violence. It will readily be seen, then, that in concentrating our attention on the stylistic peculiarities of works of art, we are confining it to a consideration of accidents, and really only amusing ourselves with a psychological analysis of personalities; not by any means penetrating to what is constant and essential in the art itself.

The manual operation of the artist is called servile, because similitude is with respect to the form; in writing down, for example, the form of a musical composition that has already been heard mentally, or even in performance as such, the artist is no longer free, but an imitator of what he has himself imagined. In such a servility there is certainly nothing dishonorable, but rather a continued loyalty to the good of the work to be done; the artist turns from intellectual to manual operation or vice versa at will, and when the work has been done, he judges its "truth" by measuring the actual form of the artifact against the mental image of it that was his before the work began and remains in his consciousness regardless of what may happen to the work itself. We can now perhaps begin to realize just what we have done in separating artist from craftsman and "fine" from "applied" art. We have assumed that there is one kind of man that can imagine, and another that cannot; or to speak more honestly, another kind whom we cannot afford, without doing hurt to business, to allow to imagine, and to whom we therefore permit a servile and imitative operation *only*. Just as the operation of the artist who merely imitates nature as closely as possible, or as an archaist merely imitates the forms and formulae of ancient art without attempting any recreation of ideas in terms of his own constitution, is a servile operation, so is that of the mason required to carve, whether by hand or machinery, innumerable copies or "ornaments" for which he is provided with ready-made designs, for which another man is responsible, or which may be simple "superstitions," that is to say "art forms," of which the ideal content is no longer understood, and which are nothing but the vestiges of originally living traditions. It is precisely in our modern world that everyone is nominally, and no one really "free." Art has also been defined as "the imitation of nature in her manner of operation": that is to say, an imitation of nature, not as effect, but as cause. Nature is here, of course, "Natura naturans, Creatrix, Deus," and by no means our own already natured environment. All traditions lay a great stress on the analogy of the human and divine artificers, both alike being "makers by art," or "by a word conceived in intellect." As the Indian books express it, "We must build as did the Gods in the beginning." All this is only to say again in other words that "similitude is with respect to the form." "Imitation" is the embodiment in matter of a preconceived form; and that is precisely what we mean by "creation." The artist is the providence of the work to be done.

All of our modern teaching centers round the posed model and the dissecting room; our conceptions of portraiture are as a matter of historical fact associated in their origins with the charnel house and death mask. On the other hand, we begin to see now why primitive and traditional and what we have described as normal art is "abstract"; it is an imitation, not of a visible and transient appearance or "effect of light," but of an intelligible form which need no more resemble any natural object than a mathematical equation need look like its locus in order to be "true." It is one thing to draw in linear rhythms and abstract light because one must; another thing for anyone who is not by nature and in the philosophical sense a realist, deliberately to cultivate an abstracted style.

The principles of traditional criticism follow immediately from what has been said above. The work of art is "true" to the extent that its actual or accidental form reflects the essential form conceived in the mind of the artist (it is in this sense that the workman still speaks of "trueing" the work in hand); and adequate, or apt, if this form has been correctly conceived with respect to the final cause of the work, which is to be used by the patron. This distinction of judgments, which normally coincide in unanimous cultures, is of particular value to the modern student of ancient or exotic arts, for which we have no longer a practical use. The modern aesthetician thinks that he has done enough if he "feels into" the work, since he holds that the secret of art resides in a peculiar sensibility outwardly manifested as an aesthetic urge to express and communicate a feeling; he does not realize that ancient works of art were produced devoutly, indeed, but primarily to serve a purpose and to communicate a gnosis. What was demanded of the traditional artist was first and foremost to be in possession of his art, that is to be in possession of a knowledge, rather than a sentiment. We forget that sensation is an animal property, and knowledge distinctly human; and that art, if thought of as distinctly human and particularly if we think of art as a department of the "higher things of life," must likewise have to do much more with knowledge than with feeling. We ought not, then, as Herbert Spinden so cleverly puts it, to "accept a pleasurable effect upon our unintelligent nerve ends as an index of understanding."

The critic of ancient or exotic art, having only the work of art before him, and nothing but the aesthetic surfaces to consider, can only register reactions, and proceed to a dimensional and chemical analysis of matter, and psychological analysis of style. His knowledge is of the sort defined as accidental, and very different from the essential and practical knowledge of the original artist and patron. One can in fact only be said to have understood the work, or to have any more than a dilettante knowledge of it, to the extent that he can identify himself with the mentality of the original artist and patron. The man can only be said to have understood Romanesque or Indian art who comes very near to forgetting that he has not made it himself for his own use; a man is only qualified to translate an ancient text when he has really participated in, and not merely observed, the outer and inner life of its time, and identified this time with his own. All this evidently requires a far longer, more round about, and self-denying discipline than is commonly associated with the study of the history of art, which generally penetrates no farther than an analysis of styles, and certainly not to an analysis of the necessary reasons of iconographies or logic of composition.

There is also a traditional doctrine of beauty. This theory of beauty is not developed with respect to artifacts alone, but universally. It is independent of taste, for it is recognized that as Augustine says, there are those who take pleasure in deformities. The word deformity is significant here, because it is precisely a formal beauty that is in question; and we must not forget that "formal" includes the connotation "formative." The recognition of beauty depends on judgment, not on sensation; the beauty of the aesthetic surfaces depending on their information, and not upon themselves. Everything, whether natural or artificial, is beautiful to the extent that it really is what it purports to be, and independently of all comparisons; or ugly to the extent that its own form is not expressed and realized in its tangible actuality. The work of art is beautiful, accordingly, in terms of perfection, or truth and aptitude as defined above; whatever is inept or vague cannot be considered beautiful, however it may be valued by those who "know what they like." So far from that, the veritable connoisseur "likes what he knows"; having fixed upon that course of art which is right, use has made it pleasant.

Whatever is well and truly made, will be beautiful in kind because of its perfection. There are no degrees of perfection; just as we cannot say that a frog is any more or less beautiful than a man, whatever our preferences may be, so we cannot possibly say that a telephone booth as such is any more or less beautiful than a cathedral as such; we only think that one is more beautiful than the other in kind, because our actual experience is of unlovely booths and really beautiful cathedrals.

It is taken for granted that the artist is always working "for the good of the work to be done"; from the coincidence of beauty with perfection it follows inevitably that his operation always tends to the production of a beautiful work. But this is a very different matter from saying that the artist has always in view to discover and communicate beauty. Beauty in the master craftsman's atelier is not a final cause of the work to be done, but an inevitable accident. And for this reason, that the work of art is always occasional; it is the nature of a rational being to work for particular ends, whereas beauty is an indeterminate end; whether the artist is planning a picture, a song, or a city, he has in view to make that thing and nothing else. What the artist has in mind is to do the job "right," *secundum rectam rationem artis*: it is the philosopher who brings in the word "beautiful" and expounds its conditions in terms of perfection, harmony, and clarity. A recognition of the fact that things can only be beautiful in kind, and not in one another's kinds, and the conception of the formality of beauty, bring us back again to the futility of a naturalistic art; the beauties of a living man and of a statue or stone man are different in kind and not interchangeable; the more we try to make the statue look like a man, the more we denature the stone and caricature the man. It is the form of a man in a nature of flesh that constitutes the beauty of this man; the form of a man in a nature of stone the beauty of the statue; and these two beauties are incompatible.

Beauty is, then, perfection apprehended as an attractive power; that aspect of the truth for example which moves the will to grapple with the theme to be communicated. In medieval phraseology, "beauty adds to the good an ordering to the cognitive faculty by which the good is known as such"; "beauty has to do with cognition." If we ourselves endeavor to speak well, it is for the sake of clarity alone, and we should much rather be called interesting than mellifluent. To quote a Hasidic example: if any should say, "'Let us now hear you talk of your doctrine, you speak so beautifully,' 'May I be struck dumb ere I speak beautifully.'" But if beauty is not synonymous with truth, neither can it be isolated from the truth: the distinction is logical, but there is coincidence *in re*. Beauty is at once a symptom and an invitation; as truth is apprehended by the intellect, so beauty moves the will; beauty is always ordered to reproduction, whether a physical generation or spiritual regeneration. To think of beauty as a thing to be enjoyed apart from use is to be a naturalist, a fetishist, and an idolater.

Nothing more enrages the exhibitionist of modern art than to be asked, What is it about? or What is it for? He will exclaim, You might as well ask what it looks like! In fact, however, the question and answer are on altogether different planes of reference; we have agreed that the work of art by no means needs to look like anything on earth, and is perhaps the worse the more it tends to create an illusion. It is another matter if we demand an intelligibility and functional efficacy in the work. For what are we to do with it, intellectually or physically, if it has no meaning and is not adapted to be used? All that we can do in this case is to like it or dislike it, much as bulls are said to love green and hate red.

The intelligibility of traditional art does not depend on recognitions but, like that of script, on legibility. The characters in which this art is written are properly called symbols; when meaning has been forgotten or ignored and art exists only for the comfort of the eye, these become "art forms" and are spoken of as "ornaments"; we speak of "decorative" values. Symbols in combination form an iconography or myth. Symbols are the universal language of art; an international language with merely dialectic variations, current once in all milieus and always intrinsically intelligible, though now no longer understood by educated men, and only to be seen or heard in the art of peasants. The content of symbols is metaphysical. Whatever work of traditional art we consider, whether a crucifix, Ionic column, peasant embroidery, or trappings of a horse, or nursery tale, has still, or had, a meaning over and above what may be called the immediate value of the object to us as a source of pleasure or necessity of life. This implies for us that we cannot pretend to have accounted for the genesis of any such work of art until we have understood what it was for and what it was intended to mean. The symbolic forms, which we call ornaments because they are only superstitions for us, are none the less the substance of the art before us; it is not enough to be able to use the terms of iconography freely and to be able to label our museum specimens correctly; to have understood them, we must understand the ultimate *raison d'être* of the iconography, just why it is as it is and not otherwise.

Implicit in this symbolism lies what was equally for artist and patron the ultimately spiritual significance of the whole undertaking. The references of the symbolic forms are as precise as those of mathematics. The adequacy of the symbols being intrinsic, and not a matter of convention, the symbols correctly employed transmit from generation to generation a knowledge of cosmic analogies: as above, so below. Some of us still repeat the prayer, Thy will be done on earth as it is in heaven. The artist is constantly represented as imitating heavenly forms,—"the crafts such as building and carpentry which give us matter in wrought forms ... take their principles thence and from the thinking there" (*Enneads*, V.9). The archetypal house, for example, repeats the architecture of the universe; a ground below, a space between, a vault above, in which there is an opening corresponding to the solar gateway by which one "escapes altogether" out of time and space into an unconfined and timeless empyrean. Functional and symbolic values coincide; if there rises a column of smoke to the luffer above, this is not merely a convenience, but also a representation of the axis of the universe that pillars-apart heaven and earth, essence and nature, and is itself although without dimensions or consistency the adamantine principle and exemplary form of temporal and spatial extension and of all things situated in time or space. This was doubtless already apparent to prehistoric man, though we cannot trace it farther back in literature than perhaps a millennium and a half B.C. Vestiges of the primitive luffer survive in the eyes of domes, and of its significance in the fact that even to-day we speak of Santa Claus, a doublet of the resurrected Sun, as entering in with his gifts, not by the human door, but by the chimney.

The world-wide designation of stone weapons as "thunder-bolts" is a memory surviving from the Stone Age, when already primitive man identified his striking weapons with the shaft of lightning with which the solar Deity smote the Dragon, or if you prefer, St. Michael Satan, in the beginning; an iron age inherits older traditions, and literary evidences for an identification of weapons with lightning go back at least as far as the second millennium B.C. All traditions agree in seeing in the warp of tissues made by hand an image of the fontal-raying of the dawn-light of creation, and in their woof the representation of planes of being or levels of reference more or less removed from, but still dependent on their common center and ultimate support. Instances could be multiplied, but it will suffice to say that the arts have been universally referred to a divine source, that the practice of an art was at least as much a rite as a trade, that the craftsman had always to be initiated into the Lesser Mysteries of his particular craft, and that the artifact itself had always a double value, that of tool on the one hand and that of symbol on the other. These conditions survived in medieval Europe, and still survive precariously in the East, to the extent that normal types of humanity have been able to resist the subversive influences of civilized business.

We are thus in a position to understand in part how both the making of things by art, and the use of things made by art subserved not only man's immediate convenience, but also his spiritual life; served in other words the whole or holy man, and not merely the outer man who feeds on "bread alone." The transubstantiation of the artifact had its inevitable corollary in a transformation of the man himself; the Templar, for example, whose sword was also a cross, had been initiated as and strove to become more than a man and as nearly as possible an hypostasis of the Sun. "The sword," as Rûmî says, is the same sword, but the man is not the same man (*Mathnawî* V.3287). Now that the greater part of life has been secularized, these transformative values of art can be envisaged only in iconolatry, where the icon made by hands and subsequently consecrated serves as a support of contemplation tending towards a transformation of the worshiper into the likeness of the archetypal form to which, and "not to the colors or the art" as St. Basil says, the honor is paid. The collector who owns a crucifix of the finest period and workmanship, and merely enjoys its "beauty," is in a very different position from that of the equally sensitive worshiper, who also feels its power, and is actually moved to take up his own cross; only the latter can be said to have understood the work in its entirety, only the former can be called a fetishist. In the same way, and as we have said elsewhere, the man who may have been a "barbarian" but could look upward to the roof tree of his house and say "There hangs the Light of Lights," or down to his hearth and say "There is the Center of the World," was more completely a Man than one whose house, however well supplied with labor-saving and sanitary apparatus, is merely "a machine to live in."

It remains for us to consider the problems of artist and patron, producer and consumer, from the standpoint of ethics: to explain the traditional position, which asserts that there can be no "good use" without art; that is to say no efficient goodness, but only good intentions in case the means provided are defective. Suppose for example, that the artist is a printer; to the extent that he designs an illegible type, the book, however supremely valuable its text, will be "no good." Of a workman who bungles we say in the same way that he is "no good" or "good for nothing," or in the technical language of traditional ethics, that he is a "sinner": "sin" being defined as "any departure from the order to the end," whatever the nature of the end. Before the artist can even imagine a form there must have been a direction of the will towards a specific idea; since one cannot imagine "form" in the abstract, but only this or that form. In Indian terms, an image can only spring from a "seed." Or as Bonaventura expresses it, "Every agent acting rationally, not at random, nor under compulsion, foreknows the thing before it is, viz., in a likeness, by which likeness, which is the 'idea' of the thing (in an imitable form), the thing is both known and brought into being." The artist's will has accordingly consented beforehand to the end in view; whether a good end or bad end is no longer his affair as an artist; it is too late now for qualms, and the artist as such has no longer any duty but to devote himself to the good of the work to be done. As St. Thomas expresses it, "Art does not require of the artist that his act be a good act, but that his work be good ... Art does not presuppose rectitude of the appetite,"—but only to serve the appetite, whether for good or evil. It is for the man to decide what, if any, propaganda are desirable; for man as artist only to make the propagation effective. The artist may nevertheless come short, and in this case he is said to "sin as an artist": if, for example, he undertakes and proposes to manufacture an efficient poison gas, and actually produces something quite innocuous, or intends to fashion a Madonna, and only produces a fashion plate. The artist as such is an amoral type: at the same time there can be no good use, that is effective use, without art.

Let us now remind ourselves that the artist is also a man, and as a man responsible for all that his will consents to; "in order that a man may make right use of his art, he needs to have a virtue which will rectify his appetite." The man is responsible directly, as a murderer for example by intent if he consents to manufacture adulterated food, or drugs in excess of medical requirement; responsible as a promoter of loose living if he exhibits a pornographic picture (by which we mean of course something essentially salacious, preserving the distinction of "obscene" from "erotic"); responsible spiritually if he is a sentimentalist or pseudo-mystic. It is a mistake to suppose that in former ages the artist's "freedom" could have been arbitrarily denied by an external agency; it is much rather a plain and unalterable fact that the artist as such is not a free man. As artist he is morally irresponsible, indeed; but who can assert that he is an artist and not also a man? The artist can be separated from the man in logic and for purposes of understanding; but actually, the artist can only be divorced from his humanity by what is called a disintegration of personality. The doctrine of art for art's sake implies precisely such a sacrifice of humanity to art, of the whole to the part. It is significant that at the same time that individualistic tendencies are recognizable in the sphere of culture, in the other sphere of business and in the interest of profit most men are denied the opportunity of artistic operation altogether, or can function as responsible artists only in hours of leisure when they can pursue a "hobby" or play games. What shall it profit a man to be politically free, if he must be either the slave of "art," or slave of "business"?

We say then that if the artist as such is morally irresponsible, he is also a morally responsible man. In the normal and long-enduring types of civilization that we have been considering,—Indian, Egyptian, early Greek, medieval Christian, Chinese, Maori, or American Indian for example,—it has been man as patron rather than man as artist with whom the decision has rested as to what shall be made: the freedom of the artist involving an autonomy only within his own sphere of operation, and not including a free choice of themes. That choice remained with the Man, and amounted to an effective censorship, though not a censorship in our sense, but in the last analysis a self-control, since the artist and the man were still of one mind, and all men in some sense artists. Nothing in fact was made that did not answer to a generally recognized necessity.

All this accords with Aristotle's dictum, that "the general end of art is the good of man." General ends take precedence of private ends; it is not the private good of this or that man, and still less of this or that artist, but Man's conception of the good, that has determined what was made by art. In principle, accordingly, a censorship can be approved of as altogether proper to the dignity of Man. This need not be a legally formulated censorship so long as the responsible artist is *also* a responsible member of society. But as soon as the artist asserts an absolute independence there arises the occasion for a formulated censorship; liberty becoming license, forges its own chains.

We must not however overlook a factor essential to the current problem. Who is qualified to be a censor? Surely it is not enough to recognize a wrong, or what we think a wrong, and to rush into action guided only by a private, or little group, opinion, however firmly entertained. It is certainly not in a democracy, nor in a society trying to find a means of survival by trial and error, that a censorship can be justly exercised. Our censorships reflect at the best a variable canon of expediency; one that varies, for example, from state to state and decade to decade. To justify the exercise of a censorship, we must *know* what is right or wrong, and why; we must have read Eternal Law before we can impose a human code. This means that it is only within a relatively unanimous community, acknowledging an ascertained truth, that a censorship can properly be exercised, and only by an elite, whose vocation it is precisely to know metaphysical truth, (whence only can there be deduced and ascertained the governing principles of doing and making) that laws of conduct binding on the artist as a man can properly be promulgated. We cannot therefore expect from any legislative censorship an adjustment of the strained relations between the artist and the patron, producer and consumer; the former is too much concerned with himself, the latter too unaware of man's real needs, whether physical or spiritual,—too much a lover of quantity and by far too little insistent upon the quality of life. The source of all our difficulties, whether economic, or psychic, lies beyond the power of legislation or philanthropy; what we require is a rectification of humanity itself and a consequent awareness of the priority of contemplation to action. We are altogether too busy, and have made a vice of industry.

Under present circumstances, then, art is by and large a luxury: a luxury that few can afford, and one that need not be overmuch lamented by those who cannot afford to buy. This same "art" was once the principle of knowledge by which the means of life were produced, and the physical and spiritual needs of man were provided for. The whole man made by contemplation, and in making did not depart from himself. To resume all that has been said in a single statement,—Art *is* a superstition: art was a way of life.

Postscript

Note on Review by Richard Florsheim
of
"Is Art a Superstition, or a Way of Life?"

In reviewing my "Is Art a Superstition, or a Way of Life?" Mr. Florsheim assumes my "advocacy of a return to a more or less feudal order ... an earlier, but dead, order of things." In much the same way a reviewer of "Patron and Artist" (cf. in *Apollo*, February, 1938, p. 100) admits that what I say "is all very true," but assumes that the remedy we "Medievalists" (meaning such as Gill, Gleizes, Carey and me) suggest is to "somehow get back to an earlier social organization."

These false, facile assumptions enable the critic to evade the challenge of our criticism, which has two main points: (1) that the current "appreciation" of ancient or exotic arts in terms of our own very special and historically provincial view of art amounts to a sort of hocus pocus, and (2) that under the conditions of manufacture taken for granted in current artistic doctrine man is given stones for bread. These propositions are either true or not, and cannot honestly be twisted to mean that we want to put back the hands of the clock.

Neither is it true that we "do not pretend to offer much in the way of practical remedy"; on the contrary, we offer everything, that is to "somehow get back to first principles." Translated from metaphysical into religious terms this means, "Seek first the kingdom of God and His Righteousness, and all these things shall be added unto you." What this can have to do with a sociological archaism or eclecticism I fail to see.

A return to first principles would not recreate the outward aspects of the Middle Ages, though it might enable us to better understand these aspects. I have nowhere said that I wished to "return to the Middle Ages." In the pamphlet reviewed I said that a cathedral was no more beautiful in kind than a telephone booth in kind, and expressly excluded questions of preference, i.e., of "wishful thinking." What I understand by "wishful thinking" is that kind of faith in "progress" which leads Mr. Florsheim to identify "earlier" with "dead," a type of thinking that ignores all distinction of essence from accident and seems to suggest a Marxist or at any rate a definitely anti-traditional bias.

Things that were true in the Middle Ages are still true, apart from any questions of styles; suppose it eternally true, for example, that "beauty has to do with cognition." Does it follow from this that in order to be consistent I must decorate my house with crockets? or am I forbidden to admire an aeroplane? Dr. Wackernagel, reviewed in *The Art Bulletin*, XX, p. 123, "warns against the lack of purpose in most of our modern art." Need this imply a nostalgia for the Middle Ages on his part? If I assert that a manufacture by art is humanely speaking superior to an "industry without art," it does not follow that I envisage knights in armor. If I see that manufacture for use is better for the consumer (and we are all consumers) than a manufacture for profit, this does not mean that we are to manufacture antiques. If I accept that vocation is the natural basis of individual progress (the word has a real meaning in an individual application, the meaning namely of *werden was du bist*), I am not necessarily wrong merely because this position was "earlier" maintained by Plato and in the *Bhagavad Gita*. I do not in fact pretend to foresee the style of a future Utopia; however little may be the value I attach to "modern civilization," however much higher may have been the prevalent values of the medieval or any other early or still existing social order, I do not think of any of these as providing a ready-made blueprint for future imitation. I have no use for pseudo-Gothic in any sense of the word. The sooner my critics realize this, and that I am not out to express any views, opinions or philosophy of my "own," the sooner will they find out what I am talking about.

10

The Nature of Medieval Art

"Art is the imitation of Nature in her manner of operation: Art is the principle of manufacture." St. Thomas Aquinas

The modern mind is as far removed from the ways of thinking that find expression in Medieval art as it is from those expressed in Oriental art. We look at these arts from two points of view, neither of them valid: either the popular view that believes in a "progress" or "evolution" of art and can only say of a "primitive" that "That was before they knew anything about anatomy" or of "savage" art that it is "untrue to nature"; or the sophisticated view which finds in the aesthetic surfaces and the relations of parts the whole meaning and purpose of the work, and is interested only in our emotional reactions to these surfaces.

As to the first, we need only say that the realism of later Renaissance and academic art is just what the Medieval philosopher had in mind when he spoke of those "who can think of nothing nobler than bodies," i.e., who know nothing but anatomy. As to the sophisticated view, which very rightly rejects the criterion of likeness, and rates the "primitives" very highly, we overlook that it also takes for granted a conception of "art" as the expression of emotion, and a term "aesthetics" (literally, "theory of sense-perception and emotional reactions"), a conception and a term that have come into use only within the last two hundred years of humanism. We do not realise that in considering Medieval (or Ancient or Oriental) art from these angles, we are attributing our own feelings to men whose view of art was quite a different one, men who held that "Art has to do with cognition" and apart from knowledge amounts to nothing, men who could say that "the educated understand the rationale of art, the uneducated knowing only what they like," men for whom art was not an end, but a means to present ends of use and enjoyment and to the final end of beatitude equated with the vision of God whose essence is the cause of beauty in all things. This must not be misunderstood to mean that Medieval art was "unfelt" or should not evoke an emotion, especially of that sort that we speak of as admiration or wonder. On the contrary, it was the business of this art not only to "teach," but also to "move, in order to convince"; and no eloquence can move unless the speaker himself has been moved. But whereas we make an aesthetic emotion the first and final end of art, Medieval man was moved far more by the meaning that illuminated the forms than by these forms themselves: just as the mathematician who is excited by an elegant formula is excited, not by its appearance, but by its economy. For the Middle Ages, nothing could be understood that had not been experienced, or loved: a point of view far removed from our supposedly objective science of art and from the mere knowledge about art that is commonly imparted to the student.

Art, from the Medieval point of view, was a kind of knowledge in accordance with which the artist imagined the form or design of the work to be done, and by which he reproduced this form in the required or available material. The product was not called "art," but an "artifact," a thing "made by art"; the art remains in the artist. Nor was there any distinction of "fine" from "applied" or "pure" from "decorative" art. All art was for "good use" and "adapted to condition." Art could be applied either to noble or to common uses, but was no more or less art in the one case than in the other. Our use of the word "decorative" would have been abusive, as if we spoke of a mere millinery or upholstery: for all the words purporting decoration in many languages, Medieval Latin included, referred originally not to anything that could be added to an already finished and effective product merely to please the eye or ear, but to the completion of anything with whatever might be necessary to its functioning, whether with respect to the mind or the body: a sword, for example, would "ornament" a knight, as virtue "ornaments" the soul or knowledge the mind.

Perfection, rather than beauty, was the end in view. There was no "aesthetic," no "psychology" of art, but only a rhetoric, or theory of beauty, which beauty was regarded as the attractive power of perfection in kind and as depending upon propriety, upon the order or harmony of the parts (some would say that this implied, dependent upon certain ideal mathematical relations of parts) and upon clarity or illumination the trace of what St. Bonaventura calls "the light of a mechanical art." Nothing unintelligible could have been thought of as beautiful. Ugliness was the unattractiveness of informality and disorder.

The artist was not a special kind of man, but every man a special kind of artist. It was not for him to say what should be made, except in the special case in which he is his own patron making, let us say, an icon or a house for himself. It was for the patron to say what should be made; for the artist, the "maker by art," to know how to make. The artist did not think of his art as a "self-expression," nor was the patron interested in his personality or biography. The artist was usually, and unless by accident, anonymous, signing his work, if at all, only by way of guarantee: it was not who, but what was said, that mattered. A copyright could not have been conceived where it was well understood that there can be no property in ideas, which are his who entertains them: whoever thus makes an idea his own is working originally, bringing forth from an immediate source within himself, regardless of how many times the same idea may have been expressed by others before or around him.

Nor was the patron a special kind of man, but simply our "consumer." This patron was "the judge of art": not a critic or connoisseur in our academic sense, but one who knew his needs, as a carpenter knows what tools he must have from the smith, and who could distinguish adequate from inadequate workmanship, as the modern consumer cannot. He expected a product that would work, and not some private *jeu d'esprit* on the artist's part. Our connoisseurs whose interest is primarily in the artist's personality as expressed in style—the accident and not the essence of art—pretend to the judgment of Medieval art without consideration of its reasons, and ignore the iconography in which these reasons are clearly reflected. But who can judge whether anything has been *well* said or made, and so distinguish good from bad as judged by art, unless he be fully aware of *what* was to be said or done?

The Christian symbolism of which Emile Mâle spoke as a "calculus" was not the private language of any individual, century, or nation, but a universal language, universally intelligible. It was not even privately Christian or European. If art has been properly called a universal language, it is not such because all men's sensitive faculties enable them to recognize what they see, so that they can say, "This represents a man," regardless of whether the work has been done by a Scotchman or a Chinaman, but because of the universality of the adequate symbolism in which its meanings have been expressed. But that there is a universally intelligible language of art no more means that we can all read it than the fact that Latin was spoken in the Middle Ages throughout Europe means that Europeans can speak it to-day. The language of art is one that we must relearn, if we wish to understand Medieval art, and not merely to record our reactions to it. And this is our last word: that to understand Medieval art needs more than a modern "course in the appreciation of art": it demands an understanding of the spirit of the Middle Ages, the spirit of Christianity itself, and in the last analysis the spirit of what has been well named the "Philosophia Perennis" or "Universal and Unanimous Tradition," of which St. Augustine spoke as a "Wisdom, that was not made, but is now what it always was and ever shall be," some touch of which will open doors to the understanding of and a delight in any traditional art, whether it be that of the Middle Ages, that of the East, or that of the "folk" in any part of the world.

11

Ars sine scientia nihil

Ars sine scientia nihil ("art without science is nothing").[1] These words of the Parisian Master Jean Mignot, enunciated in connection with the building of the Cathedral of Milan in 1398, were his answer to an opinion then beginning to take shape, that *scientia est unum et ars aliud* ("science is one thing and art another"). For Mignot, the rhetoric of building involved a truth to be expressed in the work itself, while others had begun to think, as we now think, of houses, and even of God's house, only in terms of construction and effect. Mignot's *scientia* cannot have meant simply "engineering," for in that case his words would have been a truism, and no one could have questioned them; engineering, in those days, would have been called an art, and not a science, and would have been included in the *recta ratio factibilium* or "art" by which we know how things can and should be made. His *scientia* must therefore have had to do with the reason (*ratio*), theme, content, or burden (*gravitas*) of the work to be done, rather than with its mere functioning. Art alone was not enough, but *sine scientia nihil*.[2]

In connection with poetry we have the homologous statement of Dante with reference to his *Commedia*, that "the whole work was undertaken not for a speculative but a practical end ... The purpose of the whole is to remove those who are living in this life from the state of wretchedness and to lead them to the state of blessedness" (*Ep. ad Can. Grand.*, 15 and 16). That is closely paralleled in Asvaghosa's colophon to the *Saundarânanda*: "This poem, pregnant with the burden of Liberation, has been composed by me in the poetic manner, not for the sake of giving pleasure, but for the sake of giving peace." Giselbertus, sculptor of the Last Judgment at Autun, does not ask us to consider his arrangement of masses, or to admire his skill in the use of tools, but directs us to his theme, of which he says in the inscription, *Terreat hic terror quos terreus alligat error*, "Let this terror affright those whom terrestrial error holds in bondage."

And so, too, for music. Guido d'Arezzo distinguishes accordingly the true musician from the songster who is nothing but an artist:

Musicorum et cantorum magna est distancia:
Isti dicunt, illi sciunt quae componit musica.
Nam qui canit quod non sapit, diffinitur bestia;
Bestia non, qui non canit arte, sed usu;
Non verum facit ars cantorem, sed documentum.[3]

That is, "between the true 'musicians' and the mere 'songsters,'
the difference is vast: the latter vocalize, the former understand the
music's composition. He who sings of what he savors not is termed
a 'brute'; not brute is he who sings, not merely artfully, but *usefully*;
it is not art alone, but the doctrine that makes the true 'singer.'"
The thought is like St. Augustine's, "not to enjoy what we should
use"; pleasure, indeed, perfects the operation, but is not its end.
And like Plato's, for whom the Muses are given to us "that we may
use them intellectually (*meta nou*),[4] not as a source of irrational
pleasure (*eph' hêdonên alogon*), but as an aid to the circling of the
soul within us, of which the harmony was lost at birth, to help in
restoring it to order and consent with itself" (*Timaeus* 47D, cf. 90D).
The words *sciunt quae componit musica* are reminiscent of
Quintilian's "Docti rationem componendi intelligunt, etiam indocti voluptatem" (IX.4.116); and these are an abbreviation of Plato,
Timaeus 80B, where it is said that from the composition of sharp and
deep sounds there results "pleasure to the unintelligent, but to the
intelligent that delight that is occasioned by the imitation of the divine harmony realized in mortal motions." Plato's "delight" (*euphro-
sunê*), with its festal connotation (cf. *Homeric Hymns* IV.482),
corresponds to Guido's verb *sapit*, as in *sapientia*, defined by St.
Thomas Aquinas as *scientia cum amore*; this delight is, in fact, the
"feast of reason." To one who plays his instrument with art *and* wisdom it will teach him such things as grace the mind; but to one who
questions his instrument ignorantly and violently, it will only babble
(*Homeric Hymns* IV.483). *Usu* may be compared to *usus* as the *jus et
norma loquendi* (Horace, *Ars poetica*, 71, 72), and corresponds, I
think, to a Platonic *ôphelimôs* = *frui, fruitio* and Thomist *uti* = *frui,
fruitio* (*Sum. Theol.* I.39.8c).
That "art" is not enough recalls the words of Plato in *Phaedrus*
245A, where not merely art, but also inspiration is necessary, if the

poetry is to amount to anything. Mignot's *scientia* and Guido's *documentum* are Dante's *dottrina* at which (and not at his art) he asks us to marvel (*Inferno* IX.61); and that *dottrina* is not his own but what "Amor (Sanctus Spiritus) dictates within me" (*Purgatorio* XXIV.52, 53). It is not the poet but "the God (Eros) himself that speaks" (Plato, *Ion* 534, 535); and not fantasy but truth, for "Omne verum, a quocumque dicatur, est a Spiritu Sancto" (St. Ambrose on I Cor. 12:3); "Cathedram habet in caelo qui intus corda docet" (St. Augustine, *In epist. Joannis ad parthos*); "O Lord of the Voice, implant in me thy doctrine (*srutam*), in me may it abide" (AV I.1.2).

That "to make the primordial truth intelligible, to make the unheard audible, to enunciate the primordial word, such is the task of art, or it is not art"[5]—not art, but *quia sine scientia, nihil*—has been the normal and ecumenical view of art. Mignot's conception of architecture, Guido's of music, and Dante's of poetry underlie the art, and notably the "ornament," of all other peoples and ages than our own—whose art is "unintelligible."[6] Our private (*idiôtikos*) and sentimental (*pathêtikos*) contrary heresy (i.e., view that we *prefer* to entertain) which makes of works of art an essentially sensational experience,[7] is stated in the very word "aesthetics," *aisthêsis* being nothing but the biological "irritability" that human beings share with plants and animals. The American Indian cannot understand how we "can like his songs and not share their spiritual content."[8] We are, indeed, just what Plato called "lovers of fine colors and sounds and all that art makes of these things that have so little to do with the nature of the beautiful itself" (*Republic* 476B). The truth remains, that "art is an intellectual virtue," "beauty has to do with cognition."[9] "Science renders the work beautiful; the will renders it useful; perseverance makes it lasting."[10] *Ars sine scientia nihil.*

Notes

1. *Scientia autem artifices est causa artificiatorum; eo quod artifex operatur per suum intellectum, Sum. Theol.* I.14.8c.

2. "If you take away science, how will you distinguish between the *artifex* and the *inscius*?" Cicero, *Academica* II.7.22; "Architecti jam suo verbo rationem istam vocant," Augustine, *De ordine* II.34; it is the same for all arts, e.g., dance is rational, therefore its gestures are not merely graceful movements but also signs.

3. Paul Henry Lang, in his *Music and Western Civilization* (New York, 1942), p. 87, accidentally rendered the penultimate line in our verse by "A brute by rote and not

by art makes melody"; a version that overlooks the double negative, and misinterprets *usu*, which is not "by habit," but "usefully" or "profitably" *ôphelimôs*. Professor E. K. Rand has kindly pointed out to me that line 4 is metrically incomplete, and suggests *sapit usu*, i.e., "who, in practice, savors what is sung." Related material will be found in Plato, *Phaedrus* 245A; Rûmî, *Mathnawi* 1.2770.

4. The shifting of our interest from "pleasure" to "significance" involves what is, in fact, a *metanoia*, which can be taken to mean either a "change of mind," or a turning away from mindless sensibility to Mind itself. Cf. Coomaraswamy, "On Being in One's Right Mind," 1942.

5. Walter Andrae, "Keramik im Dienste der Weisheit," *Berichte der deutschen keramischen Gesellschaft* XVII (1936), p. 263. Cf. Gerhardt Hauptmann, "Dichten heisst, hinter Worten das Urwort erklingen lassen"; and Sir George Birdwood, "Art, void of its supernatural typology, fails in its inherent artistic essence" (*Sva*, London, 1915, p. 296).

6. "It is inevitable that the artist should be unintelligible because his sensitive nature inspired by fascination, bewilderment, and excitement, expresses itself in the profound and intuitive terms of ineffable wonder. We live in an age of unintelligibility, as every age must be that is so largely characterized by conflict, maladjustment, and heterogeneity" (E. F. Rothschild); i.e., as Iredell Jenkins has expressed it, in a world of "impoverished reality."

7. "It was a tremendous discovery, how to excite emotions for their own sake" (Alfred North Whitehead, *Religion in the Making*, quoted with approval by Herbert Read in *Art and Society*, London, 1937, p. 84). Much more truly, Aldous Huxley calls our abuse of art "a form of masturbation" (*Ends and Means*, New York, 1937, p. 237) : how otherwise could one describe the stimulation of emotions "for their own sake"?

8. Mary Austen in H. J. Spinden, *Fine Art and the First Americans* (New York, 1931), p. 5. No more can we understand those for whom the Scriptures are mere "literature."

9. *Sum. Theol.* I.5.4 ad 1, I-II.27.1 ad 3, and I-II.57.3 and 4.

10. St. Bonaventura, *De reductione artium ad theologiam* XIII.

12

Imitation, Expression, and Participation

"Pistoumetha de pros tous tethaumakotas ek tôn meteilêpsotôn."
Plotinus, *Enneads* VI.6.7.

As Iredell Jenkins has pointed out,[1] the modern view that "art is expression" has added nothing to the older and once universal (e.g., Greek and Indian) doctrine that "art is imitation," but only translates the notion of "imitation, born of philosophical realism, into the language and thought of metaphysical nominalism"; and "since nominalism destroys the revelation doctrine, the first tendency of modern theory is to deprive beauty of any cognitive significance."[2] The older view had been that the work of art is the demonstration of the invisible form that remains in the artist, whether human or divine;[3] that beauty has to do with cognition;[4] and that art is an intellectual virtue.[5]

While Jenkins' proposition is very true, so far as expressionism is concerned, it will be our intention to point out that in the catholic (and not only Roman Catholic) view of art, *imitation, expression*, and *participation* are three predications of the essential nature of art; not three different or conflicting, but three interpenetrating and coincident definitions of art, which is these three in one.

The notion of "imitation," (*mimêsis, anukrti, pratimâ*, etc.) will be so familiar to every student of art as to need only brief documentation. That in our philosophic context imitation does not mean "counterfeiting" is brought out in the dictionary definition: imitation is "the relation of an object of sense to its idea; ... imaginative embodiment of the ideal form"; form being "the essential nature of a thing ... kind or species as distinguished from matter, which distinguishes it as an individual; formative principle; formal cause" (Webster). Imagination is the conception of the idea in an imitable form.[6] Without a pattern (*paradeigma*, exemplar), indeed, nothing could be made except by mere chance. Hence the instruction given to Moses, "Lo, make all things according to the pattern which was shewed to thee on the mount."[7] "Assuming that a beautiful imitation could never be produced unless from a beautiful pattern, and that no sensible object (*aisthêton*, 'aesthetic surface') could be faultless unless it were made in the likeness of an archetype visible only to the intellect, God, when He willed to create the visible world, first fully formed the intelligible world, in order that He might have the use of a pattern wholly divine and incorporeal";[8] "The will of God beheld that beauteous world and imitated it."[9]

Now unless we are making "copies of copies," which is not what we mean by "creative art,"[10] the pattern is likewise "within you,"[11] and remains there as the standard by which the "imitation" must be finally judged.[12] For Plato then, and traditionally, all the arts without exception are "imitative";[13] this "all" includes such arts as those of government and hunting no less than those of painting and sculpture. And true "imitation" is not a matter of illusory resemblance (*homoiotês*) but of proportion, true analogy, or adequacy (*auto to ison*, i.e., *kat' analogian*), by which we are reminded[14] of the intended referent;[15] in other words, it is a matter of "adequate symbolism." The work of art and its archetype are different things; but "likeness in different things is with respect to some quality common to both."[16] Such likeness (*sâdrsya*) is the foundation of painting;[17] the term is defined in logic as the "possession of many common qualities by different things";[18] while in rhetoric, the typical example is "the young man is a lion."

Likeness (*similitudo*) may be of three kinds, either (1) absolute, and then amounting to sameness, which cannot be either in nature or works of art, because no two things can be alike in all respects and still be two, i.e., perfect likeness would amount to identity, (2) imitative or analogical likeness, *mutatis mutandis*, and judged by comparison, e.g., the likeness of a man in stone, and (3) expressive likeness, in which the imitation is neither identical with, nor comparable to the original but is an adequate symbol and reminder of that which it represents, and to be judged only by its truth, or accuracy (*orthotês*, *integritas*); the best example is that of the words that are "images" of things.[19] But imitative and expressive are not mutually exclusive categories; both are images, and both expressive in that they make known their model.

The preceding analysis is based upon St. Bonaventura's,[20] who makes frequent use of the phrase *similitudo expressiva*. The inseparability of imitation and expression appears again in his observation that while speech is expressive, or communicative, "it never expresses except by means of a likeness" (*nisi mediante specie, De reductione artium ad theologiam* 18), i.e., figuratively. In all serious communication, indeed, the figures of speech are figures of thought (cf. Quintilian IX.4.117); and the same applies in the case of visible iconography, in which accuracy is not subordinated to our tastes, but rather is it we ourselves who should have learned to like only what is true. Etymologically, "heresy" is what we "choose" to think; i.e., private (*idiôtikos*) opinion.

But in saying with St. Bonaventura that art is expressive at the same time that it imitates, an important reservation must be made, a reservation analogous to that implied in Plato's fundamental question: about *what* would the sophist make us so eloquent?[21] and his repeated condemnation of those who imitate "anything and everything."[22] When St. Bonaventura speaks of the orator as expressing "what he has in him" (*per sermonem exprimere quod habet apud se, De reductione artium ad theologian* 4), this means giving expression to some idea that he has entertained and made his own, so that it can come forth from within him originally: it does *not* mean what is involved in our expressionism (viz. "in any form of art ... the theory or practice of expressing one's inner, or subjective, emotions and sensations [Webster]"), hardly to be distinguished from exhibitionism.

Art is, then, both imitative and expressive of its themes, by which it is informed, or else would be informal, and therefore not art. That there is in the work of art something like a real presence of its theme brings us to our last step. Lévy-Bruhl[23] and others have attributed to the "primitive mentality" of savages what he calls the notion of a "mystic participation" of the symbol or representation in its referent, tending towards such an identification as we make when we see our own likeness and say, "that's me." On this basis the savage does not like to tell his name or have his portrait taken, because by means of the name or portrait he is accessible, and may therefore be injured by one who can get at him by these means; and it is certainly true that the criminal whose name is known and whose likeness is available can be more easily apprehended than would otherwise be the case. The fact is that "participation" (which need not be called "mystic," by which I suppose that Levy-Bruhl means "mysterious") is not in any special sense a savage idea or peculiar to the "primitive mentality," but much rather a metaphysical and theological proposition.[24] We find already in Plato[25] the doctrine that if anything is beautiful in its kind, this is not because of its color or shape, but because it participates (*metechei*) in "that," viz. the absolute, Beauty, which is a presence (*parousia*) to it and with which it has something in common (*koinônia*). So also creatures, while they are alive, "participate" in immortality.[26] So that even an imperfect likeness (as all must be) "participates" in that which it resembles.[27] These propositions are combined in the words "the being of all things is derived from the Divine Beauty."[28] In the language of exemplarism, that Beauty is "the single form that is the form of very different things."[29] In this sense every "form" is protean, in that it can enter into innumerable natures.

Some notion of the manner in which a form, or idea, can be said to be *in* a representation of it may be had if we consider a straight line: we cannot say truly that the straight line itself "is" the shortest distance between two points, but only that it is a picture, imitation or expression of that shortest distance; yet it is evident that the line coincides with the shortest distance between its extremities, and that by this presence the line "participates" in its referent.[30] Even if we think of space as curved, and the shortest distance therefore actually an arc, the straight line, a reality in the field of plane geometry, is still an adequate symbol of its idea, which it need not resemble, but must express. Symbols are projections of their referents, which are in them in the same sense that our three dimensional face is reflected in the plane mirror.

So also in the painted portrait, my form is there, *in* the actual shape, but not my nature, which is of flesh and not of pigment. The portrait is also "like" the artist ("Il pittore pinge se stesso,")[31] so that in making an attribution we say that "That looks like, or smacks of, Donatello," the model having been my form, indeed, but as the artist conceived it.[32] For nothing can be known, except in the mode of the knower. Even the straight line bears the imprint of the draughtsman, but this is less apparent, because the actual form is simpler. In any case, the more perfect the artist becomes, the less will his work be recognizable as "his"; only when he is no longer anyone, can he see the shortest distance, or my real form, directly and as it is.

Symbols are projections or shadows of their forms (cf. n. 19), in the same way that the body is an image of the soul, which is called its form, and as words are images (*eikonas, Cratylus* 439A; *eidôla, Sophist* 234C) of things. The form is in the work of art as its "content," but we shall miss it if we consider only the aesthetic surfaces and our own sensitive reactions to them, just as we may miss the soul when we dissect the body and cannot lay our hands upon it. And so, assuming that we are not merely playboys, Dante and Asvaghosa ask us to admire, not their art, but the *doctrine* of which their "strange" or "poetic" verses are only the vehicle. Our exaggerated valuation of "literature" is as much a symptom of our sentimentality as is our tendency to substitute ethics for religion. "For he who sings what he does not understand is defined as a beast.[33] ... Skill does not truly make a singer, but the pattern does."[34]

As soon as we begin to operate with the straight line, referred to above, we transubstantiate it; that is, we treat it, and it becomes for us, *as if* [35] it were nothing actually concrete or tangible, but simply the shortest distance between two points, a form that really exists only in the intellect; we could not use it *intellectually* in any other way, however handsome it may be;[36] the line itself, like any other symbol, is only the support of contemplation, and if we merely see its elegance, we are not using it, but making a fetish of it. That is what the "aesthetic approach" to works of art involves.

We are still familiar with the notion of a transubstantiation only in the case of the Eucharistic meal in its Christian form; here, by ritual acts, i.e., by the sacerdotal art, with the priest as officiating artist, the bread is made to be the body of the God; yet no one maintains that the carbohydrates are turned into proteins, or denies that they are digested like any other carbohydrates, for that would mean that we thought of the mystical body as a thing actually cut up into pieces of flesh; and yet the bread is changed in that it is no longer mere bread, but now bread with a meaning, with which meaning or quality we can therefore communicate by assimilation, the bread now feeding both body and soul at one and the same time. That works of art thus nourish, or should nourish, body and soul at one and the same time has been, as we have often pointed out, the normal position from the Stone Age onwards; the utility, as such, being endowed with meaning either ritually or as well by its ornamentation, i.e., "equipment."[37] Insofar as our environment, both natural and artificial, is still significant to us, we are still "primitive mentalities"; but insofar as life has lost it's meaning for us, it is pretended that we have "progressed." From this "advanced" position those whose thinking is done for them by such scholars as Lévy-Bruhl or Sir James Frazer, the behaviorists whose nourishment is "bread alone"—"the husks that the swine did eat"—are able to look down with unbecoming pride on the minority whose world is still a world of meanings.[38]

We have tried to show above that there is nothing extraordinary, but rather something normal and proper to human nature, in the notion that a symbol participates in its referent or archetype. And this brings us to the words of Aristotle, which seem to have been overlooked by our anthropologists and theorists of art: he maintains, with reference to the Platonic conception of art as imitation, and with particular reference to the view that things exist in their plurality by participation in (*methexis*) the forms after which they are named,[39] that to say that they exist "by imitation," or exist "by participation," is no more than a use of different words to say the same thing.[40]

Hence we say, and in so doing say nothing new, that "art is imitation, expression, and participation." At the same time we cannot help asking: What, if anything, has been added to our understanding of art in modern times? We rather presume that something has been deducted. Our term "aesthetics" and conviction that art is essentially an affair of the sensibilities and emotions rank us with the ignorant, if we admit Quintilian's "Docti rationem componendi intelligunt, etiam indocti voluptatem!"[41]

Notes

1. "Imitation and Expression in Art," in the *Journal of Aesthetics and Art Criticism*, V (1942). Cf. J. C. La Drière, "Expression," in the *Dictionary of World Literature* (New York, 1943), and R. G. Collingwood, *The Idea of Nature* (Oxford, 1944) pp. 61–62 (on participation and imitation).

2. "Sinnvolle Form, in der Physisches und Metaphysisches ursprünglich polarisch sich die Waage hielten, wird auf dem Wege zu uns her mehr und mehr entleert; wir sagen dann: sie sei 'Ornament.'" (Walter Andrae, *Die ionische Säule: Bauform oder Symbol?* Berlin, 1933, p. 65). See also Coomaraswamy, "Ornament."

3. Rom. 1:20; Meister Eckhart, *Expositio sancti evangelii secundum Johannem*, etc.

4. *Sum. Theol.* I.5.4 ad I, I-II.27.1 ad 3.

5. *Ibid.*, I-II.57.3 and 4.

6. "Idea dicitur similitudo rei cognitae," St. Bonaventura, *I Sent.*, d.35, a.unic., q.1c. We cannot entertain an idea except in a likeness; and therefore cannot think without words or other images.

7. Exod. 25:40, Heb. 8:5. "Ascendere in montem, id est, in eminentiam mentis," St. Bonaventura, *De dec. praeceptis* II.

8. Philo, *De opificio* 16, *De aeternitate mundi* 15; cf. Plato, *Timaeus* 28AB and *Republic* 601. For the "world-picture" (Sumerian *gish-ghar*, Skr. *jagaccitra*, Gk. *noêtos kosmos*, etc.), innumerable references could be cited. Throughout our literature the operations of the divine and human demiurges are treated as strictly analogous, with only this main difference that God gives form to absolutely formless, and man to relatively informal matter; and the act of imagination is a vital operation, as the word "concept" implies.

9. Hermes, *Lib.* I.8B, cf. Plato, *Timaeus* 29AB. The human artist "imitates nature (Natura naturans, Creatrix Universalis, Deus) in her manner of operation," but one who makes only copies of copies (imitating Natura naturata) is unlike God, since in this case there is no "free" but only the "servile" operation. Cf. Aristotle, *Physics* II.2.194a.20.

10. Plato, *Republic* 601.

11. Philo, *De opificio* 17 ff., and St. Augustine, Meister Eckhart, etc., *passim.*

12. *Laws* 667D ff., etc.

13. *Republic* 392C, etc.

14. *Phaedo* 74F: Argument by analogy is metaphysically valid proof when, and only when, a true analogy is adduced. The validity of symbolism depends upon the assumption that there are corresponding realities on all levels of reference—"as above, so below." Hence the distinction of *le symbolisme qui sait* from *le symbolisme qui cherche*. This is, essentially, the distinction of induction (dialectic) from deduction (syllogism): the latter merely "deducing from the image what it contains," the former "using the image to obtain what the image does not contain" (Alphonse Gratry, *Logic* [La Salle, Ill., 1944], IV.7; cf. KU II.10, "by means of what is never the same obtaining that which is always the same").

15. *Phaedo* 74, *Laws* 667D ff.

16. Boethius, *De differentiis topicis*, III, cited by St. Bonaventura, *De scientia Christi*, 2.C.

17. *Visnudharmottaram* XLII.48.

18. S. N. Dasgupta, *History of Indian Philosophy* (Cambridge, 1922), I, 318.

19. Plato, *Sophist* 234C. Plato assumes that the significant purpose of the work of art is to remind us of that which, whether itself concrete or abstract, is not presently, or is never, perceptible; and that is part of the doctrine that "what we call learning is really remembering" (*Phaedo* 72 ff., *Meno* 81 ff.). The function of reminding does not depend upon visual resemblance, but on the adequacy of the representation: for example, an object or the picture of an object that has been used by someone may suffice to remind us of him. It is precisely from that point of view that representations of the tree under which or throne upon which the Buddha sat can function as adequate representations of himself (*Mahâvamsa* I.69, etc.); the same considerations underlie the cult of bodily or any other "relics." Whereas we think

that an object should be represented in art "for its own sake" and regardless of associated ideas, the tradition assumes that the symbol exists for the sake of its referent, i.e., that the meaning of the work is more important than its looks. Our worship of the symbols themselves is, of course, idolatrous.

20. Citations in J. M. Bissen, *L'Exemplarisme divin selon Saint Bonaventure* (Paris, 1929), ch. 1. I have also used St. Thomas Aquinas, *Sum. Theol.* I.4.3, and *Summa contra gentiles* I.29. The factors of "likeness" are rarely considered in modern works on the theory of art.

21. *Protagoras* 312E.

22. *Republic* 396-398, etc.

23. For criticism of Lévy-Bruhl see O. Leroy, *La Raison primitive* (Paris, 1927); J. Przyluski, *La Participation* (Paris, 1940); W. Schmidt, *Origin and Growth of Religion*, 2nd ed. (New York, 1935), pp. 133–134; and Coomaraswamy, "Primitive Mentality."

24. "Et Plato posuit quod homo materialis est homo ... per participationem" (*Sum. Theol.* I.18.4; cf. I.44.1), i.e., in the Being of God, in whose "image and likeness" the man was made. St. Thomas is quoting Aristotle, *Physics* IV.2.3, where the latter says that in the *Timaeus* (51A) Plato equated *hulê* (primary matter, void space, chaos) with *to metalêptikon* (that which can participate, viz. in form).

25. *Phaedo* 100D; cf. *Republic* 476D. The doctrine was later expounded by Dionysius, *De div. nom.* IV.5, "pulchrum quidem esse dicimus quod participat pulchritudinem." St. Thomas comments: "Pulchritude enim creaturae nihil est aliud quam similitudo divinae pulchritudinis in rebus participata." In the same way, of course, the human artist's product participates in its formal cause, the pattern in the artist's mind.

The notion of participation appears to be "irrational" and will be resisted only if we suppose that the product participates in its cause materially, and not formally; or, in other words, if we suppose that the form participated in is divided up into parts and distributed in the participants. On the contrary, that which is participated in is always a total presence. Words, for example, are images (Plato, *Sophist* 234C); and if to use homologous words, or synonyms, is called a "participation" (*metalêpsis, Theatetus* 173B, *Republic* 539D), it is because the different words are imitations, expressions, and participations of one and the same idea, apart from which they would not be words, but only sounds.

Participation can be made easier to understand by the analogy of the projection of a lantern slide on screens of various materials. It would be ridiculous to say that the form of the transparency, conveyed by the "image-bearing light," is not *in* the picture seen by the audience, or even to deny that "this" picture *is* "that" picture; for we see "the same picture" in the slide and on the screen; but equally ridiculous to suppose that any of the material of the transparency is in what the audience sees.

When Christ said, "this is my body," body and bread were manifestly and materially distinct; but it was "not bread alone" of which the disciples partook. Conversely, those who find in Dante's "strange verses" only "literature," letting their theory escape them, are actually living by sound alone, and are of the sort that Plato ridicules as "lovers of fine sounds."

26. RV 1.164.21.

27. *Sum. Theol.* I.4.3.

28. Aquinas, *De pulchro et bone,* in *Opera omnia, Op.* VII.4, 1.5 (Parma, 1864).

29. Meister Eckhart, Evans ed., I, 211.

30. All discourse consists in "calling something by the name of another, because of its participation in the effect of this other (*koinônia pathêmatos*)," Plato, *Sophist* 252B.

31. Leonardo da Vinci; for Indian parallels see Coomaraswamy, *The Transformation of Nature in Art,* 2nd ed., 1935, n. 7.

32. From this consideration it follows that imitation, expression, and participation are always and can be only of an invisible form, however realistic the artist's intention may be; for he can never know or see things as they "are," because of their inconstancy, but only as he imagines them, and it is of this phantasm and not of any *thing* that his work is a copy. Icons, as Plato points out (*Laws* 931A) are representations not of the "visible gods" (Helios, etc.), but of those invisible (Apollo, Zeus, etc.). Cf. *Republic* 510DE; *Timaeus* 51E, 92; *Philebus* 62B.

33. Skr. *pasu,* an animal or animal man whose behavior is guided, not by reason, but only by "estimative knowledge," i.e., pleasure-pain motives, likes and dislikes, or, in other words, "aesthetic reactions."

In connection with our divorce of art from human values, and our insistence upon *aesthetic* appreciation and denial of the *significance* of beauty, Emmanuel Chapman has very pertinently asked: "On what philosophical grounds can we oppose Vittorio Mussolini's 'exceptionally good fun' at the sight of torn human and animal flesh exfoliating like roses in the Ethiopian sunlight? Does not this 'good fun' follow with an implacable logic, as implacable as a bomb following the law of gravity, if beauty is regarded only as a name for the pleasure we feel, as merely subjective, a quality projected or imputed by the mind, and having no reference to things, no foundation whatsoever in existence? Is it not further the logical consequence of the fatal separation of beauty from reason? ... The bitter failures in the history of aesthetics are there to show that the starting-point can never be any subjective, *a priori* principle from which a closed system is induced" ("Beauty and the War," *Journal of Philosophy*, XXXIX, 1942, 495).

It is true that there are no timeless, but only everlasting, values; but unless and until our contingent life has been reduced to the eternal now (of which we can have no sensible experience), every attempt to isolate knowing from valuation (as in the love of art "for art's sake") must have destructive, and even murderous or suicidal consequences; "vile curiosity" and the "love of fine colors and sounds" are the basic motives of the sadist.

34. Guido d'Arezzo, ca. A.D. 1000; cf. Plato, *Phaedrus* 265A.

35. *The Philosophy of "As If,"* about which H. Vaihinger wrote a book with the subtitle *A System of the Theoretical, Practical and Religious Fictions of Mankind,* (English ed., London, 1942), is really of immemorial antiquity. We meet with it in Plato's distinction of probable truth or opinion from truth itself, and in the Indian distinction of relative knowledge (*avidyâ,* ignorance) from knowledge (*vidyâ*) itself. It is taken for granted in the doctrine of multiple meaning and in the *via negativa* in which all relative truths are ultimately denied because of their limited validity. The "philosophy of 'as if'" is markedly developed in Meister Eckhart, who says that "that man never gets to the underlying truth who stops at the enjoyment of its symbol," and that he himself has "always before my mind this little word *quasi*, 'like'" (Evans

ed., I, 186, 213). The "philosophy of 'as if'" is implicit in many uses of *hôsper* (e.g., Hermes, *Lib.* X.7), and Skr. *iva.*

36. Cf. Plato, *Republic* 510DE.

37. Cf. Coomaraswamy, "Ornament." We say above "either ritually or by ornamentation" only because these operations are now, and according to our way of thinking, unrelated: but the artist was once a priest, "chaque occupation est un sacerdoce" (A. M. Hocart, *Les Castes,* Paris, 1938); and in the Christian Sacrifice the use of the "ornaments of the altar" is still a part of the rite, of which their making was the beginning.

38. The distinction of meaning from art, so that what were originally symbols become "art forms," and what were figures of thought, merely figures of speech (e.g., "self-control," no longer based on an awareness that *duo sunt in homine,* viz. the driver and the team) is merely a special case of the aimlessness asserted by the behavioristic interpretation of life. On the modern "philosophy of meaninglessness ... accepted only at the suggestion of the passions" see Aldous Huxley, *Ends and Means* (New York, 1937), pp. 273-277, and I. Jenkins, "The Postulate of an Impoverished Reality" in *Journal of Philosophy,* XXXIX (1942), 533., For the opposition of the linguistic (i.e., intellectual) and the *aesthetic* (i.e., sentimental) conceptions of art, see W. Deonna, *"Primitivisme et classicisme, les deux faces de l'histoire de l'art,"* BAHA, IV (1937); like so many of our contemporaries, for whom the life of the instincts is all-sufficient, Deonna sees in the "progress" from an art of ideas to an art of sensations a favorable "evolution." Just as for Whitehead "it was a tremendous discovery—how to excite emotions for their own sake!"

39. That things can be called after the names of the things impressed upon them is rather well illustrated by the reference of J. Gregory to "coins called by the name of their Expresses, as ... saith Pollux *kai ekaleito bous hoti bous eikôn enteturomenon,* from the figure of an ox imprinted," *Notes and Observations upon Several Passages in Scripture* (London, 1684). Any absolute distinction of the symbol from its referent implies that the symbol is not what Plato means by a "true name," but arbitrarily and conventionally chosen. But symbols are not regarded thus, traditionally; one says that the house *is* the universe in a likeness, rather than that it is a likeness *of* the universe. So in the ritual drama, the performer becomes the deity whose actions he imitates, and only returns to himself when the rite is relinquished: "enthusiasm" meaning that the deity is in him, that he is *entheos* (this is not an etymology).

All that may be nonsense to the rationalist, who lives in a meaningless world; but the end is not yet.

40. *Metaphysics* I.6.4. There can be little doubt that Aristotle had in mind *Timaeus* 51A, where Plato connects *aphomoioô* with *metalambanô.* That the one implies the other is also the opinion to which Socrates assents in *Parmenides* 132E, "That by participation in which (*metechonta*) 'like' things are like (*homoia*), will be their real 'form,' I suppose? Most assuredly." It is not, however, by their "likeness" that things participate in their form, but (as we learn elsewhere) by their proportion or adequacy (*isotês*), i.e., truth of the analogy; a visual likeness of anything to its form or archetype being impossible because the model is invisible; so that, for example, in theology, while it can be said that man is "like" God, it cannot be said that God is "like" man.

Aristotle also says that "thought thinks itself through participation (*metalêpsis*) in its object" (*Metaphysics* XII.7.8). "For participation is only a special case of the problem of communion, of the symbolizing of one thing with another, of mimicry" (R. C. Taliaferro, foreword to Thomas Taylor, *Timaeus and Critias*, New York, 1944, p. 14).

For the sake of Indian readers it may be added that "imitation" is Skr. *anukarana* ("making according to"), and "participation" (*pratilabha* or *bhakti*); and that like Greek in the time of Plato and Aristotle, Sanskrit has no exact equivalent for "expression"; for Greek and Sanskrit both, an idea is rather "manifested" (*dêloô, pra-kâs, vy-añj, vy-â-khyâ*) than "expressed"; in both languages words that mean to "speak" and to "shine" have common roots (cf. our "shining wit," "illustration," "clarify," "declare," and "argument"). Form (*eidos* as *idea*) and presentation (*phainomenon*) are *nâma* (name, quiddity) and *rûpa* (shape, appearance, body); or in the special case of verbal expressions, *artha* (meaning, value), *prayojana* (use), and *sabda* (sound); the former being the intellectual (*mânasa, noêtos*) and the latter the tangible or aesthetic (*sprsya, drsya, aisthêtikos, horatos*) apprehensions.

41. Quintilian IX.4.117, based on Plato, *Timaeus* 80B, where the "composition" is of shrill and deep sound, and this "furnishes pleasure to the unintelligent, and to the intelligent that intellectual delight which is caused by the imitation of the divine harmony manifested in mortal motions" (R. G. Bury's translation, LCL).

13

Samvega: "Aesthetic Shock"

The Pali word *samvega* is often used to denote the shock or wonder that may be felt when the perception of a work of art becomes
a serious experience. In other contexts the root *vij*, with or without
the intensive prefix *sam*, or other prefixes such as *pra*, "forth,"
implies a swift recoil from or trembling at something feared. For
example, the rivers freed from the Dragon, "rush forth" (*pra vivijre,
Rg Veda* X.III.9), *Tvastr* "quakes" (*vevijyate*) at Indra's wrath (*ibid.* I.
80.14), men "tremble" (*samvijante*) at the roar of a lion (*Atharva
Veda* VIII.7.15), birds "are in a tremor" at the sight of a falcon (*ibid.*
VI.21.6); a woman "trembles" (*samvijjati*) and shows agitation
(*samvegam âpajjati*) at the sight of her father-in-law, and so does a
monk who forgets the Buddha (*Majjhima Nikâya*, I.186); a good
horse aware of the whip is "inflamed and agitated" (*âtâpino samveg-
ino, Dhammapada* 144); and as a horse is "cut" by the lash, so may the
good man be "troubled" (*samvijjati*) and show agitation (*samvega*) at
the sight of sickness or death, "because of which agitation he pays
close heed, and both physically verifies the ultimate truth (*parama
saccam*, the 'moral')[1] and presciently penetrates it" (*Anguttara
Nikâya* II.116). "I will proclaim," the Buddha says, "the cause of my
dismay (*samvegam*), wherefore I trembled (*samvijitam mayâ*): it was
when I saw peoples floundering like fish when ponds dry up, when
I beheld man's strife with man, that I felt fear" (or "horror"), and
so it went "until I saw the evil barb that festers in men's hearts"
(*Sutta Nipâta*, 935-938).[2]

The emotional stimulus of painful themes may be evoked deliberately when the will or mind (*citta*) is sluggish, "then he stirs it up
(*samvejeti*) by a consideration of the Eight Emotional Themes"
(*attha-samvega-vatthûni*) (birth, old age, sickness, death and sufferings arising in four other ways); in the resulting state of distress, he
then "gladdens[3] (or thrills, *sampahanseti*, Skr. *hrs*, 'rejoice' etc.) it by
the recollection of the Buddha, the Eternal Law and the
Communion of Monks, when it is in need of such gladdening"

(*Visuddhi Magga*,135). A poignant realization of the transience of natural beauty may have the same effect: in the *Yuvañjaya Jâtaka*, the Crown Prince (*uparâjâ*) "one day early in the morning mounted his splendid chariot and went out in all his great splendor to disport himself in the park. He saw on the treetops, the tips of the grasses, the ends of branches, on every spider's web and thread, and on the points of the rushes, dew-drops hanging like so many strings of pearls." He learns from his charioteer that that is what men call "dew." When he returns in the evening the dew has vanished. The charioteer tells him that that is what happens when the sun rises. When the Prince hears this, he is "deeply moved" (*samvegappatto hutvâ*), and he realizes that "The living constitution of such as we are is just like these drops of dew;[4] I must be rid of disease, old age and death; I must take leave of my parents, and turn to the life of a wandering monk." And so it was that "using as support of contemplation simply a dew-drop (*ussâvabindum eva ârammanam katvâ*) he realized that the Three Modes of Becoming (Conative, Formal, and Informal) are so many blazing fires ... Even as the dew-drop on blades of grass when the sun gets up, such is the life of men" (*Jâtaka* IV.120-122).

Here it is a thing lovely in itself that provides the initial stimulus to reflection, but it is not so much the beautiful thing as it is the perception of its evanescence that induces recollection. On the other hand, the "shock" or "thrill" need not involve a recoil, but may be one of supersensual delight. For example, the cultivation of the Seven Factors of Awakening (to Truth), accompanied by the notion of the Arrest (of the vicious causes of all pathological conditions), of which the seventh is an Impartiality (*upekhâ*)[5] that issues in Deliverance (*vossagga* = *avasarga*), "conduces to great profit, great ease, a great thrill (*mahâ samvega*) and great glee" (*Samyutta Nikâya* V.134).

In it there is "much radical intellection, leading to the full-awakening aspect of delight" (*pîti*) or "contentment (*tutthi*) with the flavor (*rasa*) of the chosen support of contemplation that has been grasped"; body and mind are flooded or suffused; but this joyous emotion, after-effect of the shock, is a disturbance proper only to the earlier phases of contemplation, and is superceded by equanimity (Vis. 135-145).

We are told that Brother Vakkali spent his days in gazing at the beauty of the Buddha's person. The Buddha, however, would have him understand that not he who sees his body, sees himself, but "only he who sees the Dhamma, sees Me"; he realizes that Vakkali will never wake up (*na ... bujjhissati*) unless he gets a shock (*samvegan âlabhitva*); and so forbids Vakkali to follow him. Vakkali seeks to throw himself down from a mountain peak. To prevent this, the Buddha appears to him in a vision, saying, "Fear not, but come (*ehi*), and I shall lift you up." At this, Vakkali is filled with delight (*pîti*); to reach the Master, he springs into the air[6] and, pondering as he goes, he "discards the joyful emotion" and attains the final goal of Arahatta before he descends to earth at the Buddha's feet (DhA, IV.118ff.). It will be seen that the transition from shock (that of the ban) to delight (that of the vision), and from delight to understanding, is clearly presented. Vakkali, at last, is no longer "attached" to the visual and more or less "idolatrous" experience; the aesthetic support of contemplation is not an end in itself, but only an index, and becomes a snare if misused.[7]

So far, then, *samvega* is a state of shock, agitation, fear, awe, wonder or delight induced by some physically or mentally poignant experience. It is a state of feeling, but always more than a merely physical reaction. The "shock" is essentially one of the realization of the implications of what are strictly speaking only the aesthetic surfaces of phenomena that may be liked or disliked as such. The complete experience transcends this condition of "irritability."

It will not, then, surprise us to find that it is not only in connection with natural objects (such as the dew-drop) or events (such as death) but also in connection with works of art, and in fact whenever or wherever perception (*aisthêsis*) leads to a serious experience, that we are really shaken. So we read that "The man of learning (*pandito* = doctor)[8] cannot but be deeply stirred (*samvijjetheva*, i.e. *samvegam kareyya*) by stirring situations (*samvejanîyesu thânesu*). So may an ardent master monk, putting all things to the test of prescience, living the life of peace, and not puffed up, but one whose will has been given its quietus, attain to the wearing out of Ill": there are, in fact, two things that conduce to a monk's well-being, contentment and spiritual continence, viz. his radical premise, and "the thrill that should be felt in thrilling situations" (*Itivuttaka*, 30). We see from this text (and from *Samyutta Nikâya* V.134 cited above) that the "thrill" (*samvega*), experienced under suitable conditions, if it can still in some sense be thought of as an emotion, is by no means merely an interested aesthetic response, but much rather what we so awkwardly term delight of a "disinterested aesthetic contemplation,"—a contradiction in terms, but "you know what I mean."

Now there are, in particular, "Four sightly places whereat the believing clansman should be deeply moved (*cattâri kula-puttassa dassanîyâni samvejanîyâni thânâni*); they are those four in which the layman can say 'Here the Buddha was born!' 'Here he attained to the Total Awakening, and was altogether the Wake!' 'Here did he first set agoing the incomparable Wheel of the Law,' and 'Here was he despirated, with the despiration (*nibbâna*) that leaves no residuum (of occasion of becoming)!' ... And there will come to these places believers, monks and sisters, and layfolk, men and women, and so say ... and those of these who die in the course of their pilgrimage to such monuments (*cetiya*), in serenity of will (*pasannacittâ*) will be regenerated after death in the happy heaven-world" (*Digha Nikâya* II.141, 142, cf. *Aṅguttara Nikâya* I.136, II.120).

As the words *dassanîya* (*darsanîya*) "sightly," "sight-worthy," commonly applied to visible works of art (as *sravanîya*, "worth hearing" is said of audible works), and *cetiya*,[9] "monument," imply, and as we also know from abundant literary and archeological evidence, these four sacred places or stations were marked by monuments, e.g. the still extant Wheel of the Law set up on a pillar in the Deer Park at Benares on the site of the first preaching. Furthermore, as we also know, these pilgrim stations could be substituted for by similar monuments set up elsewhere, or even constructed on such a small scale as to be kept in a private chapel or carried about, to be similarly used as supports of contemplation. The net result is, then, that icons (whether "aniconic," as at first, or "anthropomorphic," somewhat later) serving as reminders of the great moments of the Buddha's life and participating in his essence, are to be regarded as "stations" at the sight of which a "shock" or "thrill" may and should be experienced by monk or layman.

Samvega, then, refers to the experience that may be felt in the presence of a work of art, when we are struck by it, as a horse might be struck by a whip. It is, however, assumed that like the good horse we are more or less trained, and hence that more than a merely physical shock is involved; the blow has a *meaning* for us, and the realization of that meaning, in which nothing of the physical sensation survives, is still a part of the shock. These two phases of the shock are, indeed, normally felt together as parts of an instant experience; but they can be logically distinguished, and since there is nothing peculiarly artistic in the mere sensibility that all men and animals share, it is with the latter aspect of the shock that we are chiefly concerned. In either phase, the external signs of the experience may be emotional, but while the signs may be alike, the conditions they express are unlike. In the first phase, there is really a disturbance, in the second there is the experience of a peace that cannot be described as an emotion in the sense that fear and love or hate are emotions. It is for this reason that Indian rhetoricians have always hesitated to reckon "Peace" (*sânti*) as a "flavor" (*rasa*) in one category with the other "flavors."

In the deepest experience that can be induced by a work of art (or other reminder) our very being is shaken (*samvijita*) to its roots. The "Tasting of the Flavor" that is no longer any one flavor is, as the *Sâhitya Darpana* puts it, "the very twin brother of the tasting of God"; it involves, as the word "disinterested" implies, a self-naughting—*a semetipsa liquescere*—and it is for this reason that it can be described as "dreadful," even though we could not wish to avoid it. For example, it is of this experience that Eric Gill writes that "At the first impact I was so moved by the (Gregorian) chant ... as to be almost frightened ... This was something alive ... I knew infallibly that God existed and was a living God" (*Autobiography*, 1940, p. 187). I have myself been completely dissolved and broken up by the same music, and had the same experience when reading aloud Plato's *Apology*. That cannot have been an "aesthetic" emotion, such as could have been felt in the presence of some insignificant work of art, but represents the shock of conviction that only an intellectual art can deliver, the body-blow that is delivered by any perfect and therefore convincing statement of truth. On the other hand, I must confess that realism in religious art I find only disgusting and not at all moving, and that what is commonly called pathos in art generally makes me laugh; and I dare say there is nothing unusual in that. The point is that a liability to be overcome by the truth has nothing to do with sentimentality; it is well known that the mathematician can be overcome in this way, when he finds a perfect expression that subsumes innumerable separate observations. But this shock can be felt only if we have learned to recognize truth when we see it. I can give one more example, that of Plotinus' overwhelming words, "Do you mean to say that they have seen God and do not remember him? Ah no, it is that they see him now and always. Memory is for those who have forgotten" (*Enneads*, IV.4.6)]. To feel the full force of this "thunderbolt" (*vajra*)[10] one must have had at least an inkling of what is involved in the Platonic and Indian doctrine of Recollection.[11] In the question, "Did He who made the lamb make thee?" there is an incomparably harder blow than there is in "Only God can make a tree," which could as well have been said of a flea or a cutworm. With Socrates,["We cannot give the name of 'art' to anything irrational"] (*Gorgias*, 465A); nor with the Buddhist think of any but significant works of art as "stations where the shock of awe should be felt."

Notes

1. The ultimate significance (*paramârtha-satyam*) as distinguished (*vijñâtam*) from the mere facts in which it is exemplified (see *Pañcavimsa Brâhmana* X.14.5, XIX.6.1 and *Chândogya Upanisad*, VII.16, 17 with Sankarâcârya's Commentary).

2. We also feel the horror; but do we see the barb when we consider Picasso's *Guernica*, or have we "desired peace, but not the things that make for peace"? For the most part, our "aesthetic" approach stands between us and the content of the work of art, of which only the surface concerns us.

3. A learned preacher's discourse is said to convince (*samâdapeti*), inflame (*samuttejeti*) and gladden (*sampahanseti*) the congregation of monks (*Samyutta Nikâya* II.280).

4. The dew-drop is here, as are other symbols elsewhere, a "support of contemplation" (*dhiyâlamba*). The whole passage, with its keen perception of natural beauty and of its lesson anticipates the point of view that is characteristic for Zen Buddhism.

5. The upekkhaka (*upa*+[root] *îks*) corresponds to the preksaka (*pra*+ [root] *îks*) of Maitri Upanisad II.7, i.e. the divine and impartial "looker on" at the drama of which all the world, our "selves" included, is the stage.

6. On levitation (lightness), see Coomaraswamy, *Hinduism and Buddhism*, 1943, n.269, to which much might be added. Other cases of levitation occasioned by delight in the Buddha as support of contemplation occur in Vis. 143-144; the same experience enables the experient to walk on the water (J. II.III). A related association of ideas leads us to speak of being "carried away" or "transported" by joy. In Matthew 14:27-28, the words, "Be not afraid ... Come" are identical with the Pali *ehi, mâ bhayi* in the DhA context.

7. "O take heed, lest thou misconceive me in human shape" (Rûmî, *Dîvân*, Ode XXV). Similarly, Meister Eckhart, "To them his [Christ's] manhood is a hindrance so long as they still cling to it with mortal pleasure"; and "That man never gets to the underlying truth who stops at the enjoyment of its symbol" (Evans ed., I, 186, 187; cf. p.194), and St. Augustine, "It seems to me that the disciples were engrossed by the human form of the Lord Christ, and as men were held to the man by a

human affection. But he wished them to have a divine affection, and thus to make them, from being carnal, spiritual ... Therefore he said to them, I send you a gift by which you will be made spiritual, namely, the gift of the Holy Ghost ... You will indeed cease from being carnal, if the form of the flesh be removed from your eyes, so that the form of God may be implanted in your hearts" (*Sermo* CCLXX.2). The "form" of the Buddha that he wished Vakkali to see, rather than that of the flesh, was, of course, that of the Dhamma, "which he who sees, sees Me" (S. III.120). St. Augustine's words parallel those of the *Prema Sâgara*, chs. 48 and 49, where Srî Krishna, having departed, sends Udho with the message to the milk-maids at Brindâban that they are no longer to think of him as a man, but as God, ever immanently present in themselves, and never absent.

8. *Docti rationem componendi intelligunt, etiam indocti voluptatem* (Quintillian, IX.4.116, based on Plato, *Timaeus* 80B). *Nam, qui canit quod non sapit, diffinitur bestia ... Non verum facit ars cantorem, sed documentum* (Guido d'Arezzo).

9. On the different kinds of *cetiya,* and their function as substitutes for the visible presence of the *Deus absconditus,* see the *Kâlingabodhi Jâtaka* (IV.228) and my "The Nature of Buddhist Art" in Rowland and Coomaraswamy, *Wall-paintings of Central Asia, India and Ceylan,* Boston, 1938.

10. "The 'thunderbolt' is a hard saying that hits you in the eye" (*vajram pratyak-sanisthuram*), *Dasarûpa* I.64. Cf. St. Augustine's "O axe, hewing the rock!"

11. Cf. *Meno* 81C and *Phaedrus* 248C.

14

What is Civilization?

From Albert Schweitzer's own writings it is clear that, aside from his more active life of good works, his theoretical interest centers in the questions: What is civilization? And how can it be restored? For, of course, he sees very clearly that the modern "civilized world," so self-styled, is not really a civilized world at all, but as he calls it, a world of "Epigoni," inheritors, rather than creators of any positive goods.

To the question: What is civilization? I propose to contribute a consideration of the intrinsic meanings of the words "civilization," "politics" and "purusa." The root in "civilization" is *kei*, as in Greek, *keisthai*, Sanskrit *sî*, to "lie," "lie outstretched," "be located in." A city is thus a "lair," in which the citizen "makes his bed" on which he must lie. We shall presently ask "Who?" thus inhabits and "economises." The root in "politics" is *pla* as in Gr. *pimplêmi*, Skr. *pr(piparmi)* to "fill," Gr. *polis*, Skr. *pur*, "city," "citadel," "fortress," Lat. *plenum*, Skr. *pûrnam*, and English "fill." The roots in *purusa* are these two and the intrinsic meaning therefore that of "citizen," either as "man" (this man, So-and-so) or as the Man (in this man, and absolutely); in either way, the *purusa* is the "person" to be distinguished by his powers of foresight and understanding from the animal man (*pasu*) governed by his "hunger and thirst."[1]

In Plato's thought there is a cosmic city of the world, the city state, and an individual body politic, all of which are communities (Gr. *koinônia*, Skr. *gana*). "The same castes (Gr. *genos*, Skr. *jâti*), equal in number are to be found in the city and in the soul (or self) of each of us";[2] the principle of justice is the same throughout, viz. that each member of the community should perform the tasks for which he is fitted by nature; and the establishment of justice and well-being of the whole in each case depends upon the answer to the question, Which shall rule, the better or the worse, a single Reason and Common Law or the multitude of moneyed men in the outer city and of desires in the individual (*Republic*, 441, etc.)?

Who fills, or populates, these cities? Whose are these cities, "ours" or God's? What is the meaning of "self-government"? (a question that, as Plato shows, *Republic*, 436B, implies a distinction of governor from governed). Philo says that "As for lordship (*kyriôs*), God is the only citizen" (*monos polites*, *Cher.* 121), and this is almost identical with the words of the Upanisad, "This Man (*purusa*) is the citizen (*purusaya*) in every city," (*sarvasu pûrsu, Brhadâranyanka Up.*, II.5.18), and must not be thought of as in any way contradicted by Philo's other statement, that "Adam" (not "this man," but the true Man) is the "only citizen of the world" (*monos kosmopolites*), *Opif.* 142). Again, "This city (*pur* is these worlds, the Person (*purusa*)) is the Spirit (*yo'yam pavate* =*Vâyu*), who because he inhabits (*sete*) this city is called the "Citizen" (*puru-sa*)," *Satapatha Brâhmana*, XIII.6.2.1—as in *Atharva Veda*, X.2.30, where "He who knoweth Brahma's city, whence the Person (*puru-sa*) is so-called, him neither sight nor the breath of life desert ere old age," but now the "city" is that of this body, and the "citizens" its God-given powers.

These macrocosmic and microcosmic points of view are interdependent; for the "acropolis," as Plato calls it, of the city is within you and literally at the "heart" of the city. "What is within this City of God (*brahmapura*, this man) is a shrine[3] and what therein is Sky and Earth, Fire and the Gale, Sun and Moon, whatever is possest or unpossest; everything here is within it." The question arises, What then is left over (survives) when this "city" dies of old age or is destroyed? and the answer is that what survives is That which ages not with our inveteration, and is not slain when "we" are killed; *That* is the "*true* City of God";[4] *That* (and by no means this perishable city that we think of as "our" self) is our Self, unaging and immortal,[5] unaffected by "hunger and thirst," (*Chândogya Up.* VIII.1.1-5, slightly abbreviated), "That art thou" (*ibid.* VI.8.7); and "Verily, he who sees That, contemplates That, discriminates That, he whose game and sport, dalliance and beatitude are in and with that Self (*âtman*), he is autonomous (*sva-râj, kreittôn heautou*, self-governing), he moveth at will in every world;[6] but those whose knowing is of what is other-than-That are heteronyomous (*anyarâj, hettôn heautou*, subject), they move not at will in any world" (*ibid.* VII.25.2).

Thus at the heart of this City of God inhabits (*sete*) the omniscient, immortal Self, "this self's immortal Self and Duke," as the Lord of all, the Protector of all, the Ruler of all beings and the Inward Controller of all the powers of the soul by which he is surrounded, as by subjects,[7] and "to Him (*Brahma*), thus proceeding in Person (*purusa*), as he lies there extended (*uttânâya sayânaye*), and enthroned (*brahmâsandhîm ârûdhâ, atrasada*), the powers of the soul (*devatâ, prânâ*), voice, mind, sight, hearing, scent, bring tribute."[8]

The word "extended" here states a meaning already implied in the etymology of the "city," *kei* including the sense to lie at full length or outstretched.[9] The root in "extended" and *ut-tâna* is that in Gr. *teinô* and Skr. *tan*, to extend, prolong, in Gr. *tonos*, a string, and hence also, tone, and in *tenuis*, Skr. *tanu*, thin.

Not only are these worlds a city, or am "I" a city, but these are populated cities, and not waste lands, because He fills them, being "one as he is in himself there, and many in his children here" (*Satapatha Brâhmana*, X.5.2.16). "That dividing itself, unmeasured times, fills (*pûrayati*)[10] these worlds ... from It continually proceed all animate beings" (*Maitri Up.* V.26). Or with specific reference to the powers of the soul within the individual city, "He, dividing himself fivefold, is concealed in the cave (of the heart) ... Thence, having broken forth the doors of the sensitive powers, He proceeds to the fruition of experience ... And so this body is set up in the possession of consciousness, He is its driver" (*ibid.* II.6.d).[11] This "division," however, is only as it were, for He remains "undivided in divided beings" (*Bhagavad Gîtâ*, XIII.16, XVII.20), "uninterrupted" (*anantaram*) and thus is to be understood as an undivided and total presence.

The "division," in other words, is not a segmentation, but an extension, as of radii from a center or rays of light from a luminous source with which they are con-tinuous.[12] Con-*tin*uity and in*tens*ity (*samtati, syntonia*) are, indeed, a necessary quality in whatever can be tensed and extended but, like the immanent Spirit, "cannot be severed" (*acchedya, Bhagavad Gîtâ*, II.23)—"no part of that which is divine cuts itself off and becomes separated, but only extends (*ekteinetai=vitanute*) itself" (Philo, *Det.* 90). It is then, the same thing to say that the Person "fills" these worlds as to say that Indra saw this Person "as the most widely extended (*tatamam*) Brahma" (*Aitareya Âranyaka*, II.4.3). In this way all the powers of the soul, projected by the mind towards their objects, are "extensions" (*tetomena*) of an invisible principle (*Republic*, 462E), and it is this "tonic power" by which it is enabled to perceive them (Philo, *Leg. Alleg.* I.30, 37). Our "constitution" is a habitation that the Spirit makes for itself "just as a goldsmith draws-out-for-himself (*tanute*) from the gold another shape" (*Brhadâranyaka Up.* IV.4.4).[13]

This is an essential aspect of the "thread-spirit" (*sûtrâtman*) doctrine, and as such the intelligible basis of that of the divine omniscience and providence, to which our partial knowledge and foresight are analogous. The spiritual Sun (not that "sun whom all men see" but that "whom few know with the mind," *Atharva Veda*, X. 8.14)[14] is the Self of the whole universe, (*Rg Veda*, I.11.5.1) and is connected to all things in it by the "thread" of his luminous pneumatic rays, on which the "tissue" of the universe is woven—"all this universe is strung on Me, like rows of gems on a thread" (*Bhagavad Gîtâ*, VII.7); of which thread, running through our intellect, the ultimate strands are its sensitive powers, as we have already seen.[15] So, just as the noonday sun "sees" all things under the sun at once, the "Person in the Sun," the Light of lights, from the exalted point and center "wherein every where and every when is focused" (*Paradiso*, XXIX.23) is simultaneously present to every experience, here or there, past or future, and "not a sparrow falls to the ground" or ever has or ever will without his present knowledge. He is, in fact, the only seer, thinker, etc., in us (*Brhadâranyaka Up.* III.8.23), and whoever sees or thinks, etc., it is by His "ray" that he does so (*Jaiminîya Up. Brâhmana*, I.28, 29).

Thus, in the human City of God which we are considering as a political pattern, the sensitive and discriminating powers form, so to speak, a body of guardsmen by which the Royal Reason is conducted to the perception of sense objects, and the heart is the guardroom where they take their orders (Plato, *Timaeus*, 70B, Philo, *Opif.* 139, *Spec.* IV.22 etc.). These powers—however referred to as Gods,[16] Angels, Aeons, Maruts, Rsis, Breaths, Daimons, etc.—are the people (*visa*, yeomanry, etc.) of the heavenly kingdom, and related to their Chief (*vispati*) as are thanes to an Earl or ministers to a King; they are a troop of the "King's Own" (*svâ*), by which he is surrounded as if by a crown of glory—"upon whose head the Aeons are a crown of glory darting forth rays" (*Coptic Gnostic Treatise*, XII), and "by 'thy glory' I understand the powers that form thy bodyguard" (Philo, *Spec.* II, 45).[17] The whole relationship is one of feudal loyalty, the subjects bringing tribute and receiving largesse—"Thou art ours and we are thine" (*Rg Veda*, VIII.92.32), "Thine may we be for thee to give us treasure" (*ibid.* V.85.8, etc.).[18]

What must never be forgotten is that all "our" powers are not our "own," but *delegated* powers and ministries through which the royal Power is "exercised" (another sense of Gr. *teino*); the powers of the soul "are only the names of His acts" (*Brhadâranyaka Up.* I.4.7, 1.5.21,. etc.).[19] It is not for them to serve their own or one another's self-interests—of which the only result will be the tyranny of the majority, and a city divided against itself, man against man and class against class—but to serve Him whose sole interest is that of the common body politic. Actually, in the numerous accounts we have of a contest for precedence amongst the powers of the soul, it is always found that none of the members or powers is indispensable to the life of the bodily city, except only their Head, the Breath and immanent Spirit.

The right and natural life of the powers of the soul is then, precisely, their function of bringing tribute to their fountain-head, the controlling Mind and very Self, as man brings sacrificial offerings to an altar, keeping for themselves only what remains. It is the task of each to perform the functions from which it is fitted by nature, the eye seeing, the ear hearing, all of which functions are necessary to the well-being of the community of the whole man but must be co-ordinated by a disinterested power that cares for all. For unless this community can act unanimously, as one man, it will be working at all sorts of cross purposes. The concept is that of a corporation in which the several members of a community work together, each in its own way; and such a vocational society is an organism, not an aggregate of competing interests and consequently unstable "balance of power."

Thus the human City of God contains within itself the pattern of all other societies and of a true civilization. The man will be a "just" (Gr. *dikaios*) man when each of his members performs its own appropriate task and is subject to the ruling Reason that exercises forethought on behalf of the whole man; and in the same way the public city will be just when there is agreement as to which shall rule, and there is no confusion of functions but every occupation is a vocational responsibility. Not, then, where there are no "classes" or "castes" but where everyone is a responsible agent in some special field.[20] A city can no more be called a "good" city if it lacks this "justice" (*dikaiosynê*) than it could be were it wanting wisdom, sobriety or courage; and these four are the great civic virtues. Where occupations are thus vocations "more will be done, and better done, and with more ease than in any other way" (*Republic*, 370C). But "if one who is by nature a craftsman or some sort of businessman be tempted and inflated by wealth or by his command of votes or by his own might or any such thing, and tries to handle military matters, or if a soldier tries to be a counselor or guardian, for which he is unfitted, and if these men interchange their tools and honors, or if one and the same man tries to handle all these functions at once, then, I take it, you too hold that this sort of perversion and being jack-of-all-trades will be the ruin of the city"; and this is "injustice" (*Republic*, 434B).

Thus the ideal society is thought of as a kind of co-operative work-shop in which production is to be for use and not for profit, and all human needs, both of the body and the soul, are to be provided for. Moreover, if the command is to be fulfilled, "Be ye perfect even as your Father in heaven is perfect," the work must be *perfectly* done.[21] The arts are not directed to the advantage of anything but their object (*Republic*, 432B), and that is that the thing made should be as perfect as possible for the purpose for which it is made. This purpose is to satisfy a human need (*Republic*, 369B, C); and so the perfectionism required, although not "altruistically" motivated, actually "serves humanity" in a way that is impossible where goods are made for sale rather than for use, and in quantity rather than quality. In the light of Plato's definition of "justice" as vocational occupation we can the better understand the words, "Seek first the kingdom of God and his *justice*, and these things shall be added unto you" (Matthew, 6:33).

The Indian philosophy of work is identical. "Know that action arises from Brahma. He who on earth doth not follow in his turn the wheel thus revolving liveth in vain; therefore, without attachment to its rewards, ever be doing what should be done, for, verily, thus man wins the Ultimate. There is nothing I needs must do, or anything attainable that is not already mine; and yet I mingle in action. Act thou, accordingly, with a view to the welfare of the world; for whatever the superior does, others will also do; the standard he sets up, the world will follow. Better is one's own norm,[22] however deficient, than that of another well done; better to die at one's own post, that of another is full of fear ... Vocations are determined by one's own nature. Man attains perfection through devotion to his own work. How? By praising Him in his own work, from whom is the unfolding of all beings and by whom this whole universe is extended (*tatam*, <*tan*). Better is a man's own work, even with its faults, than that of another well done; he who performs the task that his own nature lays upon him incurs no sin; one should never abandon his inherited[23] vocation."[24]

On the one hand the inspired tradition rejects ambition, competition and quantitive standards; on the other, our modern "civilization" is based on the notions of social advancement, free enterprise (devil take the hindmost) and production in quantity. The one considers man's needs, which are "but little here below"; the other considers his wants, to which no limit can be set, and of which the number is artificially multiplied by advertisement. The manufacturer for profits must, indeed, create an ever-expanding world market for his surplus produced by those whom Dr. Schweitzer calls "over-occupied men." It is fundamentally, the incubus of world trade that makes of industrial "civilizations" a "curse to humanity," and from the industrial concept of progress "in line with the manufacturing enterprise of civilization" that modern wars have arisen and will arise; it is on the same impoverished soil that empires have grown, and by the same greed that innumerable civilizations have been destroyed—by Spaniards in South America, Japanese in Korea and by "white shadows in the South Seas."[25]

Dr. Schweitzer himself records that "it is very hard to carry to completion a colonisation which means at the same time a true civilization ... The machine age brought upon mankind conditions of existence which made the possession of civilization difficult[26] ... Agriculture and handicraft are the foundation of civilization ... Whenever the timber trade is good, permanent famine reigns in the Ogowe region[27] ... They live on imported rice and imported preserved foods which they purchase with the proceeds of their labour ... thereby making home industry impossible ... As things are, the world trade which has reached them is a fact against which we and they are powerless."[28]

I do not consent to this picture of a *deus*, or much rather *diabolus, ex machina*, coupled as it is with a confession of impotence.[29] If, indeed, our industrialism and trade practice are the mark of our uncivilization, how dare we propose to help others "to attain a condition of well-being"? The "burden" is of our own making and bows our own shoulders first. Are we to say that because of "economic determination" we are "impotent" to shake it off and stand up straight? That would be to accept the status of "Epigoni" once and for all, and to admit that our influence can only lower others to our own level.[30]

As we have seen, in a true civilization, *laborare est orare.* But industrialism—"the mammon of in-justice" (Gr. *adikia*)—and civilization are incompatible. It has often been said that one can be a good Christian even in a factory; it is no less true that one could be an even better Christian in the arena. But neither of these facts means that either factories or arenas are Christian or desirable institutions. Whether or not a battle of religion against industrialism and world trade can ever be won is no question for us to consider; our concern is with the task and not with its reward; our business is to be sure that in any conflict we are on the side of Justice.[31] Even as things are, Dr. Schweitzer finds his best excuse for colonial government in the fact that to some extent (however slightly) such governments protect subject peoples "from the merchant." Why not protect ourselves (the "guinea-pigs" of a well known book) 'from the merchant'? Would it not be better if, instead of tinkering with the inevitable consequences of "world trade," we considered its cause, and set about to re-form (*Wideraufbauen* is Schweitzer's word) our own "civilization"? Or shall the uncivilized for ever pretend to "civilizing missions"?

To reform what has been deformed means that we must take account of an original "form," and that is what we have tried to do in historical analysis of the concept of civilization, based on Eastern and Western sources. Forms are by definition invisible to sense. The form of our *City of God* is one "that exists only in words, and nowhere on earth, but is, it seems, laid up in heaven for whomsoever will to contemplate, and as he does so, to inhabit; it can be seen only by the true philosophers who bend their energies towards those studies that nourish rather soul than body and never allow themselves to be carried away by the congratulations of the mob or without measure to increase their wealth, the source of measureless evils[32] but rather fix their eyes upon their own interior politics, never aiming to be politicians in the city of their birth" (*Republic,* 591 E, F).

Is not Plato altogether right when he proposes to entrust the government of cities to "the uncorrupted remnant of true philosophers who now bear the stigma of uselessness"[33] or even to those who are now in power "if by some divine inspiration[34] a genuine love of true philosophy should take possession of them": and altogether right when he maintains that "no city ever can be happy unless its outlines have been drawn by draughtsmen making use of the divine pattern" (*Republic*, 499, 500)—that of the City of God that is in heaven and "within you"?[35]

Notes

1. As in *Aitareya Âranyaka*, II.3.2 and Boethius, *Contra Eutychen*.

2. Plato's Immortal Soul (Self), and two parts of the mortal soul (self), together with the body itself, make up the normal number of "four castes" that must co-operate for the benefit of the whole community.

3. The kingdom of God is within you" (Luke 17: 21); *en hautô politeia* (*Republic*, 591 E). The King survives his kingdoms and "lives forever." Just as, in the traditional theory of government, the Kingship immanent in kings antecedes them and survives them, "le roi est mort, vive le roi."

4. Plato's *polis en logois* (Skr. *srute*), *kaimenê epei ges ge oudamou* (*Republic* 592A).

5. That eternally youthful Spiritual-Self of which whoever is a Comprehensor has no fear of death (*Atharva Veda*, X.8.44).

6. This liberty, so often spoken of in the Vedic tradition from *Rg Veda*, IX.123.9 onwards, corresponds to the Platonic term *autokinêsis* (*Phaedrus*, 245D, *Laws*, 895BC) and to John, 10: 9 "shall go in and out, and find pasture."

7. BU. III.8.23, IV.4.22, *Katha Up.* II.18, *Mund Up.* II.2.6. 7, *Maitri Up.* VI.7, etc.

8. *Jaiminîya Up. Brâhmana*, IV, 23.7-23.10, somewhat condensed.

9. The divine extension in the three dimensional space of the world that is thus filled is a cosmic crucifixion to which the local crucifixion in two dimensions corresponds. To the extent that we think of Him as really divided up by this extension, i.e. to the extent that we conceive of our being as "our own," we crucify him daily.

10. Causative of *pr*, the root in *pûr* and so "populates" or even "civilizes."

11. *Psyche men estin hê periagousa hêmôn pantôn, Laws*, 898C; Questi nei cor mortali é permotore, *Paradiso*, I.116; "the heart has pulled the reins of the five senses" (Rûmî, *Mathnawî*, I.3275). Throughout the Vedic tradition (most explicitly in *Katha Up.* III.3 f. and *Jâtaka*, VI. 242) as in Plato, (*Phaedrus*, 246f). Philo, (*Leg. Alleg.* I.72, 73, III. 224, *Spec.* IV. 79, etc.) and Boethius, etc., man's constitution in which the spiritual Self-of-all-beings rides as passenger for so long as the vehicle holds together, mind (*manas, nous*) holds the reins; but being twofold, clean or unclean, disinterested or interested, may either control or be run away with by the team of the senses. The "chariot," "city," "ship" and "puppet" symbols are equivalent, so that, for example, "when Mind as charioteer rules the whole living being, as a governor does a city, then life holds a straight course." (Philo, *Leg. Alleg.* III.224, cf. *Rg Veda*, VI.75.6). The whole conception of *yoga* (*yuj*, to "yoke," "harness," "join") is connected with the symbolism of the chariot and team; we still speak of "bridling" our passions.

12. Hence *viraj*, literally "distributive shining" = "ruling power."

13. Gold in such contexts is not a figure of speech, but of thought, Gold "is" (we should now say "means") light, life, immortality (*Satapatha Brâhmana, passim,* and traditionally); and to "refine" this "gold" is to burn away from our spiritual Self the dross of all that is not-Self. Hence it is a "golden" cord by which the human puppet is rightly guided (Plato, *Laws,* 644) and Blake gives us a "golden" string that "will lead you in at heaven's gate."

14. "Sun of the sun," *Mahâbhârata,* V. 46.3 and Philo, *Spec.* I.279; "invisible light perceptible only by mind," Philo, *Opif.* 31; "whose body the sun is, who controls the sun from within," *Brhadâranyaka Up.* III. 7.9; "whose body is seen by all, his soul by none," Plato, *Laws,* 898 D; "Light of lights," *Bhagavad Gîtâ,* X. 11. 17;, *Rg Veda,* I. 113.1; "that was the true Light ... of the world," John, 1:9, 9:5; "the Sun of men," *Rg Veda,* I. 146, 4 and "Light of men," John, 1:4, "seated in every heart," *Bhagavad Gîtâ,* XIII.17, *Maitri Up,* VI. 1.

15. We cannot expound the "thread-spirit" doctrine at length here. In the European tradition it can be traced from Homer to Blake. For some of the references see my "Primitive Mentality," *Quarterly Journal of the Mythic Society,* XXXI, 1940 and *"Literary Symbolism"* in the *Dictionary of World Literature,* 1943. See Philo, *Immut.* 35 and *passim;* also my "Spiritual Paternity and the Puppet Complex" in *Psychiatry,* VIII, 1945, reprinted A. K. Coomaraswamy, *The Bugbear of Literacy,* 1947.

16. Or Sons of God. Cf. Boehme, *Signatura Rerum,* XIV. 5 "Each angelical prince is a property out of the voice of God, and bears the great name of God." It is with reference to these powers that it is said that "All these Gods are in me" (*Jaiminîya Upanisad Brâhmana,* I. 14.2), that "All things are full of Gods" (Thales, cited Plato, *Laws,* 899 B) and that "Making the Man (*purusa*) their mortal house, the Gods indwelt him" (*Atharva Veda,* XI. 8.18); accordingly, "He is indeed initiated, whose 'Gods within him' are initiated, mind by Mind, voice by Voice" etc. (*Kausîtaki Brâhmana,* VII. 4). We need hardly say that such a multiplicity of Gods—"tens and thousands"—is not a polytheism, for all are the angelic subjects of the Supreme Deity from whom they originate and in whom, as we are so often reminded, they again "become one." Their operation is an epiphany (*Kausîtaki Up.* II. 12. 13.— "This Brahma, verily, shines when one sees with the eye, and likewise dies when one does not see"). These "Gods" are Angels, or as Philo calls them, the Ideas—i.e. Eternal Reasons.

17. The double meaning of Gr., *stephanos* must be remembered: (1) as "crown" and (2) as city "wall"; thus both a glory and a defense. "Children are a man's crown, towers of the 'city' (*Homeric Epigrams,* XIII). In the same way Pali *cûlikâ,* usually "turban," is also a "city wall," as in *Samyutta Nikâya,* II. 182 *nagaram ... cûlikâ-baddham.*

Philo's interpretation of the "glory" has an exact equivalent in India, where the powers of the soul are "glories" (*sriyah*) and collectively "the kingdom, the power and the glory" (*srî*) of their royal possessors; and, accordingly, the whole science of government is one of the control of these powers (*Arthasâstra,* 1. 6; see my *Spiritual Authority and Temporal Power in the Indian Theory of Government,* 1942, p. 86). *Non potest aliquis habere ordinatam familiam, nisi ipse sit ordinatus* [one cannot have discipline in his family, unless he (first) have it in himself], St. Bonaventura, *De don. S. S.* IV. 10. V, p. 475, being applicable to everyone who proposes to govern himself, a city or a kingdom.

18. On *bhakti* ("devotion," or perhaps better "fealty," and literally "participation") as

a reciprocal relationship, see my *Spiritual Authority and Temporal Power in the Indian Theory of Government*, 1942, note 5, and my *Hinduism and Buddhism*, 1943, p.20.

19. "'I' do nothing, so should deem the harnessed man, the knower of Ultimate Reality" (*Bhagavad Gîtâ*, V. 8). "I do nothing of myself" (John 8: 28, cf. 5:19). To think that "I" do" (*kartò' ham iti*) or "'I'" think" is an infatuation, Philo's *oiêsis* (*Leg. Alleg.* 1.47, 2.68, 3.33) and Indian *abhimâna*. The proposition *Cogito ergo sum* is a *non sequitur* and non-sense; the true conclusion being *Cogito ergo EST* with reference to Him "who Is" (Damascene, *De fid. orthod.* I; *Katha Up.* VI.12; *Milinda Pañha* p. 73) and can alone say "I" (Meister Eckhart, Pfeiffer, p. 261). Cf. also the references in my "*Âkimcaññâ: Self-Naughting*," *New Ind. Antiquary* 1940.

> *Nichts anders stürzet dich in Höllenschlund hinein*
> *Als das verhasste Wort (merk's wohl!): das Mein and Dein*

Nothing else will so readily cast one into the jaws of Hell as the detestable words (mark them well!) mine and thine (Angelus Silesius, *Der Cherubinische Wandersmann*, V. 238).

20. In which case, *every* occupation is a profession; not merely a way of earning one's living, but a "way of life," to abandon which is to die a death. "The man who has shifted, easily and unworried so long as the pay was good, from one job to another, has no deep respect for himself" (Margaret Mead, *And Keep Your Powder Dry*, p. 222).

21. It is a commonplace of medieval theory that the craftsman's primary concern is with the good of the work to be done, and this means that it must be at the same time *pulcher et aptus* (beautiful and appropriate). A Buddhist text defining the entelechies of the different vocational groups calls that of the householder whose support is an art "perfected work," *Anguttara Nikâya*, III.363.

22. *Sva-dharma = sva-karma*, Plato's *ta heautou prattein, kata physin*. *Dharma* is a pregnant term, difficult to translate in the present context; cf. *eidos* in *Republic* 434A. In general, *dharma* (literally "support," *dhr* as in *dhruva*, "fixed," "Pole Star," and Gr. *thronos*) is synonymous with "Truth." Than this ruling principle there is "nothing higher" (*Brhadâranyaka Up.* I.4.14); *dharma* is the "king's King" (*Anguttara Nikâya*, I.109), i.e. "King of kings"; and there can be no higher title than that of *dharma-râjâ*, "King of justice." Hence the well-known designation of the veritable Royalty as Dharmarâjâ, to be distinguished from the personality of the king in whom it temporarily inheres. One's "own dharma" is precisely Plato's "justice," viz. to perform the task for which one is naturally equipped. Justice, Gr. *dikê* (Skr. [root] *dis*, to "indicate") represents in the same way the ultimate Index and standard by which all action must be judged. Dharma is *lex aeterna*, sva-dharma *lex naturalis*.

23. For our tradition, procreation is a "debt," and its purpose is to maintain the continuity of ministerial functions in a stable society (see my *Hinduism and Buddhism*, 1943, note 146). For only so can the bases of civilization be preserved.

24. *Bhagavad Gîtâ*, III.15–35 and XVIII.18–48, slightly abbreviated.

25. Cf. My "Am I my Brother's Keeper?", *Asia and the Americas*, March 1943, reprinted in *The Bugbear of Literacy*, 1947.

26. "The machine ... is the achievement of which man is capable if he relies entirely on himself—God is no longer needed ... Eventually ... (it) transforms him into a machine himself" (Ernst Niekisch, quoted by Erich Meissner in *Germany in Peril*, 1942).

27. "When nations grow old, the arts grow cold, and commerce settles on every tree" (William Blake).

28. Albert Schweitzer, *Zwischen Wasser und Urwald*, cited in his *My Life and Thought*.

29. "I have no more faith than a grain of mustard seed in the future history of 'civilization,' which I *know* now is doomed to destruction: what a joy it is to think of!" (William Morris). "For by civilized men we now mean industrialised men, mechanised societies ... We call all men civilized, if they employ the same mechanical techniques to master the physical world. And we call them so because we are certain that as the physical world is the only reality and as it only yields to mechanical manipulation, that is the only way to behave. Any other conduct can only spring from illusion; it is the behaviour of an ignorant, simple savage. To have arrived at this picture of reality is to be truly advanced, progressive, civilized" (Gerald Heard, *Man the Master*, 1937, p. 25). It is also to have arrived at what has properly been called a "world of impoverished reality" (Iredell Jenkins), and one that can only impoverish those to whom we communicate it.

30. Cf. A. J. Krzesinski, *Is Modern Culture Doomed?* 1942, especially Msgr. G. B. O'Toole's Introduction, and Znaniecki as cited on p.54 note; and Eric Gill, *It All Goes Together*, 1944.

31. Whoever owns a single share in any manufacturing enterprise for profit is to that extent taking sides and to that extent responsible for world trade and all its consequences.

32. The body, for the sake of which we desire wealth, is the ultimate cause of all wars (*Phaedo*, 66 c); and "victory breeds hatred, because the conquered are unhappy" (*Dhammapada*, 201). World trade and world war are congeneric evils. Whatever we have said about the government of men and cities will apply, of course, to a government of the world by cooperative and disinterested nations. Every attempt to establish "balances of power" must end in war.

33. *Noblesse oblige.* In a city that has fostered "true philosophers" the latter owe it to their fosterers to participate in civic affairs and so in the traditional theory of government it is incumbent upon the representatives of the spiritual authority to oversee and guide those who exercise the temporal power; to see to it, in other words, that might supports right, and does not assert itself. On the function of such philosophers in the regeneration of modern society, cf. Gerald Heard, *Man the Master*, and Aldous Huxley, *Ends and Means*, 1937.

34. I suppose that in the history of criticism nothing more inane has ever been propounded than Paul Shorey's comment, "But we must not attribute personal *superstition* to Plato" (Loeb ed. p. 64). Solecisms such as this must be expected whenever nominalists set out to expound the doctrine of realistic philosophers, but *why* do men set out to expound philosophies in which they do not believe?

35. The work to be done is primarily one of purgation, to drive out the money changers, all who *desire* power and office, and all representatives of special interests; and secondly, when the city has been thus "cleaned up," one of considered imitation of the natural forms of justice, beauty, wisdom and other civic virtues; amongst which we have here considered justice, or as the word *dikaiosynê* is commonly translated in Christian contexts, righteousness.

It may be, as Plato says, very difficult "to bring about such a change of mind as is required if we are to 'progress' *in this way*," but as he also says, it is "not impossible"; and so we may "not cease from Mental Fight ... till we have built Jerusalem."

15

The Nature of "Folklore" and "Popular Art"

A sharp distinction is commonly drawn between "learning" and folklore, "high art" and popular art; and it is quite true that under present conditions the distinction is valid and profound. Factual science and personal or academic art on the one hand, and "superstition" and "peasant art" on the other are indeed of different orders, and pertain to different levels of reference.

We seem to find that a corresponding distinction has been drawn in India between the constituted (*samskrta*) and provincial (*desî*) languages and literatures, and between a highway (*mârga*) and a local or byway (*desî*) art; and what is *samskrta* and *mârga* being always superior to what is *desî*, an apparent parallel is offered to the modern valuation of learning and academic art and relative disparagement of superstition and folk art. When, for example, we find in *Samgîtadarpana*, I. 4-6, "The ensemble of music (*samgîtam*) is of two kinds, highway (*mârga*) and local (*desî*); that which was followed after by Siva (*druhinena*)[1] and practicsed (*prayuktam*) by Bharata is called 'highway' and bestows liberation (*vimukti-dam*); but that which serves for worldly entertainment (*lokânurañjakam*) in accordance with custom (*desasthayâ-rityâ*) is called 'local,'" and when similarly the *Dasarûpa*, I. 15, distinguishes *mârga* from *desî* dancing, the first being "that which displays the meanings of words by means of gestures,"[2] it is generally assumed that the modern distinction of "art" from "folk" music is intended. It is also true that the modern *ustâd* looks down upon what are actually folk-songs, very much in the same way that the academic musician of modern Europe looks down upon folk music, although in neither case is there an entire want of appreciation.

A pair of passages parallel to those above can advantageously be cited. In the *Jaiminîya Brâhmana*, II. 69–70, where Prajâpati and Death conduct opposing sacrifices,[3] the protagonists are aided by two "armies" or "parties," Prajâpati's consisting of the chanted lauds, recitative, and ritual acts (the sacerdotal art), and Death's of "what was sung to the harp, enacted (*nrtyate*),[4] or done, by way of mere entertainment" (*vrthâ*). When Death has been overcome, he resorts to the women's house (*patnîsâlâ*), and it is added that what had been his "party" are now "what people sing to the harp, or enact, or do, to please themselves" (*vrthâ*). In the *Sukranîtisâra*, IV. 4. 73-76, we find that whereas the making of images of deities is "conducive to the world of heavenly light," or "heavenward leading" (*svargya*), the making of likenesses of men, with however much skill, is "non-conducive to the world of heavenly light" (*asvargya*). The common reference of *vrthâ* (lit. "heretical" in the etymological sense of this word) and *asvargya* here to what is connoted by our word *desî*, previously cited, will be evident.

A similar distinction of sacred from profane musical art is drawn in *Satapatha Brâhmana*, III. 2. 4, in connection with the seduction of Vâc, who is won over from the Gandharvas by the Devas; Vâc, the feminine principle, turns away from the Vedic recitations and the hymnody and lauds in which the Gandharvas are occupied, and turns to the harp-playing and singing with which the mundane Devas propose to please her. It is significant that whereas the Gandharvas invite her attention by saying, "We verily know, we know," what is offered by the gods is to "give you pleasure" (*tvâ pramoday-isyâma*). And so, as the text expresses it, Vâc indeed inclined to the gods, but she did so "vainly" (*mogham*), inasmuch as she turned away from those who were occupied with celebration and laudation, to the dancing and singing of the gods. And "This is why women even here and now (*itarhi*) are addicted to vanity (*mogham-samhitâh*), for Vâc inclined thereto, and other women do as she did. And so it is that they take a liking most readily to one who sings and dances" (*nrtyati, gâyati*).[5] It is quite clear that *mogham* here corresponds to *vrthâ* in the *Jaiminîya* text, and that in both cases the worldly and feminine arts of mere amusement are contrasted with the sacred liturgical arts. It is also perfectly clear that the worldly arts of mere amusement are regarded literally as "deadly"—it must not be forgotten that "all that is under the sun is under the sway of death" (*mrtyun-âptam, Satapatha Br.*, X. 5. 1. 4)—and that such disparagement of the arts as can be recognized in Indian thought (especially Buddhist) from first to last is a disparagement not of the arts as such, but of the secular arts of mere amusement as distinguished from the intellectual arts that are a very means of enlightenment.[6]

Before going further it will be desirable to examine more closely some of the terms that have been cited. In connection with the passage quoted above, Dr. Bake has remarked that "The religious value of art music—*mârga*—is clearly apparent from this quotation, and actually this music, as conceived by the highest God and handed down through a succession of teachers, is felt as a means of breaking the cycle of birth." Apart from the questionable rendering of *mârga* by "art," this is absolutely true. The doctrine that human works of art (*silpâni*) are imitations of heavenly forms, and that by means of their rhythm there can be effected a metrical reconstitution (*samskarana*) of the limited human personality, dates at least from the Brâhmana period (*Aitareya Brâhmana*, VI. 27, etc.), and is implied in the Rgveda. "Sanskrit" itself is "constructed" (*samskrtam*) in just this sense; it is something more than merely "human" speech, and when the corresponding script is called *devanâgarî* this undoubtedly implies that the human script is an imitation of means of communication in the "city of the gods."

Since the Rg Veda has to do only with what is incessant (*nityam*), it is evident that all its terms are symbols rather than signs, and must be understood in their transfigured senses. Now the word *mârga*, rendered above by "highway," derives from *mrg*, to chase or hunt, especially by tracking.[7] In the Rg Veda it is familiar that what one hunts and tracks by its spoor is always the deity, the hidden light, the occulted Sun or Agni, who must be found, and is sometimes referred to as lurking in his lair. This is so well known that a very few citations will suffice. In RV. VIII. 2. 6 men are said to pursue (*mrgayante*) Indra, as one pursues a wild beast (*mrgam na*), with offerings of milk and kine (which may be compared to bait); in RV. VII. 87. 6, Varuna is compared to a "fierce beast" (*mrgas tuvismân*); in RV. X. 46. 2 the Bhrgus, eager seekers after Agni, track him by his spoor (*padaih*) like some lost beast (*pasun na nastam*). *Mârga* is then the creature's "runway," the "track to be followed" (*padavîya*) by the *vestigium pedis*. One sees thus clearly what values are implied in the expression *mârga*, "Way," and how inevitably that which is *mârga* is likewise *vimukti-da*, since it is precisely by the finding of the Hidden Light that liberation is effected. *Desî*, on the other hand, deriving from *dis*, to "indicate," and hence *dis*, "region" or "quarter," is "local"; cf. *desam nivis*, to "settle" in a given locality, *desa vyavahâra* or *desâcâra*, "local custom," "way of the world," and *desya*, "native." But these are not merely terms that could be derogatively employed by city people or courtiers to countrymen in general, but that could be employed by dwellers in the city of God or in any Holy Land with reference to those beyond the pale. Heaven lies "beyond the falcon," the worlds are "under the sun," and "in the power of death"; *loka* "world," is etymologically Latin *locus,* a place defined by given conditions; and *laukika,* "mundane" is literally "local"; it is precisely here (*iha*) in the worlds that the kindreds are "settled," "localized," and "native." "From the celestial or solar point of view, *desî* is thus mundane, human and devious, as distinct from super-mundane, divine and direct; and this distinction of *mârga* (= *svargya*) from *desî* as sacred from profane is in full agreement with the sense of the expressions *rañjaka* (pleasing, impassioning, affecting, etc.) and *vrthâ,* (wanton, random, "as you like," etc.), by which the value of *desî* has been explained above.

If we now consider the terrestrial analogy, then, looking at the matter from the Brahmans' point of view (who are "gods on earth"), whatever is geographically and/or qualitatively removed from an orthodox center, from a Holy Land (such as Aryâvarta) where the heavenly pattern is accurately imitated, will be at the same time geographically and spiritually "provincial"; those are pre-eminently *desî* who are outer barbarians beyond the pale; and in this sense *desî* is the equivalent of "heathen" or "pagan" in the primary sense of "pertaining to the heaths or wastes," as well as "pagan" in the secondary sense of worldly or sentimental (materialistic).

Highway and local or byway cultures can be pursued at one and the same time and in one and the same environment; they are not so much the cultures of ethnically different peoples or of given social strata as they are the cultures of qualitatively different kinds of people. The distinction is not nearly so much of aristocratic from peasant culture as it is one of aristocratic and peasant from bourgeoisie and proletarian cultures. Mughal painting, for example, even when more refined than Hindu painting, is a byway rather than a highway art; it is essentially an art of portraiture (from the *mârga* point of view, then, *asvargya*), and a "dated" art, which is as much as to say a "placed" (*desî*) art, for we cannot logically restrict the idea of "local" to a merely spatial significance, and indeed the two commonly associated words *kâla-desa* imply one another. From the Indian point of view, then, it is not the "primitive" (but abstract) art of the American Indian, or the peasant cultures of Europe or India, but rather the anti-traditional, academic, and bourgeoisie culture of modern Europe, and the proletarian culture of Soviet Russia, that can properly be called a devious and "byway" culture, "not heavenward leading." A traditional must not be confused with an academic or merely fashionable art; tradition is not a mere stylistic fixation, nor merely a matter of general suffrage. A traditional art has fixed ends and ascertained means of operation, has been transmitted in pupillary succession from an immemorial past, and retains its values even when, as at the present day, it has gone quite out of fashion. Hieratic and folk arts are both alike traditional (*smârta*). An academic art, on the other hand, however great its prestige, and however fashionable it may be, can very well be and is usually of an anti-traditional, personal, profane, and sentimental sort.

We think it has now been made sufficiently clear that the distinction of *mârga* from *desî* is not necessarily a distinction of aristocratic and cultivated from folk and primitive art, but one of sacred and traditional from profane and sentimental art.

We may then very well ask what is the true nature of folk and peasant art, and whether such an art differs from that of the *kavi* and *âcârya* in any other way than in degree of refinement. In traditional and unanimous societies we observe that no hard and fast line can be drawn between the arts that appeal to the peasant and those that appeal to the lord; both live in what is essentially the same way, but on a different scale. The distinctions are of refinement and luxury, but not of content or style; in other words, the differences are measurable in terms of material value, but are neither spiritual nor psychological. The attempt to distinguish aristocratic from popular motifs in traditional literature is fallacious; all traditional art is a folk art in the sense that it is the art of a unanimous people (*jana*). As Professor Child has remarked in connection with the history of ballads, "The condition of society in which a truly national and popular poetry appears ... (is one) in which the people are not divided by political organizations and book-culture into marked distinct classes;[9] in which, consequently, there is such community of ideas and feelings that the whole people form one individual."

It is only because we regard these problems from the narrow standpoint of present circumstances that we fail to grasp this condition. In a democratic society, where all men are theoretically equal, what exists in fact is a distinction between a bourgeoisie culture on the one hand and the ignorance of the uncultured masses on the other, notwithstanding that both classes may be literate. Here there is no such thing as a "folk" (*jana*), for the proletariat is not a "folk," but comparable rather to the outcaste (*candâla*) than to a fourth estate (*sûdra*): the sacerdotal (*brâhmana*) and chivalrous (*ksatriya*) classes are virtually lacking (men are so much alike that these functions can be exercised by anyone—the newsboy, for example, becoming a President); and the bourgeoisie (*vaisya*) is assimilated to the proletarian (*candâla*) masses, to form what is in effect an unanimously profane "herd" (*pasu*) whose conduct is governed only by likes and dislikes, and not by any higher principles.[10] Here the distinction of "educated" from "uneducated" is merely technical; it is no longer one of degrees of consciousness, but of more or less information. Under these conditions the distinction of literacy from illiteracy has a value altogether different from its value in traditional societies in which the whole folk, at the same time that it is culturally unanimous, is functionally differentiated; literacy, in the latter case, being quite unnecessary to some functions, where, moreover, its absence does not constitute a privation, since other means than books exist for the communication and transmission of spiritual values; and, further, under these circumstances, the function itself (*svadharma*), however "menial" or "commercial," is strictly speaking a "way" (*mârga*), so that it is not by engaging in other work to which a higher or lower social prestige may attach, but to the extent that a man approaches perfection in his own work and understands its spiritual significance that he can rise above himself—an ambition to rise above his fellows having then no longer any real meaning.

In democratic societies, then, where proletarian and profane (i. e. , ignorant) values prevail, there arises a real distinction of what is optimistically called "learning" or "science" on the part of the educated classes from the ignorance of the masses; and this distinction is measured by standards, not of profundity, but of literacy, in the simple sense of ability to read the printed word. In case there survives any residue of a true peasantry (as is still the case in Europe, but scarcely in America), or when it is a question of the "primitive" culture of other races, or even of traditional scriptures and metaphysical traditions that are of anything but popular origin, the "superstitions" involved (we shall presently see what is really implied by this very apt term) are confounded with the "ignorance" of the masses, and studied only with a condescending lack of under-standing. How perverse a situation is thus created can be seen when we realize that where the thread of symbolic and initiatory teaching has been broken at higher social levels (and modern education, whether in India or elsewhere, has precisely and very often inten-tionally, this destructive effect), it is just the "superstitions" of the people and what is apparently irrational in religious doctrine that has preserved what would otherwise have been lost. When the bour-geoisie culture of the universities has thus declined to levels of pure-ly empirical and factual information, then it is precisely and only in the superstitions of the peasantry, wherever these have been strong enough to resist the subversive efforts of the educators, that there survives a genuinely human and often, indeed, a superhuman wis-dom, however unconscious, and however fragmentary and naive may be the form in which it is expressed. There is, for example, a wisdom in traditional fairy tales (not, of course, in those which have been written by "literary" men "for children") that is altogether dif-ferent in kind from such psychological sense or nonsense as may be embodied in a modern novel.

As has been justly remarked by M. René Guénon, "The very con-ception of 'folklore,' as commonly understood, rests on a funda-mentally false hypothesis, the supposition, viz., that there really are such things as 'popular creations' or spontaneous inventions of the masses; and the connection of this point of view with the democrat-ic prejudice is obvious ... The folk has thus preserved, without understanding, the remains of old traditions that go back some-times to an indeterminably distant past; to which we can only refer as 'prehistoric.'" What has really been preserved in folk and fairy tales and in popular peasant art is, then, by no means a body of merely childish or entertaining fables or of crude decorative art, but a series of what are really esoteric doctrines and symbols of any-thing but popular invention. One may say that it is in this way, when an intellectual decadence has taken place in higher circles, that this doctrinal material is preserved from one epoch to another, afford-ing a glimmer of light in what may be called the dark night of the intellect; the folk memory serving the purpose of a sort of ark, in which the wisdom of a former age is carried over (*tiryate*) the peri-od of the dissolution of cultures that takes place at the close of a cycle.[11]

It is not a question of whether or not the ultimate significance of the popular legends and folk designs is actually understood by those who relate or employ them. These problems arise in much higher circles; in literary history, for example, one is often led to ask, when we find that an epic or romantic character has been imposed on purely mythical material (for example in the Mâhâbhârata and Râmâyana, and in the European recensions of the Grail and other Celtic material), how far has the author really understood his material? The point that we want to bring out is that the folk material, regardless of our actual qualifications in relation to it, is actually of an essentially *mârga* and not a *desî* character, and actually intelligible at levels of reference that are far above and by no means inferior to those of our ordinary contemporary "learning." It is not at all shocking that this material should have been transmitted by peasants for whom it forms a part of their lives, a nourishment of their very constitution, but who cannot explain; it is not at all shocking that the folk material can be described as a body of "superstition," since it is really a body of custom and belief that "stands over" (*superstat*) from a time when its meanings were understood. Had the folk beliefs not indeed been once understood, we could not now speak of them as metaphysically intelligible, or explain the accuracy of their formulation. The peasant may be unconscious and unaware, but that of which he is unconscious and unaware is in itself far superior to the empirical science and realistic art of the "educated" man, whose real ignorance is demonstrated by the fact that he studies and compares the data of folklore and "mythology" without suspecting their real significance any more than the most ignorant peasant.[12]

All that has been said above applies, of course, with even greater force to the *sruti* literature and, above all, the Rgveda, which so far from representing an intellectually barbarous age (as some pretend) has references so far abstract and remote from historical and empirical levels as to have become almost unintelligible to those whose intellectual capacities have been inhibited by what is nowadays called a "university education." " It is a matter at the same time of faith and understanding: the injunctions *Crede ut intelligas* and *Intellige ut credas* ("Believe, that you may understand," and "Understand, in order to believe") are valid in both cases—i. e. , whether we are concerned with the interpretation of folklore or with that of the transmitted texts.

Notes

1. Brahmâ may be meant, but the word suggests rather S?iva. Both of these aspects of deity are traditionally "authors" of the principles of music and dancing; the former in the *Nâtya Sâstra*, the latter in the *Abhinaya Darpana*.

2. The *Abhinaya Darpana* similarly distinguishes *nrtya*, or mimesis—viz., that form of the dance which has flavor, mood, and implied significance (*rasa, bhâva, vyañjana*)—from *nrtta*, or decorative dancing, devoid of flavor and mood.

3. It need hardly be pointed out that the Vedic sacrifice, constantly described as a mimesis of "what was done in the beginning," is in all its forms and in the fullest sense of the words a work of art, and a synthesis of arts liturgical and architectural, just as the same can be said of the Christian Mass (which is also a mimetic sacrifice), in which the dramatic and architectural elements are inseparably connected.

4. It should not be supposed that it is only on Death's side that there is singing to the harp, enactment (*nrt*), and a doing (*kr*); the point is that all of these acts are done by him *vrthâ*, "wantonly," for mere pleasure, and not in due form. As already remarked, the sacrifice is mimetic by nature and definition, and it is for this reason that we render *nrtyate* by "enacted" rather than by "danced"; for though there can be no doubt that the ritual, or portions of it, were in a certain sense "danced," (as "Indra danced his heroic deeds," RV. V. 33. 6), this expression would hardly convey to a modern reader the significance of the root *nrt* as employed here as well as in later stage directions, where what is intended is a signification by means of formal and rhythmic gestures. That the ritual must have been, as we said, at least in parts, a kind of dance, is evident from the fact that the gods themselves, engaged in the work of creation, are compared to dancers (*nrtyatâm iva*, RV. X. 72. 6), and that in KB. XVII. 8 the sacrificing priests are spoken of as "dancing" (*ninartyanti*), Keith justly commenting that this implies a "union of song, recitation, and dancing"—that is to say, what is later called the ensemble of music, *samgîta*. It may be added that ritual dancing survived in the Christian sacrifice at least as late as the eighteenth century in Spain.

The contests of Prajâpati with Death parallels that of Apollo with Marsyas, as to which Plato says that the man of sound mind will "prefer Apollo and his instruments to Marsyas and his" (*Republic* 399 E).

5. Similarly but more briefly in the *Taittirîya Samhitâ*, VI. VI. 1. 6. 5. 6, where also the Gandharvas who utter incantations are contrasted with the (mundane) deities who merely "sing," and Vâc follows the latter, but is restored to the former as the price of Soma. The mundane deities are, of course the immanent Breaths, the powers of the soul; it is only when they restore the Voice to the Sacerdotium that they are enabled to partake of the Water of Life; as in RV. X. 109. 5-7, where the (mundane) deities, restoring his wife (i. e. , Vâc) to Brhaspati, obtain the Soma in exchange, and are made free of their original sin.

6. The modern iconoclastic attitude towards the arts of imagery and dancing, according to which attempts are made to abolish "idolatry" and the service of Devadâsîs in temples, is of a deformative rather than a reformative nature. The intellectual limitations of the iconoclast are such that he interprets in a worldly and moralistic sense what are in themselves by no means vain and deadly but truly *mârga* and *svargya* arts; contemporary mentality reduces all things to its own *desî* level.

7. *Mrga* is "deer," but in the Old English sense of "four-footed game," without necessary reference to the Cervidae—usage that survives in the expression "small deer." The relation of *mrga*, animal, to *mrg*, to hunt, may be compared to that of our "fowl" to "fowling."

8. It may be noted that *pada* as a "word" or "phrase" is a naturally developed meaning, all formal language being a trace of the unspoken Word—"the lovely tokens (*laksmîh*) are inherent in the seers' speech," RV. X. 71. 2. In casual conversation, worldly speech, on the other hand, there is nothing more than a literal indication of perceptions, and only the estimative understanding is involved. This distinction in the verbal field corresponds to that of *mârga* from *desî* dancing, the former having an intelligible theme and embodying more than literal meanings, as is implied by the word *vyañjana*. The one kind of communication is formal (ideally informed) and intellectual, the other informal and sensitive: "Were it not for Intellect, the Word would babble incoherently" (SB. III. 2. 4. 11). It is from this point of view, and only accidentally geographically, that Sanskrit is distinguished from the vernaculars (*desî bhâsâ*), of which one may say that Apabhramsa is most of all a "byway" or "devious" and non-significant (*avyakta*) manner of communication, and that such as Braj Bhâsâ or Tamil are *desî* in the geographical sense only. In the same way one may say that all sacred languages employed in the transmission of traditional doctrines are "highway," and that languages designed or employed for purely practical purposes (Esperanto would be a good example) are "byway" tongues. Pali, nevertheless, by its confusion of certain words (e. g. *dîpa* = *dîpa* or *dvîpa*) is not *as* well fitted as Sanskrit for precise communications of ideas.

9. It need hardly be pointed out that a caste or feudal organization of society is no more a division in this sense than is the complex organization of the physical body the mark of a disintegrated personality.

10. A condition of the individual can be imagined that is superior to caste; an absolute *pramâna*, for example, is predicated of deity, for whom no function (*dharma*) is too high or too low. The proletarian condition, on the other hand, is not of this nature, but inferior to caste, alike from a spiritual and from an economic point of view; for as Plato has expressed it, "more will be done, and better done, and with more ease, when everyone does but one thing, according to his genius; and this is justice to each man as he is in himself."

11. Cf. Luc-Benoist, *La Cuisine des Anges*, 1932, pp. 74-75. "L'intérêt profond de toutes les traditions dites populaires réside surtout dans le fait qu'elles ne sont pas populaires d'origine ... Aristote y voyait avec raison les restes de l'ancienne philosophie. Il faudrait dire les formes anciennes de l'éternelle philosophie"—i. e., of the *philosophia perennis*, Augustine's "Wisdom uncreate, the same now as it ever was and the same to be for evermore." As pointed out by Michelet, V. E., it is in this sense— viz., inasmuch as "les Maîtres du Verbe projettent leurs inventions dans la mémoire

populaire, qui est un réceptacle merveilleux des concepts merveilleux" (*Le Secret de la Chevalerie*, 1930, p. 19)—and not in any "democratic" sense, that it can properly be said, *Vox populi, vox Dei*.

The beast fables of the *Pañcatantra*, in which a more than merely worldly wisdom is embodied, is unquestionably of aristocratic and not of popular origin; most of the stories in it have, as Edgerton says, "gone down" into Indian folklore, rather than been derived from it (*Amer. Oriental Series*, III, 1924, pp. 3, 10, 54). The same applies, without question, to the Jâtakas, many of which are versions of myths, and could not possibly have been composed by anyone not in full command of the metaphysical doctrines involved.

Andrew Lang, introducing Marian Roalfe Cox's *Cinderella* (1893), in which 345 versions of the story from all over the world are analyzed, remarked, "The fundamental idea of Cinderella, I suppose, is this: a person of mean or obscure position, by means of supernatural assistance, makes a good marriage." He found it very difficult to account for the world-wide distribution of the motive; of which, it may be added, there is a notable occurrence *in a scriptural context* in the Indian myth of Apâlâ and Indra. Here I will only ask the reader, of *what* "person in a mean or obscure position" is the "good marriage" referred to in the words of Donne, "Nor ever chaste until thou ravish me?" whom did Christ "love in her baseness and all her foulness" (St. Bonaventura, *Dom. prim. post Oct. Epiph.* II. 2)? and what does the *ierós gamos* imply in its final significance? And by the same token, *who* is the "dragon" disenchanted by the *fier baiser*? Who emerges with a "sunskin" from the scaly slough, who shakes off the ashes and puts on a golden gown to dance with the Prince? *Pra vasîyânsam vivâham âpnoti ya evam veda*, "More excellent is the marriage that one makes who understands that" (*Pañcavimsa Brâhmana*, VII. 10. 4)!

12. Strzygowksi, in *Jisoa*. V. p. 59 expresses his complete agreement with this statement.

16

Primitive Mentality

"The myth is not my own, I had it from my mother."
Euripides, fr. 488

There is, perhaps, no subject that has been more extensively investigated and more prejudicially misunderstood by the modern scientist than that of folklore. By "folklore" we mean that whole and consistent body of culture which has been handed down, not in books but by word of mouth and in practice, from time beyond the reach of historical research, in the form of legends, fairy tales, ballads, games, toys, crafts, medicine, agriculture, and other rites, and forms of social organization, especially those that we call "tribal." This is a cultural complex independent of national and even racial boundaries, and of remarkable similarity throughout the world;[1] in other words, a culture of extraordinary vitality. The material of folklore differs from that of exoteric "religion," to which it may be in a kind of opposition—as it is in a quite different way to "science"[2]— by its more intellectual and less moralistic content, and more obviously and essentially by its adaptation to vernacular transmission:[3] on the one hand, as cited above, "the myth is not my own, *I had it from my mother*," and on the other, "the passage from a traditional mythology to 'religion' is a humanistic decadence."[4]

The content of folklore is metaphysical. Our failure to recognize this is primarily due to our own abysmal ignorance of metaphysics and of its technical terms. We observe, for example, that the primitive craftsman leaves in his work something unfinished, and that the primitive mother dislikes to hear the beauty of her child unduly praised; it is "tempting Providence," and may lead to disaster. That seems like nonsense to us. And yet there survives in our vernacular the explanation of the principle involved: the craftsman leaves something undone in his work for the same reason that the words "to be finished" may mean either to be perfected or to die.[5] Perfection is death: when a thing has been altogether fulfilled, when all has been done that was to be done, potentiality altogether

225

reduced to act (*kṛtakṛtyaḥ*), that is the end: those whom the gods love die young. This is not what the workman desired for his work, nor the mother for her child. It can very well be that the workman or the peasant mother is no longer conscious of the meaning of a precaution that may have become a mere superstition; but assuredly we, who call ourselves anthropologists, should have been able to understand what was the idea which alone could have given rise to such a superstition, and ought to have asked ourselves whether or not the peasant by his actual observance of the precaution is not defending himself from a dangerous suggestion to which we, who have made of our existence a more tightly closed system, may be immune.

As a matter of fact, the destruction of superstitions invariably involves, in one sense or another, the premature death of the folk, or in any case the impoverishment of their lives.[6] To take a typical case, that of the Australian aborigines, D. F. Thompson, who has recently studied their remarkable initiatory symbols, observes that their "mythology supports the belief in a ritual or supernatural visitation that comes upon those who disregard or disobey the law of the old men. When this belief in the old men and their power—which, under tribal conditions, I have never known to be abused—dies, or declines, as it does with 'civilization,' chaos and racial death follow immediately."[7] The world's museums are filled with the traditional arts of innumerable peoples whose culture has been destroyed by the sinister power of our industrial civilization: peoples who have been forced to abandon their own highly-developed and beautiful techniques and significant designs in order to preserve their very lives by working as hired laborers at the reproduction of raw materials.[8] At the same time, modern scholars, with some honorable exceptions,[9] have as little understood the content of folklore as did the early missionaries understand what they thought of only as the "beastly devices of the heathen"; Sir J. G. Frazer, for example, whose life has been devoted to the study of all the ramifications of folk belief and popular rites, has only to say at the end of it all, in a tone of lofty superiority, that he was "led on, step by step, into surveying, as from some spectacular height, some Pisgah of the mind, a great part of the human race; I was beguiled, as by some subtle enchanter, into indicting what I cannot but regard as a dark, a tragic chronicle of human error and folly, of fruitless endeavor, wasted time and blighted hopes"[10]—words that sound much more like an indictment of modern European civilization than a criticism of any savage society!

The distinctive characteristic of a traditional society is order.[11] The life of the community as a whole and that of the individual, whatever his special function may be, conforms to recognized patterns, of which no one questions the validity: the criminal is the man who does not *know* how to behave, rather than a man who is unwilling to behave.[12] But such an unwillingness is very rare, where education and public opinion tend to make whatever ought not to be done simply ridiculous, and where, also, the concept of vocation involves a corresponding professional honor. Belief is an aristocratic virtue: "unbelief is for the mob." In other words, the traditional society is a unanimous society, and as such unlike a proletarian and individualistic society, in which the major problems of conduct are decided by the tyranny of a majority and the minor problems by each individual for himself, and there is no real agreement, but only conformity or nonconformity.

It is often supposed that in a traditional society, or under tribal or clan conditions, which are those in which a culture of the folk flourished most, the individual is arbitrarily compelled to conform to the patterns of life that he actually follows. It would be truer to say that under these conditions the individual is devoid of social ambition. It is very far from true that in traditional societies the individual is regimented: it is only in democracies, soviets, and dictatorships that a way of life is imposed upon the individual from without.[13] In the unanimous society the way of life is self-imposed in the sense that "fate lies in the created causes themselves," and this is one of the many ways in which the order of the traditional society conforms to the order of nature: it is in the unanimous societies that the possibility of self-realization—that is, the possibility of transcending the limitations of individuality—is best provided for. It is, in fact, for the sake of such a self-realization that the tradition itself is perpetuated. It is here, as Jules Romains has said, that we find "the richest possible variety of individual states of consciousness, in a harmony made valuable by its richness and density,"[14] words that are peculiarly applicable, for example, to Hindu society. In the various kinds of proletarian government, on the other hand, we meet always with the intention to achieve a rigid and inflexible uniformity; all the forces of "education,"[15] for example, are directed to this end. It is a national, rather than a cultural type that is constructed, and to this one type everyone is expected to conform, at the price

227

of being considered a peculiar person or even a traitor. It is of England that the Earl of Portsmouth remarks, "it is the wealth and genius of variety amongst our people, both in character and hand, that needs to be rescued now":[16] what could not be said of the United States! The explanation of this difference is to be found in the fact that the order that is imposed on the individual from without in any form of proletarian government is a *systematic* order, not a "form" but a cut and dried "formula," and generally speaking a pattern of life that has been conceived by a single individual or some school of academic thinkers ("Marxists," for example); while the pattern to which the traditional society is conformed by its own nature, being a metaphysical pattern, is a consistent but not a systematic form, and can therefore provide for the realization of many more possibilities and for the functioning of many more kinds of individual character than can be included within the limits of any system.

The actual unity of folklore represents on the popular level precisely what the orthodoxy of an elite represents in a relatively learned environment. The relation between the popular and the learned metaphysics is, moreover, analogous to and partly identical with that of the lesser to the greater mysteries. To a very large extent both employ one and the same symbols, which are taken more literally in the one case, and in the other understood parabolically; for example, the "giants" and "heroes" of popular legend are the titans and gods of the more learned mythology, the seven-league boots of the hero correspond to the strides of an Agni or a Buddha, and, "Tom Thumb" is no other than the Son whom Eckhart describes as "small, but so puissant." *So long as the material of folklore is transmitted, so long is the ground available on which the superstructure of full initiatory understanding can be built.*

Let us now consider the "primitive mentality" that so many anthropologists have studied: the mentality, that is, which manifests itself in such normal types of society as we have been considering, and to which we have referred as "traditional." Two closely connected questions must first be disposed of. In the first place, is there such a thing as a "primitive" or "alogical" mentality distinct from that of civilized and scientific man? It has been taken for granted by the older "animists" that human nature is a constant, so that "if we were in the position of the primitives, our mind being what it is now, we should think and act as they do."[17] On the other hand, for anthropologists and psychologists of the type of Lévy-Bruhl, there can be recognized an almost specific distinction between the primitive mentality and ours.[18] The explanation of the possibility of disagreement in such a matter has much to do with the belief in progress by which, in fact, all our conceptions of the history of civilization are distorted.[19] It is too readily taken for granted that we have progressed, and that any contemporary savage society in all respects fairly represents the so-called primitive mentality, and overlooked that many characteristics of this mentality can be studied at home as well as or better than in any African jungle: the point of view of the Christian or Hindu, for example, is in many ways nearer to that of the "savage" than to that of the modern bourgeoisie. What real distinction of two mentalities can be made is, in fact, the distinction of a modern from a medieval or oriental mentality; and this is not a specific distinction, but one of sickness from health. It has been said of Lévy-Bruhl that he is a past master in opening up what is to us "an almost inconceivable" world: as if there were none amongst us to whom the mentality reflected in our own immediate environment were not equally "inconceivable."

We shall consider, then, the "primitive mentality" as described, very often accurately enough, by Lévy-Bruhl and other psychologist-anthropologists. It is characterized in the first place by a "collective ideation";[20] ideas are held in common, whereas in a civilized group, everyone entertains ideas of his own.[21] Infinitely varied as it may be in detail, the folk literature, for example, has to do with the lives of heroes, all of whom meet with essentially the same adventures and exhibit the same qualities. It is not for one moment realized that a possession of ideas in common does not necessarily imply the "collective origination" of these ideas. It is argued that what is true for the primitive mentality is unrelated to experience, i.e., to such "logical" experience as ours. Yet it is "true" to what the primitive "experiences." The criticism implied, for such it is, is exactly parallel to the art historian's who criticizes primitive art as not being "true to nature"; and to that of the historian of literature who demands from literature a psychoanalysis of individual character. The primitive was not interested in such trivialities, but thought in types. This, moreover, was his means of "education"; for the type can be imitated, whereas the individual can only be mimicked.

The next and most famous characteristic of the primitive mentality has been called "participation," or more specifically, "mystical participation." A thing is not only what it is visibly, but also what it represents. Natural or artificial objects are not for the primitive, as they can be for us, arbitrary symbols of some other and higher reality, but actual manifestations of this reality:[22] the eagle or the lion, for example, is not so much a symbol or image *of* the Sun as it *is* the Sun in a likeness (the form being more important than the nature in which it may be manifested) ; and in the same way every house *is* the world in a likeness, and every altar situated at the center of the earth; it is only because we are more interested in what things are than in what they mean, more interested in particular facts than in universal ideas, that this is inconceivable to us. Descent from a totem animal is not, then, what it appears to the anthropologist, a literal absurdity, but a descent from the Sun, the Progenitor and Prajâpati of all, in that form in which he revealed himself, whether in vision or in dream, to the founder of the clan. The same reasoning validates the Eucharistic meal; the Father-Progenitor is sacrificed and partaken of by his descendants, in the flesh of the sacred animal: "This is my body, take and eat."[23] So that, as Lévy-Bruhl says of such symbols, "very often it is not their purpose to 'represent' their prototype to the eye, but to facilitate a participation," and that "if it is their essential function to 'represent,' in the full sense of the word, invisible beings or objects, and to make their presence effective, it follows that they are not necessarily reproductions or likenesses of these beings or objects."[24] The purpose of primitive art, being entirely different from the aesthetic or decorative intentions of the modern "artist" (for whom the ancient motifs survive only as meaningless "art forms"), explains its abstract character. "We civilized men have lost the Paradise of the 'Soul of primitive imagery [*Urbildseele*].' We no longer live among the shapes which we had fashioned within: we have become mere spectators, reflecting them from without."[25]

The superior intellectuality of primitive and "folk" art is often confessed, even by those who regard the "emancipation" of art from its linguistic and communicative functions as a desirable progress. Thus W. Deonna writes, "Le primitivisme exprime par l'art les idées," but "l'art évolue ... vers un naturalisme progressif," no longer representing things "telles qu'on les conçoit" [I would rather say, "telles qu'on les comprend"], but "telles qu'on les voit"; thus substituting "la réalité" for "l'abstraction"; and that evolution, "de l'idéalisme vers un naturalisme" in which "la forme [*sc.* la figure] tend à prédominer sur l'idée," is what the Greek genius, "plus artiste que tous les autres," finally accomplished.[26]

To have lost the art of thinking in images is precisely to have lost the proper linguistic of metaphysics and to have descended to the verbal logic of "philosophy." The truth is that the content of such an "abstract," or rather "principial," form as the Neolithic sun-wheel (in which *we* see only an evidence of the "worship of natural forces," or at most a "personification" of these forces), or that of the corresponding circle with center and radii or rays, is so rich that it could only be fully expounded in many volumes, and embodies implications which can only with difficulty if at all be expressed in words; the very nature of primitive and folk art is the immediate proof of its essentially intellectual content. Nor does this only apply to the diagrammatic representations: there was actually nothing made for use that had not a meaning as well as an application: "The needs of the body and the spirit are satisfied together";[27] "le physique et le spirituel ne sont pas encore séparés,"[28] "meaningful form, in which the physical and metaphysical originally formed a counterbalancing polarity, is increasingly depleted in its transmission to us; we say then that it is 'ornament.'"[29] What we call "inventions" are nothing but the application of known metaphysical principles to practical ends; and that is why tradition always refers the fundamental inventions to an ancestral culture hero (always, in the last analysis, a descent of the Sun), that is to say, to a primordial revelation.

In these applications, however utilitarian their purpose, there was no need whatever to sacrifice the clarity of the original significance of the symbolic form: on the contrary, the aptitude and beauty of the artifact at the same time express and depend upon the form that underlies it. We can see this very clearly, for example, in the case of such an ancient invention as that of the "safety pin," which is simply an adaptation of a still older invention, that of the straight pin or needle having at one end a head, ring, or eye and at the other a point; a form that as a "pin" directly penetrates and fastens materials together, and as a "needle" fastens them together by leaving behind it as its "trace" a thread that originates from its eye. In the safety pin, the originally straight stem of the pin or needle is bent upon itself so that its point passes back again through the "eye" and is held there securely, at the same time that it fastens whatever material it has penetrated.[30]

Whoever is acquainted with the technical language of initiatory symbolism (in the present case, the language of the "lesser myster-ies" of the crafts) will recognize at once that the straight pin or nee-dle is a symbol of generation, and the safety pin a symbol of regeneration. The safety pin is, moreover, the equivalent of the but-ton, which fastens things together and is attached to them by means of a thread which passes through and again returns to its perfora-tions, which correspond to the eye of the needle. The significance of the metal pin, and that of the thread left behind by the needle (whether or not secured to a button that corresponds to the eye of the needle) is the same: it is that of the "thread-spirit" (*sûtrâtman*) by which the Sun connects all things to himself and fastens them; he is the primordial embroiderer and tailor, by whom the tissue of the universe, to which our garments are analogous, is woven on a living thread.[31]

For the metaphysician, it is inconceivable that forms such as this, which express a given doctrine with mathematical precision, could have been "invented" without a knowledge of their significance. The anthropologist, it is true, will believe that such meanings are merely "read into" the forms by the sophisticated symbolist (one might as well pretend that a mathematical formula could have been discovered by chance). But that a safety pin or button is meaning-less, and merely a convenience for us, is simply the evidence of our profane ignorance and of the fact that such forms have been "more and more voided of content [*entleert*] on their way down to us" (Andrae); the scholar of art is not "reading into" these intelligible forms an arbitrary meaning, but simply reading their meaning, for this is their "form" or "life," and present in them regardless of whether or not the individual artists of a given period, or we, have known it or not. In the present case the proof that the meaning of the safety pin had been understood can be pointed to in the fact that the heads or eyes of prehistoric fibulae are regularly decorated with a repertoire of distinctly solar symbols.[32]

Inasmuch as the symbolic arts of the folk do not propose to tell us what things are like but, by their allusions, intend to refer to the ideas implied by these things, we may describe them as having an algebraic (rather than "abstract") quality, and in this respect as dif-fering essentially from the veridical and realistic purposes of a pro-fane and arithmetical art, of which the intentions are to tell us what things are like, to express the artist's personality, and to evoke an emotional reaction. We do not call folk art "abstract" because the forms are not arrived at by a process of omission; nor do we call it "conventional," since its forms have not been arrived at by experiment and agreement; nor do we call it "decorative" in the modern sense of the word, since it is not meaningless;[33] it is properly speaking a principial art, and supernatural rather than naturalistic. The nature of folk art is, then, itself the sufficient demonstration of its intellectuality: it is, indeed, a "divine inheritance." We illustrate in Figures 1 and 2 two examples of folk art and one of bourgeois art. The characteristic informality, insignificance, and ugliness of the latter will be obvious. Figure 1 is a Sarmatian "ornament,"[34] probably a horse trapping. There is a central six-spoked wheel, around which revolve four equine protomas, also wheel-marked, forming a whorl or *svastika*; and it is abundantly clear that this is a representation of the divine "procession," the revolution of the Supernal Sun in a four-horsed and four-wheeled chariot; a representation such as this has a content evidently far exceeding that of later pictorial representations of an anthropomorphic "Sun," or human athlete, riding in a chariot actually drawn by four prancing horses. The two other illustrations are of modern Indian wooden toys: in the first case we recognize a metaphysical and formal art, and a type that can be paralleled throughout a millennial tradition, while in the latter the effect of European influence has led the artist not to "imitate. nature in. her manner of operation," but simply to imitate nature in her appearances; if either of these kinds of art can be called "naïve," it is certainly not the traditional art of the folk!

Figure 1. Sarmatian (?) Ornament

Figure 2. Horse and Donkey: Folk Art and Bourgeois Art

The characteristic pronouncements of anthropologists on the "primitive mentality," of which a few may be cited, are often very remarkable, and may be said to represent not what the writers have intended, the description of an inferior type of consciousness and experience, but one intrinsically superior to that of "civilized" man, and approximating to that which we are accustomed to think of as "primordial." For example, "The primitive mind experienced life as a whole ... Art was not for the delectation of the senses."[35] Dr. Macalister actually compares what he calls the "Ascent of Man" to Wordsworth's *Ode on the Intimations of Immortality*, not realizing that the poem is the description of the descent or materialization of consciousness.[36] Schmidt remarks that "In 'heathenish' popular customs, in the 'superstitions' of our folk, the spiritual adventures of prehistoric times, the imagery of primitive insight are living still; *a divine inheritance* ... Originally every type of soul and mind corresponds to the physiological organism proper to it ... The world is conceived as being partner with the living being, which is unconscious of its individuality; as being an essential portion of the Ego; and it is represented as being affected by human exertion and sufferings ... Nature-man lives his life in images. He grasps it in his conception as a series of realities. His visions are therefore not only real; they form his objective insight into a higher world ... The talent, in the man of understanding, is only obstructed, more or less. Artistic natures, poets, painters, sculptors, musicians, seers, who see God face to face, remain all their lives eidetically rooted in their creations. In them there lives the folk-soul of dissolving images in their most perfect creative form ... Natural man, to whom vision and thought are identical ... The man of magic ... is still standing in a present world which includes the whole of primeval time ... [On the other hand] the emancipated man, vehicle of a soul ... differentiates the original magical somatopsychic unity ... Outward and Inward, World and Ego, become a duality in the consciousness."[37] Could one say more in support of the late John Lodge's proposition, "From the Stone Age until now, *quelle dégringolade*"?

If it is difficult for us to understand the primitive belief in the efficacy of symbolic rites, it is largely because of our limited knowledge of the prolongations of the personality, which forces us to think in terms of a purely physical causality. We overlook that while we may believe that the anticipatory rite has no physical effect in the desired direction, the rite itself is the formal expression of a will directed to this end, and that this will, released by the performance of the rite, is also an effective force, by which the environment in its totality must be to some extent affected. In any case, the preliminary rite of "mimetic magic" is an enactment of the "formal cause" of the subsequent operation, whether it be the art of agriculture or that of war that is in question, and the artist has a right to expect that the actual operation, if carried out on this plan, will be successful. What seems strange to us, however, is that for the primitive mentality the rite is a "prefiguration," not merely in the sense of a pattern of action to be followed, but in the sense of an anticipation in which the future becomes a virtually already existent reality, so that "the primitives feel that the future event is actually present": the action of the force released is immediate, "and if its effects appear after some time it is nevertheless imagined—or, rather, in their case, felt—as immediately produced."[38] Lévy-Bruhl goes on to point out very justly that all this implies a conception of time and space that is not in our sense of the word "rational": one in which both past and future, cause and effect, coincide in a present experience. If we choose to call this an "unpractical" position, we must not forget that at the same time "the primitives constantly make use of the real connection between cause and effect ... they often display an ingenuity that implies a very accurate observation of this connection."[39]

Now it is impossible not to be struck by the fact that it is precisely a state of being in which "everywhere and every when is focused" (Dante), that is for the theologian and the metaphysician "divine": that at this level of reference "all states of being, seen in principle, *are* simultaneous in the eternal now," and that "he who cannot escape from the standpoint of temporal succession so as to see all things in their simultaneity is incapable of the least conception of the metaphysical order."[40] We say that what seems to "us" irrational in the life of "savages," and may be unpractical, since it unfits them to compete with our material force, represents the vestiges of a primordial state of metaphysical understanding, and that if the savage himself is, generally speaking, no longer a comprehensor of his own "divine inheritance," this ignorance on his part is no more shameful than ours who do not recognize the intrinsic nature of his "lore," and understand it no better than he does. We do not say that the modern savage exemplifies the "primordial state" itself, but that his beliefs, and the whole content of folklore, bear witness to such a state. We say that the truly primitive man—"before the Fall"—was not by any means a philosopher or scientist but, by all means, a metaphysical being, in full possession of the *forma humanitatis* (as we are only very partially); that, in the excellent phrase of Baldwin Smith, he "experienced life as a whole."

Nor can it be said that the "primitives" are always unconscious of the sources of their heritage. For example, "Dr. Malinowski has insisted on the fact that, in the native Trobriand way of thinking, magic, agrarian or other, is not a human invention. From time immemorial, it forms a part of the inheritance which is handed down from generation to generation. Like the social institutions proper, it was created in the age of the myth, by the heroes who were the founders of civilization. Hence its sacred character. Hence also its efficacy."[41] Far more rarely, an archeologist such as Andrae has the courage to express as his own belief that "when we sound the archetype, the ultimate origin of the form, then we find that it is anchored in the highest, not the lowest," and to affirm that "the sensible forms [of art], in which there was at first a polar balance of physical and metaphysical, have been more and more voided of content on their way down to us."[42]

The mention of the Trobriand Islanders above leads us to refer to one more type of what appears at first sight to imply an almost incredible want of observation. The Trobriand Islanders, and some Australians, are reported to be unaware of the causal connection between sexual intercourse and procreation; they are said to believe that spirit-children enter the wombs of women on appropriate occasions, and that sexual intercourse alone is not a determinant of birth.[43] It is, indeed, implausible that the natives, "whose aboriginal endowment is quite as good as any European's, if not better,"[44] are unaware of any connection whatever between sexual intercourse and pregnancy. On the other hand, it is clear that their interest is not in what may be called the mediate causes of pregnancy, but in its first cause.[45] Their position is essentially identical with that of the universal tradition for which reproduction depends on the activating presence of what the mythologist calls a "fertility spirit" or "progenitive deity," and is in fact the Divine Eros, the Indian Kâmadeva and Gandharva, the spiritual Sun of RV I.115.1, the life of all and source of all being; it is upon *his* "connection with the field"[46] that life is transmitted, as it is by the human "sower" that the elements of the corporeal vehicle of life are planted in *his* "field." So that as the *Majjhima Nikâya*, I.265-266, expresses it, three things are required for conception, viz. conjunction of father and mother, the mother's period, and the presence of the Gandharva:[47] of which the two first may be called dispositive and the third an essential cause. We see now the meaning of the words of BU III.9.28.5, "Say not 'from semen,' but 'from what is alive [in the semen].'" "It is the Provident Spirit [*prajñâtman*, i.e., the Sun] that grasps and erects the flesh" (*Kaus. Up.* III.3); "The power of the soul, which is in the semen through the spirit enclosed therein, fashions the body" (*Sum. Theol.* III.32.11). Thus, in believing with Schiller that "it is the Spirit that fashions the body for itself" (*Wallenstein*, III.13), the "primitive" is in agreement with a unanimous tradition and with Christian doctrine: "Spiritus est qui vivificat: caro non prodest quicquam" ("it is the spirit that quickeneth; the flesh profiteth nothing," John 6:63).[48]

It will be seen that the Trobriander view that sexual intercourse alone is not a determinant of conception but only its occasion, and that "spirit-children" enter the womb, is essentially identical with the metaphysical doctrine of the philosophers and theologians. The notion that "old folklore ideas" are taken over into scriptural contexts, which are thus contaminated by the popular superstitions, reverses the order of events; the reality is that the folklore ideas are the form in which metaphysical doctrines are received by the people and transmitted by them. In its popular form, a given doctrine may not always have been understood, but for so long as the formula is faithfully transmitted it remains understandable; "superstitions," for the most part, are no mere delusions, but formulae of which the meaning has been forgotten and are therefore called meaningless—often, indeed, because the doctrine itself has been forgotten.

Aristotle's doctrine that "Man and the Sun generate man" (*Physics* II.2),[49] that of JUB III.10.4 and that of the *Majjhima Nikâya*, may be said to combine the scientific and the metaphysical theories of the origin of life: and this very well illustrates the fact that the scientific and metaphysical points of view are by no means contradictory, but rather complementary. The weakness of the scientific position is not that the empirical facts are devoid of interest or utility, but that these facts are thought of as a refutation of the intellectual doctrine. Actually, our discovery of chromosomes does not in any way account for the origin of life, but only tells us more about its mechanism. The metaphysician may, like the primitive, be incurious about the scientific facts; he cannot be disconcerted by them, for they can at the most show that God moves "in an even more mysterious way than we had hitherto supposed."

We have touched upon only a very few of the "motifs" of folklore. The main point that we have wished to bring out is that the whole body of these motifs represent a consistent tissue of interrelated intellectual doctrines belonging to a primordial wisdom rather than to a primitive science; and that for this wisdom it would be almost impossible to conceive a popular, or even in any common sense of the term, a human origin. The life of the popular wisdom extends backward to a point at which it becomes indistinguishable from the primordial tradition itself, the traces of which we are more familiar with in the sacerdotal and royal arts; and it is in this sense, and by no means with any "democratic" implications, that the lore of the people, expressed in their culture, is really the word of God—*Vox populi vox Dei.*[50]

Notes

1. "The metaphysical notions of man may be reduced to a few types which are of universal distribution" (Franz Boas, *The Mind of Primitive Man*, New York, 1927, p. 156); "The great myths of mankind are almost monotonously alike in their fundamental aspects" (D. C. Holtom, *The National Faith of Japan*, London, 1938, p. 90). The pattern of the lives of heroes is universal (Lord Raglan, *The Hero*, London,

1936). From all over the world more than three hundred versions of a single tale had already been collected fifty years ago (M. R. Cox, *Cinderella*, London, 1893). All peoples have legends of the original unity of Sky and Earth, their separation, and their marriage. "Clapping Rocks" are Navajo and Eskimo as well as Greek. The patterns of *Himmelfahrten* and the types of the active *Wunderthor* are everywhere alike.

2. The opposition of religion to folklore is often a kind of rivalry set up as between a new dispensation and an older tradition, the gods of the older cult becoming the evil spirits of the newer. The opposition of science to the content of both folklore and religion is based upon the view that "such knowledge as is not empirical is meaningless." The most ludicrous, and pathetic, situation appears when, as happened not long ago in England, the Church joins hands with science in proposing to withhold fairy tales from children as being untrue; it might have reflected that those who can make of mythology and fairy lore nothing but literature will do the same with scripture. "Men live by myths ... they are no mere poetic invention" (Fritz Marti, "Religion, Philosophy, and the College," in *Review of Religion*, VII, 1942, 41). "La mémoire collective conserve ... des symboles archaïques d'essence purement métaphysique" (M. Eliade in *Zalmoxis*, II, 1939, 78). "Religious philosophy is always bound up with myths and cannot break free from them without destroying itself and abandoning its task" (N. Berdyaev, *Freedom and the Spirit*, London, 1935, p. 69). Cf. E. Dacqué, *Das verlorene Paradies* (Munich, 1940).

3. The words "adaptation to vernacular transmission" should be noted. Scripture recorded in a sacred language is not thus adapted; and a totally different result is obtained when scriptures originally written in such a sacred language are made accessible to the "untaught manyfolk" by translation, and subjected to an incompetent "free examination." In the first case, there is a faithful transmission of material that is always intelligible, although not necessarily always completely understood; in the second, misunderstandings are inevitable. In this connection it may be remarked that "literacy," nowadays thought of as almost synonymous with "education," is actually of far greater importance from an industrial than from a cultural point of view. What an illiterate Indian or American Indian peasant knows and understands would be entirely beyond the comprehension of the compulsorily educated product of the American public schools.

4. J. Evola, *Rivolta contra il mondo moderno*, Milan, 1934, p. 374, n. 12. "For the primitives, the mythical world really existed. Or rather it still exists" (Lucien Lévy-Bruhl, *L'Expérience mystique et les symboles chez les primitifs*, Paris, 1938, p. 295). One might add that it will exist forever in the eternal now of the Truth, unaffected by the truth or error of history. A myth is true now, or was never true at all.

5. Just as Sanskrit *parinirvâna* is both "to be completely despirated" and "to be perfected". The Buddha's *parinibbâna* is a "finish" in both senses.

6. The life of "civilized" people has already been impoverished; its influence can only tend to impoverish those whom it reaches. The "white man's burden," of which he speaks with so much unction, is the burden of death. For the poverty of "civilized" peoples, cf. I. Jenkins, "The Postulate of an Impoverished Reality," *Journal of Philosophy*, XXXIX, 1942, 533 ff.; Eric Meissner, *Germany in Peril* (London, 1942), pp. 41, 42; Floryan Znaniecki, as quoted by A. J. Krzesinski, *Is Modern Culture Doomed?* (New York, 1942), p. 54, n. 8; W. Andrae, *Die ionische Säule: Bauform oder Symbol?* (Berlin, 1933) p. 65 "*mehr and mehr entleert.*"

7. *Illustrated London News*, February 25, 1939. A traditional civilization presupposes a correspondence of the man's, most intimate nature with his particular vocation (see René Guénon, "Initiation and the Crafts," *JISOA*, VI, 1938, 163-168). The forcible disruption of this harmony poisons the very springs of life and creates innumerable maladjustments and sufferings. The representative of "civilization" cannot realize this, because the very idea of vocation has lost its meaning and become for him a "superstition"; the "civilized" man, being himself a kind of economic slave, can be put, or puts himself, to any kind of work that material advantage seems to demand or that social ambition suggests, in total disregard for his individual character, and cannot understand that to rob a man of his hereditary vocation is precisely to take away his "living" in a far more profound than merely economic sense.

8. See Coomaraswamy, "Notes on Savage Art," 1946, and "Symptom, Diagnosis, and Regimen"; cf. Thomas Harrisson, *Savage Civilization* (New York, 1937).

9. E.g., Paul Radin, *Primitive Man as Philosopher* (New York, 1927); Wilhelm Schmidt, *Origin and Growth of Religion*, 2nd ed. (New York, 1935), and *High Gods in North America* (Oxford, 1933); Karl von Spiess, *Marksteine der Volkskunst* (1937), and *Vom Wesen der Volkskunst* (1926); Konrad Th. Preuss, *Lehrbuch der Völkerkunde* (Stuttgart, 1939), to mention only those best known to me. C. G. Jung is put out of court by his interpretation of symbols as psychological phenomena, an avowed and deliberate exclusion of all metaphysical significance.

10. *Aftermath* (London, 1936), preface. Olivier Leroy, *La Raison primitive, essai de réfutation de la théorie de prélogisme* (Paris, 1927), n. 18, remarks that Lévy-Bruhl "fut aiguillé sur les recherches ethnologiques par la lecture du *Golden Bough*. Aucun ethnologue, aucun historien des religions, me contredira si je dis que c'était un périlleux début." Again, "la notion que Lévy-Bruhl se fait du 'primitif' a été écartée par tous les ethnographes ... son peu de curiosité des sauvages a scandalisé les ethnographes" (J. Monneret, *La Poésie moderne et le sacré*, Paris, 1945, pp. 193, 195). The very title of his book, *How Natives Think*, betrays him. If he had known *what* "natives" think (i.e., about Europeans), he might have been surprised.

Another exhibition of the superiority complex will be found in the concluding pages of Sidney Hartland, *Primitive Paternity* (London, 1909-1910); his view that when "the relics of primeval ignorance and archaic speculation" have been discarded, the world's "great stories" will survive, is both absurd and sentimental, and rests on the assumption that beauty can be divorced from the truth in which it originates, and a notion that the only end of "literature" is to amuse. *The Golden Bough* is a glorified doctor's thesis. Frazer's only survival value will be documentary; his lucubrations will be forgotten.

11. "What we mean by a normal civilization is one that rests on principles, in the true sense of this word, and one in which all is ordered and in a hierarchy consistent with these principles, so that everything is seen to be the application and extension of a purely and essentially intellectual or metaphysical doctrine: that is what we mean when we speak of a 'traditional civilization'" (René Guénon, *Orient et occident*, Paris, 1930, p. 235)

12. Sin, Skr. *aparâddha*, "missing the mark," any departure from "the order to the end," is a sort of clumsiness due to want of skill. There is a ritual of life and what matters in the performance of a rite is that whatever is done should be done cor-

rectly, in "good form." What is not important is how one *feels* about the work to be done or life to be lived: all such feelings being tendentious and self-referent. But if, over and above the *correct* performance of the rite or any action, one also understands its form, if all one's actions are conscious and not merely instinctive reactions provoked by pleasure or pain, whether anticipated or felt, this awareness of the underlying principles is immediately dispositive to spiritual freedom. In other words, wherever the action itself is correct, the action itself is symbolic and provides a discipline, or path, by following which the final goal must be reached; on the other hand, whoever acts informally has opinions of his own and, "knowing what he likes," is limiting his person to the measure of his individuality.

13. A democracy is a government of all by a majority of proletarians; a soviet, a government by a small group of proletarians; and a dictatorship, a government by a single proletarian. In the traditional and unanimous society there is a government by a hereditary aristocracy, the function of which is to maintain an existing order, based on eternal principles, rather than to impose the views or arbitrary will (in the most technical sense of the words, a *tyrannical* will) of any "party" or "interest."

The "liberal" theory of class warfare takes it for granted that there can be no common interest of different classes, which must oppress or be oppressed by one another; the classical theories of government are based on a concept of impartial justice. What majority rule means in practice is a government in terms of an unstable "balance of power"; and this involves a kind of internal warfare that corresponds exactly to the international wars that result from the effort to maintain balances of power on a still larger scale.

14. "The stronger and more intense the social is, the less it is oppressive and external" (G. Gurvitch, "Mass, Community, Communion," *Journal of Philosophy*, XXXVIII, 1941, 488). "In a medieval feudalism and imperialism, or any other civilization of the traditional type, unity and hierarchy can co-exist with a maximum of individual independence, liberty, affirmation, and constitution" (Evola, *Rivolta*, p. 112). But: "Hereditary service is quite incompatible with the industrialism of today, and that is why the system of caste is always painted in such dark colors" (A. M. Hocart, *Les Castes*, Paris, 1938, p. 238).

15. "Compulsory education, whatever its practical use may be, cannot be ranked among the civilizing forces of this world" (Meissner, *Germany in Peril*, p. 73). Education in a primitive society is not compulsory, but inevitable; just because the past is there "present, experienced and felt as an effective part of daily life, not just taught by schoolmasters" (*idem*). For the typically modern man, to have "broken with the past" is an end in itself; any change is a meliorative "progress," and education is typically iconoclastic.

16. G.V.W. Portsmouth, *Alternative to Death* (London, 1943), p. 30.

17. G. Davy, "Psychologie des primitifs d'après Lévy-Bruhl," *Journal de psychologie normale et pathologique*, XXVII (1931), 112.

18. For a general refutation of "prélogisme," see Leroy, *La Raison primitive*, and W. Schmidt, *The Origin and Growth of Religion*, pp. 133, 134. Leroy, for example, in discussing the "participation" of kingship in divinity, remarks that all that Lévy-Bruhl and Frazer have done is to call this notion "primitive" because it occurs in primitive societies, and these societies "primitive" because they entertain this primitive idea. Lévy-Bruhl's theories are now quite generally discredited, and most anthro-

pologists and psychologists hold that the mental equipment of primitive man was exactly the same as our own. Cf. Radin, *Primitive Man as Philosopher*, p. 373, "in capacity for logical and symbolical thought, there is no difference between civilized and primitive man," and as cited by Schmidt, *Origin and Growth of Religion*, pp. 202, 203; and Boas, *The Mind of Primitive Man*, p. 156.

19. Cf. D. B. Zema on "Progress," in the *Dictionary of World Literature* (New York, 1943); and René Guénon, *East and West* (London, 1941), ch. 1, "Civilization and Progress." The latter remarks: "The civilization of the modern West appears in history as a veritable anomaly: among all those which are known to us more or less completely, this civilization is the only one which has developed along purely material lines, and this monstrous development, whose beginning coincides with the so-called Renaissance, has been accompanied, as indeed it was fated to be, by a corresponding intellectual *regress*." Cf. Meissner, *Germany in Peril*, pp. 10-11: "The shortest way of stating the case is this: during the last centuries a vast majority of Christian men have lost their homes in every sense of the word. The number of those cast out into the wilderness of a dehumanized society is steadily increasing ... the time might come and be nearer than we think, when the ant-heap of society, worked out to full perfection, deserves only one verdict: *unfit for men*." Cf. Gerald Heard, *Man the Master* (New York, 1941), p. 25, "By civilized men we now mean industrialized men, mechanical societies ... Any other conduct ... is the behavior of an ignorant, simple savage. To have arrived at this picture of reality is to be truly advanced, progressive, civilized." "In our present generation of primary and almost exclusive emphasis on mechanics and engineering or economics, understanding of people no longer exists, or at best only in very rare cases. In fact we do not want to know each other as men ... That is just what got us into this monstrous war" (W. F. Sands in *Commonweal*, April 20, 1945)

20. The anthropologist's "collective ideation" is nothing but the unanimism of traditional societies that has been discussed above; but with this important distinction, that the anthropologist means to imply by his "collective ideation" not merely the common possession of ideas, but also the "collective origination" of these ideas: the assumption being that there really are such things as popular creations and spontaneous inventions of the masses (and as René Guénon has remarked, "the connection of this point of view with the democratic prejudice is obvious"). Actually, "the literature of the folk is not their own production, but comes down to them from above ... the folktale is never of popular origin" (Lord Raglan, *The Hero*, p. 145).

21. In a normal society one no more "thinks for oneself" than one has a private arithmetic [cf. Augustine, *De ordine* II.48]. In a proletarian culture one does not think at all, but only entertains a variety of prejudices, for the most part of journalistic and propagandistic origin, though treasured as one's "own opinions." A traditional culture presumes an entertainment of ideas, to which a private property is impossible. "Where the God (*sc.*, Eros) is our teacher we all come to think alike" (Xenophon, *Oeconomicus* XVII.3); "What really binds men together is their culture—the ideas and standards they have in common" (Ruth Benedict, *Patterns of Culture*, Boston, 1934, p. 16). In other words, religion and culture are normally indivisible: and where everyone thinks for himself, there is no society (*sâhitya*) but only an aggregate. The *common* and divine Reason is the criterion of truth, "but

most men live as though they possessed a private intelligence of their own" (Heracleitus, *Fragment* 92). "Insofar as we participate in the memory of that [common and divine] Reason, we speak truth, but whenever we are thinking for ourselves (*idiasômen*) we lie" (Sextus Empiricus, on Heracleitus, in *Adversus dogmaticos* I,131-134).

22. Cf. "The lust of the goat is the bounty of God ... When thou seest an Eagle, thou seest a portion of Genius" (William Blake). "The sacrificial horse is a symbol (*rûpa*) of Prajâpati, and consubstantial with Prajâpati (*prâjâpatya*)," so that what is said to the horse is said to Prajâpati "face to face" (*sâksât*), and so "verily he wins Him visibly" (*sâksât*, TS V.7.1.2). "One day I witnessed a *Râmlilâ* performance. I saw the performers to be actual Sîtâ, Râma, Laksmana, Hanumân, and Bibhisana. Then I worshiped the actors and actresses, who played those parts" (Srî Râmakrishna). "The child lives in the reality of his imagery, as did the men of early prehistoric time" (R. R. Schmidt, *Dawn of the Human Mind*, London, 1936, p. 7), but the aesthete in the actuality of the fetish!

23. In the statement, "in some cases we cannot easily tell whether the native thinks that he is in the actual presence of some (usually invisible) being, or that of a symbol" (Lévy-Bruhl, *L'Expérience mystique*, p. 206), "we" can only refer to such profane mentalities as are intended by our authors when they speak of "civilized" or "emancipated" man or of themselves. It would not be true for a learned Catholic or Hindu to say that "this peculiarity of the symbols of the primitives creates a great difficulty for us," and one wonders why our authors are so much puzzled by the "savage," and not by the contemporary metaphysician. More truly, one does not wonder: it is because it is assumed that wisdom was born with *us*, and that the savage does not distinguish between appearance and reality; it is because we choose to describe the primitive religious cults as a "worship of nature"—we who are nature worshipers indeed, and to whom the words of Plutarch are preeminently applicable, viz. that men have been so blinded by their powers of observation that they can no longer distinguish between, Apollo and the Sun, the reality and the phenomenon.

24. Lévy-Bruhl, *L'Expérience mystique,* pp. 174, 180. Lévy-Bruhl appears to have been quite ignorant of the Platonic-Aristotelian-Christian doctrine of the "participation" of things in their formal causes. His own words, "not necessarily ... likenesses," are notably illogical, since he is speaking of "invisible" prototypes, and it is evident that these invisibles have no appearance that could be visually imitated, but only a character of which there can be a representation by means of adequate (*isos*) symbols; cf. Rom. 1:20, "invisible things ... being understood by the things that are made."

25. Schmidt, *Dawn of the Human Mind*, p. 7.

26. W. Deonna, "Primitivisme et classicisme," BAHA, IV, no. 10 (1937). For the same facts but a contrary conclusion see A. Gleizes, *Vers une Conscience plastique; la forme et l'histoire* (Paris, 1932).

27. Schmidt, *Dawn of the Human Mind*, p. 167. Was "primitive man" already a Platonist, or was Plato a primitive man when he spoke of those arts as legitimate "that will at the same time care for the bodies and the souls of your citizens" (*Republic* 409E-410A), and said that "the one means of salvation from these evils is neither to exercise the soul without the body nor the body without the soul" (*Timaeus* 88BC)?

28. Hocart, *Les Castes*, p. 63. Under these conditions, "Chaque occupation était un sacerdoce" (p. 27).

29. Andrae, *Die ionische Säule*, p. 65.

30. It is noteworthy that the word *fibule* (fibula) in French surgical language means suture.

31. "The Sun is the fastening (*âsañjanam*, one might even say "button") to whom these worlds are linked by means of the quarters ... He strings these worlds to Himself by a thread; the thread is the Gale of the Spirit" (SB VI.1I.1.17 and VIII.7.3.10). Cf. AV IX.8.38, and BG VII.7, "All 'this' is strung on Me like a row of gems on a thread." For the "thread-spirit" doctrine, cf. also Homer, *Iliad* VIII.18 ff.; Plato, *Theatetus* 153 and *Laws* 644; Plutarch, *Moralia* 393 ff.; Hermes, *Libellus* XVI.5.7; John 12:32; Dante, *Paradiso* I.116; Rûmî, *Divân*, Ode XXVIII, "He gave me the end of a thread..."; Blake, "I give you the end of a golden string..." We still speak of living substances as "tissues." See also Coomaraswamy, "The Iconography of Dürer's 'Knoten' and Leonardo's 'Concatenation,'" 1944, and "Spiritual Paternity and the Puppet-Complex," 1945.

32. See Christopher Blinkenberg, *Fibules grecques et orientales*, Copenhagen, 1926. The ornamentation of these fibulae forms a veritable encyclopedia of solar symbols.

33. See Coomaraswamy, "Ornament."

34. Reproduced by permission of the Trustees of the British Museum.

35. Earl Baldwin Smith, *Egyptian Architecture* (New York, 1938), p. 27. "It was a tremendous discovery—how to excite emotions for their own sake" (A. N. Whitehead). Was it really? "No, not even if all the oxen and horses in the world, by their pursuit of pleasure, proclaim that such is the criterion" (Plato, *Philebus* 67)!

36. Preface to Schmidt, *Dawn of the Human Mind*. The customary virtual identification of the "childhood of humanity" with the childhood of the individual, that of the mind of Cro-Magnon man with his "fully developed forehead" (Schmidt, p. 209), with that of the still subhuman child, is illogical. "Since we are forced to believe that the race of man is of one species, it follows that man everywhere has an equally long history behind him" (Benedict, *Patterns of Culture*, p. 18). That the child can in certain respects be used as an adequate symbol of the primordial state, in the sense that "of such is the Kingdom of Heaven," is quite another matter.

37. Schmidt, *Dawn of the Human Mind*, pp. 1, 13, 89, 126, 212 ff.; italics mine. The final sentence contrasts poignantly with Plato's famous prayer, "grant to me that I may become beautiful within, and that my outward and my inner man may be in fond accord" (*Phaedrus* 278C); cf. BG VI.5 and 6, on friendship or enmity between the empirical and the essential "self." Schmidt is referring, of course, to the clear distinction of subject from object which ordinary "knowledge" presupposes; it is precisely this kind of "knowing" that is, from the standpoint of traditional metaphysics, an *ignorance*, and morally an "original sin" of which the wages are death (Gen. 3); cf. Coomaraswamy, "The Intellectual Operation in Indian Art," n. 20.

The remarkable expressions of Schmidt are tantamount to the definition of the modern, civilized "man of understanding" as an atrophied personality, out of touch with his environment. That he also envisages this as an *ascent* of man can only mean that he regards the "seers, who see God face to face" and in whom the folk soul survives, as belonging to a strictly atavistic and inferior type of humanity, and thinks of the "divine inheritance" as something to be gotten rid of as soon as possible.

38. Lucien Lévy-Bruhl, *La Mentalité primitive* (Paris, 1922), pp. 88, 290. The problem of the use of apparently ineffectual rites for the attainment of purely practical ends is reasonably discussed by Radin, *Primitive Man as Philosopher*, pp. 15-18

39. Lévy-Bruhl, *La Mentalité primitive*, p. 92.

40. René Guénon, *La Métaphysique orientale* (Paris, 1939) pp. 15, 17.

41. Lévy-Bruhl, *L'Expérience mystique*, p. 295.

42. Andrae, *Die ionische Säule*, "Schlusswort."

43. M. F. Ashley Montagu, *Coming into Being among the Australian Aborigines* (London, 1937); B. Malinowski, *The Sexual Life of Savages* (London, 1929). Cf. Coomaraswamy, "Spiritual Paternity and the Puppet-Complex," 1945.

44. Montagu, *Coming into Being.*

45. "God, the master of all generative power" (Hermes, *Asclepius* III.21); "the power of generation belongs to God" (*Sum. Theol.* I.45.5); "ex quo omnis paternitas in coelis et terra nominatur" (Eph. 3:14). In Gaelic incantations (see A. Carmichael, *Carmina gadelica*, Edinburgh, 1928), Christ and the Virgin Mary are continually invoked as progenitive deities, givers of increase in cattle or man; the phrasings are almost verbally identical with those of RV VII.102.2, "Who puts the seed in the plants, the cows, the mares, the women, Parjanya." "Call no man your father upon the earth: for one is your father, which is in heaven" (Matt. 23:9).

46. "The Sun is the *âtman* of all that is motionless or mobile," RV I.115.1. "Whatsoever living thing is born, whether motionless or mobile, know that it is from the union of the Knower of the Field and the Field itself," BG XIII.26. "It is inasmuch as He 'kisses' (breathes on) all his children that each can say 'I am,' " SB VII.3.2.12; "Light is the progenitive power," TS VII.1.1.1; cf. John 1:4, "the life was the light of men"; "when the father thus actually emits him as seed into the womb, it is really the sun that emits him as seed into the womb," JUB III.10.4. Further references to solar paternity will be found in SB I.7.2.11 (Sun and Earth parents of all born beings); Dante, *Paradiso* XXII.116 (Sun "the father of each mortal life"); St. Bonaventura, *De reductione artium ad theologiam*, 21; *Mathnawî* I.3775; Plutarch, *Moralia* 368C, *phôs ... gonimon.*

In connection with the "Knower of the Field" it may be remarked that his "conjunction" (*samyoga*) with the "Field" is not merely cognitive but erotic: Skr. *jñâ* in its sense of "to recognize as one's own," or "possess," corresponding to Latin *gnoscere* and English "know" in the Biblical expression "Jacob knew his wife." Now the solar manner of "knowing" (in any sense) is by means of his rays, which are emitted by the "Eye"; and hence in the ritual in which the priest represents Prajâpati (the Sun as Father-Progenitor), he formally "looked at" the sacrificer's wife, "for insemination"; a metaphysical rite that the anthropologist would call a piece of "fertility magic." See also Coomaraswamy, "The Sunkiss," 1940.

47. For "to be present," the Pâli equivalent of Skr. *praty-upasthâ*, "to stand upon," is employed; and this is the traditional expression, in accordance with which the Spirit is said to "take its stand upon" the bodily vehicle, which is accordingly referred to as its *adhisthânam*, "standing ground" or "platform." Gandharva, originally the Divine Eros, and Sun.

48. That St. John is speaking with reference to a regeneration by no means excludes application to any generation; for as exegetical theory insists, the literal sense of the words of scripture is also always true, and is the vehicle of the transcendental significance.

49. To which correspond also the words of a Gaelic incantation, "from the bosom of the God of life, and the courses together," (Carmichael, *Carmina gadelica*, II, 119). In Egypt, similarly, "Life was an emanation of progenitive light and the creative word ... The Sun, Râ, was the creator above all others, and the means of his creative power were his eye, the 'Eye of Horus,' and his voice, the 'voice of heaven, the bolt'"; the Pharaoh was regarded as having been born, quite literally, of the Sun and a human mother (Alexandre Moret, *Du Caractère religieux de la royauté pharaonique*, Paris, 1902, pp. 40, 41).

50. The misunderstanding of the folk is accidental rather than essential; because they are not skeptical, nor moralistic, "by faith they understand." On the other hand, the literary artist (Andersen, Tennyson, etc.) who does not scruple to modify his narrative for aesthetic or moral reasons, often distorts it (cf. Plutarch, *Moralia* 358F, on "the unestablished first thoughts of poets and littérateurs") ; and so, in the transition "from ritual to romance" we often have to ask, "how far did such and such an author really understand his material?"

17

The Coming to Birth of the Spirit

"You cannot dip your feet twice into the same waters,
because fresh waters are ever flowing in upon you."
Heracleitus

The present article embodies a part of the material which I have assembled during recent years towards a critical analysis of the Indian, and incidentally neo-Platonic and other doctrines of "reincarnation," regeneration, and transmigration, as these terms are defined below.[1] These doctrines, often treated as one, appear to have been more profoundly misunderstood, if that is possible, than any other aspect of Indian metaphysics. The theses that will be proposed are that the Indian doctrine of palingenesis is correctly expressed by the Buddhist statement that in "reincarnation" *nothing*[2] passes over from one embodiment to another, the continuity being only such as can be seen when one lamp is lighted from another: that the terms employed for "rebirth" (e.g. *punar janma, punar bhava, punar apâdana* [*prati januma, nava jamma*]) are used in at least three easily distinguishable senses: (1) with respect to the transmission of physical and psychic characteristics from father to son, i.e. with respect to palingenesis in a biological sense, defined by Webster as "The reproduction of ancestral characters without change,"[3] (2) with respect to a transition from one to another plane of consciousness effected in one and the same individual and generally one and the same life, viz. that kind of rebirth which is implied in the saying "Except ye be born again" and of which the ultimate term is deification,[4] and (3) with respect to the "motion" or peregrination of the Spirit from one body-and-soul to another, which "motion"[5] necessarily takes place whenever one such a compound vehicle dies or another is generated, just as water might be poured out of one vessel into the sea, and dipped out by another, being always "water," but never, except in so far as the vessel seems to impose a temporary identity and shape on its contents, properly

247

"a water"; and thirdly, that no other doctrines of rebirth are taught in the Upanisads and Bhagavad Gîtâ than are already explicit and implicit in the Rig Veda.

"Spirit" we employ in the present introduction with reference to *âtman, brahman, mrtyu, purusa*, etc., alike, but in the body of the article only as a rendering of *âtman*, assuming as usual a derivation from a root *an* or *vâ* meaning to breathe or blow. But because the Spirit is really the whole of Being in all beings, which have no private essence but only a becoming, *âtman* is also used reflexively to mean the man himself as he conceives "himself" (whether as body, or body-and-soul, or body-soul-and-spirit, or finally and properly only as Spirit),[6] and in such contexts we render *âtman* by "self," or sometimes "self, or spirit." Capitals are employed whenever there seems to be a possibility of confusing the very Man or immanent God with the man "himself"; but it must always be remembered that the distinction of spirit from Spirit and person from Person is "only logical, and not real," in other words, a distinction without difference (*bhedâbheda*). A sort of image of what may be implied by such a distinction (which is analogous to that of the Persons as envisaged in the Christian Trinity) can be formed if we remember that the Perfected are spoken of as "rays" of the Supernal Sun, which rays are manifestly distinct if considered in their extension, but no less evidently indistinct if considered in their intension, i.e. at their source.

The Upanisads and BG are primarily concerned to bring about in the disciple a transference of self-reference, the feeling that "I am," from oneself to the Spirit within us: and this with the purely practical purpose[7] in view of pointing out a Way (*mârga*, Buddhist *magga*)[8] that can be followed from darkness to light and from liability to pain and death to a state of deathless and timeless beatitude, attainable even here and now. In the Upanisads and early Buddhism it is clear that what had been an initiatory teaching transmitted in pupillary succession was now being openly published and in some measure adapted to the understanding of "royal" and not merely "sacerdotal" types of mentality, for example in the BG.

On the other hand, it is equally clear that there existed widespread popular misunderstandings, based either on an ignorance of the traditional doctrines or on a too literal interpretation of what had been heard of them.[9] The internal evidence of the texts themselves with their questions and answers, definitions and refutations, is amply sufficient to show this. Hence, then, the necessity of those innumerable dialogues in which, alike in the Upanisads, BG and Buddhism, that which in "us" is, and that which is not, the Spirit are sharply distinguished and contrasted; the Spirit being that which "remains over"[10] when all other factors of the composite personality "identity-and-appearance," or "soul-and-body" have been eliminated. And furthermore, because "That One that breathes yet does not breathe" (RV. X,129.2) is not any what as opposed to any other what, It or He is described simultaneously by means of affirmations and denials, *per modum excellentiae et remotionis.*[11] The following analysis of the Supreme Identity (*tad ekam*), restricted to words derived from *an*, to "breathe" or *vā*, to "blow," may contribute to a better understanding of the texts:

Despirated Godhead	*avātam, nirātmā, anātmya, nirvāna*, Pali *nibbāna*. Only negative definitions are possible.
Spirit, God, Sun, "Knower of the field": King	*ātman*, Pali *attā*. In motion, *vāyu, vāta*, "Gale of the Spirit"; and *prāna*, "Spiration," the "Breath of Life" as imparted, not the breath empirically, but the "ghost" that is given up when living creatures die.[12] Being "One and many," transcendent and immanent, although without any interstice or discontinuity, the Spirit, whether as *ātman* or as *prāna* can be considered in the plural (*ātmanah, prānah*), though only "as if." Form, as distinguished from substance: Intellect.
What-is-not-Spirit; Moon; the Field, World, lower-Earth: the King's domain.	*anātman*, Pali *anattā*. The hylomorphic, physical and psychic, or lower-mental, vehicle of the Spirit, [is] seemingly differentiated by its envelopes. Mortal substance as distinguished from its informing Forms.

These are not "philosophical" categories, but categories of experience from our point of view, *sub rationem dicendi sive intelligendi*, rather than *secundum rem.*

We can scarcely argue here in detail what was really meant by the palingenesis, metempsychosis, or metasomatosis of the neo-Platonic tradition.[13] We shall only remark that in such texts as Plotinus,

Enneads III, 4.2 (Mackenna's version), where it is said that "Those (i.e. of "us") that have maintained the human level are men once more. Those that have lived wholly to sense become animals ... the spirit of the previous life pays the penalty,"[14] it must be realized that it is a metempsychosis and metasomatosis (and not a transmigration of the real person) that is in question; it is a matter, in other words, of the direct or indirect inheritance of the psycho-physical characteristics of the deceased, which he does not take with him at death and which are not a part of his veritable essence, but only its temporary and most external vehicle. It is only in so far as we mistakenly identify "ourselves" with these accidental garments of the transcendent personality, the mere properties of terrestrial human existence, that it can be said that "we" are reincorporated in men or animals: it is not the "spirit" that pays the penalty, but the animal or sensitive soul with which the disembodied spirit has no further concern.[15] The doctrine merely accounts for the reappearance of psycho-physical characteristics in the mortal sphere of temporal succession. The intention of the teaching is always that a man should have recognized "himself" in the spirit, and not in the sensitive soul, before death, failing which "he" can only be thought of as in a measure "lost," or at any rate disintegrated. When, on the other hand, it is said that the "Soul" is "self-distributed" (cf. *âtmânam vibhajya*, MU VI,26) and "always the same thing present entire" (*ibid.*, III,4.6), and that this "Soul passes through the entire heavens in forms varying with the variety of place"[16]—the sensitive form, the reasoning form, even the vegetative form" (*ibid.*, III,4.2) it is evident that it is only as it were that there is any question of "several Souls," and that what is described is not the translation of a private personality from one body to another, but much rather the peregrination of the Spirit (*âtman*) repeatedly described in the Upanisads as omnimodal and omnipresent, and therefore as occupying or rather animating body after body, which bodies or rather bodies and sensitive souls, follow one another in causally determinated series.[17]

All this is surely, too, what Eckhart (in whom the Neo-Platonic tradition persists) must mean when be says "Aught is suspended from the divine essence; its progression (i.e. vehicle) is matter, wherein the soul puts on new forms and puts off her old ones ... the one she doffs she dies to, and the one she dons she lives in" (Evans ed. I, 379), almost identical with BG II, 22 "As a man casting off worn-out garments, taketh other new ones, so the Body-dweller (*dehin = sarîra âtman*), casting off worn-out bodies, enters into new ones," cf. BU IV,4.4 "Just so this Spirit, striking down the body and driving off its nescience,[18] makes for itself some other new and fairer form."

The three sections of Upanisads translated below begin with the question, "What is most the Spirit"? That is to say, "What is this 'Self' that is not 'myself'? What is this 'Spirit' in 'me,' that is not '*my*' spirit"? It is the distinction that Philo is making in *Quaestiones ... ad Genesis* II, 59 and *De Cherubim*, 113ff. (as cited by Goodenough, *By Light, Light*, 1941, pp. 374-375) when he distinguishes "us" from that in us which existed before "our" birth and will still exist when "we, who in our junction with our bodies,[19] are mixtures (*sunkritoi*) and have qualities, shall not exist, but shall be brought into the rebirth, by which, becoming joined to immaterial things, we shall become unmixed (*asunkritoi*) and without qualities." The "rebirth" (*palingenesia*) is here certainly not an "aggregation" or palingenesis in the biological sense, but a "regeneration" (palingenesis as a being born again of and as the Spirit of Light), cf. Goodenough, p. 376, note 35.

"What is most the Self," or "most the Spirit"? As the late C. E. Rolt has said in another context (*Dionysius the Areopagite on the Divine Names and Mystical Theology*, 1920, p. 35), "Pascal has a clear-cut answer: 'Il n'y a que l'Être universel qui soit tel ... Le Bien Universel est en nous, est nous-mêmes et n'est pas nous.' This is exactly the Dionysian doctrine. Each must enter into himself and so find Something that is his true Self and yet is not his particular self ... Something other than his individuality which (other) is within his soul and yet outside of him."

"If any man come to me ... and hate not his own soul (*heautou psuchên*, Vulgate *animam suam*) he cannot be my disciple" (Luke, 14:26). The English versions shrink from such a rendering, and have "hate not his own life." It is evidently, however, not merely "life" that is meant, since those who are at the same time required to "hate" their own relatives, if, on the contrary, they love them, may be willing to sacrifice even life for their sake: what is evidently meant is the lower soul, as regularly distinguished in the neo-Platonic tradition from the higher power of the soul which is that of the Spirit and not really a property of the soul but its royal guest.[20] It is again, then, precisely from this point of view that St. Paul says with a voice of thunder, "For the word of God is quick and powerful, and sharper than any two-edged sword, piercing even to the dividing asunder of soul and spirit" (Heb. 4:12),[21] and consistently with this that "Whoever is joined unto the Lord is One Spirit" (I Cor. 6:17, cf. 12:4-13).

With this may be compared, on the one hand, BG VI, 6 "The Spirit is verily the foeman of and at war with what-is-not-the-Spirit" (*anâtmanas tu satrutve vartetâtmaiva satruvat*), where *anâtman* = Buddhist *anattâ*,[22] all that, body-and-soul, of which one says *na me so attâ*, "This is not my spirit," and on the other, with Eckhart's "Yet the soul must relinquish her existence" (Evans ed., I, 274),[23] and, in the anonymous *Cloud of Unknowing*, Ch. XLIV, "All men have matter of sorrow: but most specially he feeleth sorrow, that feeleth and wotteth that he is," and with Blake's "I will go down unto Annihilation and Eternal Death, lest the Last Judgment come and find me unannihilate, and I be seiz'd and giv'n into the hands of my own Selfhood." All scripture, and even all wisdom, truly, "cries aloud for freedom from self."

But if "he feeleth sorrow that feeleth and wotteth that he is," he who is no longer anyone, and sees, not himself, but as our texts express it, only the Spirit, one and the same in immanence and transcendence, being what he sees, *geworden was er ist*, he feels no sorrow, he is beatified,— "One ruler, inward Spirit of all beings, who maketh manifold a single form! Men contemplative, seeing Him whose station is within you, and seeing with Him,—eternal happiness is theirs, none others" (KU V,12).[24]

An "actual experience of Unknowing and of the Negative Path that leads to it" (Rolt, *ibid.*) is not easy to be had, unless for those who are perfectly mature, and like ripe fruits, about to fall from their branch. There are men still "living," at least in India, for whom the funeral rites have been performed, as if to seal them "dead and buried in the Godhead." "It is hard for us to forsake the familiar things around, and turn back to the old home whence we came" (Hermes, *Lib.* IV, 9). But it can be said, even of those who are still self-conscious, and cannot bear the strongest meat, that he specially, if not yet most specially, "feeleth joy," whose will has already fully consented to, though it may not yet have realized, an annihilation of the whole idea of any private property in being, and has thus, so to speak, foreseen and foretasted an ultimate renunciation of all his great possessions, whether physical or psychic. *Mors janua vitae.*

Notes

1. Frag. 12; cf. Fragments 30, 31a, 31b, 91a (qv), 91b, 48a, 50 and 10. The line could also be translated: "As they step into the same rivers, different and still different waters flow upon them", cf. Plut. *De apud Delphous* 3926. The original reference is to Arius, *Didyma, Dox. Gr.* 471.47 and Plato, *Theatetus* 160D, *Cratylus* 401D and 402A. The emphasis is here the unity of the World's Flux of which we are a part, at any one point one thing and another at the next.See also my "Vedic Exemplarism," *Harvard Journal of Asiatic Studies*, I, 1936 and "Rebirth and Omniscience in Pali Buddhism," *Indian Culture*, III, p. 19f. and p. 760; and René Guénon, *L'Erreur spirite*, Paris, 1930, Ch. VI.

2. *Mil.* 72, *na koci satto*, "not any being." Note that this expression is by no means necessarily exclusive of the Âtman as defined in the Upanisads by negation, of Basilides' *ouk ôn Theos*, Eriugena's God who "is not any what," Eckhart's "nonexistent" Godhead, Behmen's God who is "no thing."

3. In a number of important texts, rebirth is explicitly and categorically defined in terms of heredity, and this is probably the only sense in which the individual is thought of as returning to the plane of being from which he departs at death. It is expressly stated of the deceased that he is not seen again here (SB XIII, 8.4.12, *etaj jîvâ's ca pitaras ca na samdrsyante*, and SB. *passim, sakrd parâñcah pitarah*).

We have now RV VI,70.3: "He is born forth in his progeny according to law" (*pra prajâbhir jâyate dharmanas parî*); AB VII,13, "The father enter the wife, the mother, becoming an embryo, and coming into being anew, is born again of her" (*jâyâm pravisati, garbho bhûtvâ, sa mâtaram, tasyâm punar navo bhûtvâ jâyate*, cf. AV XI,4.20); AA II,5, "In that he both before and after birth maketh the son to become (*sa yat kumâram ... adhibhâvayati*), it is just himself as son that he maketh to become" (*kumâram ... adhibhâvayati âtmânam eva*); CU III,17. 5, "That he has procreated, that is his rebirth" (*asosteti punar-utpâdanam*); BU III,9.28, "He (the deceased) has indeed been born, but he is not born again, for (being deceased) who is there to beget him again?" (*jâta eva na jâyate, ko nv enam janayet punah*). We have also BU II,2.8 where filiation is rebirth "in a likeness" (*pratirûpah*). It would be impossible to have a clearer definition of the ordinary meaning of "reincarnation." This filial reincarnation is moreover precisely the *antapokatastasis* or "renewal of things by substitution" of Hermes, as explained by Scott (*Hermetica*, II, 322), "The father lives again in his son; and though the individuals die and return no more, the race is perpetually renewed."

It should be added that beside the natural fact of progenitive reincarnation there is also a formal communication and delegation of the father's nature and status in the world, made when the father is at the point of death. Thus in BU I,5.17-20, when this "All bequest" (*sampratti*) has been made, "the son who has been thus induced (*anusistah*) is called the father's 'mundane-representative'" (*lokyah*), and so "by means of the son the father is still-present-in (*prati-tisthati*) the world": and similarly in *Kaus. Up.* II,15 (10) where the "All-bequest of the father to the son" (*pitâpûtrîyam sampradânam*) is described in greater detail, after which bequest if perchance the father should recover, he must either live under the lordship of the son or become a wandering religious (*parivâvrajet*, i.e. become a *parivrâjaka* dead to the world at least in outward form).

4. Cf. my "Indian Doctrine of Man's Last End," *Asia*, May 1937.

5. "Motion," not a local motion, but an *omnipresence*, and as we speak, although metaphorically, of a "procession" *in divinis*. Not a local motion, but that of the Unmoved Mover, "Motionless One, swifter than thought itself ... who outgoeth others though they run" (*Isâ* 4), "Seated, He fares afar; reclining, goeth every-where" (KU II,21), being "Endless in all directions" (MU VI,17), and though "He hath not come from anywhere" (KU II,18), still "Perpetually differentiated and going everywhere" (Mund. I,2.6) and "Multifariously taking birth" (*bahudhâ jâyamânah*, Mund. II,2.6).

6. Where we say, "Do not hurt me," meaning the body, or "I know," or "my soul," the very careful teacher would say "Do not hurt this body," "this mind knows," and "the Spirit in 'me'" or "Body-dweller."

7. Cf. Edgerton, "The Upanisads, what do they seek and why?", JAOS., 51. 97; Dante, *Ep. ad. Can. Grand.* §§15, 16. The Vedic tradition is neither philosophical, mystical, nor religious in the ordinary modern senses of these words. The tradition is metaphysical; "mystical" only in the sense that it expounds a "mystery," and in that of Dionysius, *Theologia Mystica*. The Indian position has been admirably defined by Satkari Mookerjee: "*Of course* the question of salvation is a problem of paramount importance and constitutes the justification and ultimate *raison d'être* of philosophical enquiry. Philosophy in India has never been a mere speculative interest irrespective of its bearing on life ... The goal loomed large in the philo-sophical horizon, but it was recognized that there was no short cut or easy walk-over to it. The full price had to be paid in the shape of unfaltering philosophical *real-ization* of the ultimate mysteries of existence achieved through a rigorous moral dis-cipline; and mere academic and intellectual satisfaction accruing from philosophical studies was considered to be of value only in so far as it was calculat-ed to bring about the happy consummation" (in *The Cultural Heritage of India*, Vol. III, pp. 409, 410, 1937; italics mine).

8. For the meaning of this word see my "Nature of 'Folklore' and 'Popular art'" in *Quarterly Journal Mythic Society*, Bangalore, Vol. XXVII.

9. We do not say that a theory of reincarnation (re-embodiment of the very man and true personality of the deceased) has never been believed in India or else-where, but agree with M. Guénon that "it has never been taught in India, even by Buddhists and is essentially a modern European notion," and further "that no authentic traditional doctrine has ever spoken of reincarnation" (*L'Erreur spirite*, pp. 47, 199). It has been generally agreed by modern scholars that "reincarnation" is not a Vedic doctrine, but one of popular or unknown origin adopted and taken for granted already in the Upanisads and Buddhism. Neglecting Buddhism for the moment, it may be pointed out that where we have to do with a fundamental and revolutionary thesis, and not the simple expansion of doctrines previously taught, it would be inconceivable from the orthodox and traditional Hindu point of view that what is not taught in one part of *sruti* could have been taught in another; in such a matter, one cannot imagine an orthodox Hindu "choosing between" the RV and Upanisads, as though one might be right and the other wrong. This difficulty disappears if we find that the theory of reincarnation (as distinguished from the doctrines of metempsychosis and transmigration) is not really taught in the Upanisads: in this connection we call particular attention to the statement of BU IV, 3.37 where, when a new entity is coming into being, the factorial elements of

the new composite are made to say, *not* "Here comes so-and-so" (previously deceased) but, "HERE COMES BRAHMAN." This is furthermore in full agreement with the Buddhist *Mil.*, 72 where it is said categorically that no entity whatever passes over from one body to another, and it is merely that a new flame is lighted.

In differentiating reincarnation, as defined above, from metempsychosis and transmigration it may be added that what is meant by metempsychosis is the psychic aspect of palingenesis, or in other words psychic heredity, and that what is meant by transmigration is a change of state or level of reference excluding by definition the idea of a return to any state or level that has already been passed through. The transmigration of the "individual" *âtman* (spirit) can only be distinguished as a particular case of the transmigration of the *paramâtman* (Spirit, Brahman), for which last, however, it may be proved desirable to employ some such term as "peregrination"; peregrination replacing transmigration when the state of the *kâmâcârin* (Mover-at-will) has been attained.

There are doubtless many passages in the Upanisads, etc., which, taken out of their whole context, seem to speak of a "personal reincarnation," and have been thus misunderstood, alike in India and in Europe. Cf. Scott, *Hermetica*, II, pp. 193-194, note 6 ("he" in the first quoted sentence is the son of Valerius, and for our purposes "so-and-so" or Everyman; the italics are mine): "During his life on earth he was a distinct portion of *pneuma*, marked off and divided from the rest; now, that portion of *pneuma*, which was he, is blended with the whole mass of *pneuma* in which the life of the universe resides. This is what the writer (Apollonius) *must* have meant, if he adhered to the doctrine laid down in the preceding part of the letter. But from this point onward, he speaks ambiguously, and uses phrases which, *to a reader who had not fully grasped the meaning of his doctrine*, might seem to imply a survival of the man as a distinct and individual person."

The modern mind, with its attachment to "individuality" and its "proofs of the survival of personality" is predisposed to misinterpret the traditional texts. We ought not to read into these texts what we should like or "naturally" expect to find in them, but only to read in them what *they* mean: but "it is hard for us to forsake the familiar things around us, and turn back to the old home whence we came" (Hermes, *Lib.* IV, 9).

Individuality, however we may hug its chains, is a partial and definite modality of being: "I" is defined by what is "not-I," and thus imprisoned. It is with a view to liberation from this prison and this partiality that our texts so repeatedly demonstrate that our vaunted individuality is neither uniformal nor constant, but composite and variable, pointing out that he is the wisest who can most say "I am not now the man I was." This is true in a measure of all werdende things; but the "end of the road" (*adhvanah pâram*) lies beyond "manhood." It is only of what is not individual, but universal (cosmic) that perduration can be predicated, and only of what is neither individual nor universal that an eternity, without before or after, can be affirmed.

10. KU V, 4 *kim atra sisyate*? CU VIII, 5 *atisisyate ... âtman*. Note that *tad sisyate* = Sea = Ananta = Brahman = Âtman.

11. We have briefly discussed the Indian doctrine de divinis nominibus in JIH XV, 84-92, 1936, and will only remark here that RV V,44.6 *yâdrg eva dadrse tâdrg ucyate*, "As he is envisaged, so is he called" answers to St. Thomas, *Sum. Theol.*, I. XIII. [1c: *Voces referuntur ad rea significandas mediante conceotione intellectus. Secundum iqitur quod*

aliquid a nobis intellectu cognosci potest, sic a nobis potest nominari, and *ad* 3: *Pronomina vero demonstrationem ad id quod intelligitur,* and 5c: *Secundum analogium creaturum ad ipsum.*]

12. *Prâna,* like Gk. *pneuma* has the double value of *Spiritus* and *spiraculum vitae* according to the context. "It is as the Breath-of-life (*prâna*) that the Provident Spirit (*prajñâtman*) grasps and erects the flesh" (Kaus. Up. III,3), cf. St. Thomas, *Sum. Theol.,* III,32.1, "The power of the soul which is in the semen, through the spirit enclosed therein fashions the body," and Schiller, *Wallenstein,* III, 13 "Es ist der Geist der sick den Körper schart"; and JUB III,32.2. Whereas the divided *prânah* are said to move within the vectors of channels (*nadi, hita*) of the heart (see refs. Hume, *Upanisads,* ed. 2), in Hermes *Lib.* X, 13 and 17 the "vital Spirit" (*pneuma*) traverses the veins and arteries "with, but not as, the blood" and thus "moves the body, and carries it like a burden ... (and) controls the body."

The *Prâna* is identified with the *Prajñâtman*: as *Prâna,* "life," as *Prajñâtman,* "immortality"; length of days in this world and immortality in the other are complementary. As distinguished from the *Prâna,* the divided *prânah* are the currents of perception by means of the sense organs and are prior to them. Hence as in KU IV.1 one says, "The Self-existent pierced the openings outward, thereby it is that one looks forth" (but must look in to see the Seer; see the discussion of this passage in JIH XI, 571-578, 1935).

13. For many references, see Scott, *Hermetica,* II, 265ff.

14. Viz. of "shameful transmigration into bodies of another kind," Hermes Trismegistus, *Asclepius* I, 12a, cf. BU VI,2.16, CU V,10,7-8, Kaus. I.2. We understand that the result of a bestiality in "us" is that bestial types are propagated: this is the reincarnation of character in our sense (1), and it is in this way that "the sins of the fathers are visited upon their children."

"Beasts," moreover, is a symbol, just as when we say, "Don't be a beast" or refer to some man as a "worm" or some woman as a "cat." The Indian tradition regularly employs this sort of language, AA II,3.8 (a *locus classicus,* cf. the definition of "person" by Boethius, *Contra Eutychen,* II), for example, defining the spiritual man who "knows what is and what is not mundane," etc., as a "person" (*purusa*), and "others" whose knowledge is merely an affection as "cattle" (*pasu*).

For the benefit of those who believe in the folk origin of the notion of reincarnation (understood to mean a rebirth in the flesh of the very person lately deceased) it may be observed that the Sumatran Bataks devoured "captives in war to assimilate their valor and grandmothers or grandfathers as a form of pious internment. This last was frequently, if not always, at the request of the victim, in the belief that it would assure *continued existence in the form of a new soul*" (G.H. Seybold in *Asia,* September 1937, p. 641, italics mine). This cannibal belief is a belief in metempsychosis, and not a belief in "reincarnation."

15. In all these discussions it must be remembered that "soul" (*psuchê, anima,* without exact equivalent in Sanskrit, other than *nâma,* the name or "form" of a thing by which its identity is established) is a two-fold value; the higher powers of the "soul" coinciding with Spirit (*pneuma*) and/or Intellect, (*nous hêgemôn,* or *noûs*), the lower with sensation (*aisthêsis*) and opinion (*doxa*). Hence the Gnostic hierarchy of animal, psychic, and spiritual men, the former destined to be lost, the intermediate capable of liberation, and the latter virtually free, and assured of liberation at death (Bruce Codex, etc.). By "lost" understand "unmade into the cos-

The Coming to Birth of the Spirit

mos" (Hermes, *Lib.* IX, 6), and by "liberated," wholly separated from the animal soul and thus become what the higher powers already are, divine. Render *âtman* by "soul." Observe that "animal" is from *anima* = *psuchê*, "soul," *animalia* = *empsucha*; hence Scott, *Hermetica*, I. 297 renders *Solum enim animal homo* by "Man, and man alone of all beings that have soul"; it is by *nous* and not by *psuchê* that man is distinguished from animal (Hermes, *Lib.* VIII, 5). It may be noted that the Averroist doctrine of the Unity of the Intellect (for which "monopsychism" seems a peculiarly inappropriate term) was repugnant to the Christian scholastic authors of a later age, precisely because of its incompatibility with a belief in personal immortality (cf. De Wulf, *Histoire..*, II, 361, 1936): on the other hand, imagination (*phantasmata*) and memory survive the death of the body not as they are in the passive intellect (Hermetic *noêsis*, Skr. *asuddha manas*), but only as they are in the possible intellect (Hermetic *nous*, Skr., *suddha manas*) which "is in act when it is identified with each thing as knowing it" (St. Thomas, *Sum. Theol.*, I,2.67.2C). Furthermore St. Thomas says that "To say that the soul is of the Divine Substance involves a manifest improbability" (I,90.1), and Eckhart is continually speaking of the deaths and last death of the soul. It is clear at least that an immortality of the sensitive and reasoning "soul" is out of the question, and that if the soul can in any sense be called "immortal," it is with respect to the "intellectual power of the soul" rather than with respect to the soul itself. Hermes' "soul that is fastened to the body," *Lib.* XI, 24a, is no conceivably immortal principle, even supposing a temporary post-mortem cohesion of certain psycho-physical elements of the *bhûtâtman*; neither can we equate the "soul" that Christ asks us to "hate" with "man's immortal soul." The quest of "the modern man in search of a soul" is a very different one from that implied in Philo's "soul of the soul"; one may say that modern psychology and aesthetics have in view only the lower or animal soul in man, and only the subconscious. What Philo (*Quis rerum divinarum Heres*, 48, Goodenough's version, p. 378) says is that "The word 'soul' is used in two senses, with reference either to the soul as a whole or to its dominant (*hêgemonikon* = Skr. *anataryâmin*) part, which latter is, properly speaking, the soul of the soul" (*psuchê psuchês* cf. in MU III, 2 *bhûtâtman ... amrto' syâtmâ* "elemental self ... its deathless Self). The value of the European "soul" has remained ambiguous ever since.

Hence in the analysis of neo-Platonic doctrines of rebirth, and also throughout the Christian tradition from the Gospels to Eckhart and the Flemish mystics, it is indispensable to know just what "sort of soul" is being spoken of in a given context: and in translating from Sanskrit it is exceedingly dangerous, if not invariably misleading, to render *âtman* by "soul."

16. I do not know the source of this quotation; it is probably Platonic, but corresponds exactly to *Nirukta*, VII, 4, "It is because of his great divisibility that they apply many names to Him ... The other Gods, or Angels (*devâh*) are counter-members of the One Spirit. They originate in function (*karma*); Spirit (*âtman*) is their source ... Spirit is the whole of what they are," and BD I, 70-74 "Because of the vastness of the Spirit, a diversity of names is given ... according to the distribution of the spheres. It is inasmuch as they are differentiations (vibhutih, cf, BG X,40) that the names are innumerable ... according to the spheres in which they are established." Cf. MU VI, 26 "Distributing himself He fills these worlds," and for further references my "Vedic Monotheism" in JIH XV, pp. 54-92, April, 1936.

"Now there are diversities of gifts, but the same Spirit. And there are differences

57

—-

of administration, but the same Lord. And there are diversities of operations, but it is the same God that worketh in all ... The members of that body, being many, are one body" (I Cor.12:4-6 and 12).

17) For "*karma*" (= "*adrsta*") in Christian doctrine, cf. Augustine, *Gen. ad. Lit.*, VII, 24 (cited by St. Thomas, *Sum. Theol.* I,91.2), "The human body pre-existed in the previous works in their causal virtues" and *De Trin.* III, 9, "As a mother is pregnant with the unborn offspring, so the world itself is pregnant with the causes of unborn things" (cf. St. Thomas, I, 115.2 ad 4), and St. Thomas, I. 103.7 ad 2, "If God governed alone (and not also by means of mediate causes) things would be deprived of the perfection of causality."

18. Hermes Trismegistus, Lib. X, 8b, *kakia de psuchês agnôsia ... Tounantion de aretê psuchês gnôsis ... ho gar gnous ... êdê theios*, and XI.ii.21a, "But if you shut up your soul in your body, and abase yourself, and say 'I know nothing' (*Ouden noô*)..., then what have you to do with God?" *Ignorantia divisiva est errantium*, as Ulrich says in comment on Dionysius, *De div. Nom.* "Agnostic" means "ignoramus," or even *quis ignorare vult sine ignorantiam diligit*. On the contrary, "Think that for you too nothing is impossible" (Hermes, *Lib.* XI,ii.20b), cf. "Nothing shall be impossible to you" (Matt. 17:20); "Not till the soul knows all that there is to be known does she cross over to the unknown good" (Eckhart, Evans ed. I, 385); "No despiration without omniscience" (SP V, 74-75). Note that Hermes *Lib.* II,ii.20b-21a corresponds to CU VIII.1.

19. BG XIII, 26 "Whatsoever is generated, whatever being (*kimcit sattvam*, cf. *Mil.* 72 *koci satto*, cited above) whether mobile or immobile, know that it is from the conjunction (*samyogât*) of the Field with the Knower of the Field." The "Field" has been previously defined in XIII, 5-6; it embraces the whole of what we should call "soul and body" and all that is perceived by them.

20. Cf. Plutarch, *Obsolescence of Oracles*, 436F, where the soul of man is assigned to Prophecy (*hê mantikê* here = *pronoia*, Providence as distinguished from "compelling and natural causes") as its *material* support (*hulên men autê tên psychên tou anthrôpou ... apodidotes*); and BG VI.6 where the Spirit is called the enemy of what is not the Spirit (*anâtmanas tu ... âtmaiva satruvat*).

"To be willing to lose (hate) our *psuchê* must mean to forget ourselves entirely ... to live no more my own life, but let my consciousness be possessed and suffused by the Infinite and Eternal life of the spirit" (Inge, *Personal Idealism and Mysticism*, p. 102 and James, *Varieties of Religious Experience*, p. 451).

21. *merismou psuchês kai pneumatos*, cf.Hermes, *Lib.* X, 160 *ho nous tês psuchês* (*chôrixetai*).

22. *Anâtman*, similarly "un-en-spired" (not "despirated") in SB II, 2.28 where gods and titans alike are originally "un-en-spired and "mortal," and "to be un-en-spired is the same as to be mortal" (*anâtmâ hi martyah*); Agni alone is "immortal" (*amartyah*).

23. Compare the expressions used by St. Bernard, *deficere a se tota* and *a semetipsa liquescere* in *De diligendo Deo*; and as Gilson remarks, p. 156, "Quelle différence y-a-t-il donc, à la limite, entre aimer Dieu et s'aimer soi-même?"

24. *Eko vasî sarva-bhûtântarâtmâ ekam rûpam bahudhâ yah karoti: Tam âtmastham ye'nupasyanti dhîrâs tesâm sukham sâsvatam nêtaresâm* [(KUV.12).]

The force of *anu* in *anupasyanti* we can only suggest by the repeated "seeing ...

and seeing with." It is lamented by the descending souls that "Our eyes will have lit-tle room to take things in ... and when we see Heaven, our forefather, contracted to small compass, we shall never cease to moan. And even if we see, we shall not see outright" (Hermes, Stobaeus, *Exc.* XXIII, 36); "For now we see through a glass, darkly; but then face to face: now I know in part; but then shall I know even as also I am known" (I Cor. 13:12). Sight-of is perfected in sight-as, even as knowledge-of in knowledge-as (*adaequatio rei et intellectus*: to see Heaven "outright" requires an eye of Heaven's width). *Dhîrâh*, "contemplatives, those who see inwardly, not with the "eye of the flesh" (*mâmsa caksus*); who see the Spirit "above all to be seen" (*abhidhyâyeyam*, MU I, 1), "the Spirit that is yours and in all things, and than which all else is a wretchedness" (BU III, 4. 2).

Note that *ekam rûpam bahuddhâ yah karoti* corresponds to S II, 212 *eko'pi bahuddhâ homi*: and "than which all else is a wretchedness" to the Buddhist *anicca, anattâ, dukkha.*

18

Quod factum est in ipso vita erat

"ho gegonen en autô zôê ên."

These words,[1] taken from John 1:3, 4 are cited in the form in which they are given in nearly all of the earlier codices, and in which they are quoted by the Scholastics, e.g. Meister Eckhart in *Expositio S, Evangelii sec. Johannem* (ed. J. Christ and J. Koch, Stuttgart-Berlin, 1936, p. 56), and by Origen in *Comm. in Ev. Joannio*, II.16.2 I render, "What has been made (or, "has become," or "was begotten") was life in Him," or in Sanskrit *Yad bhûtam* (or *jâtam*) *tad svâtmani jîva âsît.*

Both Meister Eckhart and St. Bonaventura, the latter in *I Sent.*, d. 36, a. 2, q. 1 ad 4 citing St Augustine's *res factae ... in artifice creato dicuntur vivere*, recognize the analogy of the human and divine artificers; in both cases the pattern of what is to be made pre-exists in the maker's living mind, and is alive in it, and remains alive in it even when the *factibile* has become a *factum* or after it has been destroyed. Our intention is to indicate the immediate and universal background against which these ideas subsist.

This background is essentially that of the traditional doctrine of the "two minds," or two aspects of the mind, the one in act and the other in action. Combining Aristotle's *Metaphysics*, XII.7.8, 1072b 20f. and XII.9.5, 1074a 34f. with *De anima*, III.5, 430 a-f., we find that of these two the first, or Mind[3] "in act" (*energeia*)— "in itself" (*kath' adtên*), in its own act of being—is "apart" (*chôristos*) "from sensibles" (*tôn aisthêtôn*), "contemplative" (*theôrêtikos*), "impassible" (*apathês*), without remembrance[4] and unmixed; "it does not think," or rather, "its 'thinking' is the 'Thinking of thinking,' (*noêseôs noêsis*) i.e. the principle and sine qua non, but not the activity of thinking. In other words, "it thinks only itself" (*auton ara noei*) "throughout eternity," (*ton apanta aiôna*) without distinction of subject from object, for where both are immaterial "the thesis is both the operation and the thought," (*ho logos to pragma kai hê noêsis*) "thought and what is thought of are one and the same" (*hê noêsis tô nooumenô mia*),[5] Mind,

261

"becoming everything," (*panta ginesthai*) is what it knows. Furthermore, it is eternal and beatific (*hêdistos*) Life, the Life (*zôê*) of God himself. The second mind is creative (*poiêtikos*), and an "efficient cause (*to aition kai poiêtikon*) in that it makes everything"[6] (*tô panta poiein*); it is passible (*pathêtikos*) and mortal, and thinks of contingent things, not always of itself. It is on a plane still lower than that of its creative activity that the mind is "sensitive" (*aisthêtikos=pathêtikos*).[7]

These two (or three) minds are the same as Plato's two (or three) parts of the soul, one immortal, and the other mortal, the latter in its best part active and courageous, and in its worst part passively affected by and subject to emotions and reactions provoked by sensation (*aisthêsis*). The two minds are the "natures" in the universal doctrine of "one essence and two natures."[8] As three, they correspond to the contemplative and active lives and the life of pleasure.

In these distinctions of the theoretical from the practical mind, and in the identification of the former (Mind) with the Life (*zôê*) of God and of it's Thinking with its Thesis, or why not say "Word" (*Logos*)? there is a veritable prediction or fore-telling of St. John's "In the First Principle (as the Scholastics so often interpret *in principio* = Skr. *agre*, not so much "in the beginning" as "at the top") was the Word, and the Word was with God, and the Word was God." The "Word" that, as Aristotle says, the First Mind thinks, when in its act of being it thinks itself, is for St. John the Christ, the Son of God, "through whom all things were made" and whom St. Augustine therefore calls "as it were, God's art" (*De Trin.* VI.10)[9]—the art *by* which all things were made. "Word" and "Mind" (*logos, nous*) are for Plato often interchangeable, while if for Aristotle the Word is what the First Mind thinks, and the Thinker and the thought are one, it is clear that one might safely paraphrase St. John by "In the First Principle was the Mind, and the Mind was with God, and the Mind was God."[10]

Having so far outlined the immediate background and implications of our text, it may be shown that these are also universal, and in particular, Indian conceptions; in saying which we are very far from suggesting or implying that in their Hellenistic context they are of Indian origin. As before, and to simplify the presentation, we shall combine the evidence of several texts, notably *Brhadâranyaka Upanisad*, I.a 4.10, IV.1.6, IV.3.28, 30, 32, *Kena Upanisad*, I.2 and 5 and *Maitri Upanisad*, VI.34.6, with *Satapatha Brâhmana*, X.5.3.1, "In the beginning (or rather, "at the top")[11] there was just That Mind" (*agre...tan-mana evâsa*); a paraphrase of *Rg Veda*, X.129.1, "There was That One (*tad ekam ... âsa*), naught else whatever."

To the question, "what was it that Brahma knew, whereby he became the All?" it is replied, "In the beginning, verily, this (Self)[12] was Brahma. It knew just Itself (*âtmânam-evâvet*), thereby It became the All" (*sarvam abhavat*). And as to this Gnosis, "Verily, though he (who can say, 'I am Brahma') does not think (*na manute*) or know (*na vijânati*), yet is he one who thinks and knows, albeit he does not think or know (contingently). Forsooth, there cannot be a dissipation of the Knower's knowing, because of his imperishability. It is not, however, any second thing, divided from Himself, that he should know ... That is his highest station, that is his Beatitude" (*ânanda*).

And "What is that Beatitude? Nothing but Mind (*mana eva*). Verily, my King, it is by his Mind that He possesses himself of the Woman (i.e. *vâc*, the Voice, Theotokos),[13] a Son is born of Her, in his image (*pratirupah*); that is his Beatitude. Verily, my King, the Imperial, Supreme Brahma is just Mind." As expressed in Thomist phraseology, the generation of the Son is a vital operation, *a principio conjunctivo*.

Aristotle's "Thinking of thinking," i.e. non-discursive principle of discursive thought, is the "Mind of the mind" (*manaso manas*) of the *Kena Upanisad* where, to the question "By whom (*kena*) impelled and sent forth does the mind fly?"[14] it is answered that is by "the Mind of the mind," and that "the Contemplatives, wholly relinquishing (*atimucya*, sc, their own mind), when they depart from this world, become immortal." A subsequent verse says that "He has It in mind, who does not think It; he who thinks It, does not know It; It is unknown to those who 'know It,' but known to those who 'know it not'"; and that is precisely the thesis of Nicolas of Cusa's *Docta Ignorantia*, while "wholly relinquishing their own mind" corresponds to Philo's "He that flees for refuge from his own mind, flees for refuge to the Mind of all things" (I.93).[15]

And so, as the *Maitri Upanisad* says, "The mind is said to be twofold,[16] clean and unclean: unclean, by admixture with desire, clean when separated from desire[17] ... The means of bondage and release;[18] of bondage, when it clings to the objective, of liberation, when disconnected from the objective."

Is it not then true, as Jeremias said, that "*in den verschiedenen Kulturen findet man die Dialekte der einen Geistessprache*"?

Notes

1. In which the distinction is implied of *esse* from *essentia*, existence from being, *genesis* from *to ontôs on*.

2. Meister Eckhart quotes the gloss, *Quod in mente est, vivit cum artifice; quod fit, mutatur cum tempore.*

3. Henceforth I use the capital when the First Mind is referred to.

4. Just as for Plotinus, *Enneads*, IV.4.6, the Gods "never learn" and "do not remember": and for the same reason, viz. that where there is no forgetting, there is no occasion for learning or remembrance. It is only for the second and variable mind, our mind that has forgotten so many things, that to be taught and so reminded is desirable. What it can be taught is what it has forgotten (*Meno*, 80, etc., and also Indian doctrine), and so, as Meister Eckhart says, "Not till the soul knows all that there is to be known can she pass over to the Unknown Good."

5. To restore "that original nature in which the knower and the known are alike" is for Plato life's highest purpose (*Timaeus*, 90D); it is the beatific "synthesis" (*samâdhi*) for which the discipline of Yoga is undertaken, and in which it culminates.

6. Cf. Mahesvarânanda, *Maharthamañjarî*, p. 44, where "The suchness called Sadâsiva (*sadâ*, "eternal") is prior with respect to the principle called *îsvara* (Lord, *kurios*) which latter, by the splendor of its practical power becomes the demiurge of all things in their manifested likeness." Cf. John, "through whom all things were made," and Skr. Visvakarma, "All-maker."

Aristotle's *to aition kai poiêtikon* (*De anima* III.5, 430 12) reflects *Phaedrus*, 97C *nous ... pantôn aitios.* Cf. Hermes Trismegistus *Lib.* 1.9 "And the First Mind, which is Life and Light, gave birth to another mind, the maker of things" (*dêmiourgos*).

7. "Aesthetic" (or "pathetic") is, properly speaking, the science of the feelings, whether of plants, animals or men. Art has to do with the making of things for good use, physical and mental.

8. As in *Brhadâranyaka Upanisad*, II.3.1 (*dve rûpe*); *Maitri Upanisad*, VII.11.2. (*dvaitîbhâva*) etc.

9. Meister Eckhart's "*bildner aller dingen in sînem vater*" (Pfeiffer, p. 391). In the same way the human artist works *per verbum in intellectu conceptum* (St. Thomas, *Sum. Theol.*, 1A.45.6).

10. "The Mind was God": cf. *Satapatha Brâhmana*, X.5.3.1 "Mind" (*manas*) = *Rg Veda* X. 129.1 "That One" (*tad ekam*).

"Mind is the male, Voice the female...He, by Mind had intercourse with the Voice" (*Satapatha Brâhmana*, 1.4.4.3, 4, VI. 1.2.8); so we call a thought a concept, implying that it is the produce of a vital operation.

11. Rather than "in the beginning," since it is to a before the beginning (*ante principium*) that the text refers.

12. Not, as rendered by Hume, "this world"; for we are told that He *became*, not that He *was*, the All. "This" contrasted with "All" can be only "One."

13. Separated from Himself (Prajâpati, the Father) as a mother of whom to be born, *Pañcavimsa Brâhmana*, VII. 6; as *Agni, Jaiminîya Upanisad Brâhmana*, 1, 51.5.

14. "Mind is the swiftest of birds" (*Rg Veda*, VI.9.5).

15. "The Lord of Mind, the Lord of all minds" (Sankarâcârya on *Vedânta Sûtra*, IV.4.8).

16. "There are two minds, that of all, which is God, and that of the individual" (Philo, I. 93). Hence the possibility of a "repentance," or rather, "change of mind" (*metanoia*). Cf. my "On Being in One's Right Mind."

17. "Desire, first seed and child of Mind" (*Rg Veda*, X.129.4). To be "minded to" is to desire, and when we "mind" things, then there is "wishful thinking."

18. "By what (*kena*) ladder does the sacrificer ascend to heaven?...by the Mind" (*Brhadâranyaka Upanisad*, III.1.6). "I am born a new being of God, and I see now not with the eye but by the Mind's act" (Hermes Trismegistus, *Lib.* XIII.11a).

 It will be understood that the First Mind, throughout, is *intellectus vel spiritus*, and the other a purposeful and constructive mentality; the First, or theoretical (speculative) Mind "cares for nothing but the Truth," the other is pragmatic, and contented with fact.

19

The Hindu Tradition

The Myth

Like the Revelation (*sruti*) itself, we must begin with the Myth (*itihâsa*), the penultimate truth, of which all experience is the temporal reflection. The mythical narrative is of timeless and placeless validity, true nowever[1] and everywhere: just as in Christianity, "In the beginning God created" and "Through him all things were made," regardless of the millennia that come between the datable words, amount to saying that the creation took place at Christ's "eternal birth." "In the beginning" (*agre*), or rather "at the summit," means "in the first cause": just as in our still told myths, "once upon a time" does not mean "once" alone, but "once for all."[2] "The Myth is not a "poetic invention" in the sense these words now bear: on the other hand, and just because of its universality, it can be told, and with equal authority, from many different points of view.

In this everlasting beginning there is only the Supreme Identity of "That One" (*tad ekam*),[3] without differentiation of being from non-being, light from darkness, or separation of sky from earth. The All is for the present impounded in the first principle, which may be spoken of as the Person, Progenitor, Mountain, Tree, Dragon or endless Serpent. Related to this principle by filiation or younger brotherhood, and alter ego rather than another principle, is the Dragon-slayer, born to supplant the Father and take possession of the kingdom, distributing its treasures to his followers.[4] For if there is to be a world, the prison must be shattered and its potentialities liberated.

This can be done either in accordance with the Father's will or against his will; he may "choose death for his children's sake,"[5] or it may be that the Gods impose the passion upon him, making him their sacrificial victim.[6] These are not contradictory doctrines, but different ways of telling one and the same story; in reality, Slayer and Dragon, sacrificer and victim are of one mind behind the scenes, where there is no incompatibility of contraries, but mortal enemies on the stage, where the everlasting war of the Gods[7] and the Titans is displayed. In any case, the Dragon-Father remains a Pleroma, no more diminished by what he exhales than he is increased by what he inhales. He is the Death, on whom our life depends;[8] and to the question "Is Death one, or many?" the answer is made that "He is one as he is there, but many as he is in his children here."[9] The Dragon-slayer is already our Friend; the Dragon must be pacified and made a friend of.[10]

The passion is both an exhaustion and a dismemberment. The endless Serpent (*speirama aiônos,* coil of eternity), who for so long as he was one Abundance remained invincible,[11] is disjointed and dismembered as a tree is felled and cut up into logs.[12] For the Dragon, as we shall presently find, is also the World-Tree, and there is an allusion to the "wood" of which the world is made by the Carpenter.[13] The Fire of Life and Water of Life (Agni and Soma, the Dry and the Moist, SB. I. 6. 3. 23), all Gods, all beings, sciences and goods are constricted by the Python, who as "Holdfast" (Namuci) will not let them go until he is smitten and made to gape and pant;[14] and from this Great Being, as if from a damp fire smoking, are exhaled the Scriptures, the Sacrifice, these worlds and all beings;[15] leaving him exhausted of his contents and like an empty skin.[16] In the same way the Progenitor, when he has emanated his children, is emptied out of all his possibilities of finite manifestation, and falls down unstrung,[17] overcome by Death[18] though he survives this woe.[19] Now the positions are reversed, for the Fiery Dragon will not and cannot be destroyed, but would enter into the Hero, to whose question "What, wouldst thou consume me?" it replies "Rather to kindle (waken, quicken) thee, that *thou* mayst eat."[20] The Progenitor, whose emanated children are as it were sleeping and inanimate stones, reflects "Let me enter into them, to awaken them";[21] but so long as he is one, he cannot, and therefore divides himself into the powers of perception and consumption, extending these powers from his hidden lair in the "cave" of the heart through the doors of the senses to their objects, thinking "Let me eat of these objects"; in this way "our" bodies are set up in possession of consciousness, he being their mover.[22] And since the Several Gods or Measures of Fire into which he is thus divided are "our" energies and powers, it is the same to say that "the Gods entered into man, they made the mortal their house."[23] His passible nature has now become "ours": and from this predicament he cannot easily recollect or rebuild himself, whole and complete."[24]

We are now the stone from which the spark can be struck, the mountain beneath which God lies buried, the scaly reptilian skin that conceals him, and the fuel for his kindling. That his lair is now a cave or house presupposes the mountain or walls by which he is enclosed, *verborgen* and *verbaut*.[25] "You" and "I" are the psychophysical prison and Constrictor in whom the First has been swallowed up that "we" might be at all.[26] For as we are repeatedly told, the Dragon-slayer devours his victim, swallows him up and drinks him dry, and by this Eucharistic meal he takes possession of the first-born Dragon's treasure and powers and becomes what he was. We can cite, in fact, a remarkable text in which our composite is called the "mountain of God" and we are told that the Comprehensor of this doctrine shall in like manner swallow up his own evil, hateful adversary.[27] This "adversary" is, of course, none but our self. The meaning of the text will only be fully grasped if we explain that the word for "mountain," *giri*, derives from the root *gir*, to "swallow."[28] Thus He in whom we were imprisoned is now our prisoner; as our Inner Man he is submerged in and hidden by our Outer Man. It is now his turn to become the Dragon-slayer; and in this war of the God with the Titan, now fought within you, where we are "at war with ourselves,"[29] his victory and resurrection will be also ours, *if* we have known who we are. It is now for him to drink us dry, for us to be his wine.

We have realized that the deity is implicitly or explicitly a willing victim; and this is reflected in the human ritual, where the agreement of the victim, who must have been originally human, is always formally secured.[30] In either case the death of the victim is also its birth, in accordance with the infallible rule that every birth must have been preceded by a death: in the first case, the deity is multiply born in living beings, in the second they are reborn in him. But even so it is recognized that the sacrifice and dismemberment of the victim are acts of cruelty and even treachery;[31] and this is the original sin (*kilbisa*) of the Gods, in which all men participate by the very fact of their separate existence and their manner of knowing in terms of subject and object, good and evil, because of which the Outer Man is excluded from a direct participation in "what the Brahmanas understand by Soma."[32] The form of our "knowledge," or rather "ignorance" (*avidyâ*), dismembers him daily; and for this *ignorantia divisiva* an expiation is provided for in the Sacrifice, where by the sacrificer's surrender of himself and the building up again of the dismembered deity, whole and complete, the multiple selves are reduced to their single principle (consciously if they are "saved," unconsciously if they are "lost"). There is thus an incessant multiplication of the inexhaustible One and unification of the indefinitely Many. Such are the beginnings and endings of worlds and of individual beings: expanded from a point without position or dimensions and a now without date or duration, accomplishing their destiny, and when their time is up returning "home" to the Sea in which their life originated.[33]

Notes

1. With one "now" he has filled "always" (Plutarch, *Moralia* 393B).

2. "At that time indeed, all things took shape simultaneously" (Philo, *De Op.* VII, 28, also Plotinus, *Enneads* VI).

3. RV X.129.1-3; TS.VI.4.8.3; JB.III.359; SB.X.5.3.1, 2, etc.

4. RV X.124.4, etc.

5. RV X.13.4, "They made Brhaspati the Sacrifice, Yama outpoured his own dear body."

6. RV X.90.6-8, "They made the first-born Person their sacrificial victim."

7. The word *deva* like its cognates *theos*, *deus*, can be used in the singular to mean "God" or in the plural to mean "Gods" or sometimes "Angels"; just as we can say "Spirit" meaning the Holy Ghost, and also speak of spirits, and amongst others even of "evil spirits." The "Gods" of Proclus are the "Angels" of Dionysius. What may be called the "high Gods" are the Persons of the Trinity, Agni, Indra, Vâyu, Âditya, or Brahmâ, Siva, Visnu, to be distinguished only, and then not always sharply, from one another according to their functioning and spheres of opera-tion. The *mixtae personae* of the dual Mitrâvarunau or Agnendrau are the form of the Sacerdotium and Regnum *in divinis*; their subjects, the "Many Gods," are the Maruts or Gales. The equivalents in ourselves are on the one hand the immanent median Breath, sometimes spoken of as Vâmadeva, sometimes as Inner Man and Immortal Self, and on the other its extensions and subjects the Breaths, or powers of seeing, hearing, thinking, etc., of which our elemental "soul" is the unanimous composite, just as the body is a composite of functionally distinguishable parts that act in unison. The Maruts and the Breaths may act in obedience to their govern-ing principle, or may rebel against it. All this is, of course, an over simplified state-ment.

8. SB X.5.2.13

9. SB X.5.2.16. Also Enneads IV. 9. 2; BG XIII.27, 30, 16; XVIII.20. 16.

10. AB III.4; TS V.1.5, 6; TSYLL11.

11. On "making a friend of" the Varunya agni or Soma who might otherwise

destroy the Sacrificer, see AB III.4; TS V.1.5.6 and TS VI.1.11.

12. TA V.1.3; MU II.6 (a).

13. RV I.32, etc.

14. RV X.31.7; X.81.4; TB II.8.9,6; cf. RV X.89.7; TS VI.4.7.3.

15. RV I.54.5 *svasanasya...susnasya*; RV V.29.4 *svasantamavadânavam han*; TS II.5.2.4 *jañjabhyamânâd agnîsomau nirakrâmatâm*; cf. SB I.6.3.13-15; SB V.5.5.1 "Of old everything here was within *Vrtra*"; AB III:20 *svasasthât* (*vrtrasya*). JUB I.47,3 All is Prajâpati's: *apâna*, expiration dying breath. BU IV.5.11 *mahato bhûtasya...etâni sarvâni nihsvasitâni*: MU VI.32, etc. "For all things arise out of only one being" (Also Behmen, *Sig. Rer.* XIV.74). As in RV X.90.

16. SB I.6.3.15, 16.

17. "Is unstrung," *vyasransata*, i.e. is disjointed or dispersed so that having been jointless, he is articulated, having been one, is divided and overcome, like Makha (TA V. 1.3) and Vrtra (originally jointless, RV IV.19.3, but dissevered, I.32.7). For Prajâpati's fall and reconstitution see SB 16.3.35 and passim; PB IV.10.1 and passim; TB I.2.6.1; AA III.2.6, etc. It is with reference to his "division" that in KU V.4 the immanent deity (*dehin*) is spoken of as "unstrung" (*visransamâna*); for he is one in himself, but many as he is in his children (SB X.5.2.16) from out of whom he cannot easily come together again.

18. SB X.4.4.1.

19. PB VI.5.1. (Prajâpati); cf. SB IV.4.3.4 (Vrtra). See also *Mahâbhârata*, Vanaparva Ch. CLXXX.

20. TS II.4.12.6; SB I.6.3.17. It is noteworthy that whereas the "Person in the right eye" is usually spoken of as the Sun or solar Indra, it can equally well be said that it is Susna (the Scorcher) that is smitten and when he falls enters into the eye as its pupil, or that Vrtra becomes the right eye (SB III.1.3.11,18). That is one of the many ways in which "Indra is now what Vrtra was."

21. SB.VIII.5.3.1 Indra and Prajâpati who enters into him with the essence of food.

22. MU II.6; cf. SB III.9.1.2; JUB I.46.1,2. "Mover," as in *Paradiso*, I.116. *Questi nei cor mortali è permotore* (This is the motive force in mortal heart). Cf. *Laws*, 898C.

23. AV X.8.18; cf. SB II.3.2.3; JUB I.14.2, *mayy etâs sarvâ devatâh*. Cf. KB VII.4 *ime puruse devatâh*; TS IV.1.4.5 *prânâ vai devâ...tesu paroksam juhoti* ("The Gods in this man ... they are the Breaths ... in them he sacrifices metaphysically"). See Patanjali's *Yoga Sutras* IV-23. "The mind, though assuming various forms by reason of innumerable mental deposits, exists for the purpose of the soul's emancipation and operates in cooperation therewith." Food is quite literally *consumed* by the digestive Fire: so, when a ritual meal is announced one should say "Kindle the Fire" (*samintsvâgnim*, JUB II.15.1-3) or "Come to the feast" (*agne â vîtaye*, RV VI.69.10, etc.) by way of benedicite. KU IV.6 (cf. Ait.Up. I.3.13). *Yah pûrvam tapaso...ajâyata. guhâm pravisya ... bhutebhir vyapasyata. Colossians* I.15 *primogenitus creaturae* (= the firstborn of every creature). *Sig. Rer.* III.38 "The Being of all beings, who thus manifests himself in particular beings with the eyes of eternity." Cf. *Kaus.Up.* II.13. Climbing cf. JUB I.33.1 (center: summit: slope). DhA III.52 Mogallâna's plunge into earth and ascent Majjhena. Mt. Sineru.

24. TS V.5.2.1. *Prajâpatih prajâ srstvâ prenânu pravisat, tâbhyâm punar sambhavitum nâsaknot*; Prajâpati after creating creatures in affection entered into them; from them he could not emerge again. SB I.6.3.36 *Sa visrastaih parvabhih na sasâka samhâtum* = He was

unable to rise with his relaxed joints. BU IV.3.32 *salila eko drstâdvaito bhavati, esa brahmalokah* KB I.7. Mil.263 *mahasannidohr,* 346 *dhamma-nadî* and *dhammasâgara.*

Mathnawî III.4662: "Existence in non-existence is itself a marvel."

VI. 1622: "opposites and likes in number as the leaves of the orchard, are as a fleck of foam on the Sea that hath no like or opposite."

VI.4052: "He that finds is lost: like a torrent he is absorbed in the Ocean."

V.802: "These footprints (extend) as far as the shore of the Ocean; then the footprints are naught in the Ocean."

II.160-1: "What is a Sufi's possession? Footprints."

25. "Gott liegt verborgen und bedeckt im inwendigen Grunde" (Sermon 22 in W. Lehmann, *Johannes Tauler Predigten,* Jena, 1917).

Sherman, *Philosophical Hymns,* p. 18 uses this word verborgen in the sense of Kath.Up.II.20 *nihito guhâyâm* = is lodged in the heart.

26. Philo, LA.III.74: "When the mind (*nous*) has carried off the prizes of virtue, it condemns the corpse body to death."

LA.I.108: "Now, when we are living, the soul is dead and has been entombed in the body as in a sepulcher; whereas, should we die, the soul lives forth with its own proper life, released from the body, the baneful corpse to which it was held."

Phaedrus, 250C: "entombed in the body."

Enneads, IV.8.3: "prison or tomb of the body, cavern or cave of Kosmos." The "cave" stands for mental activity as per the *Yoga Sutra* IV.23.

Cratylus, 400.C: "the body is the tomb of the soul."

RV.: *guhâ nisîdau (agni).*

Henry Constable: "Buryed in me, unto my sowle appeare." E Bk. M. veise p.13.

Eckhart, Pfeiffer, p. 593: "hat gewonet in uns verborgenliche." Trans.: "has dwelt in us in a hidden manner."

Kath. Up. III.12: "*Esa sarvesu bhûtesu gûdho'tmâ...*" ("This Âtman, hidden in all beings...").

Philo, *Migr.* 188, 190: "man as troglodyte."

II *Cor.* 4.7: "But we have this treasure in earthen vessels, ..."

Maitri Up. VI.28: "buried treasure."

27. AA II.1.8. St. Bonaventura likewise equated *mons* (noonlain) with *mens* (mind) (*De dec. praeceptis II, ascendere in montem, id est, in eminentiam mentis*) (ascend the mountain which is the highest mind).

 This traditional image which, like so many others, must be dated back to the time when "cave" and "home" were one and the same thing, underlies the familiar symbols of mining and seeking for buried treasure (CU VIII.3.2; MU VI.28, etc.). The powers of the soul (*bhûtâni,* a word that also means "gnomes") at work in the mind-mountain, are the types of the dwarf miners who protect the "Snow-White" Psyche when she has bitten into the fruit of good and evil and fallen into her death-like sleep, in which she remains until the divine Eros awakens her and the fruit falls from her lips. Whoever has understood the scriptural Mythos will recognize its paraphrases in the universal fairy-tales that were not created by, but have been inherited and faithfully transmitted by the "folk" to whom they were originally communicated. It is one of the prime errors of historical and rational analysis to suppose that the "truth" and "original form" of a legend can be separated from its miraculous elements. It is in the marvels themselves that the truth inheres: "There is no other origin of philosophy than wonder," Plato, *Theatetus* 1556. And in the same way Aristotle who adds "therefore even a lover of fables is in a way a lover of wisdom, for fables are compounded of wonder" (*Metaphysics* 982B). Myth embodies the nearest approach to absolute truth that can be stated in words.

28. *Samyutta Nikâya*, III.86: "eaten up by my body, etc." There is a remarkable echo of the *brahma-giri* doctrine in *Majjhima Nikâya*, III.68 where the *Isigiri pabbata* in which the *isî* are living is so called in that it *isî gilati*, "swallows up the Rsis." BU III.2.13, *Sânkarabhâsya*: "*grahâtigraha laksanena mrtyunâ grastam.*"

29. BGVI.6; cf. S.I.57 = Dh.66; AI 149; Rûmî, *Mathnawî* I.267f, etc.

30. N.T. Romans, VII.24: "Who shall deliver me from the body of this death?", VI.6: "... that the body of sin might be destroyed.... ," VIII.10 "... the body is dead because of sin... "

31. TS II.5.1.2, II.5.3.6; cf. VI.4.8.1; SB I.2.3.3, III.9.4.17; SB XII.6.1.39, 40; PB XII.6.8, 9; *Kaus.Up.* III.1, etc.; cf. Bloomfield in JAOS., XV.161.

32. TS II.4.12.1; AB VII.28, etc.

33. *Mund.Up.* III.2.8; *Prasna Up.* VI.5; A.IV.198, *Udâna* 55. For further parallels see *Review of Religion*, Nov. 1941, p.18, note 2.

For the return of the "Rivers" to the "Sea" in which their individuality is merged, so that one speaks only of the "Sea": CU.VI.10.1; *Prasna Up.* VI.5; *Mund. Up.* III.2.8; A.IV.198; *Udâna* 55; and similarly Lao Tzu, *Tao Te Ching* XXXII; Rûmî, *Mathnawî* VI.4052; Meister Eckhart (in Pfeiffer's edn., p. 314), ...all to the effect that "As the drop becomes the ocean, so the soul is deified, losing her name and work, but not her essence" (Angelus Silesius, *Cherubinische Wandersmann* II.15): "And in his will is our tranquility / It is the mighty ocean, whither tends / Whatever it creates and nature makes" (Dante, *Paradiso* III.85, 86).

For "going home" (to *Agni*) RV I.66.5; V.2.6; (to *Brahmâ*) MU VI.22; (to the "Sea") *Prasna Up.* VI.5; (to the Gale) RV X.16.3; AV X.8.16 (like *Katha Up.* IV.9; BU I.5.23), JUB III.1.1,2,3,12; CU IV.3.1-3; (to the *summum bonum*, man's last end) S.IV.158; Sn.1074-6; Mil.73); (to our Father) Luke 23.46.

Eckhart I.176: "the sea of his own unfathomable nature." *Mathnawî* IV.2062: "Silence is the Sea and speech is like the river"; *Rumi Odes*, XII, XV; BU.IV.3.32; *Kaus.Up.* I.7. *Majjhima Nikâya* I.488: Buddha like *mahâsamudda*, fathomless, etc. I.499: Like river to sea every pilgrim tends towards *nibbâna*. *Samyutta Nikâya* IV.179-80: gliding downstream to *nibbâna*.

20

The Hindu Tradition
Theology and Autology[1]

The Sacrifice (*yajña*) undertaken here below is a ritual mimesis of what was done by the Gods in the beginning, and in the same way both a sin and an expiation. We shall not understand the Myth until we have made the Sacrifice, nor the Sacrifice until we have understood the Myth. But before we can try to understand the operation it must be asked, what is God? and what are we?

God is an essence without duality (*advaita*), or as some maintain, without duality but not without relations (*visistâdvaita*). He is only to be apprehended as Essence (*asti*),[2] but this Essence subsists in a two-fold nature (*dvaitîbhâva*),[3] as being and as becoming.[4] Thus, what is called the Entirety (*krtsnam, pûrnam, bhûman*) is both explicit and inexplicit (*niruktânirukta*), sonant and silent (*sabdâsabda*), characterized and uncharacterized (*saguna, nirguna*), temporal and eternal (*kâlâkâla*), partite and impartite (*sakalâkâla*), in a likeness and not in any likeness (*mûrtâmûrta*), shewn and unshewn (*vyaktâvyakta*), mortal and immortal (*martyâmartya*), perishable and the Imperishable (*ksarascâksam*), and so forth. Whoever knows him in his proximate (*apara*) aspect, immanent, knows him also in his ultimate (*para*) aspect, transcendent;[5] the Person seated in our heart, eating and drinking, is also the Person in the Sun.[6] This Sun of men, and Light of lights[7] "whom all men see but few know with the mind,"[8] is the Universal Self (*âtman*) of all things mobile or immobile.[9] He is both inside and outside (*bahir antas ca bhûtânâm*), but uninterruptedly (*anantaram*), and therefore a total presence, undivided in divided things.[10] He does not come from anywhere,[11] nor does he become anyone,[12] but only lends himself to all possible modalities of existence.[13]

The question of his names, such as Agni, Indra, Prajâpati, Siva, Brahmâ, etc.,[14] whether personal or essential, is dealt with in the usual way: "they call him many who is really one";[15] "even as he seems, so he becomes";[16] "he takes the forms imagined by his worshippers."[17] The trinitarian names—Agni, Vâyu and Âditya or

Brahmâ, Rudra and Vishnu—"are the highest embodiments of the supreme, immortal, bodiless Brahma—their becoming is a birth from one another, partitions of a common Self defined by its different operations—These embodiments are to be contemplated, celebrated, and at last recanted. For by means of them one rises higher and higher in the worlds; but where the whole ends, attains the simplicity of the Person."[18] Of all the names and forms of God the monogrammatic syllable Aum, the totality of all sounds and the music of the spheres chanted by the resonant Sun, is the best. The validity of such an audible symbol is exactly the same as that of a plastic icon, both alike serving as supports of contemplation (*dhiyâlamba*); such a support is needed because that which is imperceptible to eye or ear cannot be apprehended objectively as it is in itself, but only in a likeness. The symbol must be naturally adequate, and cannot be chosen at random; one locates or infers (*âvesyati, âvâhayati*) the unseen in the seen, the unheard in the heard; but these forms are only means by which to approach the formless and must be discarded before we can become it.

Whether we call him Person, or Sacerdotium, or Magna Mater, or by any other grammatically masculine, feminine or neuter names, "That" (*tat, tad ekam*) of which our powers are measures (*tanmâtrâ*) is a syzygy of conjoint principles, without composition or duality.[19] These conjoint principles or selves, indistinguishable ab intra, but respectively self-sufficient and insufficient ab extra, become contraries only when we envisage the act of self-manifestation (*svaprakâsatvam*) implied when we descend from the silent level of the Non-duality to speak in terms of subject and object and to recognize the many separate and individual existences that the All (*sarvam= to pan*) or Universe (*visvam*) presents to our physical organs of perception. And since this finite totality can be only logically and not really divided from its infinite source, "That One" can also be called an "Integral Multiplicity"[20] and "Omniform Light."[21] Creation is exemplary. The conjoint principles, for example, Heaven and Earth, or Sun and Moon, man and woman, were originally one. Ontologically, their conjugation (*mithunam, sambhava, eko bhava*) is a vital operation, productive of a third in the image of the first and nature of the second. Just as the conjugation of Mind (*manas*) with the Voice (*vâc*) gives birth to a concept (*sankalpa*) so the conjugation of Heaven and Earth kindles the Bambino, the Fire, whose birth divides his parents from one another and fills the intervening Space (*âkasa, antariksa*, Midgard) with light;[22] and in the same way microcosmically, being kindled in the space of the heart, he is its light. He shines in his Mother's womb,[23] in full possession of all his powers.[24] He is no sooner born than he traverses the Seven Worlds,[25] ascends to pass through the Sun-door, as the smoke from an altar or central hearth, whether without or within you, ascends to pass out through the eye of the dome.[26] This Agni is at once the messenger of God, the guest in all men's houses, whether constructed or bodily, the luminous pneumatic principle of life, and the missal priest who conveys the savor of the Burnt-offering hence to the world beyond the vault of the Sky, through which there is no other way but this "Way of the Gods" (*devayâna*). This Way must be followed by the Forerunner's footprints, as the word for "Way"[27] itself reminds us, by all who would reach the "farther shore" of the luminous spatial river of life[28] that divides this terrestrial from yonder celestial strand; these conceptions of the Way underlying all the detailed symbolisms of the Voyage and the Pilgrimage, Bridge and Active Door.

Considered apart, the "halves" of the originally undivided Unity can be distinguished in various ways according to our point of view; politically, for example, as Sacerdotium and Regnum (*brahma-ksatrau*), and psychologically as Self and Not-self, Inner Man and Outer Individuality, Male and Female. These pairs are disparate; and even when the subordinate has been separated from the superior with a view to productive cooperation, it still remains in the latter, more eminently. The Sacerdotium, for example, is "both the Sacerdotium and the Regnum"—a condition found in the *mixta persona* of the priest-king Mitrâvarunau, or Indrâgnî—but the Regnum as a separated function is nothing but itself, relatively feminine, and subordinated to the Sacerdotium, its Director (*netr* = *hêgemôn*). Mitra and Varuna correspond to *para* and *apara* Brahma, and just as Varuna is feminine to Mitra, so the functional distinction in terms of sex defines the hierarchy. God himself is male to all, but just as Mitra is male to Varuna and Varuna in turn male to Earth, so the Priest is male to the King, and the King male to his realm. In the same way the man is subject to the joint government of Church and State; but in authority with respect to his wife, who in turn administers his estate. Throughout the series it is the noetic principle that sanctions or enjoins what the aesthetic performs or avoids; disorder arising only when the latter is distracted from her rational allegiance by her own ruling passions and identifies this subjection with "liberty."[29]

The most pertinent application of all this is to the individual, whether man or woman: the outer and active individuality of "this man or woman, so-and-so" being naturally feminine and subject to its own inner and contemplative Self. On the one hand, the submission of the Outer to the Inner Man is all that is meant by the words "self-control' and "autonomy," and the opposite of what is meant by "self-assertion": and on the other, this is the basis of the interpretation of the return to God in terms of an erotic symbolism, "As one embraced by a darling bride knows naught of 'I' and 'thou,' so the self embraced by the foreknowing (solar) Self knows naught of a 'myself,' within or a 'thyself' without";[30] because, as Sankara remarks, of "unity." It is this Self that the man who really loves himself or others, loves in himself and in them; "all things are dear only for the sake of the Self."[31] In this true love of Self the distinction of "selfishness" from "altruism" loses all its meaning. He sees the Self, the Lord, alike in all beings, and all beings alike in that Lordly Self.[32] ["Loving thy Self," in the words of Meister Eckhart, "thou lovest all men as thy Self."[33] All these doctrines coincide with the Sufi ["What is Love? Thou shalt know when thou becomest me."[34]

The sacred marriage, consummated in the heart, adumbrates the deepest of all mysteries.[35] For this means both our death and beatific resurrection. [The word to "marry" (*eko bhû*, become one) also means to "die," just as in Greek, *teleô* is to be perfected, to be married, or to die.] When "Each is both," no relation persists: and were it not for this beatitude (*ânanda*) there would be neither life nor gladness anywhere.[36] All this implies that what we call the world-process and a creation is nothing but a game (*krîdâ, lîlâ, paidia, dolce gioco*) that the Spirit plays with itself, and as sunlight "plays" upon whatever it illuminates and quickens, although unaffected by its apparent contacts. We who play the game of life so desperately for temporal stakes might be playing at love with God for higher stakes—our selves, and his. We play against one another for possessions, who might be playing with the King who stakes his throne and what is his against our lives and all we are: a game in which the more is lost, the more is won.[37]

By the separation of Heaven and Earth the "Three Worlds" are distinguished; the in-between World (*antariksa*) provides the ethereal space (*âkâsa*)[38] in which the inhibited possibilities of finite manifestation can take birth in accordance with their several natures. From this first ethereal substance are derived in succession air, fire, water and earth; and from these five elemental Beings (*bhûtâni*), combined in various proportions, are formed the inanimate bodies of creatures;[39] into which the God enters to awaken them, dividing himself to fill these worlds and to become the "Several Gods," his children.[40] These Intelligences[41] are the host of "Beings" (*bhûtagana*) that operate in us, unanimously, as our "elemental soul" (*bhûtâtman*), or conscious self,[42] our "selves," indeed, but for the present mortal and unspiritual (*anâtmya, anâtmana*), ignorant of their immortal Self (*âtmânam ananuvidya, anâtmajña*),[43] and to be distinguished from the Immortal deities who have already become what they are by their "worth" (*arhana*) and are spoken of as "Arhats" (= "Dignities").[44] Through the mundane and perfectible deities, and just as a King receives tribute (*balim âhr*) from his subjects,[45] the Person in the heart, our Inner Man who is also the Person in the Sun (MUVI.1, 2), obtains the food (*anna, âhâra*), both physical and mental, on which he must subsist when he proceeds from being to becoming. And because of the simultaneity of his dynamic presence in all past and future becoming,[46] the emanated powers at work in our consciousness can be regarded as the temporal support of the solar Spirit's timeless providence (*prajñâna*) and omniscience (*sarvajñâna*). Not that this sensible world of successive events determined by mediate causes (*karma, adrsta, apûrva*) is the source of his knowledge, but rather that it is itself the consequence of the Spirit's awareness of "the diversified world picture painted by itself on the vast canvas of itself."[47] It is not by means of this All that he knows himself, but by his knowledge of himself that he becomes this All.[48] To know him by this All belongs only to our inferential manner of knowing.[49]

You must have begun to realize that the theology and the autology are one and the same science, and that the only possible answer to the question, "What am I?" must be "That art thou."[50] For as there are two in him who is both Love and Death,[51] so there are, as all tradition affirms unanimously, two in us; although not two of him or two of us, nor even one of him and one of us, but only one of both. As we stand now, in between the first beginning and the last end, we are divided against ourselves, essence from nature, and therefore see him likewise as divided against himself and from us. Let us describe the situation in two different figures. Of the conjugate birds, Sunbird and Soulbird, that perch on the Tree of Life, one is all-seeing, the other eats of its fruits.[52] For the Comprehensor these two birds are one;[53] in the iconography we find either one bird with two heads, or two with necks entwined. But from our point of view there is a great difference between the spectator's and the participant's lives; the one is not involved, the other, submerged in her feeding and nesting, grieves for her lack of lordship (*anîsa*) until she perceives her Lord (*îsa*), and recognizes her Self in him and in his majesty, whose wings have never been clipped.[54]

In another way, the constitution of worlds and of individuals is compared to a wheel (*cakra*), of which the hub is the heart, the spokes powers, and their points of contact on the felly, our organs of perception and action.[55] Here the "poles" that represent our selves, respectively profound and superficial, are the motionless axle-point on which the wheel revolves—"Due from the pole, round which the first wheel rolls"[56]—and the rim in contact with the earth to which it reacts. This is the "wheel of becoming, or birth" (*bhava cakra = ho trochos tês geneseôs =* the round of generation).[57] The collective motion of all the wheels within wheels—each one turning on a point without position and one and the same in all—that are these worlds and individuals is called the Confluence (*samsâra*), and it is in this "storm of the world's flow" that our "elemental self" (*bhûtât-man*) is fatally involved: fatally, because whatever "we" are naturally "destined" to experience under the sun is the ineluctable consequence of the uninterrupted but unseen operation of mediate causes (*karma, adrsta*), from which only the aforesaid "point" remains independent, being in the wheel indeed, but not a "part" of it.

It is not only *our* passible nature that is involved, but also *his*. In this compatible nature he sympathizes with our miseries and our delights and is subjected to the consequences of things done as much as "we" are. He does not choose his wombs, but enters into births that may be aughty or naughty (*sadasat*)[58] and in which his mortal nature is the fructuary (*bhoktr*) equally of good and evil, truth and falsity.[59] That "he is the only seer, hearer, thinker, knower and fructuary" in us,[60] and that "whoever sees, it is by his ray that he sees,"[61] who (*Îksvaku*) looks forth in all beings, is the same as to say that "the Lord is the only transmigrator,"[62] and it follows inevitably that by the very act with which he endows us with consciousness "he fetters himself like a bird in the net," and is subject to the evil, Death,[63]—or seems to be thus fettered and subjected.

Thus he is apparently submitted to our ignorance and suffers for our sins. Who then can be liberated and by whom and from what? It would be better to ask, with respect to this absolutely unconditional liberty, What is free now and nowever from the limitations that are presupposed by the very notion of individuality (*aham ca mama ca*, "I and mine"; *kartâ' ham iti*, "'I' am a doer")?[64] Freedom is from one's self, this "I," and its affections. He only is free from virtues and vices and all their fatal consequences who never became anyone; he only can be free who is no longer anyone; impossible to be freed from oneself and also to remain oneself. The liberation from good and evil that seemed impossible and is impossible for the man whom we define by what he does or thinks and who answers to the question, "Who is that?", "It's me," is possible only for him who can answer at the Sundoor to the question "Who art thou?", "Thyself."[65] He who fettered himself must free himself, and that can only be done by verifying the assurance, "That art thou." It is as much for us to liberate him by knowing who we are as for him to liberate himself by knowing Who he is;[66] and that is why in the Sacrifice the sacrificer identifies himself with the victim.

Hence also the prayer, "*What* thou art, thus may I be,"[67] and the eternal significance of the critical question "In *whose* departure, when I go hence, shall I be departing?",[68] i.e. in myself, or "her immortal Self" and "Leader."[69] If the right answers have been verified, if one has found the Self, and having done all that there is to be done (*krtakrtya*), without any residue of potentiality (*krtyâ*, BG III.17),[70] the last end of our life has been presently attained.[71] It cannot be too much emphasized that freedom and immortality[72] can be, not so much "reached," as "realized" as well here and now as in any hereafter. One "freed in this life" (*jîvanmukta*) "dies no more" (*na punar mriyate*).[73] "The Comprehensor of that Contemplative, ageless, undying Self, in whom naught whatsoever is wanting and who wanteth nothing, has no fear of death."[74] Having died already, he is, as the Sufi puts it, "a dead man walking."[75] Such a one no longer loves himself or others, but is the Self in himself and in them. Death to one's self is death to "others"; and if the "dead man" seems to be "unselfish," this will not be the result of altruistic motives, but accidentally, and because he is literally un-self-ish. Liberated from himself, from all status, all duties, all rights, he has become a Mover-at-will (*kâmâcârî*),[76] like the Spirit (*Vâyu, âtmâ devânâm*) that "moveth as it will" (*yathâ vasam carati*),[77] and as St.

Paul expresses it, "no longer under the law."

This is the superhuman impartiality of those who have found their Self,—"The same am I in all beings, of whom there is none I love and none I hate";[78] the freedom of those who have fulfilled the condition required of his disciples by Christ, to hate father and mother and likewise their own "life" in the world.[79] We cannot say what the freeman (*mukta*) is, but only what he is not,—*Trasumanar significar per verba non si poria!* ("he has gone beyond human limits through the word and not by action").

But this can be said that those who have not known themselves are neither now nor ever shall be free, and that "great is the destruction" of these victims of their own sensations.[80] The Brahmanical autology is no more pessimistic than optimistic, but only more authoritative than any other science of which the truth does not depend on our wishes. It is no more pessimistic to recognize that whatever is alien to Self is a distress, than it is optimistic to recognize that where there is no "other" there is literally nothing to be feared.[81] That our Outer Man is "another" appears in the expression: "I cannot trust myself." What has been called the "natural optimism" of the Upanishads is their affirmation that our consciousness of being, although invalid as an awareness of being So-and-so, is valid absolutely, and their doctrine that the Gnosis of the Immanent Deity, our Inner Man, can be realized now: "That art thou." In the words of St. Paul, *Vivo autem, jam non ego* ("... nevertheless I live; yet not I ... " *Gal.* 2:20).

That this is so, or that "He is" at all, cannot be demonstrated in the classroom, where only quantitative tangibles are dealt with. At the same time, it would be unscientific to deny a presupposition for which an experimental proof is possible. In the present case there is a Way[82] prescribed for those who will consent to follow it: and it is precisely at this point that we must turn from the first principles to the operation through which, rather than by which, they can be verified; in other words from the consideration of the contemplative to the consideration of the active or sacrificial life.

Notes

1. *Autology* (Chambers, 1983 ed.) has been defined as "knowledge or understanding of oneself" (*heautou epistêmê, âtmavidyâ, âtmajñâna*), not like other sciences, but the science of itself and of other sciences. See Plato, *Charmides* 165D, 166E; *Republic* 430, 432 and *Sophroniscus* in Plato's notes.

2. KU VI.13; MU IV.4, etc.

3. SB X.1.4.1; BU II.3; MU VI.15, VII.11. No trace of Monophysitism or of Patripassianism can be discovered in the so-called "monism" of the Vedanta; the "non-duality" being that of two natures coincident without composition.

4. Being and becoming, *tattva* and *bhava* correspond to Gk. *ousia* (= being) and *nemesis* (= personification of divine wrath).

5. MU VI.22; *Pras. Up.*V.2.

6. BU IV.4.24; *Tait.Up.* III.10.4; MU VI.1.2.

7. RV I.113.1, 1.146.4; BU IV.1.6; *Mund. Up.* II.2.9; BG XIII.17; *John* 1:4. AV X.8.14; Plato, *Laws* 898 D. "Since soul is what, so it seems everything go round." Every one sees the body of the sun, but no one sees his soul,—See Jowett's translation of the Dialogues of Plato, Vol. I, p. 640.

8. RV I.115.1, VII.101.6; AV X.8.44; AA III.2.4. Autology (*âtma jñâna*) is the fundamental theme of scripture; but it must be understood that this Self-knowledge differs from any empirical knowledge of an object inasmuch as our Self is always the subject and can never become the object of knowledge; in other words, all definition of the ultimate Self must be by remotion.

Atman (root *an*, to breathe, cf. *atmos, autmê*) is primarily Spiritus, the luminous and pneumatic principle, and as such often equated with the Gale (*Vâyu, Vâta*, root *vâ*, to blow) of the Spirit which "bloweth as it listeth" (*yathâ vasam carati*, RV X.168.4 as in John 3:8). Being the ultimate essence in all things, *âtman* acquires the secondary sense of "Self," regardless of our level of reference, which may be either somatic, psychic or spiritual. So that over against our real Self, the Spirit in ourselves and all living things there is the "self," of which we speak when we say "I" or "you," meaning this or that man, So-and-so. In other words there are two in us, Outer and Inner Man, psychophysical personality and very Person. It is therefore according to the context that we must translate. Because the word *âtman*, used reflexively, can only be rendered by "self" we have adhered to the sense of "self" throughout, distinguishing Self from self by the capital, as is commonly done. But it must be clearly understood that the distinction is really of "spirit" (*pneuma*) from "soul" (*psuchê*) in the Pauline sense. It is true that the ultimate Self, "this self's immortal Self" (MU III.2, VI.2), is identical with Philo's "soul of the soul" (*psuchê, psuchês*), and with Plato's "immortal soul" as distinguished from the "mortal soul" and that some translators render *âtman* by "soul"; but although there are contexts in which "soul" means "spirit" (cf. William of Thierry, *Epistle to the Brethren of Mont Dieu*, Ch. XV, on this very problem of the distinction of *anima* from *animus*; see also Philo, *Heres* 55) it becomes dangerously misleading, in view of our current notions of "psychology" to speak of the ultimate and universal Self as a "soul." It would be, for example, a very great mistake to suppose that when a "philosopher" such as Jung speaks of "man in search of a soul" this has anything whatever to do with the Indian search for the Self, or for that matter with the injunction, *Gnôthi seauton,* know thy Self. The empiricist's "self" is for the metaphysician, just like all the rest of our environment, "not my Self."

Of the two "selves" referred to, the first is born of woman, the second of the divine womb, the sacrificial fire (SB I.8.3.6); and whoever has not thus been "born again" is effectively possessed of but the one and mortal self that is born of the flesh and must end with it (JB I.17, cf. John 3:6, Gal. 6:8, I Cor. 15:50, etc.). Hence in the Upanishads and Buddhism the fundamental questions "Who art thou?", and "By which self?" is immortality attainable, the answer being, only by that Self that is immortal; the Indian texts never fall into the error of supposing that a soul that has had a beginning in time can also be immortal; nor indeed, can we see that the Christian Gospels anywhere put forward such an impossible doctrine as this.

10. BG XIII.15, 16; XV.16, 17; XVIII.20 *uttamah purusastvanyah.*

11. Cf. John 3:18.

12. KU. II.18.

13. BU.IV.4.5.

14. See AB IV.22 on Names. The following correspondences of names and functions have been drawn—Agni: sacerdotium; Indra: regnum; Prajâpati: progenitor; Siva: king; Brahmâ: lordship.

15. RV X.114.5, cf. III.5.4, V.3.1.

16. RV V.44.6.

17. *Kailayamâlai* (see *Ceylon National Review*, no. 3, 1907, p. 280).

18. *Nirukta* VII.4; *Brhad Devatâ* I.70-74; MU IV.6.

19. "There is no distinction of elder or younger between One and another." *Liturgical Homilies of Narsai* (trans. Dom Connolly, Camb. Univ. Press, 1909), Homily XXII.

20. RV III.54.8 *visvam ekam.*

21. VS V.35 *jyotir asi visvarûpam.*

22. For *vâc* as *logos* and the creation of the triple science, see SB VI.1.1.9-10.

manas = *nous*-mind, *logos*-word, *dianoia*-thought; *vâc* = *hermêneia*-interpretation, *psuchê*-soul, *aisthêsis*-sense perception; *sankalpa* = *alêtheia*-truth, *doxa*-opinion, *sophia*-wisdom. On *nous* (mind) and *êchô* (sound) see Philo, *De migr.* On *aisthêsis* and *psuchê*, *doxa* see Philo LA III.221.

23. RV VI.16.35, cf. III.29.14.

24. RV III.3.10, X.115.1, etc.

25. RV X.8.4, X.122.3.

26. For the Sun-door, the "ascent after Agni" (TS V.6.8; AB IV.20-22), etc., see my "*Svayamâtrnnâ*: Janua Coeli" in *Zalmoxis* II, 1939 (1941).

27. *Mârga,* "Way," from *mrg* = *ichneuô,* to track, hunt. The doctrine of the *vestigia pedis* is common to Greek, Christian, Hindu and Buddhist teaching and is the basis of the iconography of the "footprints." The forerunners can be traced by their spoor as far as the Sun-door, Janua Coeli, the End of the Road; beyond that they cannot be tracked.

Phaedrus 266B: "I follow this one in his tracks as if he were a god"; and *Phaedrus* 253A: "tracking on their own accord"; also *Mathnawi* II.160.1: "What is the Sufi's provision? Footprints. He stalks the game like a hunter: he sees the musk deer's track and follows the footprints." Cf. *The Original Gospel of Buddhism* (Rhys Davids), No. 680, and MU; *metallaô*, to search after other things, to explore carefully. Cf. also *Psalm* 123:6, "My soul has been delivered as a sparrow out of the snare of the fowlers." The symbolism of tracking like that of "error" (sin) as a "failure to hit the mark," is one of those that have come down to us from the oldest hunting cultures.

28. *Lo gran mar d'essere*, "through the vast sea of being," *Paradiso* I.113. The "crossing" is the *diaposeia* of Plato's *Epinomis* 986E.

29. For this whole paragraph see my "Spiritual Authority and Temporal Power in the Indian Theory of Government," American Oriental Society, XXII, 1942 (2nd edn. IGNCA).

30. BU IV.3.21 (rather freely translated), cf. I.4.3; CU VII.25.2. See *Meister Eckhart*, trans. by Evans, I, p. 368—"In the embrace of this sovran One that naughts the separated self of things, being is one without distinction ... " We are repeatedly told that the deity is "both within and without," i.e. immanent and transcendent; in the last analysis this theological distinction breaks down, and "Whoever is joined unto the Lord is *one* spirit" (I Cor. 6:17).

31. BU II.4, etc. On true "Self-Love" see references in HJAS. 4, 1939, p.135.

32. BGVI.29, XIII.27.

33. Meister Eckhart, Evans trans., vol. I, p. 239; cf. *Sutta Nipata* 705 and also Von Hilderbrand, *Liturgy and Personality* (Longman Green, 1943), p. 55.

34. *Mathnawî*, Bk.II. Introduction.
Sum. Theol. II-II.25.7 "union of wills."
Shams-i-Tabriz Ode XIII, "What is Love."
Behmen, passim, "God, the Being of all beings."
Jacofrom da Todi: "He and the soul are interfused ..."
"But if I live, and yet not I,
Have being, yet not mine,
This one-in-twain and twain-in-one
How shall my words define?"

35. SB X.5.2.11-12; BU IV.3.21, etc.

36. TU II.7, 8.

37. For this whole paragraph see my "*Lila*" in JAOS. 61, 1940.
"Thou didst contrive this 'I' and 'we' in order that
thou mightest play the game of worship with Thyself,
That all 'I's' and 'thou's' should become one life."
Rûmî, *Mathnawî* I.1787.

Per sua diffalta in pianta ed in affamo
Cambio onesto riso e dolce gioco,
("through his fault he had a short stay here
through his fault he exchanged honesty, joy
and sweet sport for tears and toil.")
Dante, *Purgatorio* XXVIII.95, 96.

Also Plotinus, *Enneads* IV.7.2 and Philo, Heres 282-3.
  Near as they can, approaching; and they can

The more, the loftier their vision. Those
That round them fleet, gazing the Godhead next.

38. *Mund. Up.* II.1.3, SB.I.4.1.23 *agne â vîtaye,* etc. RV VIII.16.6 *varivaskrt.*

39. CU I.9.1, VIII.14, VII.12.1, V.15.2; TU.II.1.1; SB.XI.2.3.4-5. Space, Ether is the origin and end of "name and aspect," i.e. of existence; the four other elements arise from it and return to it as to their prior. When, as often in Buddhism, account is taken only of four elements, these are the concrete bases of material things. Cf. St. Bonaventura, *On the Reduction of Art to Theology,* 3, *Quinque sunt corpora mundi simplicia, scilcet quatuor elementa et quinta essentia.* ("the body of the world can be reduced to five things, four elements and the fifth, essence.")

Just as also in early Greek philosophy the "four roots" or "elements" (fire, air, earth and water of Empedokles, and *Timaeus* 32, 33-52 where at the divine Nature, Maya, is described as *chôra,* void of all forms) do not include the spatial ether, while Plato mentions all five (*Epinomis* 981C), and as Hermes points out "the existence of all things that are would have been impossible, if space had not existed as an antecedent condition of their being" (*Ascl.* II.15). It would be absurd to suppose that those who speak only of four "elements" were not conscious of this rather obvious consideration.

40. MU II.6, VI. 26; that is to say, apparently (*iva*) divided in things divided, but really undivided (BG XIII.16, XVIII.20), cf. Hermes *Lib.* X.7 where "souls are 'so to speak'" (*hôsper* = as if) parceled out and partitioned off from the one All Soul.

41. *Jñânâni, prajñâ-mâtrâ,* etc., KU VI.10; MU VI.30; *Kaus. Up.* III.8.

42. MU III.2f.

43. SB II.2.2.8, XI.2.3.6, etc.

44. RVV.86.5, X.63.4, etc.

45. AV X.7.39, XI.4.19; JUB IV.23.7; BU IV.3.37, 38, etc.

46. RV X.90.2; AV X.8.1; KU IV.13; Svet.Up. III.15, etc.

47. Sankarâchârya, *Svâtmanirûpana,* 95. The "world-picture" (*Sûryasataka* 26, *jagac-citra* = *kosmos noêtos,* intelligible world order) may be called the form of the divine omniscience, and is the paradigm, apart from time, of all existence, the "creation" being exemplary. See my "Vedic Exemplarism" in HJAS. I, 1936. "A precursor of the Indo-Iranian *arta* and even of the Platonic idea is found in the Sumerian *gish-ghar,* the outline, plan, or pattern of things-which-are-to-be, designed by the Gods at the creation of the world and fixed in the heaven in order to determine the immutability of their creation" (Albright in JAOS. 54, 1934, p. 130, cf. p. 121, note 48). The "world picture" is Plato's *paradeigma aiôna,* eternal paradigm (*Timaeus* 29A, 37C), Hermes' *to archetupon eidos,* the archetypal form (*Lib.* I.8) and St. Augustine's "eternal mirror which leads the minds of those who look in it to a knowledge of all creatures, and better than elsewhere." See Bissen, *L'Exemplarisme divin selon St. Bonaventure,* 1929, p. 39, note 5); cf. St. Thomas Aquinas, *Sum. Theol.* I.12.9 and 10, "But all things are seen in God as in a certain intelligible mirror, not successively, but simultaneously." "When the body-dweller, controlling the powers of the soul that seize upon what is their own in sounds, etc., glows, then he sees the Spirit (*âtman*) extended in the world in the Spirit" (*Mahâbhârata* III.210); "I behold the world as a picture, the Spirit" (*Siddhântamuktâvalî,* p.181).

48. BU I.4.10, *Pras.* IV.10. Omniscience presupposes omnipresence, and conversely.

The Hindu Tradition: Theology and Autology

49. Bonaventura, *On the Reduction of Art to Theology*, 10: "Behold, how divine wisdom is secretly contained in sensitive knowledge." Dante, *Paradiso*, I.116: "This moves the hearts of mortal animals." St. Thomas Aquinas, *Sum. Theol.* I-II.68.4 ad 31: "The Holy Spirit is the principal mover ... Men, who are in a manner His instrument, as they are moved by Him."

50. SA.XIII; CU VI.8.7, etc.

51. TS III.4.7, Mrtyu and Kâma amongst the components of the Gandharva, the Presiding Deity of the sacrifice.

52. RV I.164.20; *Mund.Up.* III.1.1-3.

53. RV X.114.5.

54. *Mund.Up.* III.1.1-3.

55. BU II.5.15, IV.4.22; *Kaus.Up.* III.8, etc.; similarly Plotinus, *Enneads*, VI.5.5.

56. *Paradiso*, XIII.11, 12: "*il punto dello stelo al cui la prima rota va dintorno.*"

57. James 3:6. See also Sermon on Fire in Vinaya Pitaka; Philo, Somn. II.44:

kuklon kai trochon anankês ateleutêtou = a circlet and hoop of endless necessity; distinguished from the chain of Nature's activities; and *heirmon tôn tês phuseôs pragmatôn* = *hormiskos* given to Tamas. And Boehme *De incarnatione Verbi* II.10.4 "Wheel of Nature."

58. MU III.2; BG XIII.21.

59. MU II.6, VII.11.8. See my "Spiritual Authority and Temporal Power... ", 1942 edn., p. 74, the distinction of *satya* from *anrta*.

60. AA III.2.4; BU III.8.11, IV.5.15, etc.

61. JUB I.28.8, and similarly for the other powers of the soul.

62. Sankarâcârya on *Brahmâ Sutra* I.1.5, *satyam nesvarâd anyah samsâri*: this very important affirmation is amply supported by earlier texts, e.g. RV VIII.43.9, X.72.9; AV X.8.13; BU III.7.23, III.8.11, IV.3.37, 38; Svet.Up. II.16, IV.11; MU V.2, etc. See also my, "On the One and Only Transmigrant" in JAOS, Supplement No. 3, Apr.-June 1944. There is no individual transmigrant essence. Cf. John 3:13 "No man hath ascended up to heaven, but he that came down from heaven, even the Son of (the) Man which is in heaven." The figure of the land-leech in BU IV.4.3 does not imply the passing over from one body to another of an individual life other than that of the universal Spirit but only of a "part as it were" of this Spirit wrapped up in the activities that occasion the prolongation of becoming (Sankarâcârya, *Brahmâ Sutra* II.3.43, III.1.1). In other words, life is renewed by the living Spirit of which the seed is the vehicle, while the nature of this life is determined by the properties of the seed itself (BU III.9.28, *Kaus.Up.* III.3 and similarly St. Thomas Aquinas, *Sum. Theol.* III.32.11) and so as Blake expresses it, "Man is born like a garden, ready planted and sown." All that we inherit from our ancestors is a character; the Sun is our real Father. Accordingly, as in JUB III.14.10, M.I. 265/6, and Aristotle, *Physica* II.2, *anthrôpos gar anthrôpon genna hêlios* ("Man is begotten by man and by the sun as well") as rightly understood by St. Thomas Aquinas, *Sum. Theol.* I.115.3 ad 2, and Dante, *De monarchia* IX, cf. St. Bonaventura, *On the Reduction of Art to Theology*, 20 [Wicksteed's and Comford's remarks in the Loeb Library Physics, p.126, shows that they have not grasped the doctrine itself].

63. SB X.4.4.1.

64. BG III.27, XVIII.17; cf. JUB I.5.2; BU III.7.23; MU VI.30, etc. Similarly S. II.252;

287

Udâna 70, etc. To the conceit "'I' am" (*asmi-mâna*) and "'I' do" (*kartâ'ham iti*) corresponds Greek *oiêsis* = *doxa* (*Phaedrus* 92A, 244C). For Philo, this *oiêsis* is "akin to untaught ignorance" (I.93); the mind that says "I plant" is impious (I.53); "I deem nothing so shameful as to suppose that *I* exert my mind or my sense" (I.78). Plutarch couples *oiêma* with *tuphos* (II.39D). It is from the same point of view that St. Thomas Aquinas says that "In so far as men are sinners they do not exist at all" (*Sum. Theol.* I.20.2 ad 4); and in accordance with the axiom *Ens et bonum convertuntur* (= the being of a thing is itself a good) that *sat* and *asat* are not only "being" and "nonbeing" but also "good" and "evil" (e.g. in MU III.1 and BG XIII.21). Whatever "we" do more or less than correctly is "amiss" and should only be regarded as a thing not done at all. For example "What in the laud falls short is not-lauded, what is over-much is ill-lauded, what is exactly lauded is actually lauded" (JB I.356). That what is not done "right" might as well not have been done at all, and is strictly speaking "not an act" (*akrtam*, "un-that"), underlies the tremendous emphasis that is laid upon the notion of a "correct" performance of rites or other actions. The final result is that "we" are the authors of whatever is done amiss, and therefore not really "done" at all; while of whatever is actually done, God is the author. Just as in our own experience, if I make a table that does not stand, I am "no carpenter," and the table not really a table; while if I make a real table, it is not by my self as this man but "by art" that the table is really made, "I" being only an efficient cause. In the same way the Inner Person is distinguished from the elemental self as promoter (*kârayitr*) from operator (*kartr*, MU III.3, etc.). The operation is mechanical and servile; the operator being only free to the extent that his own will is so identified with the patron's that he becomes his own "employer" (*kârayitr*). "My service is perfect freedom."

65. JUB III.14, etc. Cf. my "The 'E' at Delphi," *Review of Religion*, Nov., 1941.

66. For "ransoming Self by self," see KB VIII.3.

67. TS I.5.7.6.

68. Pras. Up. VI.3; cf. answers in CU III.14.4 and Kaus. Up. II.14.

69. CU VIII.12.1; MU. III.2, VI.7. For the *hêgemôn* = leader, see AA II.6 and RV V.50.1.

70. But *krtyakrta* (AV IV.28.6, X.2.23) is evil-doer, where *krtya*, potentiality is in itself evil.

71. AA II.5; SA II.4; MU VI.30, cf. TS I.8.3.1. *Krtyakrta*, "all in act" corresponds to Pali *katamkaranîyam* in the well known "Arhat formula."

72. *Amrtattva* is literally "not dying," and so far as born beings, whether Gods or men are concerned, does not imply an everlasting duration but the "whole of life," i.e. "not dying" prematurely (SB IX.5.1.10; PB XXII.12.2, etc.). Thus the whole of man's life (*âyus* = *aiôn*) is a *hundred years* (RV I.89.9, II.27.10; AA I.2.2, etc.); that of the Gods a "thousand years" or whatever this round number is taken to mean (SB VIII.7.4.9, X.2.1.11, X.1.6.6, 15). So when the Gods, who were originally "mortal" obtain their "immortality" (RV V.3.4, X.63.4; SB.XI.2.3.6, etc.) this is to be taken only relatively; it only means that as compared with mortal men, their life is longer (SB VII.3.1.10, Sankarâcârya on *Brahmâ Sutra* I.2.17 and II.3.7, etc.). God alone, as being "unborn," or "born only as it were," is immortal absolutely; Agni, *vîsvâyus* = *pur aiônion*, eternal fire; alone "immortal amongst mortals, God amongst gods" (RV IV.2.1; SB II.2.2.8, etc.). His timeless (*akâla*) nature is that of the "now" with-

out duration, of which we, who can only think in terms of past and future (*bhûtam bhavyam*), have not and cannot have experience. From him all things proceed, and in him all are unified (*eko bhavanti*) at last (AA II.3.8, etc.). There are, in other words, three orders of "not dying," that of man's longevity, that of the God's aeviternity, and that of God's being without duration (On "aeviternity" cf. St. Thomas Aquinas, *Sum. Theol.* I.10.5).

The Indian texts lend themselves to no illusions: all things under the Sun are in the power of Death (SB.II.3.3.7); and in so far as he descends into the world, the deity himself is a "dying God"; there is no possibility of never dying in the body (SB.II.2.2.14, X.4.3.9; JUB III.38.10, etc.); birth and death are inseparably connected (BG II.27; A. IV.137; Sn. 742).

It may be observed that Gk. *athanasia* has similar values; for the "mortal immortality," cf. Plato, *Symposium* 207D-208B, and Hermes, *Lib.* XI.1.4a and *Ascl.* III.40b.

73. SB II.3.3.9; BU I.5.2, etc., Luke 20:36, John 11:26.

74. AV X.8.44, cf. AA III.2.4.

75. *Mathnawî*, VI.723f. Also attributed to *Mathnawî* is, "Die before ye die." See also Chuang Tzu, ch. 2, "buried myself," and Angelus Silesius.

76. RV IX.113.9; JUB III.28.3; SA VII.22; BU II.1.17, 18; CU VIII.5.4, VIII.1.6 (cf.D.I.72); *Taitt. Up.* III.10.5 (like John 10:9).

77. RV IX.88.3, X.168.4; cf. John 3:8; *Gylfiginning*, 18.

78. BG IX.29.

79. Luke 14:26, cf. MU VI.28, "If to son and wife and family he be attached, for such a one, no, never at all"; Sn.60, *puttam ca dâram pitaram ca mâtaram ... hitvâna*; Meister Eckhart, "As long as thou still knowest who thy father and thy mother have been in time, thou art not yet dead with the real death" (Pfeiffer, p. 462). Phaedo 68A, Philosopher, escapes from what he hated, namely, *sôma*, the body [*hôte diebeblênto* = the body by which they had been deceived].

80. BU IV.4.14; CU VII.1.6, VII.8.4, etc.

81. BU I.4.2.

82. On Way or Via see *Enneads* VI. On the pursuance of a Way, see further, *Phaedrus* 253A: *ichneuontes de par' heautôn aneuriskein tên tou spheterou theou phusin euporousi* = They prosper, following the scent of their own accord, in order to discover the nature of their own god. *Enneads* III.8.11: *ichnos tou agathou* = trace of the good. Plato, *Laws* 728D: *ichneusai de kai helein to pantôn ariston* = to track out and choose the chief good; (which when a man has found, he should take up his abode with it during the remainder of his life). *Philebus* 32D, 44D: *dei diathêreuthênai* = we must hunt down that which we are pursuing. Plato, *Republic* 432B: " ... like huntsmen, we should ... look sharp ... but you must show me the way ... the wood is dark and perplexing; still we must push on." Rumi, *Mathnawî* II.160.

Glossary of Foreign Terms and Phrases[*]

Âcârya (Sanskrit): teacher; a spiritual master learned in philosophy and realized in knowledge.

Adaequatio rei et intellectus (Latin): "the intellect (of the knower) must be adequate to the thing (known)"; a medieval epistemological maxim.

Anicca (Sanskrit): impermanence.

Aswarga (Sanskrit): literally, "non-heavenly"; worldly.

Circa factibilia (Latin): "about things made."

Cogito ergo sum (Latin): "I think therefore I am"; a saying of the French philosopher and mathematician René Descartes (1596-1650).

Cogito ergo EST (Latin): "I think, therefore Thou (God) art."

Correction du savoir-penser (French): "correctness of thinking."

Crede ut intelligas (Latin): "believe in order to understand."

Darshan (Sanskrit): literally, "viewing"; a name for the six classical schools of orthodox (*âstika*) Hindu philosophy: (1) *Nyâya* (logic); (2) *Vaisheshika* (natural philosophy, or science); (3) *Sânkhya* (cosmology); (4) *Yoga* (science of union); (5) *Pûrva-Mîmâmsâ* (meditation); and (6) *Uttara-Mîmâmsâ* (*Vedânta,* or metaphysics); also the blessing derived from beholding a saint.

Deus absconditus (Latin): the hidden or transcendent God.

Deus ex machina (Latin): any artificial or improbable device resolving the difficulties of a situation.

Dharma (Sanskrit): Truth, Reality, cosmic law, righteousness, virtue.

[*] Editor's Note: Not including foreign terms and phrases translated or explained in the main text by Ananda K. Coomaraswamy.

291

Docere, delectare, flectere (Latin): to teach, to delight, and to move.

Dolce stil nuovo (Italian): sweet new style.

Docta ignorantia (Latin): literally, "learned ignorance"; refers to the negative or apophatic way of knowing God.

Dukkha (Sanskrit): desire, thirst, craving.

Duo sunt in homine (Latin): "there are two (natures) in man," viz., the spiritual and the corporeal; a saying of St. Thomas Aquinas, *Summa Theologica* II.2, q.26, art.4.

Entasis (Latin): an architectural term pertaining to a slight convexity in an upright shaft.

Ex nihilo fit (Latin): made or created out of nothing.

Factibile (Latin): a work of art, i.e., what the artist creates.

Fons vitae (Latin): the fountain of Life.

Forma humanitatis (Latin): literally, the "form of humanity"; complete human nature.

Integritas sive perfectio (Latin): integrity (accuracy) and perfection.

Intellige ut credas (Latin): "understand in order to believe."

Karma-yogin (Sanskrit): a practitioner of *karma-yoga*, the path of selfless and disinterested action; to be distinguished from the *jñāna-yogin*, the practitioner of the path of knowledge or wisdom.

Kavi (Sanskrit): poet, seer, sage.

Krama mukti (Sanskrit): gradual, or deferred, liberation; a state of partial deliverance obtained after death, corresponding to the Heaven of the Judeo-Christian tradition; total liberation is deferred to the *pralaya* (dissolution) at the end of a *kalpa* (world-cycle); to be distinguished from *jîvan-mukti*, the state of total and immediate liberation attained during this lifetime, and *videha-mukti*, the state of total liberation attained at the moment of death.

Laborare est orare (Latin): "work is prayer."

Le symbolisme qui cherche (French): a symbolism that is seeking.

Le symbolisme qui sait (French): a symbolism that knows.

Lex aeterna (Latin): Eternal law; cf. *dharma*.

Lex naturalis (Latin): natural law.

Moksha (Sanskrit): liberation from the round of birth and death (*samsâra*); deliverance from ignorance (*avidyâ*).

Mors janua vitae (Latin): "death is the gate to life."

Nirvâna (Sanskrit): literally, "extinction" (of desire or ignorance); the state of bliss experienced after the attainment of liberation from the round of birth and death (*samsâra*).

Ouk ôn Theos (Greek): "the God who is not."

Para Brahma (Sanskrit): the "supreme" (*para*) or ultimate aspect of the Divinity (*Brahma*); as distinguished from *Apara Brahma*, the "non-supreme" or penultimate aspect of the Divinity.

Per artem et ex voluntate (Latin): "by his craft (skill) and his will."

Probare, delectare, movere (Latin): to recommend, to love, to move.

Purna svaraj (Sanskrit): complete self-rule; total autonomy; self-government.

Quelle dégringolade (French): "what a rapid deterioration."

Rationem artis (Latin): the meaning of art.

Samsâra (Sanskrit): the round of existence; the cycle of life and death; the manifested world.

Secundum rectam rationem artis (Latin): according to the correct understanding of art.

Secundum rem (Latin): according to the thing itself.

Shraddha (Sanskrit): a religious ceremony in which food and water are offered to deceased relatives.

Splendor veritatis (Latin): splendor of the True.

Sub rationem dicendi sive intelligendi (Latin): according to the reasons (understanding) taught and understood.

Sub specie aeternitatis (Latin): under the aspect of eternity.

Summum bonum (Latin): the Highest or Supreme Good.

Sva-dharma (Sanskrit): literally, "own-law"; one's vocation.

Sva-karma (Sanskrit): literally, "own-activity"; to perform work in accordance with one's own inner law or nature.

Tirthankara (Sanskrit): literally, "ford-maker"; a title for the twenty-four Jain masters who conveyed the principles of Jain belief over the centuries, the last of whom was Mahavira (6th century B.C.E.), the founder of Jainism.

Vox populi vox Dei (Latin): "the voice of the people is the voice of God."

Werden was du bist (German): "become what you are."

Yuga (Sanskrit): age; Hindu cosmology distinguishes four ages: Krita (or Satya) Yuga, Treta Yuga, Dvapara Yuga, and Kali Yuga, which correspond approximately to the Golden, Silver, Bronze, and Iron Ages of Greco-Roman mythology; according to Hindu cosmology humanity is presently situated in the Kali Yuga, the "dark age" of strife.

For a glossary of all key foreign words used in books published by World Wisdom, including metaphysical terms in English, consult:
www.DictionaryofSpiritualTerms.org.
This on-line Dictionary of Spiritual Terms provides extensive definitions, examples and related terms in other languages.

Bibliographical References[*]

Marco Pallis, Prologue: "A Fateful Meeting of Minds: A. K. Coomaraswamy and R. Guénon": *Dilip*, Vol. V, No. 1 (n.d.); and *Studies in Comparative Religion*, Vol. 12, Nos. 3, 4 (1978).

1. "A Figure of Speech or a Figure of Thought?": Ananda K. Coomaraswamy, *Figures of Speech or Figures of Thought: Collected Essays on the Traditional or "Normal" View of Art* (London: Luzac, 1946); *Coomaraswamy 1: Selected Papers, Traditional Art and Symbolism*, edited by Roger Lipsey (Princeton: Bollingen Series, Princeton University, 1977); and *The Door in the Sky: Coomaraswamy on Myth and Meaning*, edited by Rama P. Coomaraswamy (Princeton: Bollingen Series, Princeton University, 1997).

2. "The Bugbear of Literacy": *Asia Magazine*, New York (February 1944); Ananda K. Coomaraswamy, *Am I My Brother's Keeper?* (New York: John Day, 1947; London: Dennis Dobson, 1947); and Ananda K. Coomaraswamy, *The Bugbear of Literacy* (London: Perennial Books, 1979).

3. "On the Pertinence of Philosophy": Ananda K. Coomaraswamy, *What is Civilization? And Other Essays* (Ipswich: Golgonooza Press, 1989).

4. "Eastern Wisdom and Western Knowledge": *Isis*, Vol. XXIV, Cambridge, Massachusetts (1943); *Am I My Brother's Keeper?*; and *The Bugbear of Literacy*.

5. "Beauty and Truth": *Art Bulletin*, Vol. XX, New York (1938); Ananda K. Coomaraswamy, *Why Exhibit Works of Art?* (London: Luzac, 1943); and Ananda K. Coomaraswamy, *Christian and Oriental Philosophy of Art* (New York: Dover, 1956).

---

[*] Editor's Note: the interested reader is referred to the complete bibliographical listing of Ananda K. Coomaraswamy's works in James Crouch, *A Bibliography of Ananda Kentish Coomaraswamy* (New Delhi: Manohar Publishers, 2002).

6. "The Interpretation of Symbols": *What is Civilization? And Other Essays.*

7. "Why Exhibit Works of Art?": *Journal of Aesthetics,* New York, Fall Issue (1941); *Why Exhibit Works of Art?,* and *Christian and Oriental Philosophy of Art.* Originally an address delivered before the American Association of Museums at Columbus, Ohio, and Newport, R.I., in May and October, 1941.

8. "The Christian and Oriental, or True, Philosophy of Art": *Why Exhibit Works of Art?,* and *Christian and Oriental Philosophy of Art.* Originally a lecture delivered at the Walter Vincent Smith Art Gallery, and at Boston College, 1939, and printed as a *John Stevens Pamphlet,* Newport, 1939.

9. "Is Art a Superstition, or a Way of Life?": *Why Exhibit Works of Art?,* *Christian and Oriental Philosophy of Art;* and as "Art, Man and Manufacture," in *Our Emergent Civilization,* edited by Ruth Nanda Anshen (New York: Harper and Brothers, 1947). Originally a lecture given at the Metropolitan Museum of Art, New York, April, 1937, and at Harvard University (Summer School), July, 1937. Printed in the *American Review,* Summer Number (1937), and as a *John Stevens Pamphlet,* Newport, 1937.
"Postscript: Note on a Review by Richard Florsheim of 'Is Art a Superstition, or a Way of Life?'": *Art Bulletin,* Vol. XX, New York (1937); *Why Exhibit Works of Art?,* and *Christian and Oriental Philosophy of Art.*

10. "The Nature of Medieval Art": *Arts of the Middle Ages,* Museum of Fine Arts, Boston (1940); *Why Exhibit Works of Art?,* and *Christian and Oriental Philosophy of Art.*

11. "*Ars sine scientia nihil*": *The Catholic Art Quarterly,* Vol. VI (1943); *Figures of Speech or Figures of Thought;* and *Coomaraswamy 1: Selected Papers.*

12. "Imitation, Expression, and Participation": *Journal of Aesthetics and Art Criticism,* Vol. III (1945); *Figures of Speech or Figures of Thought; Coomaraswamy 1: Selected Papers;* and *The Door in the Sky: Coomaraswamy on Myth and Meaning.*

13. "*Samvega*: 'Aesthetic Shock'": *Harvard Journal of Asiatic Studies,* Vol. VII (1943); *Figures of Speech or Figures of Thought*; and *Coomaraswamy 1: Selected Papers.*

14. "What is Civilization?": *What is Civilization? And Other Essays.*

15. "The Nature of 'Folklore' and 'Popular Art'": *Quarterly Journal of the Mythic Society* (July-October 1936); *Indian Art and Letters,* London (1937); *Why Exhibit Works of Art?*; and *Christian and Oriental Philosophy of Art.*

16. "Primitive Mentality": *Quarterly Journal of the Mythic Society,* Vol. XX (1940); *Figures of Speech or Figures of Thought*; and *Coomaraswamy 1: Selected Papers.* Originally published in French in *Études traditionelles,* Vol. XLVI (1939).

17. "The Coming to Birth of the Spirit": *What is Civilization? And Other Essays.*

18. "*Quod factum est in ipso vita erat*": *What is Civilization? And Other Essays.*

19. "The Hindu Tradition: The Myth": Ananda K. Coomaraswamy, *Hinduism and Buddhism* (New York: Philosophical Library, 1943; New Delhi: Munshiram Manoharlal, 1975; Bloomington: World Wisdom, forthcoming, 2005).

20. "The Hindu Tradition: Theology and Autology": *Hinduism and Buddhism.*

Biographical Notes

ANANDA K. COOMARASWAMY was born in 1877, the son of Sir Mutu Coomaraswamy, one of the leading men of Sri Lanka, and Lady Elizabeth Clay Bibi, an Englishwoman from an aristocratic Kent family. After graduating from London University with Honors in Geology, he became—at age 25—Director of the Mineralogical Survey in Ceylon (Sri Lanka). His interests were soon, however, to be consumed by the arts and crafts of the region, which he expertly interpreted in the light of their underlying metaphysical principles. In 1917 Dr. Coomaraswamy relocated to the USA where he became Keeper of Indian and Islamic Art at the Boston Museum of Fine Arts, establishing a large collection of Oriental artifacts and presenting lectures on their symbolic and metaphysical meaning. An encounter with the seminal writings of Traditionalist author René Guénon served to confirm and strengthen his view of the perspective of the perennial philosophy, or "transcendent unity of religions"—the view that all authentic Heaven-sent religions are paths that lead to the same summit. From this period onwards Dr. Coomaraswamy began to compose his mature—and undoubtedly most profound—works, adeptly expounding the perspective of the perennial philosophy by drawing on his unparalleled knowledge of the arts, crafts, mythologies, cultures, folklores, symbolisms, and religions of the Orient and the Occident. In 1947 he had planned to retire from his position as curator at the Boston Museum of Fine Arts and return to India, with the intention of completing a new translation of the Upanishads and taking on *sannyasa* (renunciation of the world). These plans, however, were cut short by his sudden and untimely death.

RAMA P. COOMARASWAMY was born in New York in 1929, the son of Ananda and Doña Louisa Coomaraswamy. He received his early education in Canada, India, and England, before undertaking undergraduate studies at Harvard University, and medical studies at New York University, where he graduated in 1959. Subsequent post-graduate studies at the Albert Einstein College of Medicine in New York City saw him specialize in both general and thoracic and cardiovascular surgery. Parallel with his distinguished medical career, Dr. Coomaraswamy has retained a deep interest in theological matters and was professor of Ecclesiastical History at St. Thomas Aquinas Seminary in Ridgefield, Connecticut for a period of five years. He is one of the most forceful exponents of traditional Christian teachings—he converted to Catholicism at age 22—and is the author of over fifty articles, as well as

The Essential Ananda K. Coomaraswamy

The Destruction of the Christian Tradition (1981), *The Problems with the New Mass* (1990), and *The Invocation of the Name of Jesus: As Practiced in the Western Church* (1999). Dr. Coomaraswamy is also co-editor of *The Selected Letters of Ananda Coomaraswamy* (1988).

MARCO PALLIS was born of Greek parents in Liverpool, England in 1895, received his education at Harrow and Liverpool University, and served in the British army during the Great War. He was widely respected as a teacher and writer of religious and metaphysical works, and was also a gifted musician and composer, as well as a mountaineer, traveler and translator of Traditionalist works. For many years he corresponded with the eminent Traditionalist writers Ananda Coomaraswamy, René Guénon, and Frithjof Schuon. His writings include the best-selling *Peaks and Lamas* (1939; new edition forthcoming from World Wisdom), an account of his mountain experiences in Tibet before its invasion by Chinese Communist troops, and *The Way and the Mountain* (1960; new edition forthcoming from World Wisdom), a collection of articles on Tibetan Buddhist themes informed by a universalist perspective. He also wrote many articles for the British journal *Studies in Comparative Religion*, the most important of which appeared in a compendium of his writings entitled *A Buddhist Spectrum* (World Wisdom, 2003). Marco Pallis died in 1990.

ARVIND SHARMA was born in Varanasi, India. He earned a B.A. in History, Economics, and Sanskrit from Allahabad University in 1958 and continued his interests in economics at Syracuse University, earning an M.A. in 1970. Pursuing a life-long interest in comparative religion, Dr. Sharma gained an M.T.S. in 1974 and then a Ph.D. in Sanskrit and Indian Studies from Harvard University in 1978. He was the first Infinity Foundation Visiting Professor of Indic Studies at Harvard University and succeeded Wilfred Cantwell Smith to the Birks Chair of Comparative Religion at McGill University in Montreal, Canada. He has published over fifty books and five hundred articles in the fields of comparative religion, Hinduism, Indian philosophy and ethics, and the role of women in religion. Often cited as an authority on Hinduism, amongst his most noteworthy publications are *The Hindu Gita: Ancient and Classical Interpretations of the Bhagavadgita* (1986), *The Experiential Dimension of Advaita Vedanta* (1993), *Our Religions: The Seven World Religions Introduced by Preeminent Scholars from Each Tradition* (1994), and *The Study of Hinduism* (2003).

Index

Index

189, 193, 196, 201, 205, 207, 208, 211, 222, 223, 237, 241, 258, 264, 269, 272, 280, 281, 288, 289
Goodenough, 251, 257
Grail (Holy), 83, 220
Great Work, 79
Greater mysteries, 61, 228
Greek Archaic art, 115
Greek Geometric art, 115
Greek miracle, 114
Greek Orthodox (Church), 94
Gregorian chant, 197
Grierson, Sir George A., 59
Guénon, René, 1, 8-16, 19, 82, 84-95, 151, 219, 240, 242, 245, 253, 254
Guido d'Arezzo, 146, 147, 178, 179, 189, 199
Gulag Archipelago, 16
Harrisson, Tom, 58, 65
Hasidic saying, 108, 165
Heaven, 18, 31, 50, 61, 76, 77, 80, 83, 85, 130, 149, 166, 196, 206, 208, 209, 210, 216, 244, 245, 246, 259, 265, 276, 278, 286, 287
Heaven and Earth, 18, 166, 276, 278
Heavenly Door, 130
Hegemon, Philo's, 134
Hehaka Sapa (Black Elk), 18
Heracleitus, 78, 243, 247
heresy, 38, 179, 183
Hermeneia of Athos, 104
Hermes Trismegistus, 44, 133, 187, 189, 244, 245, 252, 253, 255, 256, 257, 258, 259, 264, 265, 286, 289
hero, heroes, 25, 28, 34, 60, 114, 139, 140, 228, 229, 231, 236, 238, 242, 268
Hesiod, 35, 43, 93
Highlanders, of Scotland, 57, 63, 93
Hinduism and Buddhism, 5
History of Indian and Indonesian Art, The
hogan, American Indian, 121
Holdfast, 268
Holy Ghost, 120, 134, 199, 270
Holy Land, a, 216
Homer, 25, 48, 105, 120, 210, 244
humanist, humanism, 70, 135, 140, 154, 173
Hyde, Douglas, 56, 64

Ibn 'Arabî, 74, 78
Ibn 'Arabî and an-Nizâm, 81
iconoclast, iconoclasm, 45, 104, 142, 143, 222
iconography, 29, 44, 50, 102, 103, 105, 136, 145, 154, 160, 165, 166, 175, 183
iconolatry, 143, 167
Ideal City (Platonic), 23-25, 37
idolater, 143, 167
imagination, 34, 55, 105, 116, 132, 134, 181, 187, 257
imitation (*mimêsis*), 24, 25, 26, 27, 28, 29, 37, 38, 45, 79, 113, 120, 134, 154, 161, 162, 172, 173, 178, 181-91, 215
immortality, 74, 75, 80, 81, 148, 184, 210, 234, 256, 257, 281, 284, 288
Indra, 72, 193, 203, 213, 221, 223, 270, 271, 275, 284
Indrâgnî, 277
induction, 68, 187
industrial society, industrial system, industrialism, 17, 34, 37, 47, 53, 54, 92, 116, 117, 207, 227, 239
ingenium, Augustinian, 134
initiation, 71, 79, 240
Inner Man, 60, 244, 269, 270, 277, 278, 279, 282, 283
inspiration, 34-36, 48, 117, 120, 131, 133, 134, 150, 178, 204
intellect, 23, 37-39, 40, 42, 49, 50, 71, 74, 82, 83, 84, 106, 114, 126, 131, 134, 144, 148, 159, 162, 182, 185, 204, 219, 222, 249, 251, 257
Intellectual Realm, 77, 80
Introduction to the Study of the Hindu Doctrines, 12, 87
intuition, 46, 131, 132
Inward Controller, 202
Jafna, 2
Jenkins, Iredell, 180, 181, 190, 212, 239
Jesuit missionaries, 61
jîvan-mukta, 281
jñâna, 46, 71
John, Saint (Evangelist), 246, 262
Johnson, Charles, 61
Josquin des Prés, 101
Jupiter Terminus, altar of, 121

Titles in The Perennial Philosophy Series by World Wisdom

A Buddhist Spectrum by Marco Pallis, 2003

The Essential Ananda K. Coomaraswamy, edited by Rama P. Coomaraswamy, 2004

The Essential Titus Burckhardt: Reflections on Sacred Art, Faiths, and Civilizations, edited by William Stoddart, 2003

Every Branch in Me: Essays on the Meaning of Man, edited by Barry McDonald, 2002

Islam, Fundamentalism, and the Betrayal of Tradition: Essays by Western Muslim Scholars, edited by Joseph E. B. Lumbard, 2004

Journeys East: 20th Century Western Encounters with Eastern Religious Traditions by Harry Oldmeadow, 2004

Living in Amida's Universal Vow: Essays in Shin Buddhism, edited by Alfred Bloom, 2004

Paths to the Heart: Sufism and the Christian East, edited by James S. Cutsinger, 2002

Returning to the Essential: Selected Writings of Jean Biès, translated by Deborah Weiss-Dutilh, 2004

Science and the Myth of Progress, edited by Mehrdad M. Zarandi, 2003

Seeing God Everywhere: Essays on Nature and the Sacred, edited by Barry McDonald, 2003